Object-Oriented
Systems Design
An Integrated Approach

Object-Oriented Systems Design

An Integrated Approach

Edward Yourdon

YOURDON PRESS
Prentice Hall Building
Englewood Cliffs, New Jersey 07632

Yourdon, Edward
    Object-oriented systems design: an integrated approach/
Edward Yourdon
        p. cm. -- (Yourdon Press computing series)
    Includes bibliographical references and index.
    ISBN 0-13-636325-3
    1. Object-oriented programming (Computer science) 2. System design
        I. Title. II. Series.
QA76.64.Y72   1994
005.1--dc20   93-6098
CIP

Editorial/production supervision: *Ann Sullivan*
Cover design: *Tommyboy Graphics*
Jack photo: *Ron Victor Technagraphy*
Buyer: *Alexis Heydt*
Acquisitions editor: *Paul W. Becker*
Editorial assistant: *Maureen Diana*

©1994 by P T R Prentice Hall
Prentice-Hall, Inc.
A Paramount Communications Company
Englewood Cliffs, New Jersey 07632

The publisher offers discounts on this book when ordered in bulk quantities. For more information, contact:

> Corporate Sales Department
> PTR Prentice Hall
> 113 Sylvan Avenue
> Englewood Cliffs, NJ 07632
> Phone: 201-592-2863
> FAX: 201-592-2249

Printed in the United States of America
10 9 8 7 6 5 4 3 2 1

ISBN 0-13-636325-3

Prentice-Hall International (UK) Limited, *London*
Prentice-Hall of Australia Pty. Limited, *Sydney*
Prentice-Hall Canada Inc., *Toronto*
Prentice-Hall Hispanoamericana, S.A., *Mexico*
Prentice-Hall of India Private Limited, *New Delhi*
Prentice-Hall of Japan, Inc., *Tokyo*
Simon & Schuster Asia Pte. Ltd., *Singapore*
Editora Prentice-Hall do Brasil, Ltda., *Rio de Janeiro*

Dedication

To my children — the objects of my affection:

Jenny
  first-born, lover of life, economist extraordinaire

Jamie
  actor, writer, and reincarnation of Pele

David
  guitar-playing rock-'n'-roller masquerading as math whiz

Thanks for allowing me to be a part of your life!

Contents

Preface

This is not the first book on object-oriented systems development, and it certainly won't be the last. It covers a lot of ground and, addresses some issues of importance to systems developers today. But it doesn't try to answer every question—and it may not be helpful for those who have a very specific object-oriented problem to tackle. Thus the most important thing I can do in this brief preface is tell you what the book is about and for whom it's intended; I'd also like to acknowledge the help that several people have provided in making the book better than it was in its earlier incarnations.

First and foremost, this book is a synopsis and an integration of several popular object-oriented development methods, with particular emphasis on OO analysis and design. It does not address object-oriented programming in any detail, nor does it have anything particularly useful to say about object-oriented databases. When I first began writing the manuscript, I referred to it as a "synthesis" of OO methods. But in addition to howls of indignation that I had stolen a term that Meilir Page-Jones and Steve Weiss (of Wayland Systems Inc.) have already appropriated for their methodology, several reviewers quite correctly pointed out that I have not achieved a true synthesis—that is, something resembling a "unified field theory" of object-orientation—in this book. So, a synthesis it's not; an integration it might be called; a synopsis it definitely is.

One reason I didn't try any harder to achieve a technical synthesis of OO methods (aside from the fact that it would probably have been beyond my abilities) is that I was more concerned with a variety of management and cultural issues surrounding the practice of OO methods. Some reviewers complained that my treatment of several technical issues in the book is rather simplistic, and this is undoubtedly true. However, a full treatment of the technical issues would have filled an 800-page book and would have dealt with issues that are already discussed in detail in many other fine OO books; more important, it would have detracted from the management issues that I've discussed in the first seven and the last six chapters.

Object orientation is an important technology, and it has already made an important contribution to the software engineering field; there is still a great deal to learn about OO, and a number of technical problems to solve, so we will no doubt see quite a variety of additional OO books over the next several years, before the topic becomes passé. But OO, like all other technologies, does not exist in a vacuum; it is used within a larger context of project management and organizational cultures. It may be a sign of creeping middle age, but I have become more and more aware of the impact these managerial and cultural issues have on the success or failure of technologies like object orientation, CASE technology, structured methods, and so on.

This perspective may help identify the intended audience for the book: it is not intended for the "pure" technician whose primary interest is rigorous theory and formal methods. It is aimed at the "practitioner": the systems developer or manager who has to make OO work in the "real world"—a world filled with ugly politics, demanding deadlines, and increasing pressure for rapid solutions to urgent problems. Because the book is concerned more with analysis and design issues than with programming issues in C++ or Smalltalk, it will be of interest primarily to systems analysts, designers, software architects, and project managers.

Aside from programming, one major issue the book does not address at all is maintenance. Yes, I know that we spend 50 percent, or 80 percent, or maybe even 99.99 percent, of our software budget on maintenance. But most of that maintenance budget is associated with the care and feeding of old software, developed in the Dark Ages before OO came along. In any case, the plain truth is that I have very little experience with the long-term problems of maintaining a system developed with OO techniques; I don't think very many others do, either. Someone else will have to write an OO maintenance book, and I don't think we'll see it for a few more years.

Whatever merit this book does have is the result of suggestions, comments, clever ideas, and useful feedback that I've received from several thousand students and seminar attendees over the past few years in North America, South America, Europe, Africa, Australia, and Asia. Indeed, one of the most interesting things that I've noticed about the OO "phenomenon" is that everyone is aware of it, and software engineers all over the world are rushing to gain competitive advantage by being the first in their city, state, or country to gain expertise in the field.

A few people deserve special mention for going over earlier versions of this manuscript with a fine-tooth comb. Mark Lorenz, Adrian Bowles, Julian Morgan, John Connell, James Odell, Robert Glass, Don Firesmith, Ron Norman, and Alan Davis all gave me the benefit of their insight and experience in the OO field; they caught a number of egregious errors and debated a number of points where my opinions were expressed sloppily. In addition, Paul Becker, Ann Sullivan, and Sally Ann Bailey at Prentice Hall did their usual super-human job of turning a rough manuscript into a published book. Of course, any errors that remain are my responsibility; I welcome any comments and suggestions from readers, and look forward to continuing the dialogue on this exciting and important technology of object orientation.

Ed Yourdon
New York City
email: 71250.2322@compuserve.com

PART I   INTRODUCTION

1

Introduction

As TV talk-show host Arsenio Hall says to his audience, "Let's get *busy!*" This book is about object-oriented (OO) development methodologies, and there's a great deal to talk about. But before we plunge into the details, there are three important points to make:

- OO software engineering methodologies are the greatest thing since sliced bread. In computer-related terms, object-oriented techniques are the most important development since the introduction of structured techniques during the 1970s and 1980s.

- Just because OO is wonderful does not mean that we have to throw away everything we learned in the 1970s and 1980s. There are some fundamental principles of good software design and analysis that transcend the various techniques that sweep through the industry every decade. In a recent book, Don Firesmith seems to echo the feeling of many younger software engineers with the comment, "I have even heard one so-called software engineer say that 'good engineering is timeless.'"[1] But some principles of software engineering—modularity, information hiding, coupling, cohesion, and so on—*are* timeless, and any good methodology will embrace them. Furthermore, some of the notation and strategies of older methodologies can also be used effectively within the larger framework of a new OO methodology.

---

[1]Donald G. Firesmith, *Object-Oriented Requirements Analysis and Design: A Software Engineering Approach* (New York: John Wiley and Sons, 1993), p. 2.

1

- Object-oriented methodologies (or for that matter, *any* software engineering methodology) involve a lot more than programming techniques. Even after five years of active discussion in the literature, most practitioners and almost all software managers seem to think that the OO means nothing more than learning how to program in C++. But the programming issues are almost trivial in comparison to the larger issues of OO-analysis and OO-design.

1.1 WHAT IS AN OBJECT? WHAT IS OBJECT ORIENTATION?

The word "object" is thrown around rather loosely in the software field, and most vendors of CASE tools, programming languages, and database packages are scurrying to attach the OO adjective to their products. But what does object orientation really mean?

Here is a useful summary:

A system built with object-oriented methods is one whose components are encapsulated chunks of data and function, which can inherit attributes and behavior from other such components, and whose components communicate via messages with one another.

If someone tries to sell you a software tool, language, product, or application that has these characteristics, it is probably reasonable to conclude that it is indeed an OO product; whether it is a good product requires closer examination. On the other hand, if someone describes his software system as OO without these characteristics, he is stretching the truth, at best.

1.1.1 Definitions of Class and Object

Before we discuss the finer points of this definition—the concepts of inheritance, encapsulation, and so on—we need to begin with the basics. What is an object? What is a class? Pete Coad and I defined "object" and "class" in the following way in one of our earlier books on the subject:

Object. An *abstraction* of something in a problem domain, reflecting the capabilities of the system to keep information about it, interact with it, or both; an *encapsulation* of Attribute values and their exclusive Services. (synonym: an Instance)

Class. A collection of one or more Objects with a uniform set of Attributes and Services, including a description of how to create new Objects in the Class.[2]

There are several variations on this definition; indeed, it seems that every author of an OO book or methodology has a slightly different nuance in his description of an object. For example, the Object Management Group (OMG), an influential nonprofit consortium of software vendors, offers the following definition in a recent document:

An object is a thing. It is created as the instance of an object type. Each object has a unique identity that is distinct from and independent of any of its characteristics. Each object offers one or more operations.[3]

Don Firesmith provides the following definition in his book:

An **object** is defined as a software abstraction that models all relevant aspects of a single tangible or conceptual entity or thing from the application domain or solution space. An object is one of the primary software entities in an object-oriented application, typically corresponds to a software module, and consists of a set of related attribute types, attributes, messages, exceptions, operations, and optional component objects.[4]

Grady Booch offers a slightly different perspective:

From the perspective of human cognition, an object is any of the following:
• A tangible and/or visible thing
• Something that may be apprehended intellectually
• Something toward which thought or action is directed

An object has state, behavior, and identity; the structure and behavior of similar objects are defined in their common class; the terms instance and object are interchangeable.[5]

---

[2]Peter Coad and Edward Yourdon, *Object-Oriented Analysis*, 2nd ed., (Englewood Cliffs, NJ: Yourdon Press/Prentice Hall, 1990) p. 53.

[3]Object Management Group (OMG), *Object Analysis and Design*, Volume 1, *Reference Model*, Draft 7.0 (Framingham, MA: OMG, October 1, 1992), p. 32.

[4]Firesmith, *Object-Oriented Requirements Analysis and Designs*, p. 29.

[5]Grady Booch, *Object-Oriented Design, with Applications* (Redwood City, CA: Benjamin/Cummings, 1991).

Sally Shlaer and Stephen Mellor offer a similar explanation:

> An *object* is an abstraction of a set of real-world things such that
> - all the things in the set—the instances—have the same characteristics, and
> - all instances are subject to and conform to the same set of rules and policies.[6]

The definition provided by Ivar Jacobson and coworkers is admirably succinct:

> An **object** is characterised by a number of operations and a state which remembers the effect of these operations.[7]

Finally, James Martin and James Odell offer an equally succinct definition of an object:

> An object is any thing, real or abstract, about which we store data and those methods which manipulate the data.[8]

There are many other authors, books, and papers that offer additional nuances; however, there are some common elements in virtually all the definitions, and we will use them through the remainder of this book:

- An object is a real-world thing *or* an abstraction of that thing; thus it is equally meaningful to talk about a real-world object like a "pencil" or about a software representation of a pencil which we intend to specify, design, and eventually program. Computer people tend to deal almost exclusively in abstractions; thus we automatically think of a pencil in terms of how we will represent it in some binary format, how we will arrange lists and arrays of pencils, et cetera. But during the analysis portion of a systems development project, we are dealing with users for whom abstractions are often irrelevant, confusing, and difficult. To a user, a pencil is more likely to be the physical object, consisting of a stick of graphite surrounded by yellow-painted wood. While it might be

---

[6]Sally Shlaer and Stephen J. Mellor, *Object Lifecycles: Modeling the World in States* (Englewood Cliffs, NJ: Yourdon Press/Prentice Hall, 1992).

[7]Ivar Jacobson, Magnus Christerson, Patrik Jonsson, and Gunnar Övergaard, *Object-Oriented Software Engineering: A Use Case Driven Approach* (Reading, MA: Addison-Wesley, 1992).

[8]James Martin and James J. Odell, *Object-Oriented Analysis & Design* (Englewood Cliffs, NJ: Prentice Hall, 1992).

useful to use terms like A-object and RW-object to distinguish between abstract and real-world forms of objects, most practitioners and most textbooks don't bother. We won't bother in this book, either; so please remember that while most of the objects that *we* talk about are abstract objects, many of our users prefer to think in terms of real objects.

- A real-world object can be tangible or intangible; Embley, Kurtz, and Woodfield make a similar distinction between "physical" objects and "conceptual" objects,[9] as does Firesmith. A pencil, as discussed, is clearly tangible: we can touch it, bite it, and use it to make markings on paper. Of course, there are many other objects that are far less tangible, but nevertheless important and meaningful to our end users: plans, strategies, styles, directions, et cetera. It might be convenient to classify these intangible objects as "abstract," in the sense used earlier—but *our* abstractions are typically quite different from the user's abstractions. An end user might think of a "plan" in terms of a textual description or a series of flowcharts and diagrams; a software engineer might have a very different abstraction of that same intangible object.

- An object is a single occurrence, or "instance" of a real-world thing or abstraction. Thus, when discussing people, we recognize that John is an object and Mary is a different object. Implicit in this statement—but quite essential to an OO methodology—is the assumption that each object/instance can be uniquely identified and distinguished from other objects.

- A set of objects with the same characteristics (i.e., the same descriptive attributes and the same behavior) is usually referred to as a *class* or an *object type*. In this book, we will use the term *"class"* to minimize confusion.

Note, though, that in many discussions of basic OO principles, it doesn't matter whether we refer to a class, or to the objects within the class; our choice of "object" or "class" or "instance" will sometimes depend on what sounds more natural and "English-like" in the context of the discussion.

---

[9]David W. Embley, Barry D. Kurtz, and Scott N. Woodfield, *Object-Oriented Systems Analysis: A Model-Driven Approach* (Englewood Cliffs, NJ: Yourdon Press/Prentice Hall, 1992).

1.1.2 The Key Characteristics of an Object-Oriented Method

From the preceding discussion, it is obvious that any OO software development methodology must be based on objects and classes. But what else is involved? When evaluating an allegedly object-oriented software system, what kind of checklist can be used to determine whether it has been faithful to the OO paradigm?

In this book, we emphasize three fundamental characteristics of an object-oriented approach to developing systems:

- *Abstraction*—any mechanism that allows us to represent a complex reality (e.g., a set of detailed components) in terms of a simplified model (e.g., a single higher-level component). Of course, virtually every software development approach incorporates some kind of abstraction—for example, a "top-down design" methodology is usually based on the concept of decomposing functions into smaller, simpler subfunctions. OO methodologies are often based on *data* abstraction, using concepts analogous to the subtype/supertype concept found in various information engineering methodologies; however, functional abstraction may still play a role in an OO methodology!

- *Encapsulation*—any mechanism that allows us to "hide" the implementation of the object, so that other components of the system will not be aware of (or be able to take advantage of) the "innards" of the data stored in the object.[10] As a practical matter, this means that an object's data (or attributes) and the functions that operate on the data (typically known as "methods," "operations," or "services") are packaged together. Not only is this important as a programming mechanism, but also as a design and analysis concept; most earlier methodologies went to great lengths to *separate* the data and functional components of a system. The other practical consequence of this concept is that an OO system depends heavily on communication *between* objects; the communication usually takes the form of "messages" that are sent to specific "methods" or functions within the receiving object.

---

[10]Veteran software engineers will find this a familiar concept: techniques such as David Parnas's information hiding have been well known since the 1970s. But what makes the OO approach is that such concepts are typically *enforced* (through CASE tools and/or OO programming languages) and combined with the other OO concepts of abstraction and inheritance.

- *Inheritance*—any mechanism that allows an object to incorporate all or part of the definition of another object as part of its own definition. In practical terms, this usually means that OO systems involve hierarchies of objects, with "subordinate" objects inheriting all or part of their definition (i.e., the definition of their attributes and their functional behavior) from higher-level "parents" or "superclasses." Exactly *how* this should be accomplished is a matter of a great deal of debate and controversy, and the variations are particularly extreme at the level of programming languages.

As mentioned earlier, it is hard to imagine any software engineering methodology—or any of the CASE tools, languages, and packages that software engineers use to build systems—which do not have some form of abstraction. So it is usually the presence or absence of encapsulation and inheritance that determines the degree to which the methodology/tool/language can legitimately be called "object-oriented."[11]

Thus it is not at all uncommon to hear vendors describe their products as "object-based," or "object-compatible," or "object-like" just to associate the magical marketing properties of the "O" word without actually lying. "Object-based," for example, is frequently used to describe programming languages like Ada, which have the fundamental property of encapsulation but lack the equally fundamental property of inheritance. As for the various other marketing terms, the best advice is: *caveat emptor*.

1.1.3 What Else Do OO Methodologies Include?

Does the term "object-oriented" imply anything above and beyond the fundamental characteristics of abstraction, encapsulation, and inheritance? Some believe it does; James Rumbaugh and coworkers, for example, also include the concept of *polymorphism*:

> There is some dispute about exactly what characteristics are required by an object-oriented approach, but they generally include four aspects: identity, classification, polymorphism, and inheritance.[12]

---

[11]For example, Ada 83 supports encapsulation, but very little in the way of inheritance; consequently, it is usually described as being "object-based" rather than "object-oriented."

[12]James Rumbaugh, Michael Blaha, William Premerlani, Frederick Eddy, and William Lorensen, *Object-Oriented Modeling and Design* (Englewood Cliffs, NJ: Prentice Hall, 1991).

And the Object Management Group describes the key features of OO in terms of the fundamental characteristics described above, *plus* the concepts of polymorphism and reuse:

> The key features of object modeling which differentiate this subject area from the others are:
> - **Abstraction**: which defines a relationship between a group of object types such that one object type represents a set of characteristics which are shared by other object types.
> - **Encapsulation**: which implies the packaging of operations and data together into an object type such that the data is only accessible through its interface.
> - **Reuse**: which is the ability to reuse object types during the design of a system and object classes within the implementation of a system.
> - **Specialisation**: which occurs when an object type inherits operations, attribute types and relationship types from one or more supertypes (with possible restrictions).
> - **Object communication**: which, in object oriented systems, takes the form of one object sending requests to other objects.
> - **Polymorphism**: which occurs when an operation can apply to several types. There are two main forms of polymorphism:
>   - Inherent polymorphism: where operations are inherited by every subtype.
>   - Ad hoc polymorphism: where different operations on different types have the same name.[13]

As the OMG points out, polymorphism is usually defined as a mechanism that allows different operations (typically described as methods, services, or functions) on different object types to have the same name; as a practical consequence, this means that an object can send a message to another object without necessarily knowing (or caring) the precise *class* to which the object belongs. Thus the message "move" might be sent to an "animal" object, without knowing whether that object is a fish, a bird, a snake, or a mammal. Each of these different types of animals knows how to interpret and carry out the "move" message— for example, by swimming, flying, wiggling, or walking—thereby eliminating the necessity of the sending object to first ask, "What kind of object are you?" and then sending a specific message like "swim."[14]

---

[13]OMG, *Object Analysis and Design*, p. 29.

[14]In a software environment, a similar example might be the "display yourself" message sent to an object in the "figure" class or a "compute your current balance" message sent to an object in the "invoice" class.

From this simple example, it should be evident that polymorphism can be a tremendously useful concept during the design and implementation of a system. Whether it is equally important and useful during the analysis phase of a project, when system requirements are being negotiated with an end user is more questionable; the OOA book by Embley and colleagues, the OOA/OOD books by Coad and Yourdon,[15] and the two OOA books by Shlaer and Mellor,[16] for example, do not even mention the term. On the other hand, the textbooks by Booch, Firesmith, Rumbaugh and colleagues, Jacobson and colleagues, as well as Martin and Odell *do* make a point of emphasizing polymorphism, and, as we have seen, so does the OMG. At the time this book is being written, software engineers can decide for themselves whether they want to emphasize polymorphism in their OO approach, but it appears that the trend is toward giving this concept the same stature as inheritance and encapsulation.[17]

What about reuse? While the OMG includes it in their list of OO characteristics, most methodologists and software engineers consider it a more "universal" concept that should apply to *all* software engineering methodologies. It *is* true that many of the earlier methodologies treated reuse as a Boy Scout virtue (like loyalty, bravery, and thrift) without offering any specific strategies or techniques for accomplishing it, and it *is* true that the fundamental OO concept of inheritance forms the technical basis for reusability.[18] But, as we will discuss further in Chapter 6, an OO methodology does not guarantee *any* reuse, and it hardly seems fair to penalize an OO methodology, tool, or product that fails to elevate reuse to the same level of importance as inheritance and encapsulation. If reuse is considered to be a mandatory component of OO, then the same argument

---

[15]Coad and Yourdon, *Object-Oriented Analysis*; Peter Coad and Edward Yourdon, *Object-Oriented Design* (Englewood Cliffs, NJ: Yourdon Press/Prentice Hall, 1991).

[16]Sally Shlaer and Stephen J. Mellor, *Object-Oriented Systems Analysis: Modeling the World in Data* (Englewood Cliffs, NJ: Yourdon Press/Prentice Hall, 1988); also Shlaer and Mellor, *Object Lifecycles: Modeling the World in States.*.

[17]It should be noted that software engineers have implemented the concept of polymorphism without explicitly endorsing the rest of the OO religion; a good example is the use of Ada generics to implement polymorphism.

[18]When reviewing the manuscript for this book, author Mark Lorenz disagreed with this point and argued that far more reuse occurs via delegation *across* the class hierarchy than downward through inheritance; class hierarchies, he notes, are typically wide and relatively shallow. See Mark Lorenz, *Object-Oriented Software Development: A Practical Guide* (Englewood Cliffs, NJ: Prentice Hall, 1993).

would apply to other Boy Scout virtues such as maintainability, simplicity, flexibility, quality, and portability.

Indeed, Martin and Odell make the valid point that object-oriented technologies (specifically OO analysis and design, in their discussion) are just one item in a list of "killer" technologies for software development; the rest of the list includes CASE, visual programming, code generators, repositories, repository-based methodologies, information engineering, object-oriented databases, nonprocedural languages, inference engines, client-server technology, and class libraries that maximize reusability.[19] While some may quibble about individual items on this list (e.g., Do OO methodologies replace information engineering, and does one *really* have to use inference engines for conventional applications today?), it is important to remember that OO is just part of a bigger picture. We will discuss this further in Chapter 7.

Not included on our list are two additional items identified by Grady Booch: concurrency and persistence. Booch defines concurrency as "the property that distinguishes an active object from one that is not active."[20] He goes on to argue that:

> One of the realities about concurrency is that once you introduce it into a system, you must consider how active objects synchronize their activities with one another as well as with objects that are purely sequential. . . . In the presence of concurrency, it is not enough simply to define the methods of an object; we must also make certain that the semantics of these methods are preserved in the presence of multiple threads of control.[21]

For obvious reasons, emphasis on the concurrency characteristics of a system typically occurs in the realm of programming and design; for real-time and on-line systems, it may also be a sufficiently important issue that it will be represented in the analysis model, after discussions with the user. For the purposes of this book, we will treat concurrency as a useful and relevant design/implementation concept, but *not* as a fundamental, required feature of the OO paradigm.

Similarly, the concept of *persistence* is often discussed within the context of OO methodologies: some objects are transient, and disappear shortly after they are created, while other objects "persist" long

---

[19]Martin and Odell, *Object-Oriented Analysis & Design*, p. 5.
[20]Grady Booch, *Object-Oriented Design*, p. 67.
[21]Ibid., p. 68.

after the execution of the associated program that created them. Booch defines persistence as follows:

> Persistence is the property of an object through which its existence transcends time (i.e., the object continues to exist after its creator ceases to exist) and/or space (i.e., the object's location moves from the address space in which it was created).[22]

Traditional programming languages typically deal only with relatively transient data, for example., variables that exist only within a block of code, or during the execution of the program. Data that survives between different versions of the same program, or from one transaction to the next, or that outlives the very existence of the program has traditionally fallen under the control of database management systems (DBMS); in OO systems, such a distinction between the programming language and the DBMS is typically blurred considerably.[23] In any case, persistence is typically an issue of concern in the design and programming stages of a project, and typically not discussed in great detail during the analysis stage (where it is usually assumed that *all* objects are persistent). Thus, for the purposes of this book, we will not treat persistence as a fundamental criterion of OO methodologies (since all systems must eventually deal with the issue, no matter how clumsily); however, the issue of *how* an OO methodology deals with persistence at the design and implementation stage will be discussed in Part IV.

While many of the commercially available OOA and OOD methodologies address the OO issues discussed in this section in somewhat different ways, virtually all of them provide some mechanism for implementing the fundamental concepts. On the other hand, recent comparisons of conventional and OO methodologies[24] have noted that many OO methodologies do *not* have capabilities for such traditional activities as top-down decomposition of functions.

---

[22]Ibid., p. 70.

[23]Or to put it another way, conventional DBMS's have always provided for the storage of persistent *data*, but have rarely provided any mechanism for storage of the "methods" associated with that persistent data. This is beginning to change with recent DBMS products that allowed "stored procedures" or "triggers" to be stored along with the data, but since an OO approach encapsulates data and function together, it is important to indicate which objects are transient and which are persistent.

[24]See, for example, Robert G. Fichman and Chris F. Kemerer, "Object-Oriented and Conventional Analysis and Design Methodologies," *IEEE Computer*, October 1992, pp. 22–39.

1.2 WHAT OBJECT ORIENTATION IS *NOT* ABOUT

Veterans of the computer field know there is a tendency toward introducing new products and concepts with an ever-increasing amount of "hype." This trend has become even stronger in the 1980s and 1990s with personal computers, mass-marketed software packages, and the presence of start-up companies financed by venture capitalists. Indeed, the tendency to describe new products and technologies as "revolutionary" predates the computer field by several centuries,[25] and during the past decade, we have witnessed the attempt to associate supernatural powers to CASE technology, expert systems, pen-based computing, relational database technology, graphical user interfaces—and now, object-oriented technology.

So it is crucial to emphasize, at this early point of discussion in the book, that OO is not magic; it is not a new silver bullet guaranteed to eliminate the problems of productivity and quality that have plagued the software industry for the past several decades. Carefully practiced, and combined with various other software engineering disciplines—for example, metrics, reuse, CASE tools, testing, and quality assurance—OO can help bring about dramatic improvements in the performance of a software organization. But it will not turn an ugly duckling into a swan.

Also, object orientation is *not* just a collection of programming tricks. Whether a programming language supports single or multiple inheritance, how it implements the functional behavior of an object (in terms of methods, slots, etc.), whether it supports dynamic binding rather than static, compile-time binding, and various other implementation details—all these issues may be the *raison d'être* for programmers, but they are only a small part of the overall OO paradigm.

1.3 WHAT THE BOOK IS ALL ABOUT

Having now introduced the concept of objects, the first part of this book concludes with a look at the popularity of the OO paradigm. Chapter 2 discusses the extent of OO usage, as of 1991–92, and the reasons many software organizations are being attracted to the approach. But equally important, Chapter 2 explains why some organizations are consciously, deliberately choosing *not* to implement OO software methodologies—at least, for the time being.

---

[25]For a good discussion of this, see George Basalla, *The Evolution of Technology* (New York: Cambridge University Press, 1988).

Part II of the book discusses a number of "management" issues associated with the OO paradigm. Many software project managers are ready to embrace the technical concepts of OO analysis, design, and programming—and frankly don't care which of the dozen commercial forms of OO methodology their project team uses—but they want to make sure they can still *manage* the project to assure that it will be finished on time, within budget, and with an acceptable level of quality. Thus individual chapters in Part II discuss the subjects of software life cycles, project management, configuration management, software reuse, and techniques that complement OO methodologies.

Part III discusses the broad area of object-oriented *analysis*, or OOA. There are now so many different OOA methodologies that it is important to begin with an overview of what needs to be accomplished in the OOA phase of a project. Separate chapters then discuss the critical problem of object *discovery*, object attributes, object behavior, object structures and relationships, and object methods and services.

Part IV continues with a discussion of object-oriented *design*, or OOD. The problem of design notation is considered; while it would be impossible for this book to consolidate all the different OOD graphical notations into a single diagramming representation, we should agree on the important *issues* for OOD notation. Separate chapters then examine the topics of OOD architectures and databases, as well as the design of the human interface. The impact of programming languages on OOD is discussed, though this is not intended to be a detailed, comprehensive coverage of object-oriented programming. Guidelines and criteria for distinguishing good designs from bad designs are also discussed; a final chapter addresses the eternal problem of testing.

Part V discusses CASE technology for OO methodologies. One lesson we have learned from the 1970s and 1980s is that any software engineering methodology, applied to a large, complex project, requires good tool support. Fortunately, we are beginning to see a number of new tools emerging; separate chapters review desirable features of OO CASE tools as well as survey some of the more popular products in the marketplace.

Finally, Part VI discusses the organizational question now being debated in software development shops around the world: *how do we get started?* The choices between revolution and evolution are examined; subsequent chapters then discuss the process of "justifying" or "selling" OO technology in a large organization, as well as training and technology transfer problems.

2

Pros and Cons
of Object Orientation

Object Orientation has been heralded as a silver bullet, a paradigm shift, a killer technology, and even a cure for whatever ails the U.S. software industry (and by extension, whatever ails the software industries of other countries). In this chapter, we explore the extent of OO popularity and summarize both the reasons why it is popular in some organizations and why other organizations have consciously decided *not* to join the OO revolution.

2.1 THE EXTENT OF OO POPULARITY

It's almost impossible for a software engineer or a software manager *not* to have heard of OO as we march further into the 1990s; it has definitely escaped from the lunatic fringe and shows some evidence of gradually becoming a respectable technology. Various surveys in industry trade journals indicate that 75 percent of the *Fortune* 100 companies[1] are now using OO to some degree. Similarly, a cover story by *Business Week* magazine in October 1991 proclaimed OO as one of the most important software technologies of the last 20 years and predicted that it would help revitalize software productivity.[2]

---

[1]For readers outside the United States and for Americans who don't read magazines, the term *"Fortune* N" means the N largest companies, as measured by *Fortune* magazine. One typically hears of the *Fortune* 50, or *Fortune* 100, or *Fortune* 500.

[2]In 1990, *Business Week* lavished similar praise on CASE technology, effectively suggesting that CASE would save the American form of capitalism. Since then, the fortunes of most CASE vendors have gone straight downhill, the victims of overhype and the sea change of mainframe technology to PC-based client-server technology.

If magazines like *Business Week* are discussing OO, then it must be entering the mainstream! And indeed it is: banks, insurance companies, and other organizations that one would normally regard as highly conservative are aggressively pursuing a technology that was regarded as the domain of the technology freaks and propeller heads only a few years ago. As Smalltalk guru Sam Adams puts it,

> The long wait for object technology to enter the mainstream is over. The business community, long dominated by mainframe COBOL applications, is beginning to use Smalltalk for its "line of business" applications. Until recently, only those companies willing to make a bold move into the future were seriously considering object technology. . . . A few organizations have decided that the reward for redesigning their business computing around object technology is worth the risk.[3]

Perhaps more important, we have begun to see OO software technology used for large, complex "industrial-strength" systems and applications. Throughout the late 1980s, the overwhelming majority of OO projects discussed in magazine articles and at software conferences were 3-person projects that lasted 6 months. The claim that 3 people could accomplish in 6 months what would have taken 30 people 60 months in a conventional third-generation language is indeed impressive (though rarely documented in an objective fashion by neutral observers), and tended to add to the excitement already associated with prototyping and various "rapid application development" approaches to software development. But there was always the nagging suspicion that OO might collapse when applied to projects that are intrinsically so large and complex that, regardless of the technology employed, an army of 200–300 people is required.

Happily, we are beginning to see that OO can be used in such projects; perhaps the most widely circulated example of such a project is the System-7 operating system for the Apple Macintosh, a complex system involving the efforts of approximately 200 software engineers.[4] Ericsson, the Swedish telecommunications company,

---

[3]Sam Adams, "Getting down to business with Smalltalk," *American Programmer*, October 1992, p. 8.

[4]In fairness, it should be noted that System-7 was at least one year late, and perhaps even two years late, depending on whose published schedule one believes. On the other hand, the equivalent effort from IBM—OS/2—is rumored to have involved an army of 2000 software engineers and was *also* so late that nobody can remember when it was originally promised.

used Ivar Jacobson's ObjectOry methodology for the development of its AXE telecommunications software; this system is not only large, but it has the added complexity of real-time behavior.

Indeed, real-time systems are often regarded as the litmus test for the practicality of software development methodologies, languages, operating systems, and CASE tools. With regard to OO for real-time systems, Brian Barry, the Vice President of Research and Development at Ottawa-based Object Technology International, has observed that

> Those few who have taken the plunge into real-time OOPS know the reality: object-oriented technology is a winner for real-time and embedded applications . . . . Looking ahead, it seems clear that as OO technology matures, microprocessors continue to deliver more computational bang for the buck, and the demand for real-time and embedded applications increases, you will hear much less about the efficiency and performance problems with OOPS and much more about the productivity and quality advantages they bring to a project. . . . Real-time OO technology has finally arrived, and it is definitely here to stay.[5]

This doesn't mean that the entire software community is ready to begin coding "hard" real-time systems in Smalltalk; there are often serious performance problems with OO programming languages, as we will see in Chapter 17. But as hardware continues to become cheaper and faster, the performance concerns for real-time systems can typically be localized to a few "hot spots"—and even if these portions of the system have to be hand coded in a non-OO fashion, the rest of the system (as well as the analysis and design that preceded the code) can be done quite effectively with an OO approach.

2.2 POPULARITY SURVEYS

But while OO is definitely becoming more popular, it is still a technology used by a small minority of the software community. The trade magazines that report OO usage in 75 percent of the *Fortune*

---

[5]Brian M. Barry, "Real-Time Object-Oriented Programming Systems," *American Programmer*, October 1991, pp. 11–20.

100 companies don't emphasize, for example, that *most* of that usage consists of experimentation and pilot projects. Nor does it emphasize that *most* of what goes on in a so-called "object-oriented" project is a lot of programming in C++, with little or no regard for the analysis, design, and other software engineering activities that should also be addressed from an OO perspective.

The "bottom line" is that OO is being used in a serious fashion by only 3–5 percent of the software engineering community. A 1991 Sentry Research study, for example, found the distribution of methodologies shown in Figure 2.1. Of course, things have undoubtedly changed since the survey was conducted in 1991, and it is reasonable to expect that OO usage has increased—most likely, at the expense of the various forms of structured analysis and design. But even if the combined use of *all* OO methodologies has increased to 5 percent, it is still a very small piece of the pie.

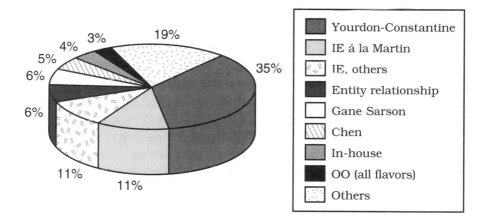

Figure 2.1: Usage of software methodologies

Another survey, conducted by Systems Development, Inc., in 1991, produced similar figures for OO. Covering a wide variety of modern software technologies, the survey found the figures given in Table 2.1:[6]

---

[6]Chris Pickering, *Survey of Advanced Technology—1991* (Denver: Systems Development, 1991).

Table 2.1: Success Rate With Modern Technologies

Technology	Projects Used on	Success	Effective Penetration
OO/OOPS	3.8%	91.7%	3.5%
Structured methods	71.4	90.2	64.4
Fourth-generation languages	20.6	86.6	17.8
Relational DBMSs	39.3	84.2	33.1
Model-based systems	23.1	80.7	18.6
End-user computing	25.0	75.0	18.8
Packages with models	9.4	73.1	6.9
Imaging	4.4	70.0	3.1
PC/workstation-based development	27.5	67.8	18.7
Executive information systems	6.9	63.1	4.4
CASE technology	28.8	59.7	17.2
AI/expert systems	3.9	55.3	2.2

Note that in this survey, OO technology was used by a very small percentage of the population, but was associated with a very high level of success on the projects where it was used; in contrast, CASE technology was used in slightly less than 30 percent of the projects, and was deemed successful in slightly less than 60 percent of those projects. One is tempted to conclude from these figures that OO is used by a tiny group of enthusiastic, highly successful, fanatics, that is, the very people whose job is to "champion" the technology within the organization.[7]

2.3 WHY ARE PEOPLE USING OO TECHNOLOGY?

Before one is stampeded into using a technology that has achieved such public notoriety, it is reasonable to ask, "Why?" What are the benefits of OO? In this section, we review the "traditional" arguments in favor of OO technology, as well as the practical arguments in favor of "abandoning" an older methodology in favor of OO.

But within a few years, all this may be moot: OO is likely to become such a pervasive technology that we cannot escape it. The

---

[7]Some additional caveats regarding this survey: the relative mix of "advanced" technologies has undoubtedly changed since 1991; however, it is still reasonable to assume that the majority of OO usage has been associated with programming, not analysis/design. Note also that "success" was judged by the project manager and may not be entirely objective.

older generation of software engineers may remember the violent arguments over the relevance of operating systems and high-level languages; more recently, companies like Apple Computer had to do a lot of evangelizing to convince an IBM-dominated world that graphical user interfaces (GUIs) might be a lot more productive than a character-based "dumb terminal" interface. And it was only a few years ago that many of us asked, "Why do I need a fax machine, anyway?"

But now all these technologies are ubiquitous. Nobody would dream of using a modern computer without an operating system, only the truly demented program in assembly language, and even IBM acknowledges that GUIs and PCs are more popular (even if less profitable) than mainframes. As for fax machines: they are effectively free, since they are bundled into the data modems we computer people must have, and they are so universal that our children fax their homework assignments to their teachers. And so it is likely to be with objects: all our operating systems, languages, and tools—indeed, the entire infrastructure with which we build software—will be object-oriented by the mid- to late-1990s.[8]

2.3.1 The Productivity Argument in Favor of OO Technology

The primary arguments in favor of OO technology involve two words: *productivity* and *speed*. There are strong claims in the computer trade magazines, and some limited evidence, to suggest that a system built with OO techniques can increase the productivity of the project team by as much as an order of magnitude, and that it can reduce the project schedule (in terms of calendar time) by as much as an order of magnitude. A profession that has lived through multiple generations of order-of-magnitude hardware improvements—a profession that is now using computers approximately 1 million times more powerful than the computers at the dawn of the computer age 50 years ago—is so jaded that it typically ignores improvements of merely 10 percent.[9] Our adrenaline begins to flow when we hear

---

[8]A contrarian opinion, offered by Robert Glass, is that OO and various other methodologies may eventually be seen as "domain-dependent", for example, highly applicable for some application domains, but useless in others. OO methodologies seem quite appropriate, for example, where the natural "metaphor" for the application involves distributed, communicating components, but it may be inappropriate for a batch payroll system.

[9]In addition to being jaded by hardware improvements, we also suffer from the short attention span of a young industry. It is interesting to note that the United States overtook England as the world's leading industrial economy in the early twentieth century because its productivity exceeded England's by a mere 1 *percent* each year from the end of the Civil War. Compounding of percentages, as any banker will tell you, can achieve miracles—in the long run.

claims of 10-fold improvements—and along with CASE tools and other silver bullets, that is what OO has been promising.

But how could OO achieve such enormous productivity gains? Why is it that someone programming in Smalltalk or C++ can claim to achieve 10 times the productivity of someone programming in COBOL? If the discussion degenerates to the level of *programming* productivity, then part of the answer has to do with the "level" of the languages involved: the same claims have been made about 4GLs since the early 1980s, and most people are prepared to admit that a 4GL is likely to increase software productivity *during the programming phase of the project* by as much as 10 percent over third-generation languages like COBOL or PL/I. We should not be surprised by similar claims for OO languages like Smalltalk or Eiffel; to the extent that the languages provide single-statement constructs that require 10–100 primitive statements in the older languages, they will naturally be more productive. This is particularly true for today's GUI-oriented applications, where it takes as much as six pages of code in C simply to open a window on the user's screen.

But there is more to the argument than the intrinsic power of the OO programming languages; indeed, the primary reason why OO projects achieve dramatically higher levels of productivity comes from the extensive *reuse* of classes and objects. We have long known that reuse is one of those silver bullet technologies, with which some organizations have achieved near-miraculous results. In the worst case, a software organization steeped in the "not-invented-here" culture may achieve 0 percent reuse; at the other extreme, a few organizations have reported as much as 94 percent reuse as they build common applications over and over again.

OO technology achieves reuse through libraries of classes and objects but in particular, through the concept of inheritance discussed in Chapter 1. From a technical perspective alone, OO reuse *is* likely to be easier to achieve than reuse in other software development methodologies. But there are still two fundamental questions: first, is a high level of reuse *guaranteed* if one follows an OO approach? And, second, is a high level of reuse impossible if one avoids an OO approach? The answers to both questions are "No!"; the reasons will be discussed in detail in Chapter 6.

For the moment, though, we can say the following: OO projects are likely to achieve substantially higher levels of productivity, because reuse is more natural and easier to achieve. But there are no guarantees.

2.3.2 The Rapid-Development Argument

If productivity in a software project is substantially increased, one would naturally assume that the project will be finished more quickly. But this is not necessarily true: OO technology could conceivably allow a project to be accomplished with 3 people instead of 30, but it could still drag on for three years. What is it about OO that could make it possible for a project schedule to be reduced from three years to three months?

The primary answer is the same as before: reuse. The OO software engineer typically has available a robust library of reusable classes and objects, and he can easily create a specialized subclass of an existing object for his own unique needs, through the mechanism of inheritance. This not only reduces the time spent for programming, but also for testing (because the reusable classes and objects have already been tested) and for design (because one doesn't have to spend time thinking about how to implement the classes and objects).

But there is an even more powerful reason for the dramatic reduction in OO project schedules: *prototyping*. The classical waterfall methodology, in which the life-cycle activities are carried out sequentially over a long period of time, is typically ignored in OO projects. If you approach an OO software engineer in the midst of a project and ask, "What are you doing now?" the answer is likely to be, "A little of everything: a little analysis, a little design, a little coding, and a little testing."

Prototyping and reuse go hand in hand: it is much easier to quickly develop a prototype for the end user if one has available a robust library of reusable objects. But it takes more than reusable objects to succeed with prototyping. Indeed, the same two questions that we saw at the end of the previous section recur: Is one guaranteed to achieve prototyping by using an OO approach? And is it impossible to achieve prototyping without using an OO approach? As we will see in Chapter 3, the answers to both questions are "No."

Nevertheless, prototyping does appear to be more likely to occur, and easier to achieve, in an OO project than in non-OO projects. But there are no guarantees.

2.3.3 Additional Arguments in Favor of OO Technology

Productivity and rapid systems development are not the only arguments in favor of OO—they are simply the most compelling in today's competitive environment. But there are two other justifications one often hears in the "veteran" OO development shops: *quality* and *maintainability*.

Quality has many dimensions, and it is beyond the scope of this book to explore the topic in detail. For the moment, let's focus on just one aspect of quality: absence of defects. OO advocates typically argue that their systems are more likely to be bug-free than systems developed using other methodologies, and that if a bug does occur, their systems are more likely to degrade gracefully than conventionally developed software that often halts abruptly if something goes wrong.

The greater emphasis on reuse is one of the reasons for experiencing fewer defects in an OO system: a component that has been reused hundreds of times is more likely to have had the bugs shaken out of it. The other reason (and a reason that partially explains the phenomenon of graceful degradation) is the strong emphasis on encapsulation: objects protect themselves and their associated data, so that if one object goes berserk, it is less likely to randomly clobber other objects in the same system.[10] There is also a tradition in many OO projects that says, "If my object receives a message that it does not understand, it simply replies to its sender that it is unable to process the message, rather than hemorrhaging, running amok, and destroying itself."

What about the maintainability argument? OO enthusiasts typically answer that this comes from the fundamental paradigm itself: rather than basing the overall architecture of the system on a hierarchy of functions (which tends to be rather volatile, as end users change their ideas about what functions they want the system to carry out), the architecture is based on a network of collaborating objects. Because of encapsulation, an object can be replaced with a

---

[10]The degree to which this can actually be accomplished is very much a function of the programming language and the amount of run-time support provided by the compiler, operating system, and even the hardware. A similar degree of encapsulation could be accomplished in older methodologies like structured design (where it was typically described as "information hiding") but typically is not. The culture and the mind-set of encapsulation tends to be stronger and more pervasive in OO projects.

new implementation—sometimes while the rest of the system is running—without affecting the other objects.[11]

2.3.4 Where Are the Numbers?

The arguments in this section are intuitively appealing, and they have been demonstrated in a number of specific projects and examples. Nevertheless, the typical reaction of a jaded software manager—someone who has spent the past 20 years listening to silver bullet promises of increased productivity and quality—is, "Where are the numbers?"

Indeed, there is essentially no proof that OO technology will increase productivity or quality by any specific amount. Indeed, as of early 1993, there are not even any large-scale surveys demonstrating that a large sample of, say, 10,000 projects achieved an increased productivity of, say, 25 percent. An OO skeptic can revel in the absence of such statistical evidence.

For the OO enthusiasts, it may be a consolation to learn that there was never any proof that structured techniques, or information engineering, or CASE technology, or any other new technology would work as promised. And during the early days of the technology's life cycle, there was precious little data to justify the optimistic expectations of the pioneers using the technology. As with OO, there were intuitively appealing arguments—"it makes *sense* that we should do things this way"—combined with a sense of frustration that old techniques weren't working, combined with the exuberance of a few other first-time users.

Virtually all the evidence supporting OO technology today falls into the category of "anecdotal war stories," that is, individual projects that have been reported in the trade magazines, or by project managers and participants in computer conferences, or by vendors whose objectivity is often suspect. The description of these OO projects can usually be summarized as, "We tried it, and it worked real good for us!" But was the success due to extraordinarily talented project per-

---

[11]However, it should also be emphasized that widespread use of OO methodologies is so new that we have few, if any, large OO-based applications that have survived a 5-year or 10-year maintenance period. Although there is some anecdotal evidence supporting the claim of improved maintainability, there are also some serious skeptics who argue that OO-based systems could turn out to be more difficult to maintain than conventionally designed software, because of the relatively "flat" architecture involving hundreds of objects all sending messages to one another.

sonnel, or superfriendly users? Did the reported productivity increase actually include all the paperwork, administrative effort, and other "hidden" costs? Was the project a small effort, and if so, would it "scale up" with similar benefits on larger projects? The questions go on and on—and they are essentially the same questions that skeptics asked of the structured methods evangelists in the 1970s and the CASE evangelists in the 1980s.

Ultimately, we will begin to see statistical data from larger samples of OO projects, and they will, it is hoped, confirm the informal success stories from the pioneers and evangelists. But overall, the proliferation of OO technology through the software industry is likely to follow the same trend we have seen for other new technologies. As we will discuss in Chapter 26, it is primarily the innovators and early adopters who are embracing OO today; *those organizations typically do not rely on detailed statistical evidence to justify their decision.* The more conservative organizations that demand a detailed cost-benefit calculation will jump on board the OO bandwagon a few years later.

2.4 ARGUMENTS FOR ABANDONING OLD METHODOLOGIES

In an earlier book,[12] Peter Coad and I discussed the reasons why older software methodologies such as structured analysis and design should be replaced with an OO approach. In summary, the most important reasons are these:

- *Problems with older methodologies.* This is especially so with the structured or information engineering methodologies that separate the process (function) model from the data model. In practice, the two models are often developed by separate teams of people, using separate CASE tools. When it comes time to combine the two models, incompatibilities and contradictions are discovered—and the process often degenerates into a political argument about which of the two models will be accepted as the dominant (correct) one. The other model is often discarded, leaving the project to continue with only half its essential characteristics documented in a formal model.

---

[12]Peter Coad and Edward Yourdon, *Object-Oriented Analysis*, 2nd ed. (Englewood Cliffs, NJ: Yourdon Press/Prentice Hall, 1990).

- *Radically different types of systems being developed.* The earlier generation of methodologies was designed for the mainframe, batch, third-generation days. Today's systems involve PCs, client-server networks, and (perhaps most important) graphical user interfaces. Some project managers have said simply, "We abandoned the old methodologies because, in this new world, they simply don't work; our projects are guaranteed to fail unless we adopt an OO approach." In addition, today's systems are often 10 times larger than the systems of the 1970s and early 1980s,[13] and they are taking place in a much more competitive environment that requires delivery of finished applications as quickly as possible; hence the issues of productivity and speed of development have become crucial, and concepts such as reuse have evolved from a whimsical Boy Scout virtue to a critical success factor.

- *Radically different programming languages, development environments, and CASE tools.* One reason we didn't use OO development technologies in the 1970s is that we didn't have any available; we didn't use it in the 1980s because we weren't aware of the early versions of Smalltalk and C++. Until recently, there were no OO CASE tools; there were no commercial libraries of reusable classes and objects. Whether or not it is justified, we tend to use the technology that is available to us; so when COBOL is upgraded to OO-COBOL (which is happening as this book is being written), it is reasonable to expect that the software development community will gradually take advantage of the new technology.[14]

While these arguments are obvious and straightforward, it is important to remember the converse: if you don't have problems, if your users don't require new kinds of systems, and if you don't have new technology available—then perhaps it doesn't make sense to consider a shift to OO methods. Not everyone is at the leading edge;

---

[13]Maintenance gurus such as Nicholas Zvegintzov have published reports showing that vintage-1990 systems are 50 times larger than vintage-1980 systems.

[14]If you *don't* have an object-oriented programming language available, should you still consider object-oriented analysis and design? In theory, it should be possible, for analysis/design activities should be independent of the programming language; in practice, it doesn't work very well. If you're going to do a good job with OOA and OOD, I strongly recommend making the transition to an OOPL; the reasons are discussed in more detail in Chapter 3.

our field is now so large, and has so much inertia, that it cannot revolutionize itself overnight.

I was reminded of this in a presentation on object-oriented analysis and design that I made in Argentina in 1991. At the end of a two-day lecture, one of the seminar participants rushed up to me, his face beaming with enthusiasm, and said, "This is very exciting technology! I plan to adopt it as soon as I get back to my company tomorrow morning!" When I asked exactly what he would be applying OO technology to, he responded, "Oh, we have mostly batch systems, written in RPG-III for an AS/400 minicomputer. We do have a few on-line applications, and they use a character-based interface with IBM 3270 terminals. However, it doesn't seem to matter: our users are very happy with what they have now." Conclusion: OO might be very exciting for this software engineer from a technology perspective, but it's hard to imagine there being a pressing business need in his case.

2.5 REASONS *NOT* TO USE OO TECHNOLOGY

The encounter with my Argentinean colleague raises an obvious question: Are there circumstances when one should *not* use OO technology—or at least, not yet? The skeptics in a conservative DP organization—who often have a considerable investment in older tools, methods, reputations, and political empires—might well respond to this question with a chortle of glee, "No, don't use OO now, because it's just a fad! If we wait for a couple of years, it will all blow over, and we can get back to business as usual!"

It's difficult to imagine that we will ever return to "business as usual," if that means the kind of software development that many of us remember from the 1970s; on the other hand, the steadily growing popularity of OO technology makes it increasingly difficult to dismiss it as a short-term fad. But this does not necessarily mean that OO should be the highest priority for a software development organization attempting to improve its productivity and quality.

In many organizations, for example, "peopleware" is the area where the greatest leverage can be obtained: before concentrating on OO, it would be wise to ensure that the software development organization is staffed by talented people who are well trained, and well motivated and surrounded by a supportive infrastructure.[15] In other organizations, the fundamental problem is the lack of a well-defined software process: the organization is populated by cowboy programmers who operate in a state of utter anarchy.[16]

The 1991 survey by Systems Development, Inc., that showed OO technology being used by only 3.8 percent of current projects also documented the reasons why the remaining 96.2 percent chose *not* to use OO; their reasons, which are instructive, are given in Table 2.2:

Table 2.2: Reasons for Not Using OO Technology

Reasons for Not Using	% of Total
Not aware of technology	31.0%
Benefits not demonstrated	3.5
No business need	17.2
Technology too costly	0.9
Organization unprepared	19.8
Technology too immature	19.8
Other	7.8

As mentioned earlier, the software development community is enormous—some 3 million people are employed, worldwide, as programmers, systems analysts, and software engineers—and not everyone is on the leading edge of technology; it is a sobering, but nevertheless realistic, discovery that some 30 percent of our industry is not yet aware of OO technology.

The organizations who report that they have not seen a demonstration of the business needs, and those that argue that there *is* no business need, should not be dismissed as software Luddites. They may simply be following a conservative path, and they may still be living in a mainframe, batch-oriented, non-GUI world. The world *will* change for these people, and when it does, they will be more likely to embrace OO.

---

[15]The best single reference on the subject of peopleware is a book with the same name: *Peopleware*, by Tom DeMarco and Timothy Lister (New York: Dorset House, 1987).

[16]In other words, introducing OO technology into an organization that operates at level 1 on the Software Engineering Institute's process maturity model is unlikely to bring any sustained improvement. For more details on the SEI model, and the five levels of process maturity, see Watts Humphrey's *Managing the Software Process* (Reading, MA: Addison-Wesley, 1989).

The most sobering item in this survey is the group reporting that its organization is unprepared for OO technology; the lack of preparation may involve training, familiarity with new concepts, or a more fundamental problem involving a formal, standardized Software Engineering Institute–like systems development process. The organizations in this category are realists: no matter how wonderful OO technology may be, it will fail if the organization is not ready for it.

Note also that nearly 20 percent of the respondents to this survey argue that the technology is too immature. The skeptics in this category often argue (justifiably) that there are too many OO analysis and design methodologies, each with its own vocabulary, rules, and diagramming notation. Others point to a lack of industrial-strength applications of OO; still others bemoan the lack of OO CASE tools, languages, class libraries, or other components of technology. While each of these points might be debated, it is difficult to argue that OO is a "mature" technology[17] in the same way that relational database management systems, structured techniques, and information engineering is mature.

2.6 CONCLUSION

OO technology is getting much more attention, and is growing more popular with each passing day. On the other hand, it is currently used by only a small minority of software developers and is still considered "leading-edge" technology.

The arguments in favor or OO technology—productivity, rapid systems development, increased quality and maintainability—are intuitively appealing, and have been demonstrated on a number of individual projects. But for some organizations, there are still rational arguments for postponing or ignoring OO.

Perhaps the most important message of this chapter is that, despite the popularity and the intuitive appeal of OO, it is not a panacea. In the discussion of how to implement OO technology, in Part VI of this book, we will further elaborate on some of the problems that can sometimes prevent OO technology from achieving its full promise of improved productivity and quality.

---

[17]But some organizations *would* argue that OO is mature. Companies like Apple Computer have been using OO technology for much of their systems software for over a decade; languages like Smalltalk and C++ have been available for over 10 years, and companies like Ericsson made a fundamental commitment to an OO approach as early as 1976. But these are isolated examples and do not represent the "mainstream" of DP organizations.

PART II   MANAGEMENT ISSUES

3

Object- Oriented
Project Life Cycles

Imagine the reaction of a software project manager who has just been told that his company has adopted OO as the new "company standard" methodology and that, henceforth, all projects will be implemented in C++. After the first howls of complaint have died away, the manager's most likely question is: "OK, I'm willing to go along with this newfangled OO stuff, but how am I supposed to *manage* projects now?"

To put it another way, many software managers have said to me during the past few years, "Look, I don't care *which* OO methodology we use—it doesn't matter whether it's Coad-Yourdon, Booch, Rumbaugh, Martin-Odell, Shlaer-Mellor, Jacobson, or someone else. What I want to know is whether the project is under control and whether my people are doing the right thing at the right time."

With this perspective, it's easy to see why many managers are very skeptical about OO-based projects. As mentioned in Chapter 2, the behavior of the project team members is the antithesis of what the manager wants to see: when the manager asks the team members what they are doing, the answer is, "A little bit of everything: some analysis, some design, a little coding, and a little testing." The manager naturally worries that such behavior may lead to the worst characteristic of a software project: nothing is done until it's all done, and nobody knows *when* it will be done—until, magically, with no warning, *voilà!* it's done.

Of course, OO projects are not required to exhibit such behavior; indeed, OO projects can be just as well managed and carefully orchestrated as any other kind of software project. But with new methodologies, new kinds of activities (e.g., discovering objects, rather than creating bubbles in a data flow diagram), and new notation, the project manager's "road map" is likely to be different: different phases, different milestones, different checkpoints.

3.1 THE OO LIFE CYCLE

Perhaps the most important thing to say at the outset is that there *are* OO project life cycles. Object orientation is not an excuse for unmitigated "hacking" at software development, and it does not mean that all the software engineers have to disappear into a dark room to start writing C++ code on the first day of the project.

For software development projects, a "life cycle" is traditionally understood to mean the "steps" or activities that must be carried out during the project. We'll defer the question of whether the steps should be carried out sequentially or in parallel until Section 3.2; our first question is: What are the steps that an OO project must go through?

Veteran project managers will be relieved to learn that, at the highest level of abstraction, the steps are exactly the same as they have been for previous software methodologies: there is more to an OO project than object-oriented programming. At a minimum, we need to include the steps of analysis, design, coding, and testing.[1] If OO is going to be applied to the enterprise as a whole (as opposed to a single-project usage), then we should also consider OO-based enterprise modeling. And if we are going to worry about legacy systems (as most large organizations must), then we should also include OO-based maintenance and reengineering.

The Object Management Group (OMG) has apparently recognized the universal nature of these life-cycle activities, and has proposed the following model of the OO project life cycle (see figure 3.1).

---

[1]In *Software Conflict* (Englewood Cliffs, NJ: Prentice Hall, 1991), consultant Robert Glass points out that the software life cycle is merely a specific form of a universal problem-solving paradigm; so it should come as no surprise that OO approaches use the same paradigm. But this notion will be regarded with suspicion by the younger OO revolutionaries, for they assume (incorrectly) that a methodology that involves these classical life-cycle activities must necessarily be an inefficient, bureaucratic waterfall approach.

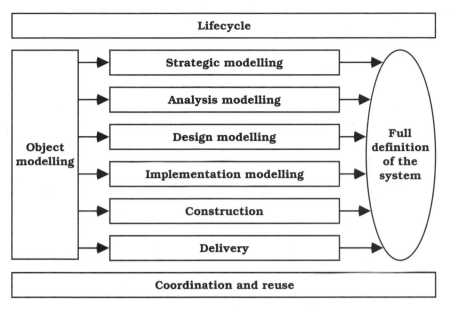

Figure 3.1: The OO life cycle proposed by OMG

Several of the life-cycle activities are summarized in the paragraphs that follow.

3.1.1 Object Modeling

One of the important characteristics of an OO project is that *all* the life-cycle activities share common vocabulary, notation, and strategies—that is, *everything* revolves around objects. Whether the project is involved in the analysis stage, the design stage, or the programming stage, the project team will be involved in discovering, documenting, prototyping, and/or developing objects, and in *all* of the life-cycle activities, the fundamental OO concepts of abstraction, encapsulation, and inheritance play a large role. In simplistic terms, the software development process could be considered as a sequence of first developing "core" business-related objects, then adding application-specific objects, and then surrounding those objects with implementation-related objects that deal with the hardware/software architecture.

This is in stark contrast to the development activities in projects using the older, conventional methodologies: the activities of the data modeling group often seem utterly unrelated to the activities of the project modeling group, and the notations used by each group look as if they were invented on different planets. The design team is likely to throw away the results produced by the analysis team, while the programmers ignore all of the modeling activities because it seems unrelated to their programming language.

3.1.2 Strategic Modeling

Strategic modeling, as used by the OMG, is approximately the same as "enterprise modeling" in methodologies such as information engineering. The objective of this activity is to develop a model of a large business unit, or organizational enterprise that may contain a number of distinct systems; as such, it is a concept that is primarily of interest to those building business-oriented information systems.

When strategic modeling was first introduced into software development methodologies, its primary emphasis was on discovering the *commonality* between systems. In classical, non-OO terms, what individual systems have in common is their data; hence many organizations invested considerable effort during the mid-1980s developing enterprise data models, typically documented with entity-relationship diagrams. Whether or not such models were successful is a matter of heated debate, and precisely *why* they were sometimes unsuccessful is the subject of another debate. Suffice it to say, for the purposes of this book, that the objectives were noble, and the efforts were well intentioned. Unfortunately, far too many organizations found that after spending several years and several millions of dollars, they had an enterprise data model that was incomplete, incomprehensibly complex to the audience of senior executives for whom it was intended, and generally ignored by everyone else in the systems development organization.

This does not bode well for the development of OO-based enterprise models, but some organizations are making a fresh start at this high-level process. If they do, they are likely to find that an OO approach gives them more "bang for the buck" than the older methodologies, because an object contains both data and behavior. Thus a strategic, or enterprise-level, object model might include an object called "customer"—that not only contains the standard attributes of a customer, but also the "methods" that determine how a new instance of customer can be created, how it can be deleted, how a customer can place an order with the enterprise, and so on.

More recently, strategic modeling has become associated with another hot buzzword in the field: *business reengineering*. In organizations around the world, many senior executives are asking, "What business are we *really* in? What do we need to know, and what do we need to *do*, to carry out the business? How can we dramatically streamline the business? How can we move the elements of the business closer to the customer that needs it?" These questions can be answered from an object-oriented perspective, although (as we will see in Chapter 8), the perspective and mind-set of the business executive asking those questions may exert a strong influence on *how* we go about discovering the relevant objects.

In any case, the strategic modeling activity typically produces a number of documents and/or decisions in addition to a high-level model of the enterprise: a set of recommendations of high-level business policies, a proposed plan for development of various systems within the enterprise, and a list of high-level requirements for individual systems.

3.1.3 Analysis Modeling

The concept of analysis modeling is familiar to most software engineers; whether it takes the form of object-oriented analysis modeling or structured-analysis, or information-engineering, it consists of activities of discovering and documenting user requirements for a specific system.

Unfortunately, this is a bit of a culture shock for many of the younger generation of software engineers, for whom OO means extemporaneous creation of working prototypes in a Smalltalk or C++ environment. The activity of analysis is based on the premise that it is valuable to *formalize* the requirements of an application (which does not preclude building prototypes). On the other hand, another important premise of the analysis activity is that the environment in which those applications will be used is well understood and relatively stable and that the end user has a reasonably good idea of what she wants from the application; obviously, there are many environments today where that assumption is questionable.

In all analysis methodologies, the analysts try to ignore the constraints of hardware, operating systems, programming languages, database management systems, and other familiar components of implementation technology; the model they create is the "perfect technology" model. Thus, even though everyone *knows* that the system will be implemented in C++, that knowledge should not taint the analysis model (who knows? maybe C++ will be replaced with

C+++ someday!). Even though everyone knows that a GUI interface is what prompted the project team to consider object orientation in the first place, the implementation issues of windows, scroll bars, and graphical "drag-and-drop" icons should not taint the analysis model (who knows? maybe GUIs will be replaced by voice recognition in a couple of years!).

OO-based analysis differs from structured analysis and information engineering in a number of technical dimensions, as we will see in later chapters. However, the final product still serves the same purpose: a formal, detailed model of *what* the user expects the system to accomplish. But there is one major difference between OO-analysis projects and projects using older methodologies: there is more of a tendency to invoke the magic of reuse. Obviously, *any* project can look for opportunities to reuse components, but in the older-methodology projects, this tends to occur in the later stages of design and coding; even in the relatively modern information engineering methodologies, the emphasis on reusing data components (entities) tends to ignore or overshadow the possibility of reusing methods (or business rules). The cultural heritage of the OO methodology enthusiasts is such that they more commonly begin looking for ways of reusing whole objects—data *and* behavior—at the earliest possible opportunity.[2]

3.1.4 Design Modeling

The OMG describes design modeling in the following way:

> The purpose of design modeling is to specify the external view of a set of object types. Typically the results of this activity are:
> - Rigorous specifications of the object types (typically object types which represent the user interface, business logic, database components of the application and encapsulated reused legacy applications)
> - Complete specifications of operations and interfaces

---

[2]Obviously, users will still ask for customized solutions to their problems; however, if the analysis dialogue can take place in terms of "variations" and "exceptions" from an established "base" set of requirements, then the OO concept of inheritance can be used to advantage. Also, many users are beginning to think of their "shrink-wrapped" PC-based software products (spreadsheets, file management programs, word processors, etc.) as "objects" that they wish to manipulate, modify, and "hook together" to build applications to solve their problems. Some OO-based development tools allow these "building blocks" to be represented as icons in a modeling environment; applications are created by drawing lines to "connect" the building blocks.

- Clustering of object types into design models
- Designs to meet quality requirements[3]

Thus it is at the design modeling stage that the software engineer has to worry about backup, recovery, error checking,[4] and various other "dirty" aspects of the implementation. It is at the design stage that the capabilities and the constraints of the operating system, the programming language, the database management system, and various other system-level components begin to exert an influence on the analysis-level model developer earlier. As part of this activity, analysis-level objects may be clustered into more suitable design-level objects, or they may be split apart (e.g., to support the requirement for normalization).

Traditionally, the modeling of the user interface has been considered a design-level activity—simply because it involves the details of the available input-output devices, windowing mechanisms, and so on. Because the user interface has taken on such importance in today's systems, some projects consider it part of the analysis phase of the project; others simply understand that it is a design-level activity that must be prototyped as early as possible. In either case, the user interface typically involves the development of a separate "family" of objects whose primary purpose is to act as an intermediary between the user and the business-level objects identified during the analysis activity.

Sequencing, timing, coordination, and synchronization also become important issues in the design phase of a project, even though they may be of little interest to the analyst and the user (except, of course, on real-time projects, where they are an important part of the requirements of the system). Thus, in an OO project, one often finds the designer paying much closer attention to the time-dependent *behavior* of each object (using modeling tools such as a state transition diagram) and the *communication* between objects (e.g., studying how much time is consumed by a "thread" of messages through several objects).

---

[3]Object Management Group, *Object Analysis and Design*, Volume 1, *Reference Model*, Draft 7.0 (Framingham, MA: OMG, October 1, 1992).

[4]Some of the error checking will have been specified during the requirements analysis phase of the project, but error checking associated with the hardware/software environment is typically deferred until design.

3.1.5 Implementation Modeling

Implementation modeling is typically concerned with the distribution of objects across different hardware/software components in a client-server network. Thus much of the modeling activity involves the *linkage* between objects; this may involve platform-level linkages, networking linkages, and object communication "brokers" such as the OMG's proposed Object Request Broker.

The project team must also define a *strategy* for determining how objects and classes will be distributed throughout various components of the operational hardware/software environment. It must determine at what point the objects will be "bound" to one another, for example, at compile time, link-edit time, or runtime; this decision can have a significant impact on the ability to reuse classes and objects.

3.2 MIXING OF METHODOLOGIES IN AN OO PROJECT

For many organizations, the decision to embrace objects is not an "all-or-nothing" proposition; they may decide to use an OO approach for some project activities, but not for others. From an intellectual and a practical perspective, this should be avoided, as we will see shortly, but it is likely to be a common phenomenon for the next several years.

What kind of "mixing and matching" of methodologies, or system development approaches, are we likely to see? Here are some examples:

- The strategic, or enterprise-level, modeling activities are carried out with one methodology, but all the individual systems-level projects identified by the strategic modeling activity are performed with an OO approach.
- The analysis of end-user requirements is performed with structured analysis or information engineering, but the design and implementation is done with an OO approach. (Or, by extrapolation, the analysis *and* design are carried out with an older methodology, but the programmers announce that, by golly, they plan to program the system in C++.)
- Conversely, the analysis and design are performed with an OO approach, but the programmers plan to implement the system in a non-OO language like COBOL.

- Analysis, design, and implementation are all done with an OO approach, but the resulting system must interface with a relational database, using DB2 and SQL.
- A maintenance project team decides to add a major new component to a 20-year-old legacy system and announces that the new portion will be developed using object-oriented programming.
- etc., etc., etc.

Why would anyone do such a silly thing as combining non-OO analysis with OO design and OO programming? Indeed, how could *any* of the scenarios just proposed actually take place? If we ignore the obvious explanations of ignorance and pig-headed obstinacy (which may be the most common reasons, but which are beyond the scope of this book!), there is one simple explanation: it is almost impossible to revolutionize *everything*, all at once, about the way an organization develops its information systems.

The most obvious example of this involves the database scenario posed: even if an organization instantaneously adopts an OO approach for strategic modeling, analysis, design, and programming, it can't get rid of the database it has created over the past 25 years. Most business organizations today have vast quantities of data; if they are relatively advanced, all that data may exist in a relational form, but most organizations also have a variety of IDMS, IMS, VSAM, and dBASE files. Consequently, an OO development methodology must take this into account, because it is likely to be another 5–10 years before organizations will seriously contemplate making the switch to an object-oriented database.

As for the other scenarios, the simple explanation is that most organizations must introduce OO (or any other new technology) through a process of evolution, rather than revolution; we will discuss the politics of this choice more fully in Chapter 25. But, for now, imagine the scenario where senior executives and end users are reasonably comfortable with entity-relationship diagrams and various other models for the initial stages of enterprise modeling and analysis. Why would they want to change to an OO approach? Conversely, the analysts may fall in love with OO methodologies, but the programmers may complain that they're stuck with a third-generation programming language; a common variation on this problem today is that the designer/programmer group is stuck with older-style CASE tools that support only the older methodologies of structured analysis/design or entity-relationship diagrams. And the addition of a new OO-style subsystem to an older-style legacy application is a commonplace occurrence; as long as the new subsystem can be kept separate, with simple, clean interfaces to the old legacy code, there may not be any problems.

Aside from the natural intellectual desire to make everything consistent in a project, why should we care what form of methodology is used in the various project activities? There is a simple answer to this question for the "waterfall" form of project, and a more important answer for the common iterative, or rapid-development, kind of project favored by many organizations today:

- In a waterfall project, each project activity is done once, in strict sequence. But the essential requirement is that the *output* of one activity must serve as *input* to the next activity: the results of the analysis activity are the input to the design activity, and so forth. If two activities are conducted with different methodologies, there is likely to be a communication problem: the OO design group may have trouble understanding the DFD models from the analysis team, which are supposed to be the basis for their work.[5] More important is the *traceability* issue: for obvious reasons, we want to ensure that everything in the design model corresponds to something in the analysis model—no more and no less. If the two models are created using entirely different notations, semantics, and vocabulary, this becomes difficult to accomplish.

- With prototyping, iterative, or rapid-development projects, the problem is compounded the fact that the various activities are conducted several times, for example, once for each iteration or version of the system. Thus, even if the project team can tolerate the tedious effort of translating a non-OO analysis model into an OO design model (or vice versa) *once*, it becomes increasingly unlikely that they will bother to do it a second, third, or fourth time. Sooner or later, the team will throw away one of the models (typically the models produced in the earlier stages, since most of the emphasis and attention in the prototyping projects is on tangible, executable implementations of those models) and preserve only the model with which they feel most comfortable.

---

[5]To put it another way, it will be difficult for the designer/programmer to provide an object solution if the objects in the problem were not identified during analysis.

The discussion in this section does *not* mean that one has to abandon all the fundamental concepts of software engineering, or the many good ideas we have learned from older methodologies; nor does it mean that an OO approach can use only one kind of modeling notation. Indeed, much of the discussion in subsequent chapters of this book will demonstrate how concepts of dataflow diagrams, state-transition diagrams, event-driven specifications, and so on, can be used within an OO framework.

But there is a limit to the amount of "mix-and-match" activity that a project can endure without disintegrating. Imagine, for example, a project where the requirements are written in German, the design is documented in French, and the programs are written in English[6]—that is the level of confusion we're likely to find when we mix structured analysis with a Warnier-Orr design and an object-oriented programming language. There is likely to be much more consistency, and much less confusion, if all three activities are carried out in the same language, but this doesn't eliminate the need to use common principles for clarity and organization, nor does it eliminate the opportunity to occasionally include a French phrase in the middle of the English document.

Ultimately, the success of a "mix-and-match" combination of methodologies in a systems development project is going to depend on adequate CASE tools that can translate models from one methodological format to another. But this is easier said than done, and as this book is being written in 1993, none of the familiar CASE vendors offers such a capability. Further, as we will discuss in Chapters 23 and 24, it is unlikely that the newer OO-CASE vendors will bother: their allegiance is to OO *per se*, not to preserving the heritage of older methodologies. Thus, if a CASE-based mix-and-match capability does occur, it is likely to come from the older, traditional CASE vendors (those that survive the trauma of moving from a mainframe

---

[6]If it were a simple matter of translating one French word into one equivalent English word, this might not be such a major problem. But the problem is infinitely more complicated—which is why we have never really succeeded with computerized language translation. The Eskimo language has some 45 words for "snow"; English has only 1. Some languages have words for which there is simply *no* comparable counterpart in another language, some languages put the verb at the beginning of a sentence, while others put it at the end of the sentence, and so on. As linguists have often told us, languages influence the way we think; in software engineering, modeling notations and methodologies influence the way we think. If we *think* about requirements, design, and implementation from entirely different perspectives, which we articulate with entirely different words and symbols, then it will be difficult at best to provide a translation between the steps.

environment to the client-server environment of the 1990s) who want to evolve, along with their customers, from an older SA/IE methodology to a newer OO methodology.

3.3 WATERFALL VERSUS PROTOTYPING

The problems and limitations of a waterfall software development methodology are well known and have been documented exhaustively in numerous software engineering textbooks.[7] Typically, nothing of substance can be demonstrated to the end user until the final stage of the waterfall life cycle is completed; the acceptability of the final code is dependent on the user's ability to adequately describe his requirements and the analyst's ability to understand those requirements; and so on.

Ironically, even though hardly anyone has a good word to say about the waterfall life cycle, it survives—and it will continue to survive well into the next millennium. Informal surveys in most of my software engineering seminars indicate that while everyone favors prototyping, spiral life-cycle models, iterative systems development, and all the other modern buzzwords, the development of large, complex systems ultimately depend on a classical waterfall approach. Why? Because the different activities in the large megaprojects are often carried out by different organizational entities, separated by contractual barriers; because the end user wants a detailed cost estimate at the beginning of each activity, and is unwilling (or unable) to consider the frequent adjustments that might be required by an iterative life cycle; and because it is quite difficult for a project manager to coordinate the *concurrent* execution of life-cycle activities that are the *raison d'être* of iterative projects. As Grady Booch argues,

> This incremental, iterative approach inherent in object-oriented design makes it orthogonal to traditional waterfall life-cycle approaches to software development. Actually, to be very critical, our experience is that a rigid waterfall life cycle is a fundamentally poor process, and generally violates many of the principles of sound engineering practice.[8]

[7]See, for example, John Connell and Linda Brice Shafer, *Structured Rapid Prototyping* (Englewood Cliffs, NJ: Yourdon Press/Prentice Hall, 1989), and Peter DeGrace and Leslie Hulet Stahl's *Wicked Systems, Righteous Solutions: A Catalogue of Modern Software Engineering Paradigms* (Englewood Cliffs, NJ: Yourdon Press/Prentice Hall, 1990).

[8]Grady Booch, *Object-Oriented Design with Applications* (Redwood City, CA: Benjamin/Cummings, 1991), p. 189.

But it is not the purpose of this book to defend or attack the waterfall life cycle, and it is interesting to note that some OO authors ignore the issue entirely.[9] Suffice it to say that the decision to use an OO approach in developing a system can be made independently of the decision to use a waterfall versus prototyping approach. If it is desirable or politically advisable to use a waterfall approach, the life-cycle activities summarized in Section 3.2 can be carried out in strict sequence. Or the project manager may decide to make it an option, as Don Firesmith suggests:

> The assembly development teams may optionally perform some initial, incremental OOD and traditional rapid prototyping. The primary objective of this step is to develop common reusable software identified with OODA [object-oriented domain analysis]. This step can also be used to develop any high-risk objects and classes and the main reusable classes of the classification hierarchies.[10]

But of course, this lack of emphasis is anathema to most OO enthusiasts; indeed, many believe the benefits of object-orientation may be more closely associated with the emphasis on iteration, prototyping, and iterative systems development than anything else—perhaps even more important than encapsulation and inheritance! This raises an obvious question: Why couldn't we carry out iterative systems development and prototyping before OO came along? The obvious answer: we could! we did! we do! But in addition to being more enthusiastic (if not obsessive) about prototyping, the OO practitioners are generally more *successful* with their prototyping efforts than practitioners of older, more conventional methodologies. So this raises a more serious, more practical question—one that is particularly pertinent to the use of OO methods and techniques in a systems development project: What is required for successful prototyping?

3.4 WHAT'S REQUIRED FOR SUCCESSFUL PROTOTYPING?

The *first* requirement for success in prototyping (or any of its variations) is a political acceptance of the paradigm. This may sound

---

[9]For example, the two Shlaer-Mellor books on object-oriented analysis and design make no mention in the index of prototyping, waterfall, or project life cycles. But they are excellent books nonetheless.

[10]Donald G. Firesmith, *Object-Oriented Requirements Analysis and Logical Design: A Software Engineering Approach* (New York: John Wiley and Sons, 1993), pp. 246–247.

obvious, but it is not trivial: an organization that has spent the last 25 years building new systems according to a strict waterfall methodology often has an incredibly difficult time changing to a project approach that seems to border on anarchy.

It is interesting to note that OO methodologies are sometimes brought into an organization with a great deal of revolutionary fervor, for example, as part of the revolution that includes replacing mainframes with PCs, introduction of client-server networks, replacement of character-based interfaces with GUIs, and so on. And as part of the revolution, the OO paradigm brings along prototyping to replace the waterfall life cycle. (And as part of the revolution, it may sweep the "old guard"—the MIS manager and the mainframe COBOL programmers—right out the door.) So, in many cases, the technical aspects of OO have little to do with the introduction of prototyping, but OO *does* serve as the catalyst that makes it politically acceptable.

A second issue for successful prototyping is a common framework for all the life-cycle activities. As mentioned in Section 3.1.1, an important characteristic of a total OO methodology is that all the life-cycle activities are based on the single concept of an object; in simpler terms, software engineers are likely to draw the same kind of object diagrams during analysis, design, and construction of a system. By contrast, older methodologies often involved entity-relationship diagrams during strategic modeling, data flow diagrams during analysis, and structure charts during design.

This is more important than a cosmetic distinction between bubbles and boxes on a diagram: the abrupt shift in diagramming notation (and vocabulary, rules, semantics, etc.) has typically exacerbated the tendency toward following the waterfall approach. As discussed in Section 3.2, even if the project team members can successfully transform an analysis model documented with one notation into a design model documented in another notation, they don't want to do it more than once; hence, an iterative approach to systems development is doomed. As James Rumbaugh and coworkers observe,

> The seamlessness of object-oriented development makes it easier to repeat the development steps at progressively finer levels of detail. Each iteration adds or clarifies features rather than modifies work that has already been done, so there is less chance of introducing inconsistencies or errors.[11]

---

[11]James Rumbaugh, Michael Blaha, William Premerlani, Frederick Eddy, and William Lorensen, *Object-Oriented Modeling and Design* (Englewood Cliffs, NJ: Prentice Hall, 1991).

By the same token, OO enthusiasts are often more successful at prototyping and iterative systems development because they work with an integrated software engineering "environment": the *same* workstation, libraries, diagramming tools, compilers, and debuggers are used throughout analysis, design, and construction of the system. By contrast, the older methodologies frequently have different tools at different stages of the project: one CASE tool may be used for strategic modeling, while another is used for analysis, and so on. Of course, the integrated tool environment is not unique to OO; several non-OO CASE vendors claim to support a "womb-to-tomb" environment for the software engineer. And with those integrated (non-OO) environments, one is quite likely to find the project team building systems in an iterative fashion.

The nature of the project team is the final criterion to identify: as mentioned in previous chapters, OO projects have tended to involve relatively small groups of developers, working in closer concert with relatively small groups of end users. In such an environment—for example, with five developers all working in the same office, and with close daily contact with two or three key users—it is easy to see how an iterative systems development approach would work. Conversely, if an OO approach is used on a mammoth project with 200 developers, and if the project involves interactions with 200 key users in five different continents, it is much more difficult to imagine a pure prototyping approach. To the extent that an OO approach can deliver the same amount of end-user functionality (expressed in function points or some other neutral metric) with 10 times fewer developers than a non-OO approach, it stands to reason that OO projects will tend to involve much more iterative development. But notwithstanding this felicitous characteristic of OO projects, it continues to be true that massive megaprojects will almost certainly continue to exhibit some aspects of a conservative waterfall approach.

But the choice of prototyping versus waterfall life cycles is only one of the decisions that a project manager must make. In subsequent chapters, we will examine some of the other project management issues: estimating, configuration management, reuse, and so on.

4

Managing Object-Oriented Projects

Regardless of what methods and techniques their technicians use on a software development project, managers have some basic questions: How long will the project take? How many people are needed, and when? How can I tell how much progress has been made on the project—are we ahead of schedule or behind schedule?

The stark truth is that we have very little data from previous OO projects with which to make such estimates and calculations; from a software metrics perspective, most managers will be "flying blind" on their first OO development effort. But this does not mean that the manager should abdicate responsibility and simply allow the software engineers to do whatever they want, whenever they want. This chapter explores some of the steps the project manager can take to achieve a modicum of control and predictability in his or her projects.

4.1 THE LACK OF OO DATA, AND WHAT TO DO ABOUT IT

Before discussing some specific suggestions for managing OO projects, it is important that we first understand our level of ignorance. While a few organizations have developed a substantial track record of OO software development over the past 5–10 years, most organizations are just beginning;[1] as we saw in Chapter 2, only about 3 percent of the software community is using OO on a regular basis—and most

---

[1] Even a long track record is no guarantee that a software organization will be able to estimate its projects with great accuracy. As mentioned in Chapter 2, Apple Computer was over a year late with its object-oriented development of the System-7 operating system for the Macintosh. And another long-time OO enthusiast, Borland International, has been notoriously late in the delivery of its Paradox and Quattro products for Microsoft Windows 3.1.

of those organizations are simply using the programming features of an OO language.

By contrast, classical systems development projects (e.g., those developed using structured methods or information engineering) can draw on a vast library of estimating algorithms and computer-based estimating tools. According to Capers Jones, there are some 45 commercial software estimating tools available in the United States (although he also notes, ironically, that only about one-third of MIS project managers use such tools today.)[2] Many of these are based on the COCOMO model ("COnstructive COst MOdel") developed over a decade ago by Barry Boehm at TRW.[3] But most important, the traditional estimating tools and algorithms are derived from vast quantities of statistical data from previous projects; the ESTIMACS package from Computer Associates, for example, is based on a database of over 8000 projects.

But there is no substantial industrywide database of OO projects as of early 1993, when this book was being written. As software metrics expert Capers Jones told me in a recent telephone interview, "Most of the OO projects are either being carried out by hackers who don't measure, or they're still in progress—so there's no data. There is lots of data about object-oriented programming languages, but none about object-oriented analysis and design. So we don't know, for example, the extent to which object-oriented methods affect the problem of "creeping requirements" that plagues many projects."[4]

Estimating expert Howard Rubin, the creator of the ESTIMACS package, agrees: "There is a paucity of data about object-oriented projects at the present time. Indeed, estimating models lag reality by a few years; we're still finding difficulties, for example, computing 5-year maintenance estimates for information engineering methodologies with the data that was captured in 1992—because it's hard to find any IE projects that had finished the development phase in 1987."

So what should a project manager do? In the absence of any other formulas, models, or tools, there appear to be only two basic

[2]Capers Jones, "Risky Business: The Most Common Software Risks," *American Programmer*, September 1992, p. 21.

[3]Barry Boehm, *Software Engineering Economics* (Englewood Cliffs, NJ: Prentice Hall, 1981).

[4] When OO metrics data and estimating models do appear, Jones's company, Software Productivity Research, is likely to be one of the first suppliers, with appropriate changes to its CHECKPOINT estimating model. Other aspects of the metrics problem can be found in Capers Jones's *Applied Software Measurement* (New York: McGraw-Hill, 1991).

options: rely on the classical estimating models, or abandon all hope of making *any* accurate estimates. The first option is the most intuitively appealing one, and is likely to be practiced almost subconsciously by most managers: simply keep on estimating the way you've been doing in the past. The danger, of course, is that the behavior of an OO project could be dramatically different from that of previous projects; if productivity and project schedules are indeed reduced 10-fold, as some OO projects have reported, then many of the classical estimating parameters are essentially useless.

On the other hand, it may turn out that the existing estimating models can continue to be used, with relatively minor modifications. Larry Putnam, one of the foremost estimating gurus in the field, argues that "estimating object-oriented projects is primarily a sizing problem. If you can translate the concept of an 'object' into function points or lines of code, then you can make the appropriate transformations in any of the standard estimating models."[5] Howard Rubin concurs: "It doesn't appear that OO will 'bust' the traditional estimating models. *Something* will bust them sooner or later, but OO will probably only require some adjustments—for example, a scaling factor—to the basic calculations."

On the other hand, one aspect of OO systems that is typically very different from "classical" systems is the human interface. Most estimating models are still based on relatively simple character-based human interfaces (e.g., on-line screens with an IBM 3270 dumb terminal), but almost all OO systems interact with their end user through a sophisticated window-oriented graphical user interface. In some cases, that GUI interface might have to be programmed manually, but already there is a strong trend in the software industry to use existing GUI-builders or class libraries to accomplish the task. In any case, the parameters for project estimation are likely to be quite different in a system in which 75 percent of the executable logic is concerned with the human interface![6]

---

[5]For more details on the estimating models developed by Larry Putnam at Quantitative Software Management, see Lawrence H. Putnam and Ware Myers, *Measures for Excellence: Reliable Software on Time, Within Budget* (Englewood Cliffs, NJ: Yourdon Press/Prentice Hall, 1992). As of February 1993, Putnam's initial OO-related data suggested that a typical object represented about 75–100 lines of code in a language like C++.

[6]This unsubstantiated figure comes from Bill Joy, at a presentation at the 1989 OOPSLA conference in New Orleans. Whether the typical figure is 75 percent or 50 percent is not terribly important; the main point is that it's typically *much* larger than one would expect in an older-style system. And while it's true that the same argument could be made about the difficulty of estimating "GUI-heavy" systems built with non-OO techniques, it's not as common a

But even if the parameters are different, the *process* of estimating schedules, resource requirements, and costs in an OO project could be performed just as in previous projects. If an OO project followed a classical waterfall life cycle, for example, the manager could break the project into its component activities (analysis, design, coding, etc.) and then break each of those activities into appropriate tasks and subtasks; the people assigned to performing those tasks could then estimate time, effort, and cost parameters. For projects following an iterative development process, similar estimating activities could be carried out for each version, or deliverable, of the system.

Beyond the scope of a single project, the obvious solution is to gather data about OO projects, to build managerial experience and to provide the parameters for an estimating model. It is reasonable to assume that most of the 45 commercial vendors of estimating tools are beginning to do that already; in the meantime, individual organizations can do the same thing—*if* they have a decent software metrics initiative underway. Unfortunately, a comprehensive software metrics program is usually associated with level 4 on the Software Engineering Institute's scale of process maturity, and hardly any organizations have achieved it; whatever metrics do exist in a typical DP organization are typically ad hoc, scattered, and downright suspect.

If we can't wait five years for a comprehensive OO metrics database to emerge, what *can* we do? For most organizations, the simple and obvious answer is: pilot projects. The data gleaned from two or three pilot projects (or even one) is not statistically sound, but it is better than nothing—especially when we may be dealing with order-of-magnitude variations from previous forms of software projects. Of course, there are many other reasons for recommending pilot projects, and we will discuss the concept in much more detail in Chapter 26.

4.2 HOW DOES OO AFFECT ESTIMATION OF SCHEDULES?

In the good old days, a project manager could examine a high-level statement of user requirements and make an educated guess that it would take, say, 12 months to build the desired system for the user. Based on previous experience, the manager could assume that

---

phenomenon. Traditional estimating techniques were developed for non-GUI, non-OO systems, and most non-OO systems are still being developed *without* GUI interfaces; by contrast, those systems that are being built with GUI interfaces are more commonly being built with OO techniques, and it is those systems that are difficult to estimate.

the first 2–3 months would be spent developing formal, detailed analysis model, the next 2–3 months might be spent developing a detailed software design, the next 1–2 months would be spent programming; and the remainder of the time would be spent testing. What should the manager do if he or she is now suddenly told that the project will be carried out with a full-scale OO approach?

As mentioned, the first thing to do—in the absence of any other data—is to begin with *existing* estimating parameters. After all, it's better to be off by one order of magnitude in one's estimates than two or three orders of magnitude.[7] Second, examine the project as if it were going to be carried out with a classical waterfall life cycle, and perform a classical work breakdown process to identify project tasks. Of course, if many of those tasks involve object-oriented technology with which the project team members are unfamiliar, then it may be difficult to estimate time and resource requirements, but at least the extent of the team's estimating difficulties is bounded and scoped. One can also use some very rough "rule-of-thumb" guidelines for OO projects; Don Firesmith, for example, makes the following recommendation:[8]

> Schedules should take into account the front-end loading of effort on projects using OOD and programming languages (e.g., Ada) that are also design languages and that have a separation of specification and body. . . . On such projects, managers can expect the following:
> - Requirements analysis and design   50–60%
> - Coding   10–15%
> - Integration and testing   25–35%

Still, this is a largely unsatisfying recommendation: most veteran project managers would feel extremely nervous venturing into a large-scale OO project with all their estimates based on past methodological approaches. For precisely this reason, the strongest advice we can give the project manager is this: abandon the waterfall life-cycle approach, and rely instead on an iterative life cycle!

---

[7]On large, complex projects, such estimates might *not* be *off* by an order of magnitude. Metrics gurus like Capers Jones have long observed that on large, complex projects, a number of nonprogramming tasks—for example, defect removal, documentation, travel to and from meetings, and hiring and relocation costs—are likely to dwarf all others.

[8]Donald G. Firesmith, *Object-Oriented Requirements Analysis and Logical Design* (New York: John Wiley and Sons, 1993), pp. 475 to 476.

There are many other good reasons to recommend an iterative (or "rapid-development") life cycle, but it is particularly important when one is using new technology (e.g., new hardware, a new operating system, or a new programming language) or a new methodology that could dramatically affect the time spent on the various project activities. The manager's strategy is quite simple: develop an initial model as best you can, but then be prepared to revise that estimate with the completion of each version/iteration of the system. Equally important, make sure that end users and higher levels of management understand that the estimates will be revised![9]

In Chapter 3, we used the terms "prototyping" and "iterative development" as if they were equivalent. In some situations, they *are* equivalent, but from the manager's perspective of estimating the project schedule, they are quite different. In most organizations today, prototyping means *throw-away* prototyping; as a result, the project proceeds as shown in Figure 4.1:

---

[9]Of course, this is easy to say but usually quite difficult to achieve politically: most project managers find that they have been "locked" into their initial estimate. This book does not provide any brilliant political solutions to the problem, nor does the introduction of an OO methodology that replaces whatever was used before it; however, if nothing else, the project manager should be prepared to write "cover-your-ass" memos to document the situation just described.

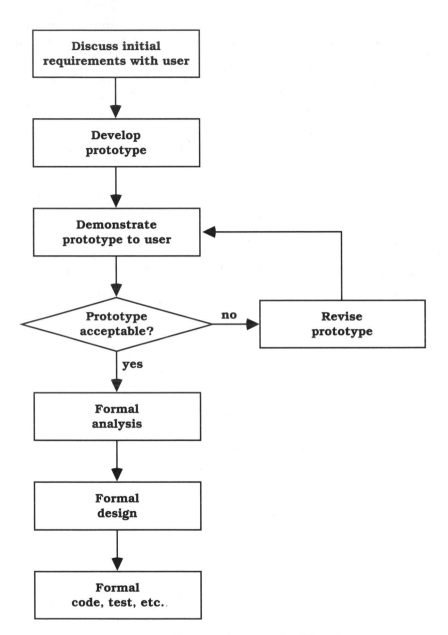

Figure 4.1: The typical prototyping life cycle

The problem with this approach is that even if the prototype is perfectly acceptable to the user, the manager still doesn't know how long it will take to do a formal analysis, design, and implementation using OO techniques. Of course, the situation is often more complicated: the prototype may have been developed with OO techniques, so perhaps it *can* be used to adjust the subsequent estimating parameters. And in some cases (e.g., on a relatively small system, implemented in Smalltalk), the prototype need not be thrown away. Nevertheless, the project manager typically does face the risk, on a medium or large project, that the prototyping effort might require 1 month, but the remainder of the "formal" effort of the project may take another 12 months, during which time there is no opportunity to revise the estimates.

Consequently, the project manager is strongly advised to consider an iterative approach wherever possible. Because prototyping is indeed such a valuable activity for discovering true user preferences and needs, we have included it in the life-cycle model shown in Figure 4.2.

Each "version" of the system should have tangible, demonstrable functionality; in the ideal case, that functionality should be "operational" from the user's perspective, and the user should expect to be able to put that version of the system into limited production. This is particularly important to ensure that the project team has not built a "mock-up" prototype and that it has actually implemented the required components for performance, backup, security, and other operational details of that version.

From the project manager's perspective, the most important activity is the last one of each version: *revise estimates*. By comparing the *actual* time and effort spent on analysis, design, coding, and testing for version N against the *estimated* time and effort, the manager is in a better position to improve the estimates for the next version.[10] In Barry Boehm's "spiral" life-cycle model, this activity is enlarged to be come a full-scale risk analysis effort.[11]

---

[10]But two things must be kept in mind: first, the project team is likely to have learned a lot about OO from their experiences in version N, so its members will presumably be more efficient at performing those same tasks in version $N + 1$. Second, if version N was delivered behind schedule, there will be a natural tendency to work harder to "catch up" on the overall schedule. These phenomena are typical of the "systems dynamics" that take place within any software project; for a fascinating discussion of modeling the "system for building systems," with its feedback loops and time delays, see Tarek Abdel-Hamid and Stuart Madnick, *Software Project Dynamics: An Integrated Approach* (Englewood Cliffs, NJ: Prentice Hall, 1991).

[11]For a discussion of the spiral life-cycle model and several interesting variations, see Peter DeGrace and Leslie Hulet Stahl, *Wicked Systems, Righteous Solutions: A Catalog of Modern Software Engineering Paradigms* (Englewood Cliffs, NJ: Yourdon Press/Prentice Hall, 1990). For a good discussion of spiral life cycle-models in an OO environment, see Mark Lorenz, *Object-Oriented Software Development: A Practical Guide* (Englewood Cliffs, NJ: Prentice Hall, 1993).

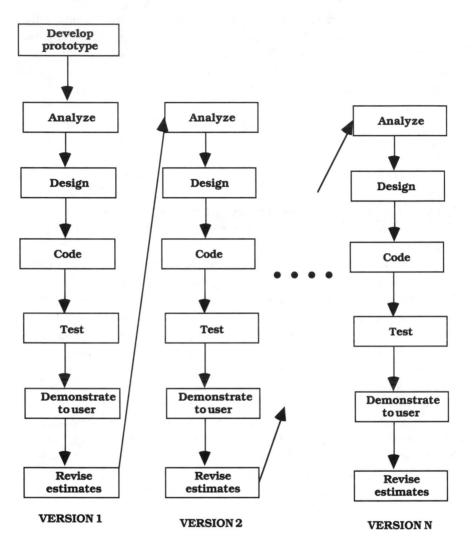

Figure 4.2: The iterative life cycle

There is another reason for emphasizing the iterative life-cycle approach with OO technology: it helps the project manager distinguish between *actual* progress and *perceived* progress. With any new analysis/design methodology, there is a danger that the project team will invest a great deal of effort in the creation of abstract models, for example, the kind of diagrams discussed in detail in Parts III and IV of this book. This can easily lead to the infamous "90 percent done" syndrome: the project team may report to its manager, "We just finished drawing all the object diagrams with our CASE tool, boss, and they look real good! We think we're 90 percent done—all that's left is a simple matter of programming!" But delivering a demonstrable, functionally operational *version* of a system is a different matter altogether: those abstract diagrams have to be converted into running code on the machine. For first-time practitioners of a new systems development methodology, this is a sobering experience!

On the other hand, the disadvantage of any form of iterative life cycle is that the project team and/or the user may fall prey to the temptation of endless iteration. The user's tendency to continue embellishing a prototype or an intermediate version of a system is well known; this phenomenon existed long before OO came along, and it is likely to continue into the foreseeable future. And there is a natural tendency to continue iterating the human interface portion of a system; GUI interfaces offer a whole new dimension of "polishing" for the systems developer and the user. But in addition to all that, the OO paradigm provides a new opportunity for iteration: the systems developers have a tendency to continue refining the class hierarchy of their objects long after the user has expressed complete satisfaction with the functional behavior of the system. The project manager must be aware of this phenomenon: if "gilding the lily" was a problem with conventional methodologies in an iterative life cycle, it will be even more of a problem with an OO methodology![12]

There is one last point to emphasize about estimating the schedule for developing an OO system: as mentioned in Chapter 2, one the most common characteristics of a "good" OO project is a high level of reuse. This must be taken into account by the project manager, with the following provisos: first, many first-time OO projects will have little experience in the "culture" of reuse (which is discussed in Chapter 6); hence it may not be much of a factor. Second, intraproject reuse is not likely to be as significant as interproject reuse; hence the higher levels of reuse may not be evident until the second, third, or fourth OO project. Finally, the extent, or degree, of potential reuse should be estimated at the beginning of each version, and that estimate should be revised at the end of each version of the system.

---

[12]To be fair to the developers, it should be pointed out that sometimes this ongoing iteration is performed for the sake of improving the reusability of the classes and objects. But the project manager may have difficulty justifying this, as the benefits of such activities will accrue to some other project.

A cautious project manager might take a different approach to the estimating dilemma discussed in this section: simply use the traditional estimating approach that would have been used before OO was introduced. Then, if OO technology does provide dramatic productivity improvements, the manager is a hero! Indeed, this is often a practical approach for the *first* OO project within the organization, for the "learning curve" problems discussed in Chapter 27 are likely to negate whatever productivity gains would have been achieved. But there is likely to be a more serious political problem: the introduction of OO within the organization is likely to be accompanied with the "hype" of order-of-magnitude productivity improvements, so the manager will be *forced* to come up with an estimate that shows faster development schedules and/or higher levels of productivity—otherwise, the investment in OO technology won't be justified!

4.3 ESTIMATING PERSONNEL REQUIREMENTS

In addition to estimating the project schedule, the second major activity carried out by project managers is estimating resources: How many people will I need and when will I need them? In general, the advice in this area is the same as in the previous section: begin with estimates based on classical parameters; use a work breakdown approach to identify the tasks that need to be done; use an iterative life cycle to provide an opportunity to revise those estimates; recognize that higher levels of reuse may dramatically affect the number of people required by the project.

What else can we tell the project manager about resource requirements for an OO project? Perhaps the most important thing, as discussed in earlier chapters, is that the OO project team is more likely to be small and highly cohesive than in previous kinds of projects. If the technology of OO allows the project to be implemented with a team of 5 people instead of 50, it eliminates much of the administrative infrastructure that bogs down many projects, for example, a proliferation of secretaries, administrators, coordinators, facilitators, team leaders, supervisors, and so on. There is likely to be less need for status reports, staff meetings, conference rooms, and other forms of communication—for the project team can fit into one office and communicate via osmosis. This may seem like a minor point, but on medium and large projects, it often seems that the people doing useful work are overwhelmed by all the administrators trying to ensure that everyone is doing the right thing at the right time (and building political empires along the way).

It is also quite likely that there will be a different mix of skills in an OO project than in a conventional project. With a robust library of reusable objects, there is likely to be much less "programming," in the conventional sense, but there may be a greater need to have someone on the project who is adept at finding and adapting components in the library; thus an OO project may have "class librarians" and "class developers." We will discuss this further in Chapter 7.

Also, the class library concept of OO, together with the inheritance concept, places a much greater emphasis on *configuration management:* if someone makes a change to the attributes or behavior of a class, that change ripples down through the inheritance hierarchy to all the subordinate classes. This is discussed in Chapter 5.

Naturally, with any new methodology, it is useful to have a "methods guru" who can advise other team members, as well as project management, on the best way to practice the particular OO methodology being used. On small projects, this role might be carried out by a part-time advisor, but on larger projects, it is likely to be a full-time responsibility.

5

Object-Oriented
Configuration Management

Configuration management has long been recognized as a basic principle of good software engineering. A large system consisting of thousands of individual components experiences myriad changes during each of the life-cycle activities described in previous chapters. To avoid utter chaos, the project team must distinguish between various versions of each component and must have an orderly process to ensure that changes are made to versions in a consistent, controlled fashion.

Configuration management was once considered a programming problem, for it was during the programming and testing phases of the project that the most significant changes occurred; thus the *tools* associated with configuration management typically consisted of library management packages intended to control changes made to source-code and object-code libraries. But during the past decade, with the gradual increase in analysis/design modeling techniques, and with the advent of code-generators and CASE tools that transform those models directly into executable code, configuration management has come to be seen as an important issue throughout the *entire* life cycle of a system—from the first moment of systems analysis until the last maintenance change is made and the system is retired.

At the same time, configuration management tools have been elevated to the status of a full-fledged CASE tool; managing the "configuration" of the system, regardless of what stage of development it is currently in, is essentially a task of ensuring that the appropriate elements within the CASE *repository* are managed properly. While not all CASE vendors actually have adequate version-control and change-control mechanisms to ensure consistency of their repository elements, it is clearly a major trend underway in the industry.

What does all this have to do with OO? Quite simply, configuration management is even more important for OO projects than for "conventional" projects, and it will probably require new tools or modifications to existing tools. It may also influence the way in which the OO project is organized and managed.

While this chapter is mercifully brief, the issues must not be ignored by the project manager—especially if the OO project team is larger than a handful of people who can fit into one office. This chapter addresses the special problems of OO configuration management and suggests what steps should be taken.

5.1 WHY IS CONFIGURATION MANAGEMENT IMPORTANT IN OO?

Those with any familiarity with OO technology can easily guess why configuration management assumes such importance: *inheritance* and the desire to emphasize reuse. The fundamental OO paradigm as discussed in Chapter 1 virtually guarantees that a class will inherit aspects of its data attributes and its behavior from one or more levels of superclasses above it.

For example, suppose we have the kind of class hierarchy in our system shown in Figure 5.1.

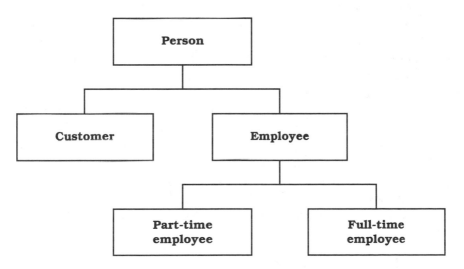

Figure 5.1: A typical class hierarchy

Suppose that one of the data attributes of the **person** superclass is "age," which has been defined as an integer with values between 0 and 99; we might also imagine that the superclass has an associated "method" that will retrieve the age of a specified instance of *person* on demand and a method that will validate the age attribute.[1] By definition, the subclasses of **employee**, **part-time employee**, and **full-time employee** inherit that attribute and methods (along with any other attributes and methods of **person**). The subclasses might have additional attributes and methods, as we will see in Part III of this book; for example, the **part-time employee** subclass might not allow a new instance to be added if the "age" attribute is less than 18, and the **full-time employee** subclass might have a method that causes an instance to be retired (which may or not involve deleting the instance entirely!) if the "age" attribute is greater than 65.

Now consider the following simple change announced by one of the application programmers on the project, after the system has been analyzed and designed and is in the midst of the programming life-cycle phase: she decides that the "age" attribute, defined in **person**, should be three digits—after all, quite a few people today live well past the age of 100 (including, it is hoped, the author and all his readers!). What impact does that have on **part-time employee** and **full-time employee**? From the description given, the optimistic answer is: "None!" But are you really sure? Would you really be willing to make such a change to a system without carefully studying the subclass methods to see if they are impacted? And meanwhile, what about the **customer** subclass? Is it affected by a simple change in the definition of "age"? Who knows?

Meanwhile, the programmer returns a day later and announces that the change she had made wasn't quite what she intended: after all, a three-digit (decimal) data field would allow instances of **person** with an age of 999 years. What she *really* meant was that the legal values of "age" were being defined as, say, 0 to 200. This might require more bytes of data than had originally been allocated, but the main point is that the *method* that validates the age attribute needs to

---

[1]Note that this implies that age is a relevant attribute for *all* persons, including members of the subclass of **customer**. If our customers don't wish to have their age recorded, then "age" would have to be demoted to the subclass of **employee**.

be modified. After implementing this change, the programmer returns and announces (as many veteran programmers would have suspected all along) that the very concept of an "age" attribute was faulty, because a person's age is constantly changing. So, she announces that **person** will have a new attribute called "birthdate" and a new method called "compute_current_age." What impact does *that* have on the various subclasses?

If all this seems too obvious and trivial, consider one last change: the organization for which the system is being developed announces, in the middle of the project, that it has just acquired a new subsidiary—a small firm called FormerLives Ltd, which deals in the occult and supernatural. Since FormerLives believes in reincarnation, the instances of **person** that it wants to incorporate into the system may have birthdates as old as 5000 B.C.; furthermore, it wishes to maintain instances of a person's "former self," for whom "age" should be represented as a *negative* integer. What changes would that require? The realistic answer, of course, is that the entire class hierarchy would probably have to be changed, but the moral of the story is that subclasses in an OO class hierarchy are, by their very nature, tightly coupled to the classes above them. A change in a superclass ripples down through all the subclasses below; the consequences of such changes have to be carefully controlled.

In addition to the inheritance argument, configuration management is also important because of the *delegation* phenomenon in OO systems: if an object is unable to carry out a requested activity by itself (e.g., because it does not understand a message it has received), then it will delegate the activity to another object. Thus, if a change is made to an object, the various "collaborators" involved in this delegation must be examined to see if they are impacted by the change.

And there is another reason for emphasizing configuration management in OO projects: the interactive nature of an iterative, rapid-prototyping type of life cycle discussed in Chapter 3. This can be a problem in non-OO projects, too, of course; conversely, we can imagine OO projects that proceed in a strict waterfall sequence of life-cycle activities. But the reality is that most OO projects are composed of relatively small groups of people who work together in an intensely iterative manner; the classes they create are constantly being extended, modified, and corrected throughout the project. Without proper configuration management, chaos is inevitable.

5.2 TOOLS FOR OO CONFIGURATION MANAGEMENT

All this suggests that configuration management tools will be essential for an OO project. While the same could be argued for non-OO projects, it is obvious from the preceding example that there is one critical difference between OO and non-OO tools: the OO configuration management tools must be intimately familiar with the concept of inheritance.

The two basic components of an OO configuration management tool are these:

- *Impact analysis.* If a change is made to one component, what is the impact on other components? As we have seen in the example earlier, our immediate concern is the impact up and down an inheritance hierarchy. But this is just the beginning: as we will see in Part III of this book, objects can have "instance connections," or "relationships" with other objects, and, as part of the basic OO paradigm, objects *communicate* with other objects via messages. Thus the "ripple effect" of a change in one object could potentially be widespread; for a large system, with thousands of objects, an impact analysis tool is crucial.

- *Version control.* Most software development projects make a distinction between "private" libraries and "public" libraries. Each software engineer wants the freedom of his own private library, where he can store various versions of a component with little or no controls imposed on him; this allows him to experiment with different ideas and debug individual components without affecting anyone else. When a component is relatively stable, it can be transferred to a public library, where changes may continue to be made—but under much stricter control. The impact analysis tool might dictate that if object X is changed from version 1 to version 2, then its subclasses Y and Z must also be upgraded. The objective of the version control tool is to ensure that the entire system consists of consistent and compatible versions of its components; in addition, such tools normally contain a number of administrative mechanisms to log a history of changes, maintain copies of previous versions, and so on.

One good example of a configuration management system for Smalltalk development projects is the ENVY product from Object Technology International;[2] similar products exist for the control and management of C++ class libraries. However, as mentioned at the beginning of this chapter, it is likely that the growing popularity of OO analysis and design will gradually move the focus of configuration management into full-blown life-cycle management tools. James Rumbaugh and coworkers make the following observation about OO configuration management tools:

> Tools for *system-building* and *change control* are essential for large projects but are also suitable for individual programmers. . . . Experience has shown that the use of conventional building tools, such as UNIX *make*, are too crude for many purposes. Finer-grained development environments are needed but are only recently available.[3]

Such new development environments, typically described as OO CASE tools, are discussed in more detail in Chapters 23 and 24.

5.3 CONFIGURATION MANAGEMENT SPECIALISTS FOR OO

In addition to tools, an OO project is far more likely to need a strong configuration management *person* (or group of people) than a conventional project. Aside from the technical issues just discussed, the main reason is that OO projects traditionally place much more emphasis on *reuse* of objects and classes in a common library. While the tools described in the previous section can carry out much of the tedious administrative activities, a human presence is also needed.

The configuration management person is often described as the "librarian" or the "repository administrator" or the "object manager." These are familiar terms from other forms of software development methodologies, but the emphasis on management is often much stronger in OO projects; thus one often hears job titles like "Conan the

---

[2]Object Technology International is located at 2670 Queensview Drive, Ottawa, Ontario, Canada K2B 8K1. Phone 613-820-1200; fax 613-820-1202

[3]James Rumbaugh, Michael Blaha, William Premerlani, Frederick Eddy, and William Lorensen, *Object-Oriented Modeling and Design* (Englewood Cliffs, NJ: Prentice Hall, 1991), p. 323..

Librarian" or "Repository Gatekeeper" or "Object Lord" in OO projects. Grady Booch describes the configuration management specialist as a "librarian," with the following duties:

> The duties of the librarian are to maintain the class library for a project. Without active effort, such a library can become a vast wasteland of junk classes that no developer would ever want to walk through. Also, it is often necessary to be proactive to encourage reuse, and a librarian can facilitate this process by scavenging the products of current design effort.[4]

One can easily imagine the duties of Conan the Librarian for the kind of changes proposed for the class hierarchy shown in Figure 5.1. Most of the proposed changes involved modifications to an attribute or method *inside* an object; the question, of course, was what impact the proposed change would have on other objects.

But a more serious kind of change involves the class hierarchy itself. Here are some examples:

- *New class versus subclass.* For the example illustrated in Figure 5.1, suppose that one of the project team members proposes to add a new class of objects called **supplier**? Should this be treated as a new class, entirely distinct from **person**, with its own inheritance hierarchy? Or is a **supplier** simply a new subclass of person, at the same level as **employee** and **customer**? In most cases, Conan the Librarian will pointedly ask the question, "Why can't you make this proposed class a subclass of something that already exists?"

- *Proposed reusable class.* Regardless of whether **supplier** turns out to be an entirely new class, or a subclass of something that already exists, Conan the Librarian is concerned with its potential for reuse; the software engineer who first proposed **supplier** is probably more concerned with solving his immediate problem, within a narrower problem domain. The Librarian will be concerned with the applicability of the proposed new class throughout the rest of the project, and possibly within a broader context in the organization; this will lead to questions about whether the proposed object has the right attributes and methods to be as reusable as possible;

---

[4]Grady Booch, *Object-Oriented Design, with Applications* (Redwood City, CA: Benjamin/Cummings, 1991), p. 214.

this investigation might indicate that there is already a class within the overall class library, created by a different project, called **vendor**. But equally important, the librarian wants to ensure that the proposed new class has an adequate level of *quality* to be trusted by other project team members. Has it been reviewed, or subjected to a design inspection? Has it been properly tested, with adequate samples of test data to exercise thoroughly the code in all its methods?

- *Changing the existing hierarchy.* The most potentially disruptive event in an OO project is a change to the class hierarchy. This may be the result of a major, unanticipated change imposed by the user, for example, the introduction of reincarnation in our earlier example. But it may also come from the project team members themselves, who gradually decide that the initial "factoring" of classes into subclasses was far from optimal, and could be improved. For example, if we examined Figure 5.1 in more detail, it would probably occur to us that we need to make a distinction between **corporate customer** and **individual customer**; if the additional subclass of **supplier** is introduced, we would probably also want to distinguish between a corporate supplier and an individual supplier. Indeed, this might lead the project team to consider the possibility of distinguishing between individual and corporate employees—something that probably never occurred to anyone up to this point in the project. And, inevitably, someone in the project team would observe that an instance of **person** could simultaneously be an employee, a customer, and a supplier.[5] It is not at all difficult to imagine a major change to the class hierarchy in Figure 5.1 as a result of such discussions; but it is the librarian's job to ensure that such drastic changes are made carefully and, in a controlled fashion, to avoid chaos.

---

[5]Exactly how we choose to model a situation like this might well depend on whether we decide to allow *multiple* inheritance, a concept that will be further discussed in Chapter 10. An alternative would be to define a class of *roles*, which are separate and distinct from the class of *person*. Then we could determine whether the user's policy is to allow a person to play one role at a time or multiple simultaneous roles.

5.4 CONCLUSION

Most software engineers are more interested in the *technology* of their work than in the *management* of their work; thus it is unlikely that programmers, designers, and systems analysts will show much interest in the subject of configuration management.

With managers, the problem is different. As Grady Booch observes,

> A manager already faced with scarce human resources may lament that powerful tools, as well as designated librarians and toolsmiths, are an unaffordable luxury. We do not deny this reality for some resource-constrained projects. However, in many other projects, we have found that these activities go on anyway, usually in an *ad hoc* fashion. We advocate explicit investments in tools and people to make these *ad hoc* activities more focused and efficient, which adds real value to the overall development effort.[6]

Until now, most OO projects have been small enough that an ad hoc effort would suffice. However, if OO methodologies are to be used on a large, complex, industrial-strength application, managers ignore configuration management at their peril. Explicit investments are indeed crucial.

[6]Booch, *Object-Oriented Design*, p. 214.

6

Object-Oriented Software Reuse

6.0 INTRODUCTION

Software reusability will go down in history as one of the major technical contributors to software productivity and quality in the 1990s.[1] Even though most software organizations have endorsed the concept of reusability since the 1960s (or before), it has rarely been practiced effectively.

In this chapter, we first review the reasons why software reusability is so important. Then we examine why reusability is not being practiced in many organizations. Next we take a closer look at the definition of "reusability" and see that there are many "levels" of reusability. Finally, we examine the technological and organizational means of achieving higher levels of reusability. But while technological solutions—including object orientation—are important, the organizational solutions are far more important.[2]

---

[1]This chapter is adapted from Chapter 9 of the author's *Decline and Fall of the American Programmer* (Englewood Cliffs, NJ: Yourdon Press/Prentice Hall, 1992).

[2]Alan Davis, author of *Software Requirements: Analysis & Specification* (Englewood Cliffs, NJ: Prentice Hall, 1990), put it much more bluntly when he reviewed the manuscript for this book: ". . . reuse and OO are not synonyms. Reuse can be practiced extremely well with or without OO. OO can be practiced well with or without reuse. An OO project can also fail miserably at practicing reuse." Unfortunately, many popular magazine articles have created the impression that OO and reuse are synonyms; as we saw in Chapter 1, this has even crept into some of the publications from the Object Management Group. Even worse, the impression has been created that reuse is easy—all you need to do is practice a little OO. The purpose of this chapter is to dispel these two myths.

6.1 WHY DOES IT MATTER?

Like loyalty, thrift, and bravery, software reusability is something that everyone believes in and that most people try to practice from time to time. Here is a simple rule of thumb: the best DP organizations are achieving reusability levels of 70 to 80 percent, while the typical shop achieves levels more on the order of 20 to 30 percent. Thus, when faced with the task of building a system requiring 100,000 lines of code, the good shop writes 20,000–30,000 lines of new code and reuses 70,000–80,000 lines of code from a library of reusable components. The bad shop treats the 100,000-line system as an intellectual exercise never before tackled by the human race and writes 70,000–80,000 lines of new code, with only 20,000–30,000 lines taken from a library. To make matters worse, the bad shop has little or no control over the manner in which the code is reused; the typical approach is to make a physical copy of the code to be reused and then make slight alterations as needed.

The primary benefit of software reusability is, of course, higher productivity. In a superficial sense, the DP shop that achieves 80 percent reusability is four times as productive as the DP shop with 20 percent reusability. However, the savings are rarely this great, because the benefits of reusability require:

- An investment to create the reusable components in the first place. This "capital investment" can then be amortized over the number of new systems or programs that make use of those components. Obviously, the more often the components can be reused, the less onerous the initial capital investment.

- An investment to perform higher levels of testing and quality assurance than would normally be expected for unique software components. Higher levels of testing and quality assurance are required by, and justified by, the higher levels of usage. Most organizations find that they need two to four times as much testing for reusable components as for unique components. As we suggested in Chapter 5, this task might fall to a project librarian.

- An investment to maintain libraries, browsers, and other facilities so that software engineers can *find* the reusable components when they need them. This can range from a simple index of available components to an on-line, interactive expert system search facility based on keywords, and so on.

Nevertheless, it is not unusual to see DP shops achieving productivity increases of 50 to 200 percent from serious, deliberate use of software reusability; indeed, as we suggested in Chapter 2, this may be the primary reason for the substantial productivity increases associated with object orientation.

There is another reason to emphasize reusability: *increased quality*. As mentioned, a reusable software component always requires more testing and quality assurance than its nonreusable brethren, simply because the consequences of an error are that much more serious. But if this is the bad news, the good news is that modules with heavy reuse will, by definition, have higher quality than will ordinary modules; in simple parlance, the bugs are shaken out much more quickly and thoroughly. Thus building a new system with a large percentage of reusable modules means that we are using modules with the "Good Housekeeping Seal of Approval"; while we may still suffer from problems of poor specifications or bad designs, at least the basic software building blocks will be solid.

There is another benefit that is often overlooked: reusability can provide a mechanism for prototyping, which, as we saw in Chapter 3, is a common approach in OO projects. Many current approaches to prototyping depend on high-level languages and/or screen-painting tools to build a quick-and-dirty "skeleton" version of a system; the problem is that while the external facade of the system may look impressive to the user, there is nothing behind the facade—no functionality that the user can exercise to see if the prototype is actually doing something useful. But as researchers at the Software Productivity Consortium observed to me a few years ago, "Reusability and prototyping are two sides of the same coin." A prototype built from reusable components can provide full functionality, since it is built from fully coded and fully tested components; because the components already exist, the prototype should be just as easy and quick to build as any other form of prototype.

6.2 WHY AREN'T WE DOING IT?

If reusability is such a good thing, why aren't we doing more of it? Is it simply because we haven't been following an OO systems development methodology all these years? I believe that the *technology* of systems development is only one of the factors; altogether, there are four major reasons for relatively low levels of reuse in most organizations today:

- Software engineering textbooks teach new practitioners to build systems from "first principles"; reusability is not promoted or even discussed.
- The "not-invented-here" (NIH) syndrome, and the intellectual challenge of solving an interesting software problem in one's own unique way, mitigates against reusing someone else's software component.
- Unsuccessful experiences with software reusability in the past have convinced many practitioners and DP managers that the concept is not practical.
- Most organizations provide no reward for reusability, productivity is measured in terms of *new* lines of code written, and reused lines of code are typically discounted by 50 percent or more.

Thus the emphasis in this book is on the managerial and organizational problems that have served as barriers to reuse. This does not deny the fact that there are still some very difficult technical problems to solve, but it is interesting to note that some organizations have been able to achieve remarkably high levels of reuse, and their success has consistently been associated with management practices rather than some mysterious new software technology.

Let's examine each of these problems in more detail.

6.2.1 Software Textbooks Don't Teach Reusability

Almost every textbook and every university course in programming, systems design, systems analysis, or software engineering teaches the student how to solve problems, design systems, and write code "from scratch." In a few rare cases, the student might be taught a form of "bottom-up" design, in which she begins with existing library modules and composes larger aggregates to solve the desired problem. But in most cases, the student is given a blank sheet of paper (or an empty CASE workstation) and is instructed to analyze/design/code "top-down," for example, by identifying major functions and decomposing them into smaller subfunctions. Nowhere is the student told that the problem she is solving has probably been solved hundreds of times before and that the most practical approach is to find an *existing* approximate solution and refine it to meet her special needs. Indeed, most universities would consider this a form of plagiarism and would penalize the student heavily for such "unethical" behavior!

Not surprisingly, this educational bias becomes deeply ingrained and stays with the student when she joins the work force. No wonder so many junior programmers experience severe culture shock when they learn that their first job (possibly for several years) will be to maintain musty old programs written by previous generations of programmers.

6.2.2 The NIH Syndrome

The NIH syndrome is pervasive in American industry; it is certainly not confined to software development. In every field of business, science, and engineering, people have an innate urge to reinvent the wheel, solving age-old problems over and over again.

The NIH syndrome is particularly acute in software development, perhaps because each design problem appears to the novice software engineer to be such a novel puzzle. And as we know, any software problem—no matter how small—has myriad possible solutions. Some solutions are faster, some are slower; some are larger, some are smaller; some are more elegant, some less so; indeed, some solutions are more reusable, and others are less reusable. But all the solutions can be correct; like a game of chess, there are an infinite number of ways to play the game and win.

The important thing to realize is that the novice software engineer derives great intellectual pleasure from solving familiar problems—whether it is a binary sort, a missile trajectory calculation, or a FICA tax calculation—on her own, with the possibility of *possibly* finding a better solution.

In most cases, software engineers eventually grow tired of reinventing solutions to problems *they themselves* have already solved; sooner or later, the novelty and excitement wane. The journeyman software engineer gradually builds his own personal library of previously solved problems, which he rummages through whenever faced with a new problem that has familiar overtones.

We should not fault the curiosity of fledgling software engineers, or their desire to find a better solution to age-old software problems; after all, this is how progress is made. However, it is important for a DP shop to provide the appropriate encouragement, incentive, and education so that the software engineer can begin focusing his intellectual energy on problems that have *not* been solved, while reusing existing solutions to problems that *have* been solved. As we will see shortly, this encouragement is often lacking.

6.2.3 Unsuccessful Experiences with Reusability

Obviously, the notion of software reusability is not a new concept—and it would be unfair and inaccurate to suggest that no one has tried to accomplish it. Indeed, many DP shops did try to implement reusable libraries in the 1960s and 1970s; however, the results were often so unimpressive that the effort was abandoned.

Why have previous results been unsuccessful, and what can we learn from the failures? In my experience, the difficulties with software reusability have been pure management failures, pure technical failures, or a combination of the two. The most common causes were the following:

Management Failures

- *Inadequate resources or investment.* Reusability doesn't happen merely as a result of management slogans and exhortations. The resources required to build, maintain, and manage a reusable library obviously depend on a number of factors, but the dollar investment can be quite high: one division of Motorola estimated the cost at $1 million (but was easily able to justify the cost with a return-on-investment calculation).
- *Not creating a separate group to create reusable software components.* As discussed shortly, it is unrealistic to assume that software engineers will have the time, energy, and foresight to create reusable software components while trying to develop software for a specific project. A separate group of reusable component producers is needed.
- *Not rewarding software engineers for reusability.* This is discussed in more detail in Section 6.2.4.

Management/Technical Failures

- *Inadequate configuration control.* If the organization can't keep track of which version of which reusable components are currently used in which systems, the reusability effort will get out of control and eventually collapse. As we discussed in Chapter 5, this problem is exacerbated in OO projects because of the highly iterative, iterative nature of development, and because of the technical concept of inheritance.
- *Inadequate searching/browsing/lookup mechanisms.* If you don't know where the reusable components are, or if you can't find one that meets your needs, you won't use it. Developing an

adequate searching mechanism is partly a technical problem and a potentially nontrivial problem: some have suggested the need for expert system AI technology to match the needs of a component user with the features of library components. But it's also a management problem: if management doesn't invest resources to build a library retrieval mechanism, it will never get built. In OO projects, those who succeed with reuse inevitably have good development environments with powerful browsing mechanisms; the Smalltalk environment is a common example.

- *Too little control over what gets put into the library.* The result is often an enormous amount of low-quality junk, with overlapping functionality, undocumented features, and so on. As an example, Tom DeMarco (former president of the U.S. Modula-2 User's Group) recently described the Modula-2 library: "it has 30,000 procedures and is virtually useless." As we mentioned in Chapter 5, the presence of a strong "Conan the Librarian" is essential to maintaining a high-quality library of reusable components.

Technical Failures

- *Including software components that are too large and/or have too many side effects.* This was one of the most common problems with reusable libraries in the 1960s: there was a tendency to create "general-purpose" components that attempted to do all things for all people under all conditions. The result typically was that the component didn't do anything terribly well for anyone, and often had disastrous, and totally unacceptable, side effects (such as clearing a CRT screen before displaying some desired text). A better example of reusable components—indeed, the *ideal* example, in my opinion—is the UNIX library, whose components are tiny (often less than 10 lines of code) and with no side effects.[3]

- *Undocumented interfaces.* If the software engineer can't figure out what input parameters are required, and what output parameters are produced by the reusable software component—that is, the details of the *messages* understood by an object—it's virtually impossible to use.

---

[3]Interestingly, this has led to some suggestions about appropriate metrics for judging the likely reusability of an object, based on the depth of its inheritance hierarchy, and also based on the number of methods contained with the class. We will discuss this further in Chapter 21.

- *No facility for exceptions and overrides.* In many cases, the software engineer will say, "I need something like module X in the library . . . but just a little bit different." The "little bit different" may involve slightly more or slightly less functionality, different data parameters, a different calling sequence, and so on. Traditional software development techniques couldn't deal with this: one had to use all the reusable module or none of it, and consequently, the software engineer often decided not to use any of it. With today's workstation environments and Macintosh-like graphical user interfaces, the programmer can, in the most primitive case, use a "cut and paste" approach to scavenge (and thus partially reuse) source code from a library; a far better approach is provided by the OO paradigm, which allows the software engineer to create subclasses of existing objects to create the needed overrides and exceptions.

- *Software overhead required to compile, link, and execute the reusable module.* If a reusable module could be found in the 1960s and 1970s, it often imposed an unacceptable overhead of CPU cycles and/or memory for compilation, link editing, and execution. While the overhead still exists today, it is much easier to tolerate with multimegabyte memory space and processors that are typically 10 to 100 times faster than predecessor machines.

6.2.4 No Rewards for Software Reusability

Many DP shops *do* emphasize productivity today. Indeed, productivity—whether measured in lines of code or function points—has been one of the most important measures of a DP shop's effectiveness for three decades or more.

But the sad fact is that almost all DP shops measure productivity in terms of *new* code written by the software engineer; no credit is given for modules or software components that have been reused. No reward or recognition is offered to the software engineer who has a higher level of reusability in his code than his peers.

Some organizations *do* count reused code, but with only a fraction the value of new code. Thus a system consisting of 100,000 lines of new code and 100,000 lines of code taken from a reusable library will be given the same productivity value as 150,000 lines of new code. What the organization *should* be doing is measuring the productivity of *delivered* functionality to the end user, not the number of lines of newly invented code that frequently repeats the intellectual effort done by dozens of previous software engineers.

Within reasonable limits, software engineers behave just like Pavlov's dogs: if they are rewarded for writing new code, they will write more new code; if their efforts to reuse existing code are effectively penalized, then they will avoid making the effort.

Sometimes the problem is more insidious. The DP shop may promote the benefits of reusability, and may even give full credit to the software engineer who reuses existing code in lieu of writing new code. But there is still a problem: Where does the reusable components come from in the first place? As mentioned earlier, additional effort—over and above what one would expect for a "normal" software component—is required to design, code, test, and perform quality assurance on a software component that is intended *from the outset* to be reusable; a good rule of thumb is that such reusable components will take twice the effort of a "one-shot" component. For the software engineer and the DP manager working to finish a specific project on time and within budget, the question is: Where is the time, where is the budget to invest in the creation of reusable software components? This is more than an academic question, for without such an investment, there may be no library of reusable components, and without a library, there will be no reusability.

The problem is typically the result of the *focus* of productivity efforts in most DP shops. Most DP organizations tend to concentrate on *individual* productivity improvements through tools, techniques, training, and so on. A few focus on *project-level* productivity, using networked CASE tools, JAD sessions, and so on. But software reusability should be aimed at *enterprise productivity*, and the DP organization must treat it as a capital investment rather than hoping each software engineer will have the inspiration, dedication, and energy to create reusable software components for the good of the enterprise in his or her spare time.

Indeed, this strongly suggests that the DP shop should have a separate group of software engineers devoted to the development of highly reusable software components. We will discuss this in more detail in Section 6.5.

6.3 LEVELS OF REUSABILITY

Much of the foregoing discussion implied that the major "asset" to be reused in a software development organization is *code*, that is, executable statements in Smalltalk, C++, or the older procedural languages like Pascal, COBOL, and FORTRAN. As we will see, reusability involves much more than just code, but since code is what everyone talks about, let's start with code.

6.3.1 Reusing Code

What's involved in reusing code? The phrase "code reuse" usually conjures up images of making a subroutine call to a module in a library, but it can take any of the forms listed here:

- *Cut and paste of source code.* This has been taking place since programs were first written on punched cards and stone tablets. In some cases, the code is reused in exactly the same form as the original; in other cases, as mentioned, it may be modified to suit slightly different circumstances. Obviously, this approach is better than no reuse at all, but it is the most primitive of all forms of reuse. In earlier days, there was a significant clerical cost associated with transcribing the code to be reused, but that has largely disappeared with today's cut and paste text editors; nevertheless, the software engineer runs the risk of introducing errors during the copying (and modification) of the original code. Worse is the configuration management problem: it is generally impossible for the DP manager to keep track of the multiple mutated uses of the original "chunk" of code. Nevertheless, this is probably the most commonly practiced form of reuse today—*and it continues to exist in DP shops using the most advanced OO methodologies.*
- *Source-level "includes."* Most high-level programming languages contain a mechanism for copying, or "including," source program text from a library. In COBOL, for example, the COPY statement is used for this purpose; in C and C++, the INCLUDE statement does the same job. In some languages, the specified library file is copied verbatim; in others, parameter substitution can be used to accomplish a minor amount of customization. Most often, the "include" facility is used to copy standard data definitions or parameter values,

which we will discuss further in Section 6.3.2; however, it can also be used to copy executable program statements. In the latter case, a disadvantage of the "include" facility is that a copy of the specified statements is made *each* time the include statement is invoked; thus it tends to be used primarily for "tiny" macros or functions that involve only two or three executable statements.

- *Binary links.* Most programming languages also provide for "external" calls to subroutines, procedures, or functions contained in a library. These external functions have already been compiled or assembled, but they must still be incorporated into the program that invokes them; this is usually done during a "load" or "link-edit" step after compilation of the main program. The primary advantage of this form of reuse is that only one physical copy of the reused component needs to be included, regardless of the number of times it is invoked; the linkage is accomplished through subroutine calls or function invocations.

- *Execution time invocation.* The problem with all three forms of source code reuse mentioned is that programmers must know, at the time they write their code, *which* component they wish to reuse; the "binding" of the reused component takes place at coding time, compile time, or link-edit time. In some cases, though, programmers may need the flexibility to allow their program to determine, *at execution time*, which component should be invoked. Some (but not all) object-oriented programming languages, facilitate this by allowing the definition of *dynamic* functions/procedures, the identity (or address) of which will be resolved at run time. *This is another point to remember about the OO paradigm: the degree to which the OOPL supports dynamic binding may strongly influence the degree of reusability in the organization.*[4]

---

[4]To put it another way, a software component may have been designed initially to operate within a certain environment or "context," for example, by interacting or collaborating with other objects to carry out its job. But to be reusable, it must be possible for that software component to be placed into a variety of different environments. This should be possible without requiring that the entire system be recompiled and relinked; the "connection" between the software component and the rest of its environment should take place at run time via dynamic binding.

6.3.2 Reusing Data

As mentioned, source code "include" or "copy" mechanisms are typically used by programmers to reuse data declarations, for example, table layouts, record definitions, and "global" parameter assignments. When I was a novice programmer, one of my mentors passed on the advice, "The only literal constants you should ever have in a program are zero and one—and I'm not even sure about those!" That's still good advice in the 1990s, even for "natural" constants like 3.14159, which should *always* be defined with a symbolic parameter in a separate parameter file and "include-d" in any program that needs the value.

With the advent of CASE technology, the obvious manifestation of reusable data is the CASE repository, and, as OO methodologies proliferate, we will eventually see object repositories that allow the software engineer to reuse both the data and the processes associated with an object. This will make possible not only reusable data declarations, but also reusable declarations of all kinds: OOA and OOD models, data flow diagrams, entity-relationship diagrams, physical database designs, structure charts, and the like. The most trivial form of reuse facilitated by a CASE repository is code reuse and parameter-definition reuse that the programmer is concerned with; the more important forms are *design* reuse and *analysis* reuse, discussed shortly.

6.3.3 Reusing Designs

The major problem with any form of code reuse is that coding takes place after the hard part is done in a project: analysis and design. For years, we have known that coding consumes only 10 to 15 percent of the time and effort of a project, so any attempt to increase coding productivity—whether through reuse, higher-level languages, or pure black magic—can have only a limited impact on overall project productivity. Nevertheless, almost all the historical attempts at implementing reuse were focused on code-level components.

Today, the world-class software organizations realize that much more significant results can be achieved through reuse at the design or specification level. As Biggerstaff and Lubars point out[5], code

---

[5]Ted J. Biggerstaff and Mitchell D. Lubars, "Recovering and Reusing Software Designs: Getting More Mileage from Your Software Assets," *American Programmer*, March 1991.

reuse typically occurs only at the bottom levels of a system design hierarchy; design reuse, though, typically results in whole "branches" of the tree structure being reused. This is illustrated in Figure 6.1.

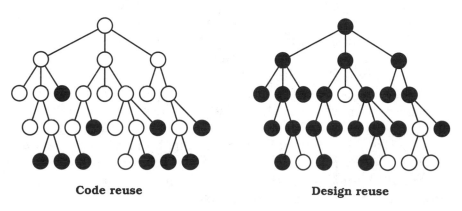

Code reuse   **Design reuse**

Figure 6.1: Code reuse versus design reuse

6.3.4 Reusing Specifications

If design reuse is good, then analysis reuse—the reuse of specifications—is even better, for it allows us to eliminate completely the effort involved in designing, coding, and testing an implementation of that specification. In the 1970s, specification-level reuse was virtually impossible, as most software organizations depended on textual "Victorian novel" documents to describe user requirements. By the 1970s, with the advent of graphical techniques such as structured analysis, specification-level reuse was an interesting concept—but still largely impractical, since the specifications were typically developed as paper documents and generally not kept up to date.

However, world-class software organizations are now moving aggressively toward specification-level reuse, because the specification "models"— object-oriented analysis models as well as the older forms of models such as data flow diagrams, entity-relationship diagrams, state-transition diagrams, "structured English" process specifications, and so on—are maintained in CASE repositories. Thus, during the analysis phase of a project, the systems analyst should be able to browse through a corporate repository of previously completed projects, looking for similar specifications that could be used as the starting point for the next new project. One of the more exciting forms of specification-level reuse will be CASE templates, discussed in Section 6.4.3.

In Chapter 5, we discussed the configuration management problems associated with the object-oriented feature of inheritance. But if used properly, inheritance is a "plus" that contributes mightily to the concept of reuse; indeed, one could argue that inheritance *is* reuse—it's a particular way of achieving the reuse of attributes and methods of higher-level superclasses when a new subclass is created.

It should also be emphasized that the object-oriented concept of *encapsulation* contributes substantially to the concept of reuse. It's much easier to reuse an object-oriented software component when the software engineer knows that (1) all the methods have been encapsulated with the data and (2) no *other* components within the system will be making pathological references to the object's data without accessing the object's methods.

6.3.5 Miscellaneous Examples of Reuse

While code, data, designs, and specifications are the most obvious candidates for reuse, they are not the only ones. World-class software organizations are looking at *all* work-products in a system development project to see if they can be captured and stored in a form for subsequent reuse. Some of the possible candidates are:

- Cost-benefit calculations and estimates
- User documentation
- Feasibility studies
- Test cases, test procedures, test drivers, test stubs

Finally, consider one component that *cannot* be stored in a repository: the people who make up the project team. The experience, infrastructure, and camaraderie formed by a project team during one project should be carried over, that is, reused, in the next project wherever possible. While this may seem to be common sense, it is not common in the typical software shop: teams are busted apart at the end of the project, and the individuals are scattered to the wind and reassigned to other projects. As we will discuss in Chapter 7, *peopleware* approaches to software productivity often achieve results several times greater than technical approaches; this applies to reuse, too.

6.4 TECHNOLOGICAL APPROACHES TO REUSABILITY

From a technical perspective, software reusability can be accomplished by any of the following mechanisms:

- Component libraries
- Object-oriented development techniques
- CASE templates
- Design recovery

Each of these is discussed next.

6.4.1 Component Libraries

The foregoing discussion suggests that modern CASE repositories will gradually become the "storehouse" of reusable software components. But, today, most organizations equate reusability with "libraries"—typically source code libraries of functions, subroutines, or classes. "Parameter files," COPY libraries, and libraries of file layouts and record definitions are also common examples.

Thus, if I wanted to verify that a software development organization was "serious" about reusability, I would look closely at its existing library; for an organization anticipating miraculous reusability benefits from its recent adoption of the OO paradigm, I would look closely at its class library. How well documented are the library components? What kind of configuration management is used to keep track of current and previous versions of the library components? How well tested are the components?[6] What kind of browsing and searching mechanisms are available to help software engineers find useful components? Who is allowed to insert new components into the library? Without satisfactory answers to these questions, the mere existence of a "reusable class library" is hardly noteworthy.

---

[6]To see how serious an organization is in this area, check to see if it distinguishes between different *levels* of testing for its library components. Some components may be completely untested; others may have been informally tested by the developer; some may have been tested by a separate quality-control group that can certify that a formal inspection of the component was conducted or that a complete "branch coverage" was performed with test cases. If none of this information is available, the appropriate documentation for the user of the software component is: *caveat emptor*.

If the organization is emphasizing code-level reuse, then it is also interesting to ask these questions: How many components are in the library, and how big are they? Successful organizations typically have libraries with 200 to 400 components; an organization with more than 1000 components is likely to have very little usage of its components. This strongly suggests that the real-world mechanism for effective reuse is that the software engineers gradually "internalize" the identity and basic features of those 200 to 400 components; they may not remember all the technical details (e.g., the calling sequence or the detailed behavior), but when faced with the need for a module to carry out function X, they will remember, "Oh, yeah, there's some class in the library that does something like X—the whatchamacallit class, I can't remember the exact name, but I know it's there . . .". With 1000 or more components, there is no hope that the average software engineer will *ever* remember what's in the library.

Successful code-level libraries also typically contain *small* components; in the case of the Smalltalk class library and the UNIX library, the components are typically only 5 to 10 statements in the source program language. Small components typically carry out one well-defined, functionally cohesive task, typically without imposing unreasonable performance or memory overhead. On the other hand, a library with gargantuan components—each consisting of 100,000 lines of code that attempt to do everything for everyone—are less successful. Software engineers will typically argue that they can't afford the overhead of the gargantuan component, nor can they tolerate the various side effects it may have.

6.4.2 Object-Oriented Development Techniques

As we have discussed in earlier chapters, one of the most attractive promises of OO methodologies is that of greater reuse. In addition to the benefits of encapsulation of data and functions into an integrated whole, the OO approach uses inheritance to facilitate reuse. This feature is found in many of the object-oriented programming languages (e.g., C++, Eiffel, and Smalltalk, but not Ada), but it won't be of much help to the COBOL community until the appearance of an object-oriented COBOL language.[7] In the meantime, various OO

---

[7]The CODASYL Committee formed an Object-Oriented COBOL Task Group in November 1989 and a draft standard of a new COBOL language is expected to emerge in the 1993–94 time frame. In the meantime, it is likely that we will see "unofficial" versions of OO-COBOL (or COBOL++) from one or more compiler vendors even before the draft standard emerges.

analysis and design methodologies are emerging to help software engineers focus on the benefits of inheritance at an earlier stage in the software development life cycle.

And there are alternative approaches to achieving the inheritance benefits usually associated with object orientation. One of the most attractive is the Bassett frame technology approach developed by Paul Bassett at Netron, Inc.[8] While the conventional OO approach uses only a "same-as, *plus*" inheritance metaphor (i.e., the subclass is the same as the parent, plus additional specialized attributes and methods), the Bassett approach also uses a "same as, *except*" metaphor. Indeed, this is exactly what a software engineer is thinking when he considers reusing a component in a library: "Gee, this component does exactly what I need, *except* that it also does X and Y, which I don't want . . .".

6.4.3 CASE Templates

As mentioned earlier, CASE tools will be an important component of software reusability technology in the 1990s; far more important than the drawing tools and error-checking features of the PC-based tools is the concept of a common *repository* for storing a wide variety of analysis, design, code, and data elements.

While this much is obvious, there is an interesting corollary: we may begin to see *reusable application programs* provided to the marketplace in the form of fully loaded CASE repositories; at least one vendor has begun referring to such a class of products as *designware*.[9] This is an exciting development for the software industry, because it promises a higher-level, more aggressive form of reuse—and it offers an alternative to the customary approach of buying commercial software packages and attempting to customize the package at the source program level.

If I want a common class of generic application program—a payroll system, for example, or an inventory control system—it is often more economical to buy a commercial package than develop it myself. But to tailor the package to my organization's specific needs, I either have to hope that the vendor has provided a great deal of

[8]Paul G. Bassett, "Engineering Software for Softness," *American Programmer*, March 1991. The Bassett frame technology concept has been widely applied in conventional third-generation languages such as COBOL. Additional information can be obtained from Netron, Inc., at 99 St. Regis Crescent North, Downsview, Ontario M3J 1Y9 Canada. Phone 416-636-8333; fax 416-636-4847.

[9]Ken Orr refers to such an approach as RAM, or *reusable application model*(s).

flexibility through parameterization, or (shudder) I have to resort to modification of the vendor's source code. But instead of buying the source code, why not buy a repository full of object-behavior diagrams, inheritance diagrams, and object-interaction diagrams? It's quite likely that 90 percent of the specification and design of the generic application will be satisfactory, but the 10 percent that must be modified should be modified at the analysis and design level, and then—through the use of a code generator attached to the CASE product—I should be able to generate a fully customized version of the package for my own use.

CASE vendors that are also in the service or consulting business—for example, Andersen Consulting—have an obvious opportunity to create such designware products. For less rational reasons, that is, the obsessive decision not to provide COBOL code generation, some of the DBMS vendors have also begun providing designware products. During the 1990s, we should expect to see a number of additional "players" in this business (though not the CASE vendors who are strictly "toolmakers" in nature), and ultimately the package vendors themselves will find it necessary to follow this trend.

6.4.4 Design Recovery

For the organization that wants to focus its efforts on software reuse, one of the immediate problems to be faced is that the library of reusable components is initially empty. Where do the components come from? How long does it take to fill the library with enough components to provide a meaningful contribution to the organization?

The idea of a Software Parts Department—a group whose only job is to create reusable components—is discussed shortly. But regardless of which people create the components, a common assumption is that the components cannot be created until after the organization has decided to "get serious" about reuse. A different approach was pursued by researchers at MCC, and it warrants serious attention if you want a "jump start" on creating a reusable library: consider your existing portfolio of old software, which, in most organizations, consists of tens of millions of lines of code, as a source of reusable components. This approach, which has a different focus and objective than the usual software reengineering techniques, is described by Biggerstaff and Lubars as *design recovery*.[10]

[10]Biggerstaff and Lubars, "Recovering and Reusing Software Design." AMERICAN PROGRAMMER, March 1991.

Two research projects, DESIRE and ROSE, developed tools and techniques for finding and extracting nuggets of reusable gold from the oceans of old code.

An interesting point is that the lack of documentation for old software means that expert system technology will probably be necessary to help us find useful patterns for reuse. MCC's expert systems looked at variable names, comments in the code, and even the formatting of source code to obtain clues to the behavior of alien code. Of course, *your* organization may have sufficient documentation that this may not be necessary, but the basic idea remains the same: harvest your old software in order to populate the empty library of reusable components. In an object-oriented world, this often means putting object "wrappers" around nuggets of non-OO legacy code to create reusable classes and objects.

6.5 ORGANIZATIONAL APPROACHES TO REUSABILITY

While technological approaches are obviously important, the key ingredient for achieving high levels of software reusability in organizations is *management*. There are three things that management must do:

- Provide a reward mechanism to instill a greater awareness of the desirability of reusability.
- Provide "proactive" leadership at the beginning of system development projects to encourage reusability.
- Change the DP organization to create a group whose sole job is to create reusable modules.

Each of these topics is discussed in more detail now.

6.5.1 Providing a Reward System

As mentioned earlier, software engineers will not be motivated to seek opportunities for reusability if they see no benefit in such action; management must provide some recognition and reward to encourage a greater awareness. At the very least, lines of code (or function points) taken from a reusable library should be given the same value, when measuring the work done by a software engineer, as lines of new code. Since it will, it is hoped, be somewhat easier to find a reusable module in a library than to create a new one from scratch, this should encourage the software engineer in the right direction.

Slogans, commendations, letters of praise, and other such public recognition of individual reusability efforts may also be useful, though the first reaction on the part of the typical software engineer is likely to be one of mild suspicion. The important thing is to ensure that the software engineers understand and believe that this is not a short-term management "fad," to be forgotten when the next budget crunch occurs, but rather a long-term, deeply felt part of the overall DP culture. In the best case, the software engineer will gradually begin to feel guilty every time he writes a new module of his own and will wonder why he couldn't find an appropriate candidate in the library of reusable components.

Several DP shops around the world are now experimenting with the idea of direct financial rewards—usually in the form of royalties—to software engineers to encourage them to create reusable software components.[11] Of course, this may open a Pandora's box of management problems—in the case of one software shop in Germany, it even created an outcry from the company's labor union—but it could also show that management is serious about recognizing the value of creating reusable software assets. If your company provides recognition and reward for patentable inventions, or other forms of intellectual property that are trademarked and copyrighted, it should consider doing the same for software components.

6.5.2 Provide a Proactive Management Approach

Most software development organizations exhibit a very passive attitude toward reusability: aside from occasional management slogans and exhortations, nobody pays much attention to the concept until the end of a development project. Then—and only then—someone might ask, "Hmmm, I wonder how much reusability we achieved on this project?" If anyone bothers to take a close look at the finished system, the answer might be, "Gee! What a surprise! This time we achieved a level of 34 percent reusability! I wonder how we did that?"

After the reusability concept has been practiced for a few years in an organization, it might be appropriate to set an overall organiza-

---

[11]The extent of the royalties would presumably be based on the number of times the reusable components were accessed. This suggests that perhaps some compensation should be provided to people who aggressively *use* components in the library as well as those who *create* components for the library; managers might also be rewarded based on the degree to which their projects employ high levels of reuse. GTE Data Services is one example of a U.S. firm aggressively exploring such approaches; on the other hand, countries like Germany have found that such an explicit reward mechanism runs afoul of labor union policies.

tional goal of, say, 50 percent or 60 percent for *all* projects. But in the early days, this is clearly not appropriate. In any case, the practical thing is to estimate consciously, deliberately, the likely and desirable level of reusability for each project at the *beginning of the project*. That is, the project manager and the senior software engineers involved in the early stages of analysis and design should be able to say, "Hmmm . . . this looks like another inventory control system, almost the same as the last inventory control system we built. We should be able to achieve a level of 80–85 percent reusability on this project."

How do we know that this is a serious estimate and not just fanciful dreaming? By building the reusability estimate into the project schedule and budget! If 80–85 percent of the code in the new system can be obtained from a reusable library, then the time required to design, code, and test new modules should be reduced considerably—and the project schedule and budget should reflect that.[12]

Obviously, the initial estimates of reusability have to be tracked as part of an overall program of software metrics in the organization. Project management should compare the *actual* level of reusability at the end of the project against the original estimates and should keep track of the overall trend of reusability across all projects on an ongoing basis.

6.5.3 Create a Software Parts Department

As mentioned earlier, it is unreasonable to expect that software engineers will have the time, energy, or foresight to create general-purpose reusable modules while working under the normal project pressures of schedules, deadlines, and budgets. Anything created in this environment will have been *first* created as a special-purpose and then, if time permits, revised in some fashion to make it more general.

A far better approach—and the only one that is likely to create a stable, useful library of reusable parts—is to create a separate group whose only job is to create reusable parts. This will typically be a small group—perhaps only 2 or 3 software engineers in an organiza-

---

[12]I must admit that I did not think of this clever idea myself. It was described to me during a visit to Toshiba Company's Software Factory in October 1988. I don't know if *every* Japanese software company uses this approach, but it was common among the half-dozen large software companies I visited in Tokyo. By contrast, a project team in New Zealand told me that their project managers are required to do the opposite, as well: not only must they estimate how much they can take *out* of a reusable library, but they must also estimate how much they can put *into* the library.

tion of 100–300 professional staff—but there should be more than one to create some flexibility, personnel backup, and a sense of shared enterprise. These software parts producers should be part of an overall "Software Parts Department," whose organizational structure might look like Figure 6.2:

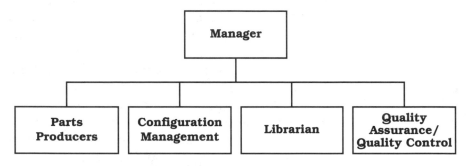

Figure 6.2: The software parts department

This does not mean that the Software Parts Department would refuse to consider submissions from the rest of the organization; however, such submissions would be examined carefully to see whether they are appropriate candidates for inclusion in the library and checked carefully for completeness, correctness, and overall quality. It is highly likely than any software components submitted by other parts of the DP organization would be considered a "rough draft" for the official reusable parts producers to revise, rewrite, and/or improve.

How would the Reusability Parts Department know what kind of reusable components to produce? One obvious way would be to respond to requests from other parts of the organization that see (or anticipate) the need for such components. But an equally important source would be the initiative of the Parts Department itself, *based on its ongoing analysis of "normal" modules developed by the rest of the organization*. Of course, this implies that all software developed throughout the organization is maintained in a central library or CASE repository and is available for review and analysis by a central group. If appropriate, the Software Parts Department could create new reusable components and suggest that other software engineers replace their specialized modules with the newly developed reusable ones.

7

Beyond Objects: Critical Success Factors for Software Projects

With the exception of a few hysterical CASE vendors and methodology zealots, most software professionals agree that there is no "silver bullet"—not even object orientation—that will solve our problems of software productivity and software quality.[1] But that doesn't mean we should give up and accept defeat; as Fred Brooks points out in a classic paper on software engineering,

> Even though no technological breakthrough promises to give the sort of magical results with which we are so familiar in the hardware area, there is both an abundance of good work going on now, and the promise of steady, if unspectacular progress.[2]

There is growing awareness that software organizations must begin paying attention to the problems of software productivity and software quality if they are to become (or remain) world-class competitors. But though the global scale of competition may be new, the problems themselves are not. For years, we have known that the day-to-day operation of our companies has depended on software-intensive computer systems. And for decades, we have known that the productivity of our software engineers is abysmally low; the figures produced by metrics guru Capers Jones in the 1990s are now expressed in function points,[3] but we first began to hear reports of 10 to 15 lines of debugged code per person per day in the 1960s. Nearly a decade ago, Tom DeMarco pointed out that 25 percent of large sys-

---

[1]This chapter is a revised, updated adaptation of Chapter 2 of the author's *Decline and Fall of the American Programmer* (Englewood Cliffs, NJ: Yourdon Press/Prentice Hall, 1992).

[2]Fred Brooks, "No Silver Bullets," *IEEE Computer*, April 1987.

[3] One of the great difficulties, of course, is that everyone measures different software development activities in different ways. Capers Jones documents minimum, median, and maximum productivity rates for 25 different software development activities (e.g., requirements analysis, coding, unit testing, and management) and a wide range of industries.

tem development projects *never* finish,[4] and a more recent study by Capers Jones[5] documented the gloomy statistic that the average MIS development project is one year late and 100 percent over budget.

Senior executives in world-class software organizations must be familiar with the kinds of "good work" going on in the software field today and must develop long-term plans to implement the "steady, unspectacular progress" suggested by Fred Brooks in tools, techniques, and other forms of improved productivity and quality. Without this awareness, there is a tendency to view software productivity problems as the end result of a programmer shortage. Indeed, this is exactly how the general public often hears about the situation; for example, during Japan's booming economy of the mid-1980s, the powerful Ministry of International Trade and Industry extrapolated the supply and demand for software engineers from 1985 through the year 2000 and predicted a shortage of nearly a million people by the end of the 1990s.[6]

Of course, OO methodologies are seen by many as the silver bullet that will solve our current productivity and quality problems. As we have suggested in the previous chapters, there is some doubt whether OO really has all the magical powers to which it has been ascribed. But even if it does, we have already seen that there are some complementary technologies that are absolutely essential to ensure its success: proper project management and software life cycles, configuration management, and adequate management of software reusability. These could be considered as "critical success factors" to make OO work—and on a larger scale, they are part of the arsenal of critical success factors, or general-purpose silver bullets, that can help solve our productivity and quality problems.

But is that all we need? Is OO, combined with reuse and configuration management, enough? A moment's thought will provide the answer: "No!" It's no good, for example, to attempt OO in a software organization populated by low-caliber, unmotivated people. And, as

---

[4]Tom DeMarco. *Controlling Software Projects* (Englewood Cliffs, NJ: Yourdon Press/Prentice Hall, 1982).

[5]Capers Jones, *Applied Software Measurement* (New York: McGraw-Hill, 1991).

[6]Edward Yourdon, "Japan Revisited," *American Programmer*, February 1990. However, the worldwide recession in the late 1980s and early 1990s appears to have affected the Japanese software industry, too; for the first time, there are reports of bankruptcies, layoffs of programmers, and all the problems experienced in other parts of the world. For an interesting perspective, see Tomoo Matsubara's, "Illusions About Japan's Software Industry," *American Programmer*, March 1993.

we have hinted in previous chapters, it's probably not a good idea to attempt an aggressive implementation of OO methodologies without adequate CASE tools. The situation is analogous to the TV commercials one often sees for low-calorie "miracle diet" foods: the fine print of the commercial usually acknowledges that the miracle diet product works only when it is "part of a balanced diet and a program of regular exercise."

In addition to configuration management and reusability, a "balanced diet" of software engineering tools, techniques, practices, and policies—all of which are necessary to make the software organization truly succeed—is likely to include some combination of the following:

1. Better people
2. More rigorous software *processes*
3. Better programming languages
4. Automated (CASE) tools
5. JAD, RAD, and prototyping
6. Structured techniques
7. Information engineering
8. Software reengineering
9. Software metrics

7.1 BETTER PEOPLE

Mediocre people with good tools and languages will still develop mediocre systems, but good people, even when burdened with poor tools and mediocre languages, can turn out damn good software. This has been true in the past, and it will continue to be true for the foreseeable future. As DeMarco and Lister argue,

> The major problems of our work are not so much *technological* as *sociological* in nature. . . . Most managers are willing to concede the idea that they've got more people worries than technical worries. *But they seldom manage that way.* [7]

Because of this, many organizations are focusing their software improvement efforts on the human resource component—often referred to as "peopleware." Attention to peopleware issues can literally cause 10-fold productivity improvements, while investments

[7] Tom DeMarco and Lister, *Peopleware* (New York: Dorset House, 1987).

in CASE, methodologies, or other technology-based silver bullets rarely cause more than a 30–40 percent improvement.

Peopleware efforts are directed at several related issues:

- *Hiring the best people.* Obviously, no manager would admit consciously to hiring incompetent people, but many managers are loath to spend a little extra money to hire someone with more specialized skills or more years of experience; it's often tempting to hire an relatively inexpensive person right out of college. And while all companies scrutinize resumes and references and subject the candidate to multiple interviews, hardly any use aptitude tests or "audition" techniques or request that the candidate bring a portfolio of his or her typical work to the interview. OO technology is obviously no panacea for hiring stupid people; on the contrary, it is every bit as intellectually demanding as any other software engineering methodology.

- *Engaging in the ongoing training and education of existing staff.* World-class companies invest as much as 20 days per year of training for each of their software engineers; typical companies may provide 5 days, and a distressingly large number provide none at all! Introducing OO into an organization unwilling to support it with training is an utter waste of time and resources. We will discuss the training issues associated with OO in Chapter 27; one of the obvious questions to be discussed is whether and older generation of software engineers, steeped in third-generation programming languages and non-OO methodologies, can ever be transformed into productive OO software engineers.

- *Motivating people for higher levels of performance.* Motivation can take many forms, of which higher salary levels is only one (and typically not the most important one). The subject of motivating software people is beyond the scope of this book, but it is wise to remember DeMarco's and Lister's advice from *Peopleware:*[8] most software people are already highly motivated, and the most important thing is for management to remove obstacles and constraints, so that the motivation can be channeled into productive work. In any case, some

---

[8]DeMarco and Lister, *Peopleware*

organizations have such an atmosphere of gloom and low morale that an outsider can smell death in the air when he walks into the office; in this kind of environment, it is hard to imagine that a newly introduced OO methodology will succeed.

- *Developing performance management ideas to align personal goals with corporate goals.* Typical organization goals are higher productivity and higher quality; however, short-term goals of higher profits for the next financial quarter or successful competition for a major contract may communicate a very different message to the software engineers in the organization. A typical example is the statement, "We're committed to higher quality—as long as it doesn't jeopardize our schedule for finishing the project on time!" Meanwhile, individual software engineers see the organization's efforts to achieve these goals—through the introduction of OO methodologies, new tools, standards, and so on—as an effort to change their behavior, and to cause them to do things differently than they did before. Individuals evaluate the *personal consequences* of such requests for behavior changes as being either "positive" or "negative," the consequences are judged as "immediate" or "future," and they are judged as "certain" or "uncertain." Software engineers, like all rational humans, tend to gravitate toward situations whose consequences are positive, immediate, and certain; they tend to avoid situations whose consequences are negative, immediate, and certain; and they are ambivalent and uncertain about the various other combinations of consequences. Thus, while OO may be a very desirable corporate objective, its personal consequences have to be examined carefully to see if it will be accepted enthusiastically or quietly sabotaged by the software engineers.

- *Offering an adequate working environment, with particular emphasis on adequate office facilities rather than the chicken coops in which most software engineers find themselves squatting for 10 hours a day.* OO can't compensate for abysmal working conditions. Period.

- *Placing more emphasis on creating and maintaining effective teams of people who can work together to create high-quality software products.* Many software engineering methodologies and tools tend to promote higher levels of productivity and quality at the *personal* level. However, as discussed earlier, very few software projects today are the work of a single person; no matter how powerful the language or CASE tool, the trend toward large, complex systems inevitably involves the joint efforts of *teams* who must collaborate, coordinate, and communicate their ideas. As mentioned in Chapter 5, OO creates its own special demands in this area, as the inheritance mechanism makes it dangerous to modify objects without carefully checking the impact on other objects in the class hierarchy. But aside from this, OO has little or nothing to say about the growing field of *groupware*, which is based on Robert Rockwell's observations that "software is more like a mortgage than a house."[9] And groupware *tools* do not address the complex cultural issues associated with building cohesive teams of professionals; these issues *must* be addressed by the organization if it is to succeed with OO (or any other methodology) on complex projects.

7.2 MORE RIGOROUS SOFTWARE PROCESSES

Any method or technique can improve productivity in a software development methodology, if it is practiced rigorously and consistently; indeed, many consultants offer the simple advice to their clients, "Pick a method—*any* method. Then practice it!"

Conversely, *any* technique can fail if it is practiced informally, sporadically, or in an *ad hoc* fashion. The blunt reality is that most software organizations will fail to implement structured techniques, information engineering, or object-oriented techniques successfully, simply because they allow each software engineer and/or each project manager to determine where, when, and how to apply the technique.

While this situation has always been a problem, the Software Engineering Institute (SEI) has made it much easier to characterize the extent or "level" of formality with which an organization (or a project team within an organization) practices a software development "process," by publishing a "process maturity" model.[10] The essence of the SEI model is that software development organizations can exist at one of five levels of maturity:

[9]Robert Rockwell, "The Coming of EuroCASE," *American Programmer*, November 1992.

[10]While the SEI model was in the process of being revised as this book was being written, the original form is still quite adequate for a basic understanding. A detailed description is given in Watts Humphrey's *Managing the Software Process* (Reading, MA: Addison-Wesley, 1991).

- *The initial level*—characterized by a "random" process, or anarchy, where every software engineer follows his own process for developing software. Level 1 organizations may succeed at developing software systems, but they have little or no ability to predict schedules and budgets with any accuracy. Also, a level 1 project is typically vulnerable to the loss of a key software engineer in the middle of the project; nobody else is willing or able to pick up the departing engineer's work and carry it on.

- *The repeatable level*—characterized by a "tribal folklore" that creates a culture where everyone instinctively understands "the way things get done around here." A level 2 organization generally succeeds at delivering systems on time and within budget by rigorous project management activities, but its projects are generally vulnerable to the loss of the project manager (who creates and instills the culture that the team members follow), and it is generally quite vulnerable to major "perturbations" (e.g., a technology perturbation such as a shift from mainframe software to client-server software or an organizational perturbation like a merger or acquisition).

- *The defined level*—where the software process has been defined, documented, and institutionalized throughout the entire organization. It is particularly interesting that the SEI advises that new technologies, such as OO or CASE, should not be introduced on a wide-scale basis, unless the organization is at level 3. While this might seem like good advice, it should also be pointed out that over 95 percent of the DP organizations in the United States are below level 3.[11]

- *The managed level*—characterized by the introduction of software metrics throughout the organization. Of course, the metrics should be used to quantify important characteristics of the *product*, that is, the software system being developed. However, the level 4 organization also has comprehensive *process* metrics to help it understand how much time

[11]This figure is based on conference presentations by Watts Humphrey and other members of the Software Engineering Institute, circa 1991: approximately 85 percent of U.S. organizations assessed by SEI were at level 1, and approximately 12 percent were at level 2. It is reasonable to assume that there has been some improvement since then, but the vast majority of software organizations are still likely to be below level 3. If the assessments were done only at the project level, the results would be somewhat more optimistic.

and effort is required for various activities in the software life cycle, how many errors are detected at each stage, and so on.

- *The optimizing level*—characterized by continuous process improvement. At level 5, the software metrics are used to identify weak parts of the software development process, so they can be improved.

The key point is not whether there are 5 levels, or 10 levels, or 347 levels, but, rather, that there are marked, recognizable differences between organizations as they progress from anarchy to maturity. The assessment is based on interviews and a complex questionnaire, involving over 100 questions; the questionnaire and the assessment process has its strengths and weaknesses, but the overall rating summary is tremendously useful for organizations that want to know where they stand.

In particular, the SEI process maturity model helps to prioritize the things an organization must do to improve; a similar approach is provided by the ISO 9000 quality standard, which many European organizations have begun following. A primitive DP organization at level 1 does *not* need OO to improve; it needs much more basic things, such as the ability to estimate the size of its projects and a rational process for deciding when it must *refuse* to accept schedule or budget constraints imposed upon the project.

7.3 BETTER PROGRAMMING LANGUAGES

Newer and more powerful programming languages are a perennial favorite of the techies in the organization. If third-generation languages didn't solve our productivity problems, then fourth-generation languages will; if fourth-generation languages won't do the job, then fifth-generation languages will.

Hardly anyone will argue with the assertion that high-level languages are better than low-level languages. However, such an argument typically ignores the problem of maintaining *existing* programs written in older languages during the past 30 years; of course, these older languages are virtually guaranteed to be non-OO languages, and the methodology used to develop those programs (if there was a methodology at all) was almost certainly not an OO approach. Since we typically spend at least 50 percent of our DP budget maintaining these old systems, perhaps *that* is what we should be focusing on: upgrading the new systems and projects from a 3GL to a 4GL, or from a non-OOPL to an OOPL, may be a great idea, but the focus has to start with the existing legacy systems, in whatever generation of programming language they were written.[12]

Similarly, the argument about newer and better programming languages typically ignores the problem of retraining existing *programmers* who have spent the past 5 to 10 years of their careers muddling around in old languages. An upgrade from COBOL '74 to COBOL '85 is hard enough for these folks; an upgrade from COBOL '85 to object-oriented COBOL (which will appear at around the time this book is published) is likely to knock their socks off. An upgrade from FORTRAN to Ada, or from Pascal to Smalltalk is equally mind-blowing. An upgrade from C to C++ may appear simpler, because C is a proper subset of C++, but of course, this just masks the problem—old programmers may continue to write old programs in their new language. In any event, a new language is typically *not* something you can just drop into the organization the way you might replace an 80286 PC with an 80386 or a Mac Plus with a Macintosh Quadra. Unless you give the existing programmers a lobotomy and "refresh" their memories with the elements of a new programming language, it's going to be an expensive, time-consuming process.

But the real problem with programming languages as the silver bullet solution to software problems is that it puts the emphasis at the wrong level: *better coding techniques may do nothing more than help you arrive at a disaster sooner than before.* Better programming languages, used without anything else, may be just what your programmers need to develop a brilliant solution to the wrong problem. Certainly one major lesson we have learned from the past 25 years of software engineering experience is that there is more to be gained from attention to design, analysis, and business strategy issues than from attention to programming-level issues.

Ultimately, most of us won't care very much about the issue of programming languages, because it will be hidden by the CASE tools we use. As an analogy, hearken back to the days of the 1960s when the concept of "high-level" third-generation languages was relatively new and many programmers distrusted compilers. *Everyone* insisted that the compilers generate assembly language as

---

[12]Obviously, the issue of software maintenance transcends the discussion of programming languages: the real question is when and how *any* new technology can be introduced into an environment of "legacy" applications. As noted in the preface, this book does not address the issue of OO technology for a maintenance environment.

their output rather than a direct translation to machine language. Why? So the programmers could examine the compiler output to see if it was as tight and efficient as they could have done on their own; also (although we often forget it), the assembly language code was important during debugging sessions, since the debugging tools available to the programmer typically didn't operate at the same level as the third-generation language.

Today, we have a comparable situation. Everyone insists that modern CASE tools generate COBOL, even though nobody in his or her right mind should want to *look* at the COBOL. But we're all curious about the quality of the code produced by the CASE code generators. And besides, if the code doesn't work, we have to use our COBOL debugging tools rather than debugging at the level of data flow diagrams, action diagrams, or some other high-level abstraction.

Sometime during this decade, this will seem like an anachronism. Programming languages will still be a matter of some academic interest, but the world-class software organization will greet the announcement of yet another new and sexy language (the seventh generation? maybe the eighth) with a loud yawn. The real productivity gains are to be found elsewhere. Based on this expectation, we won't discuss new/better/higher-level programming languages any further in this book; our only concern will be the impact of OOPL and non-OOPL languages on the software design architecture created by OOD.

7.4 AUTOMATED TOOLS

Automated tools—in particular, CASE tools—are currently a favorite approach to improving software quality and productivity; from a shaky beginning as avant-garde toys in the mid-1980s to robust, industrial-strength tools in the early 1990s, CASE is becoming a mainstream technology: by the middle of the 1990s, market forecasters expect that 50 percent of the professional software engineers in the United States will have their own personal CASE tools.

This is clearly a technology that is separating the world-class players from the mediocre shops. One reason for the separation between the "big guys" and the "little guys" is the cost issue: as of 1991, the cost for a reasonably well-equipped CASE environment in the United States is \$30,000–50,000 per person,[13] and a more recent analysis[14] found that costs remain high. While this kind of investment can usually be justified by a 20–30 percent improvement in productivity, it nevertheless represents a "big-ticket" investment: one study[15] estimated that installation and five-year maintenance costs of CASE tools for a 200-person MIS shop would be approximately \$6.5 million.

No matter what the cost-benefit study says, or how reasonable the return on investment looks, \$6.5 million investments in productivity tools can easily be delayed, sidetracked, or mothballed in tough economic times. On the other hand, one of the ironic conclusions from the technology survey discussed in Chapter 2 is that cost is the least likely reason for an organization to avoid adopting OO technology; however, this may simply reflect the naive opinion of many organizations that OO is a *programming* technology and that the cost of the technology is simply the cost of a C++ compiler.

The situation is compounded by some short-term problems: CASE users often experience a productivity *decrease* for the first 3 to 6 months, and it often takes 12 to 18 months before productivity gains are visible. So the organization expecting a "quick fix" from the CASE silver bullet can be in for a rude shock.[16] If it's any consolation, the same productivity decrease is inevitable with the introduction of *any* new technology—including OO!

But even with short-term problems, there is a growing consensus that CASE will be a necessary component of the software development community in the 1990s—just as the software development

[13]One would expect the cost of this technology to drop over the next several years, as the CASE vendors recoup their development expenses and as they look forward with greater confidence to large-volume sales. On the other hand, the functionality offered by today's CASE tools is only a small fraction of what we expect to find in the fully integrated CASE tools of the mid-1990s; thus it is quite possible that the price tag will remain relatively constant over the next several years as the functionality of the tools increase. More on this is found in Chapter 6.

[14]Jerrold M. Grochow, "The Cost of CASE Revisited," *American Programmer*, November 1992.

[15]Edward Yourdon, "The Future of CASE," Technical Report TR-3 (New York: *American Programmer*, 1990).

[16]There is another interesting "backlash" problem associated with CASE tools: if the organization does not measure unpaid overtime, then it may not see any visible evidence of productivity improvement from the introduction of CASE tools (other than a small decrease in the electric utility bills caused by programmers turning off the office lights when they go home at 5 P. M.). It's quite possible for CASE to make the software engineers happy, but managers frustrated.

community began arguing about the efficacy of dumb time-sharing terminals in the late 1960s and finally concluded sometime in the 1970s that sooner or later everyone would move away from the IBM 029 keypunch machines and insist on having a terminal on their desk. In 1991, only 10–15 percent of the software engineers in the United States had the luxury of a personal CASE workstation; thus this is an area where the world-class companies have an opportunity to move ahead of their competition.

As we have already mentioned in this book, success with OO methods will inevitably require associated OO CASE tools, which we will discuss in Chapters 23 and 24. But as we have mentioned in the preceding "peopleware" discussion, CASE is taking on a broader definition, with new emphasis on groupware tools; in addition, OO technology will demand an investment in library management tools to keep track of complex class libraries of reusable objects. Hence, to make OO succeed will require more than just an investment in a narrowly focused group of tools to support OO analysis diagrams.

7.5 JAD, RAD, AND PROTOTYPING

JAD is not a new software engineering technology, but it has been given a new life. "Joint application design," as it was originally called, was created by IBM Canada in the 1970s as a mechanism for bringing users and systems analysts together for intensive, highly productive mediated sessions to elicit the requirements of a new system. JAD was widely practiced in North America for several years, but gradually lost its glamour and pizzazz until the advent of CASE tools revived the concept. Today, there are a number of books, articles, and consultants supporting the JAD concept;[17] it is indeed alive and well and is credited with providing significant improvements in software productivity.

A modern variant of JAD is known as RAD, for "rapid application development." RAD is usually described as a combination of JAD sessions to determine user requirements quickly, as well as CASE tools, prototyping techniques, Rambo-style SWAT teams, and

---

[17]For a good discussion of JAD and RAD concepts, see Judy August's *Joint Application Design: The Group Session Approach to System Design* (Englewood Cliffs, NJ: Prentice Hall, 1991); Jane Wood and Denise Silver's *Joint Application Design* (New York: John Wiley and Sons, 1989); Inez Marino Hill's "Not All JADs Are Created Equal," *American Programmer*, January 1991; Jane Wood's "The 10-Minute JAD Quiz," *American Programmer*, January 1991; and Tony Crawford's "People Considerations for a More Successful JAD," *American Programmer*, January 1991.

a formal software development methodology to implement those requirements quickly; in some cases, though, RAD is interpreted simply as a form of prototyping. As a *combination* of tools and techniques, RAD has much to offer, but any of the techniques used alone—whether JAD sessions, prototyping, or CASE tools—almost certainly will *not* turn out to be the silver bullet that some vendors are promising.

It is particularly important to emphasize this point about prototyping, since many current languages, tools, and methodologies emphasize the benefits of prototyping. Everyone knows the benefits of building a prototype for an end user who is unsure of his or her requirements, but prototyping cannot eliminate the need for formal analysis and design work on large, complex projects. While most of the textbook descriptions and commercial versions of RAD use older methodologies such as information engineering or structured techniques, it is highly likely that we will soon see OO-based versions of RAD.

7.6 STRUCTURED TECHNIQUES

For a software development organization that has no methodology, structured techniques may indeed appear to be a life-saver; it has become the silver bullet solution for some organizations looking for dramatic improvements in productivity and quality. And for the organization that wants CASE support of its methods, structured techniques are attractive: nearly every major CASE vendor offers support for the Gane-Sarson, or Yourdon-DeMarco, or Ward-Mellor, or Yourdon-Constantine variant of structured analysis and structured design.

Unfortunately, some of these CASE tools provide automated support for only the older dialects of structured techniques developed in the mid-1970s.[18] The original form of these methodologies were fine for their time, but they are woefully inadequate by today's

---

[18]It is important to note that the "bibles" of structured analysis are Tom DeMarco's *Structured Analysis and System Specification*, published by Yourdon Press in 1978 and still available from Prentice Hall in its original first edition form, as well as Chris Gane and Trish Sarson's *Structured Analysis: Tools and Techniques*, first published by Improved Systems Technologies in 1977 and also still available from Prentice Hall in its first edition form. Larry Constantine and I published *Structured Design* in 1975 and made only cosmetic changes in the Prentice Hall version, which appeared in 1978. For an interesting history of the early days of the structured movement, see Paul Ward's "The Evolution of Structured Analysis: Part I—The Early Years," *American Programmer*, November 1991.

standards. In particular, the original form of structured analysis gave great emphasis to the modeling of *functions* in a system, using the ubiquitous data flow diagram as the graphical modeling tool. The *data* component was incorporated in structured analysis, but was not given proper emphasis; not until the mid-1980s did more "modern" forms of structured analysis appear, incorporating the entity-relationship diagram for data modeling and the state-transition diagram for models of real-time systems. McMenamin and Palmer added a crucial concept of events and event *partitioning*, as well as a critical emphasis on modeling the "essence" of a system. [19]A number of current textbooks[20] discuss these modern variants of structured analysis and design.

Much of this important work, unfortunately, seems to have escaped the attention of many CASE vendors; their tools are still based on vintage-1978 versions of the structured techniques. This does not mean that something is wrong with the concept of structured techniques, but merely that an organization hoping that structured techniques will be its silver bullet could be badly disappointed. If you are going to adopt structured techniques, be sure that you pick a modern variant, and make sure that your CASE vendor supports a modern variant.

But the situation just described suggests that something more fundamental is going on: new software development methodologies are constantly being created and introduced into the field. If they survive, inevitably they evolve over a period of time. Meanwhile, CASE tools evolve too, but the key point is that they may lag behind the methodologies (by several years, in the case of structured techniques) *until the CASE tools themselves become the driving force for methodology creation and evolution.*

Of course, the current wave of methodologies—and the one that serves as our primary focus in this book—is OO. Many software engineers naturally assume that they must make a binary choice between OO and SA/SD—or, in any case, a mutually exclusive choice between OO and various other forms of software engineering methodologies. But as we will see in later chapters of this book, sev-

---

[19]Stephen McMenamin and John Palmer, *Essential System Analysis* (Englewood Cliffs, NJ: Yourdon Press/Prentice Hall, 1984)

[20] For typical examples, see my text, *Modern Structured Analysis* (Englewood Cliffs, NJ: Yourdon Press/Prentice Hall, 1989); Paul Ward and Stephen J. Mellor's *Structured Development of Real-Time Systems* (Englewood Cliffs, NJ: Yourdon Press/Prentice Hall, 1985); and Charles Martin's *User-Centered Requirements Analysis* (Englewood Cliffs, NJ: Prentice Hall, 1988).

eral of the fundamental principles of structured techniques have survived and have been incorporated into current OO methodologies. The concepts of coupling and cohesion are one example; the McMenamin-Palmer concept of event-partitioning is another.

7.7 INFORMATION ENGINEERING

Information engineering, as popularized by James Martin[21] and others, found itself in an interesting position at the beginning of the 1990s: as a methodology, it was used by only 10 percent as many DP organizations as those using structured techniques, but it had nevertheless acquired the momentum and fervor that had been associated with structured techniques in the late 1970s and early 1980s. At the beginning of the 1990s, various trade magazines indicated that the combination of all IE methodologies (the Martin version and its various derivatives) was the fastest growing of the systems development methodologies.

Information engineering emphasizes *data* as a corporate asset and as the basis for systems analysis and design. Although it can be for the analysis and design phases of individual projects, information engineering is most often perceived as a methodology for *enterprisewide* modeling activities. By contrast, structured analysis is generally perceived as a methodology for modeling individual systems within an organization, but it can be (and has been) used to model entire enterprises.

Because information engineering is a somewhat newer (and less widely used) methodology, the CASE "methodology lag" discussed earlier does not exist: there are fewer full-spectrum information engineering CASE vendors, and those that exist support an up-to-date version of the information engineering methodology. But here again, there is an interesting issue lurking behind the surface: one reason for the adherence of CASE tools like Texas Instruments' IEF and KnowledgeWare's IEW CASE products to the "official" information engineering methodology is the business relationship that existed in the developmental stage of the product, between the CASE vendor and the methodology developer. This is in stark contrast to the large number of CASE vendors who claim, for example, to support the DeMarco form of structured analysis, but who have never spoken to

[21]James Martin, *Information Engineering*, Volumes. 1–3 (Englewood Cliffs, NJ: Prentice Hall, 1990).

Tom DeMarco and who have evidently never read past Chapter 2 of his book on the subject.

With the advent of OO methodologies, IE enthusiasts are faced with the same question plaguing SA/SD aficionados: Is it necessary to burn all the old methodology manuals to embrace the new OO concepts? In addition to the obvious advice that much of the fundamental software engineering principles of IE are still relevant in an OO world,[22] there is another important message: the *data* emphasis of IE is typically much more compatible with OO methodologies than the *functional* emphasis of structured analysis/structured design.

This does not mean that you should necessarily trust an IE vendor who suddenly announces one day that his product is object-oriented; the basic form of IE methodologies typically lack the crucial OO concepts of inheritance, encapsulation of data and function into an integrated whole, and message passing between objects. But it may be easier for an IE vendor to evolve its methodology and associated CASE products and training manuals into a legitimate OO format than would be the case for an SA/SD vendor.

Meanwhile, as we discussed in Chapter 2, many organizations may have concluded that it is *not* yet time for them to move to an OO methodology. For those organizations, IE or SA/SD may be the methodologies that will be used as the foundation for eventually evolving into OO; if nothing else, they provide the basis for a rigorous software process, as was discussed in Section 7.2.

7.8 SOFTWARE REENGINEERING

It is no secret that many organizations spend more than half their MIS resources keeping old software alive. Whether it's called maintenance, enhancement, upgrades, ongoing development, refurbishing, or bug fixing, it all has to do with *existing* systems rather than the more glamorous work of developing new systems from scratch.

For the organization spending 50–80 percent of its DP dollars in this fashion, greater productivity gains may be achieved in the maintenance area than in the new systems area. This may be achieved in

---

[22]Perhaps the most important principle of IE is that an overall corporate information model is a good foundation for modeling the individual systems within the organization; in this sense, it is a top-down methodology as compared to the bottom-up structured methodologies. But this can be a good principle for OO enthusiasts too: perhaps it is a good idea to develop an overall OO "domain" model, as discussed in Chapter 3, before plunging into an OO model of an individual system.

the form of reduced defects (or increased mean time between failures) in existing systems or a shorter time to respond to requests from the users for new features. Or it may be achieved in the form of a reduced staff requirement for maintenance—after all, if some of the maintenance programmers can be freed up to work on new systems, it should make everyone happy![23]

One of the technologies that has long been advocated for decreasing maintenance costs is *restructuring*—transforming old, unstructured code into functionally equivalent structured code. While it does offer some benefits, only about 10 percent of the candidate companies are currently making significant use of this technology. Most companies that have invested time and money in this area are currently using a variety of *reengineering* tools from companies such as Micro Focus and ViaSoft that provide the means for maintenance programmers to understand more easily "alien" programs written years earlier by people no longer with the organization. There is also a slow but steady growth of interest in *reverse engineering*, which attempts to reconstruct design models and specification-level models directly from the source code.

Reengineering technologies are considered by many to be a subset of CASE technology; indeed, reengineering does depend heavily on automated tools. But as with most of the other software productivity technologies, success in reengineering depends heavily on management issues and cultural factors. This is particularly true in a software maintenance environment, where a single individual may be the "sole living expert" who keeps a mission-critical system alive.

But if there are management problems here, there are also management opportunities. After all, the organization may only have the opportunity to develop one or two major new systems each year, but it has an existing portfolio of 20 years of accumulated software, upon which the entire enterprise depends. A significant improvement in this existing mass of software can have profound consequences for the organization, and the world-class software shop looks at this opportunity from a variety of different perspectives. For example, what better place to look for potential reusable components for the software reusability library than the inventory of existing applications?

---

[23]On the other hand, this hope of reduced maintenance costs may be a myth: consultant Robert Glass reports that recent studies indicate that software development methods cost more to maintain, because customers find such systems easier to modify and therefore request more changes.

7.9 SOFTWARE METRICS

The Software Engineering Institute's process maturity model suggests that the introduction of metrics comes toward the end of the process improvement process, that is, that only the most sophisticated organizations have implemented a metrics initiative. But it is hard to imagine an organization making *any* improvement to its productivity or quality if it doesn't measure what it is doing. As Tom DeMarco has observed, "You can't control what you can't measure."

Unfortunately, hardly any DP shop measures anything at all about the way it develops its primary work product. For the individual software engineer, there may be very little motivation to indulge in software metrics. This is a serious problem, which won't be overcome by the decision to introduce OO or CASE tools

The fundamental motivation for software metrics is quite simple: it is *the desire to improve*. If we were all basically satisfied with what we were doing, there would be no need to measure. For some 20 years, it has been blindingly obvious that our senior management and our end users aren't satisfied with what we're doing, but that hasn't seemed to matter very much: *we* have been satisfied, or at least reasonably confident that we were doing as well as could be reasonably expected. So why bother measuring?

Today, the world-class software company knows that it cannot be satisfied with what it's doing—even if its current performance is pretty damn good. Software is now a global industry, and a lot of hungry people around the world are aching to eat your lunch. Even if you're good, they aim to be better. To stay in business, *you* have to be better—better than you were last year, better than you were yesterday. *But you can't improve if you don't know your current situation.*

Software metrics is a major technology in its own right, and it is beyond the scope of this book; however, there are now a number of excellent textbooks on the subject.[24] Suffice it to say that metrics should be part of your regular software diet.

---

[24] See, for example, Tom DeMarco's classic *Controlling Software Projects* or Capers Jones's *Applied Software Measurement*. Also, for advice on introducing a software metrics initiative into an organization, see Robert Grady and Deborah Caswell, *Software Metrics: Establishing a Company-Wide Program* (Englewood Cliffs, NJ: Prentice Hall, 1987), and Robert Grady, *Practical Software Metrics for Project Management and Process Improvement* (Englewood Cliffs, NJ: Prentice Hall, 1992).

7.10 CONCLUSION

Of course, there are many other productivity tools and methods besides the ones here. And individual organizations will assign different priorities to the productivity approaches we have discussed. But each is important and deserves to be reviewed thoroughly on an ongoing basis.

No rational DP organization can implement all these productivity approaches simultaneously. It would cost too much, and it would throw the technical staff into such a state of hysteria that the organization would never recover. But management must have a plan for implementing these and other productivity techniques over a period of 3, 5, or possible even 10 years.[25]

There is no one single bullet—not OO, not CASE, and not software reusability. But taken together, perhaps a collection of small silver pellets will help to slay the werewolves of software development quality and productivity.

---

[25]For a discussion of the problems associated with implementing such organizational changes, and some good strategies for overcoming these obstacles, see Barbara Bouldin's *Agents of Change* (Englewood Cliffs, NJ: Yourdon Press/Prentice Hall, 1988). See also the March 1992 issue of *American Programmer*, a special issue on technology transfer.

PART III
OBJECT-ORIENTED ANALYSIS

8

Overview Of OOA

In this part of the book, we develop an object-oriented model of the *user requirements* for a system; the process is described as object-oriented analysis, or OOA. To illustrate and explain the OOA process, we introduce two examples in this chapter—a traditional business data processing system for managing the publication of a magazine and a process control system for controlling an elevator.

Naturally, these two examples have been simplified and scaled down to fit within a textbook; this is an unfortunate limitation in all software engineering textbooks! But they should nevertheless illustrate the principles of OOA, and they should help the reader understand how OOA could be applied to a variety of other applications, including much larger ones. Indeed, the purpose is not so much to present a finished, polished example of these two applications as to use them as the starting point in a discussion that says, "Now, if you had to do this on *your* application, here's what you would do. . ."

A typical narrative specification of the two examples is provided in this chapter; this is followed with a general discussion of issues that will need to be addressed by the formal OOA analysis. At the end of the chapter, we summarize the major steps, activities, and models of OOA; these activities are discussed and illustrated in several of the following chapters.

8.1 THE *SMALLBYTES* SUBSCRIPTION SYSTEM

8.1.1 Description of the Problem

A *small*, independent software journal, *Small Bytes*, has asked you to design a new system for managing its subscriptions; they have a jury-rigged system today using various Macintosh-based spreadsheet, word processing, and flat-file database packages, and it has gotten completely out of hand. While the concept of managing subscriptions is quite straightforward, the details are numerous, as will be seen shortly.

Small Bytes is published on a monthly basis; a typical monthly issue consists of 5–10 articles, each written by one or more authors in the software engineering field. Although the authors receive no payment for their articles, they do receive a year's free subscription as a token of appreciation for their efforts; if they already have a subscription, then the expiration date is extended for a year. Most authors have written only one article during the journal's five-year history, but a few have written several; management is concerned with keeping track of this information, for it wants to avoid publishing more than one or two articles from any one author in a single year.

Small Bytes also has an editorial board of advisors, some of whom may also be authors from time to time; the editorial board normally serves for a one-year or two-year term, and they too receive a complimentary subscription to the magazine. The editorial board reviews submitted articles and also makes suggestions to *Small Bytes*'s publisher and managing editor about topics for future issues and prospective authors who should be contacted to write articles on those topics. As with most magazines, issues are scheduled and planned months in advance; hence the editor is dealing with several issues and its associated authors simultaneously, as well as receiving numerous unsolicited articles from a variety of past, current, and would-be authors.

Small Bytes is sold on a subscription basis; most subscriptions are for a one-year period, but the publisher accepts subscriptions for periods longer than or shorter than a year by simply prorating the annual subscription price. There are only a few thousand subscribers; most are "corporate" subscribers, but some are individuals who have *Small Bytes* sent to their home address in a plain brown wrapper. Most of them are "single-copy" subscribers; however, it is not uncommon for large companies to order multiple copies, all which are sent to the same person. (However, in some cases, the organization is adamant that a *person* not be named in the subscription and that the magazine be sent to a *title*, such as "Technical Librarian," instead). Multiple-copy subscriptions typically involve a small discount from the single-copy price; in addition, various other discounts have been offered from time to time, though the overwhelming majority of subscriptions are at a standard price. (Note, however, that the "standard" price is different for North American subscriptions and international subscriptions, to cover the higher cost of shipping overseas.)

There are a few cases of multiple-copy subscriptions where the subscribing organization asks that the constituent copies be sent to named individuals; of course, it is important to keep track of the "primary" subscriber from whom payment is received and to whom any correspondence should be addressed. Generally, these issues are sent to multiple people within one "site" (for example, one division or department, located at a single corporate address); however, in a few cases, the multiple copies are sent to individuals in different sites within the corporation. In any case, the publisher finds it convenient to identify subscribers within a site and the various sites associated with an organization.

Most subscriptions are received directly from the subscriber; however, the publication also deals with a number of agencies, or subscription service bureaus, such as EBSCO, Faxon, and Readmore. These agencies receive a small commission for the subscriptions they provide, though this fact is generally kept hidden from the subscriber; it means, though, that the publisher must keep track of the "retail" price that the subscriber is being charged, as well as the commission paid to the agency.

In addition, the magazine is distributed in several foreign countries by distributors who have a quasi-exclusive right to market the magazine in their territory. The distributors receive a somewhat larger discount for a bulk shipment of magazines (in addition to paying for the shipping costs, which can be substantial), which they then distribute to their subscribers. Typically, some "direct" subscriptions from the distributor's country existed prior to the distributor-publisher agreement, and *Small Bytes* continues to supply those subscriptions directly. In addition, the distributor is supposed to supply the names and addresses of his own subscribers (in case he goes out of business) to the publisher; in practice, this has not been done consistently in the past, but the publisher is determined to enforce this provision when the new system is developed.

As noted earlier, contributing authors and members of the editorial board of advisors receive a complimentary one-year subscription to the magazine; in addition, the publisher provides a limited number of additional complimentary subscriptions to respected gurus and in the field, as well as a few friends and relatives. This list of "comps" is reviewed from time to time to see if any should be deleted. Also, the "comp" list is queried periodically to confirm that recipients still wish to receive their complimentary copy of *Small Bytes*.

A large percentage of existing subscribers renew their subscription from one year to the next; the renewal activity is typically the result of renewal notices that the publisher begins sending several months before the actual expiration. On the final month of a subscription, the publisher includes a large note with the magazine that says "THIS IS YOUR LAST COPY." For several months after the subscription has expired, the publisher continues to send renewal notices. (Note also that the subscription service bureaus make their own solicitation efforts to their subscribers, in addition to the publisher's direct letters to those same subscribers.) Renewals can straggle in several months after a subscription has expired, so it is vital to maintain the subscription records on the database indefinitely.

Payments for new subscriptions and renewals are normally received by check; the check may be accompanied with a subscription offer or a renewal notice, but such notices are not considered "invoices" in the normal sense of the word. In some cases, subscribers ask that a formal invoice be generated, with a purchase order number, so that it can be submitted to their accounting department for proper payment. Some subscribers pay by credit card, but the publisher insists (because its bank insists) that credit card payments be accompanied by a signature; this means that the credit card orders and renewals are typically sent by fax or mail.

In addition to full-year subscriptions, the publisher also sells limited numbers of individual copies of *Small Bytes*. In most cases, these are "back-issue" orders; they may be paid, as has been indicated, by check, credit card, or invoice. On rare occasions, a customer will order multiple copies of a back issue, in which case a discount is offered. And on even rarer occasions, a customer (typically an author, or a vendor whose product was favorably reviewed in the magazine) will order several thousand copies of an individual article in an issue and will ask that it be packaged as a "mini-issue" of the magazine; each of these special orders is priced separately, depending on volume; and so on.

Although there are only a small number of subscribers, the publisher has a large list of "prospects" that it has accumulated from various sources over the years. Many of these prospects have asked for sample copies of *Small Bytes*; some have received a "trial" subscription for a few months, but then decided not to "convert" to a paid subscription. Many others have received various promotional mailings from time to time, including unsolicited sample copies and/or trial subscriptions. Obviously, all this information is useful to the publisher.

8.1.2 Notes and Comments About the *Small Bytes* System

From the description just given, it is evident that the *Small Bytes* system is a classical business data processing application. While the details may seem overwhelming at first, it is clearly not a megaproject requiring hundreds of people; indeed, we would expect that such a system could be implemented by one or two people within a relatively brief period of time.

Also, it is not immediately apparent why such a system *must* be approached from an OO perspective; a structured analysis or information engineering approach, particularly if combined with a CASE tool and/or a 4GL, might do just as well. As will become more and more evident in the next several chapters, this application does lend itself to an OO approach, and large productivity gains might be expected if, for example, the publisher decides to add a new journal to its list of publications. And while the description in Section 8.1.1 says nothing about the implementation of the system, we can easily imagine that a graphical user interface will be highly desirable to the user, especially since the publisher and editor have used Macintosh packages to carry out the business activity up to this point. Thus it may well turn out that the biggest argument for adopting an OO approach is not because it improves the *analysis* phase of the project, but rather because it facilitates a subsequent OO design and implementation activity.

Note also that the most dominant characteristic of this application is its *data*. Clearly, *Small Bytes* is not a real-time system; while it will presumably be implemented as an on-line application, and while much of the activity revolves around a monthly cycle of publication, we don't have to worry about microsecond response times, concurrency, synchronization, and all the other difficult issues of real-time systems. Similarly, the processing, or number-crunching, component of the system is likely to be fairly trivial; it will involve such things as multiplying the number of copies times the unit price of the magazine to compute the total subscription price charged to a customer. This is hardly the stuff that requires functional decomposition and elaborate structure charts.

On the other hand, the problem description abounds with data descriptions. There are various items in the problem description that immediately cry out to be recognized as "objects" or "classes"; veteran information engineering practitioners would recognize the same items as "entities." There are clearly relationships between various items—for example, between subscribers and their subscriptions—and there are numerous attributes associated with each item. All this will be the primary focus of our analysis activity.

Other applications, such as the elevator problem described shortly, may have a different dominant theme. As a result, our strategy for discovering objects, which we will discuss in Chapter 9, might be quite different from the strategy we would use on the *Small Bytes* system.

8.2 THE ELEVATOR PROBLEM

8.2.1 Description of the Problem[1]

The general requirement is to design and implement a program to schedule and control four elevators in a building with 40 floors. The elevators will be used to carry people from one floor to another in the conventional way.

Efficiency: The program should schedule the elevators efficiently and reasonably. For example, if someone summons an elevator by pushing the down button on the 4th floor, the next elevator that reaches the 4th floor traveling down should stop at the 4th floor to

---

[1]This description is taken from Appendix G of the author's *Modern Structured Analysis* (Englewood Cliffs, NJ: Yourdon Press/Prentice Hall, 1989), which also presents a real-time structured analysis model of user requirements for the application. The elevator control problem is a classic example in many software engineering texts; for a more succinct description, see Stephen R. Schach, *Software Engineering*, (Homewood, IL: Aksen Associates, 1990), p. 272.

accept the passenger(s). On the other hand, if an elevator has no passengers (no outstanding destination requests), it should park at the last floor it visited until it is needed again. An elevator should not reverse its direction of travel until its passengers who want to travel in its current direction have reached their destinations. (As we will see, the program cannot really have information about an elevator's actual *passengers*; it only knows about destination button presses for a given elevator. For example, if some mischievous or sociopathic passenger boards the elevator at the 1st floor and then presses the destination buttons for the 4th, 5th, and 20th floor, the program will cause the elevator to travel to and stop at the 4th, 5th, and 20th floors. The computer and its program have no information about actual passenger boardings and exits.) An elevator that is filled to capacity should not respond to a new summons request. (There is an overweight sensor for each elevator. The computer and its program can interrogate these sensors.)

Destination Button: The interior of each elevator is furnished with a panel containing an array of 40 buttons, one button for each floor, marked with the floor numbers (1 to 40). These destination buttons can be illuminated by signals sent from the computer to the panel. When a passenger presses a destination button *not already lit*, the circuitry behind the panel sends an interrupt to the computer (there is a separate interrupt for each elevator). When the computer receives one of these (vectored) interrupts, its program can read the appropriate memory mapped eight-bit input registers (there is one for each interrupt, hence one for each elevator) that contains the floor number corresponding to the destination button that caused the interrupt. Of course, the circuitry behind the panel writes the floor number into the appropriate memory-mapped input register when it causes the vectored interrupt. (Since there are 40 floors in this application, only the first six bits of each input register will be used by the implementation; but the hardware would support a building with up to 256 floors.)

Destination Button Lights: As mentioned earlier, the destination buttons can be illuminated (by bulbs behind the panels). When the interrupt service routine in the program receives a destination button interrupt, it should send a signal to the appropriate panel to illuminate the appropriate button. This signal is sent by the program's loading the number of the button into the appropriate memory-mapped output register (there is one such register for each elevator).

The illumination of a button notifies the passenger(s) that the system has taken note of his or her request and also prevents further interrupts caused by additional (impatient?) pressing of the button. When the controller stops an elevator at a floor, it should send a signal to its destination button panel to turn off the destination button for that floor.

Floor Sensors: There is a floor sensor switch for each floor for each elevator shaft. When an elevator is within eight inches of a floor, a wheel on the elevator closes the switch for that floor and sends an interrupt to the computer (there is a separate interrupt for the set of switches in each elevator shaft). When the computer receives one of these (vectored) interrupts, its program can read the appropriate memory mapped eight-bit input register (there is one for each interrupt, hence one for each elevator) that contains the floor number corresponding to the floor sensor switch that caused the interrupt.

Arrival Lights: The interior of each elevator is furnished with a panel containing one illuminable indicator for each floor number. This panel is located just above the doors. The purpose of this panel is to tell the passengers in the elevator the number of the floor at which the elevator is arriving (and at which it may be stopping). The program should illuminate the indicator for a floor when it arrives at the floor and extinguish the indicator for a floor when it leaves a floor or arrives at a different floor. This signal is sent by the program's loading the number of the floor indicator into the appropriate memory-mapped output register (there is one register for each elevator).

Summons Buttons: Each floor of the building is furnished with a panel containing summons button(s). Each floor except the ground floor (floor 1) and the top floor (floor 40) is furnished with a panel containing two summon buttons, one marked UP and one marked DOWN. The ground floor summon panel has only an UP button. The top floor summon panel has only a DOWN button. Thus there are 78 summon buttons altogether, 39 UP buttons and 39 DOWN buttons. Would-be passengers press these buttons to summon an elevator. (Of course, the would-be passenger cannot summon a *particular* elevator. The scheduler decides which elevator should respond to a summon request.) These summon buttons can be illuminated by signals sent from the computer to the panel. When a passenger presses a summon button *not already lit*, the circuitry behind the panel sends a vectored interrupt to the computer (there is one interrupt for UP buttons and another for DOWN buttons). When the computer receives one of these two (vectored) interrupts, its program can read the appropriate memory mapped eight-bit input register that contains the floor number corresponding to the summon button that caused the interrupt. Of course, the circuitry behind the panel writes the floor number into the appropriate memory-mapped input register when it causes the vectored interrupt.

Summon Button Lights: The summon buttons can be illuminated (by bulbs behind the panels). When the summon button interrupt service routine in the program receives an UP or DOWN button vectored interrupt, it should send a signal to the appropriate panel to illuminate the appropriate button. This signal is sent by the program's loading the number of the button in the appropriate memory-mapped output register, one for the UP buttons and one for the DOWN buttons. The illumination of a button notifies the passenger(s) that the system has taken note of his or her request and also prevents further interrupts caused by additional pressing of the button. When the controller stops an elevator at a floor, it should send a signal to the floor's summon button panel to turn off the appropriate (UP or DOWN) button for that floor.

Elevator Motor Controls (Up, Down, Stop): There is a memory-mapped control word for each elevator motor. Bit 0 of this word commands the elevator to go up, bit 1 commands the elevator to go down, and bit 2 commands the elevator to stop at the floor whose sensor switch is closed. The elevator mechanism will not obey any inappropriate or unsafe command. If no floor sensor switch is closed when the computer issues a stop signal, the elevator mechanism ignores the stop signal until a floor sensor switch is closed. The computer program does not have to worry about controlling an elevator's doors or stopping an elevator exactly at a level (home) position at a floor. The elevator manufacturer uses conventional switches, relays, circuits, and safety interlocks for these purposes so that the manufacturer can certify the safety of the elevators without regard for the computer controller. For example, if the computer issues a stop command for an elevator when it is within eight inches of a floor (so that its floor sensor switch is closed), the conventional, approved mechanism stops and levels the elevator at that floor, opens and holds its doors open appropriately, and then closes its doors. If the computer issues an up or down command during this period (while the door is open, for example), the manufacturer's mechanism ignores the command until its conditions for movement are met. (Therefore, it is safe for the computer to issue an up or down command while an elevator's door is still open.) One condition for an elevator's movement is that its *stop button* not be depressed. Each elevator's destination button panel contains a stop button. This button does not go to the computer. Its sole purpose is to hold an elevator at a floor with its door open when the elevator is currently stopped at a floor. A red emergency *stop switch* stops and holds the elevator at the very next floor it reaches irrespective of computer scheduling. The red switch may also turn on an audible alarm. The red switch is not connected to the computer.

Target Machine: The elevator scheduler and controller may be implemented for any contemporary microcomputer capable of handling this application.

8.2.2 Notes and Comments About the Elevator Problem

Clearly, this is a very different kind of problem from the *Small Bytes* system: it involves the control of a physical device, and it has characteristics of a real-time system, even though the time constraints are not likely to be overwhelmingly difficult to manage.

While there are obviously a number of items in the problem description that will be identified as objects, and while many of those objects do have a number of interesting data-related characteristics, our attention is drawn in the problem description to the *behavior* of the objects. Our focus is on such issues as: When does an elevator have to go up or down? *How* does the summons button communicate with the summons light, and with what other objects must it communicate? Under what circumstances is it legal for the elevator motor control to respond to an "up" or "down" command?

Within this context, it is also evident that the elevator problem cries out to be modeled as a number of asynchronous, communicating "things"—whether we call those things objects or entities or poobahs is less important than the fact that we want to stay away from a classical, synchronous structured design model in which a single "executive" module controls the execution of a number of subordinate modules. By contrast, since the *Small Bytes* problem exhibits no real-time characteristics, the issue of asynchronous behavior doesn't arise; a classical transaction-based model would suffice just as well. Note that an IE approach, which deals with "entities," is less appealing than an OO approach for the elevator problem: a key characteristic of the application is the *communication* between various components, which the OO approach handles naturally with the concept of messages between objects.

There is one other characteristic of the elevator problem description that must be emphasized: there is a great deal of discussion of *implementation technology*. Unlike the *Small Bytes* problem description, which was basically technology independent, the elevator problem description talks about microprocessors, memory-mapped input registers, relays, vectored interrupts, interrupt service routines, sensors, signals, and a "scheduler." Some of these details may be associated with the electromechanical "environment" in which our computer system will be placed; other details obviously involve the user's assumption about the hardware and software technology that will be employed to implement the system. An important task for the systems analyst—regardless of whether he uses an OO approach or any other methodology—is to eliminate as many as possible of these irrelevant technology details from the analysis model, to provide a "perfect technology" model of the essential user requirements.

8.3 DEVELOPMENT OF THE OOA MODEL

Most software projects begin with some kind of high-level problem description like the ones just provided. They may have more or less detail; they may be provided verbally; and they may be given to a systems analyst who has a deeper understanding of the "business" than we can assume you, the reader, is likely to have about magazine subscriptions or elevators.

Even with such a sketchy problem description, there may be good reason to begin building a prototype for demonstration to the user; the reasons for this were discussed in Chapter 3. However, the next several chapters make the assumption that, sooner or later, it will be desirable to construct a formal, detailed model of the user requirements; this will be followed, in Part IV, with a model of the design, or software architecture, for the two applications.

In an earlier book,[2] Peter Coad and I emphasized the development of a *single* object-oriented model of user requirements that would be presented to the user in a series of "layers." Such an approach is ideal for a business-oriented application like the *Small Bytes* system, since the data-oriented characteristics of the system are the dominant feature; our primary concern is how to avoid overwhelming the user with details, and a layered approach is quite convenient for doing this.

The single-model approach also has the advantage of only having to "train" the end user to read one kind of diagramming notation. Nevertheless, the prevailing trend in the OO methodology field—as evidenced in the various textbooks by authors such as Booch, Jacobson, Rumbaugh, Shlaer-Mellor, Martin-Odell, Firesmith, and others—is a "multimodel" approach, with several different diagrams that illustrate different aspects of the problem. While it may not be necessary (or even desirable) for the *Small Bytes* system, it is highly desirable for the elevator control problem: depending on our perspective, we may wish to focus our attention on (1) the essential objects of the problem and the class hierarchies to which they belong, (2) the internal behavior of each object and the "life cycle" which they exhibit, and (3) the communication between objects.

While the diagramming details will continue to vary from one methodology textbook to another, it seems evident that the multimodel approach will prevail; hence we have chosen this approach for the subsequent chapters of this book. Chapter 9 begins with the fundamental questions: What objects are present in the problem, and how do we find them? Subsequent chapters then explore the class hierarchies (or inheritance structures) of classes and objects, the (static) relationships between objects; the attributes of the objects, the dynamic behavior of the objects, and the methods/functions encapsulated within the objects. These aspects of the OOA model will be illustrated with the *Small Bytes* system and the elevator control system.

---

[2]Peter Coad and Edward Yourdon, *Object-Oriented Analysis*, 2nd ed. (Englewood Cliffs, NJ: Yourdon Press/Prentice Hall, 1990).

9

Discovering Objects

There is nothing more central, more crucial, to any object-oriented methodology than the process of discovering *which* classes and objects should be included in the model. If a systems analyst can't determine which classes and objects are essential to the user, his OOA model will be a disaster. If a designer can't decide which objects are needed to form the central core of his software architecture, the architecture he builds will be a house of cards. There is a great deal of detail surrounding any OO model—messages and relationships, attributes and hierarchies, and so on—but the heart of the model is the set of classes and objects. We must begin there if we are to build a sound methodology.

Aside from the requirements of the methodology itself, our motivation for discovering objects as part of a requirements model is the belief that an object-oriented *technical* representation of the system will be closer to, and more compatible with, the user's conceptual view of the world than would be true with any other kind of model. This is tantamount to saying, "Users don't think in terms of functions or entities; they think in terms of *objects*. Objects correspond to real things that the users see in their world, things with descriptive attributes *and* behavior." This is an intuitively appealing argument, and is quite possibly true for a large class of users—but we have no proof. Indeed, no two users are alike: some may prefer an OO model of their requirements, while others may prefer some other representation. More important, some may resists *any* abstract model, favoring a working prototype instead.[1]

---

[1] There is another problem, too: What if the user has spent the past five years learning how to read analysis models based on data flow diagrams or entity-relationship diagrams? His question is likely to be, "Why should I change?" We will discuss this question further in Chapter 26.

Aside from the user's conceptual mind-set, our desire to express the requirements in terms of objects is typically based on the nature of the application itself; as mentioned in earlier chapters, objects provide a natural "metaphor" for describing some kinds of applications—and this is becoming more and more common for systems that involve GUI front-ends, client-server architectures, and distributed data and processing. Indeed, it may also be a better metaphor for the organizational environment in which our systems are built, as the enterprises of the 1990s move from a hierarchical "control-oriented" structure to a flat, decentralized group of communicating "clusters."

As we will see in this chapter, our approach to the discovery of essential objects in a system depends a great deal on our *perspective*: Are we looking at the system from a data perspective, from a functional perspective, or from a behavioral perspective? As we suggested in our initial discussion of the *Small Bytes* and elevator case studies, the system itself will often exhibit a dominant characteristic: the *Small Bytes* system, for example, seems to be intrinsically data-oriented, while the elevator system is intrinsically behavioral in nature. This does not mean that we should ignore the other perspectives altogether, but merely that the dominant perspective will usually suggest the starting point in our search for classes and objects.

Also, the user's "mind-set" will often have a dramatic influence on our search for objects. Despite the suggestion that users will find the object-oriented model intuitively appealing, it may still be true that when we first begin interviewing them, their "mental model," or frame of reference, may be intrinsically functional, or behavioral, or data-oriented in nature. Unless the systems analyst is as expert in the underlying application as the user himself, it is folly to fight the user's way of thinking when carrying out these interviews; the information thus gleaned may be packaged and rearranged in other forms, but the object discovery process can be made easier and more pleasant if it follows the user's natural way of thinking.

Thus, this chapter will discuss the task of object discovery from all three perspectives. Then we will discuss some criteria for evaluating the "reasonableness" of candidate objects that have been discovered through the analysis process. For large systems, where there may be hundreds of classes and objects, it is also important to group classes and objects into aggregate units; in the Coad-Yourdon approach, these are known as *subjects*, and we will discuss them as a final step in the discovery process. Finally, we will illustrate the process by returning to the *Small Bytes* and elevator case studies.

9.1 GRAPHICAL NOTATION FOR CLASSES AND OBJECTS

But first we must decide how to represent the classes and objects we discover. Ever since Tom DeMarco characterized text-based analysis models as Victorian novels where there is never any sex until the last page,[2] there has been a common tendency to represent user requirements in a graphical fashion. Thus structured analysis and information engineering have relied heavily on such familiar diagramming tools as data-flow diagrams (DFDs) and entity-relationship diagrams (ERDs). For OOA, the obvious question is: What kind of diagrams should we draw?

Unfortunately, every methodologist and textbook author seems to have his own answer to this question. Whereas the structured analysis methodology evolved only two common variants on DFDs— the DeMarco "bubbles" and the Gane-Sarson "bubtangles"—there are at least a dozen different graphical representations of classes and objects. The major differences in graphical notation will become more evident as we discuss additional aspects of the OOA model in subsequent chapters—for example, different ways of representing inheritance and object communication, and so on—and the differences in the diagrams for simple classes and objects tend to be more cosmetic than substantive.

In an earlier book,[3] Pete Coad and I proposed a simple graphical notation for classes and objects; over the years, I have continued to find it simple and convenient, and will continue to use it in this book. It has the added convenience of now being supported by numerous CASE tools; however, it should be emphasized that the notations proposed by Booch, Rumbaugh, and various other methodologists are also supported by various CASE vendors.

---

[2] Tom DeMarco, *Structured Analysis and System Specification* (Englewood Cliffs, NJ: Yourdon Press/Prentice Hall, 1978)

[3] Peter Coad and Edward Yourdon, *Object-Oriented Analysis*, 2nd ed. (Englewood Cliffs, NJ: Yourdon Press/Prentice Hall, 1990).

Throughout this book, our graphical notation for a *class* will look like that shown in Figure 9.1.

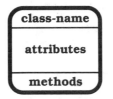

Figure 9.1: Graphical representation for a class

Recall from Chapter 1 that various books and OOA methodologies refer to Figure 9.1 as an "object type" or an "object template." We will discuss the details of "attributes" and "methods" in subsequent chapters; in this chapter, we are concerned only with discovering which "class-names" are relevant.

In most cases, we will be dealing with classes for which "instances," or individual objects, are known to exist. Some OOA methodologies refer to this situation as an "instantiated class" or simply refer to the individual objects within the class. In conformance to the original Coad-Yourdon notation, this book will use the graphical notation shown in Figure 9.2 to represent objects *and the class to which they belong*:

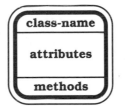

Figure 9.2: Graphical representation for class and objects

The distinction between the two diagrams is obviously the thin line surrounding the class boundary; it merely signifies that instances of the class are presumed to exist.

As an example of the contrasting graphical notation between various methodologies, here is the Booch representation for a class and object;[4] the icons shown in Figure 9.3 are typically referred to as "clouds":

[4]Grady Booch, *Object-Oriented Design with Applications* (Redwood City, CA: Benjamin/Cummings, 1991).

Figure 9.3: Representing a class in the Booch methodology

Note also that Booch identifies a "class utility," which represents "either a single free subprogram or a collection of subprograms."[5] While it may be a useful concept in some environments, and perhaps even more useful in the design and implementation phase of a project, we have chosen to not to include the concept in the notation used in this book; our perspective instead will be that *all* classes should be maintained in a common library of reusable components and thus should *all* be considered as "utilities" for use in other systems.

The Rumbaugh and coworkers notation[6] is similar to the Coad-Yourdon notation, except that rectangles are used instead of ovals or clouds (see Figure 9.4):

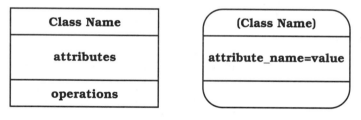
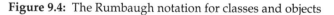

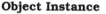

Figure 9.4: The Rumbaugh notation for classes and objects

Several OOA methodologies use even simpler notations that make no distinction between the classes and the instances within the class. The Martin-Odell[7] and the Embley-Kurtz-Woodfield[8] methodologies, for example, use a simple rectangle containing only the

[5] Ibid.

[6] James Rumbaugh, Michael Blaha, William Premerlani, Frederick Eddy, and William Lorensen, *Object-Oriented Modeling and Design* (Englewood Cliffs, NJ: Prentice Hall, 1991).

[7] James Martin and James J. Odell, *Object-Oriented Analysis & Design*. (Englewood Cliffs, NJ: Prentice Hall, 1992).

[8] David W. Embley, Barry D. Kurtz, and Scott N. Woodfield, *Object-Oriented Systems Analysis: A Model-Driven Approach* (Englewood Cliffs, NJ: Yourdon Press/Prentice Hall, 1992).

name of the class; Shlaer and Mellor[9] use a similar simple notation (with the convention that the identifying "key" attribute is highlighted with an asterisk) as shown in Figure 9.5:

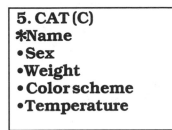

Figure 9.5: The Shlaer-Mellor notation for classes and objects

In contrast to the rather simplified modeling notations, Ivar Jacobson and coworkers[10] have chosen a notation in which different *kinds* of objects have their own distinct icons: they distinguish among "entity" objects, "interface" objects, and "control" objects, as shown in Figure 9.6:

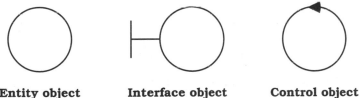

Entity object   **Interface object**   **Control object**

Figure 9.6: Jacobson notation for objects

Entity objects are characterized primarily by their data content, although they do exhibit "behavior" in the normal object-oriented sense; interface objects are primarily concerned with the interactions that take place between the user and the system (e. g., window objects in a GUI environment); and control objects are primarily concerned with coordinating and synchronizing the activity of other objects in the system.

[9] Sally Shlaer and Stephen J. Mellor, *Object Lifecycles: Modeling the World in States* (Englewood Cliffs, NJ: Yourdon Press/Prentice Hall, 1992).

[10]Ivar Jacobson, Magnus Christerson, Patrik Jonsson, and Gunnar Övergaard, *Object-Oriented Software Engineering: A Use Case Driven Approach* (Reading, MA: Addison-Wesley, 1992).

Finally, Don Firesmith's notation (see Figure 9.7) is even more elaborate, with separate icons to represent a variety of different categories of objects:

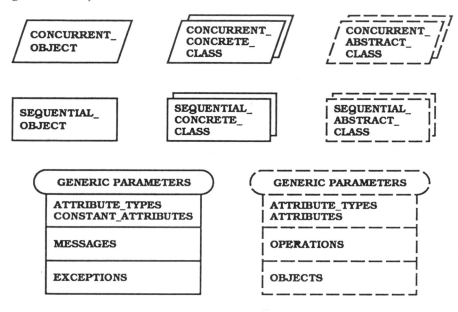

Figure 9.7: Firesmith's ADM_4 object notation

Ultimately, the systems analyst must choose a notation that "works" for his or her purposes: it must be rich enough to express all the nuances that are important in the project; it must be sufficiently formal and rigorous to avoid ambiguity and confusion; yet it must also be simple enough that a typical end user can understand the diagrams without first having to obtain a graduate degree in computer science. But even more, it should conform to what the user thinks is aesthetically pleasing: some like rectangles, some like circles, and some like neither. One could imagine, for example, that some users would find the whimsical informality of Booch's "cloud" icons appealing; others might dislike them precisely because of that whimsical informality.

Thus, in some circumstances, Firesmith's elaborate notation may be necessary and appropriate; in others cases, it will be overwhelming. For many real-time projects like the elevator control case study, Jacobson's distinction among "entity," "interface," and "control" objects may be quite useful, but for the *Small Bytes* case study, it would be less useful. The issue of simplicity versus complexity may not seem very serious with the diagrams shown thus far; however, as we will see in subsequent chapters, each variant of OOA methodology adds several more graphical icons—often a dozen or more—to represent class hierarchies, object-to-object relationships, messages between objects, and so on.

The fact that this book will use the original Coad-Yourdon notation should not be seen as a rejection of other notational schemes; indeed, it is important to avoid distracting "religious" arguments about whether rectangles are better than ovals or clouds for representing an object. The analyst should choose whatever notation works best within his or her organizational and project context; it is hoped that, as time goes on, more and more CASE tools will support a multitude of graphical OO notations.

Having given so much emphasis to graphical notation, our final comment will seem ironic indeed: in the beginning stages of object discovery, the diagrams aren't necessary. It will often be sufficient simply to provide a textual listing of the classes and objects, as we will see in the case study discussions in Sections 9.7 and 9.8. The true value of the graphics becomes evident in the next several chapters, as we begin constructing hierarchies of objects, documenting the relationships between objects, and detailing the message communication between objects.

9.2 FINDING OBJECTS: THE DATA PERSPECTIVE

For many business data processing applications, *data* is the dominant characteristic of the system, even from the first moment of systems analysis; this would probably be true, for example, in the *Small Bytes* case study. As a result, the strategy for discovering objects in such systems is very similar to the strategy used to discover "entities" in classical data modeling methodologies. Indeed, this is almost a disappointment to many systems analysts who have been reared in ERD-based methodologies: the beginning steps of an OOA project look so familiar, they are apt to complain, "What's so different about OOA? Isn't this the same old stuff we've been doing all along?"[11]

---

[11]As we will see in subsequent chapters, what *is* different is the inheritance features of class hierarchies, which are typically more powerful and extensive than the subtype-supertype concept in data modeling methodologies. Even more important is the encapsulation of data and function within objects, and the message communication between objects, which the data modeling methodologies lack entirely.

In any case, the data-oriented strategies for discovering objects should come as no surprise; the only thing that *is* surprising is that many OOA textbooks and methodologies ignore the topic altogether, apparently in the belief that the process is so intuitive and easy that it does not bear discussing. Shlaer and Mellor were among the first to popularize guidelines for data-oriented object discovery;[12] several OO design and programming books, such as Firesmith[13] and the excellent text by Wirfs-Brock and coworkers, also present excellent advice on object discovery[14] Earlier , Pete Coad and I suggested the following places to look for objects:[15]

- Look at the problem space itself, together with any diagrams, pictures, and textual information provided by the user.
- Look at other systems and "external terminators" that communicate or interact with the system being modeled.
- Look at physical devices that will exist in the environment and interact with the system, regardless of the technology used to implement the system itself.
- Look at events that must be recorded and remembered by the system.
- Look at roles played by different people who interact with the system.
- Look at physical or geographical locations and sites that may be relevant to the system.
- Look at organizational units (departments, divisions, and so on) that may be relevant to the system.

There is no guarantee, of course, that this checklist will discover all the objects in a system; all it can do is provide the analyst with a starting point for his or her investigations. Even with an OO perspective, the classic problems of systems analysis remain: the user may not know exactly what he wants his system to do and may be unwilling or unable to articulate his needs. If the analyst is unfamiliar with the underlying application, he may not know what questions to

---

[12]Sally Shlaer and Stephen J. Mellor, *Object-Oriented Systems Analysis: Modeling the World in Data* (Englewood Cliffs, NJ: Yourdon Press/Prentice Hall, 1988).

[13]Donald G. Firesmith, *Object-Oriented Requirements Analysis and Logical Design* (New York: Addison-Wesley, 1993).

[14]Rebecca Wirfs-Brock, Brian Wilkerson, and Lauren Wiener, *Object-Oriented Software* (Englewood Cliffs, NJ: Prentice Hall, 1990).

[15]Coad and Yourdon, *Object-Oriented Analysis*.

ask—even with the assistance of this checklist. Thus a prototyping life cycle may continue to be an extremely important "safety factor" for ensuring that no essential objects have been left undiscovered when the final version of the system goes into production.

On the other hand, a common problem with OOA is the discovery of too *many* objects. Enthusiasm and a naive belief that "more is better" when it comes to adding objects to the OOA model may lead the analyst to the creation of objects that really don't deserve to exist. We will discuss this problem further in Section 9.5.

9.3 FINDING OBJECTS: THE FUNCTIONAL PERSPECTIVE

During an OO presentation at Apple Computer a few years ago, I submitted a standard data-oriented perspective on discovering objects; while talking to users and examining any textual documentation they may have had, I suggested that the analysts should look for *nouns*: nouns are typically good indicators of the existence of an object in the model.

> "Wrong!" bellowed a bushy-haired software engineer in the back of the room. "Look for *verbs*!"

I was so startled that I made no reply to his outrageous statement; my immediate reaction was that it was just one more bit of evidence that everyone in Silicon Valley was part of an alien species, descended from the planet Zork in a distant galaxy.

It was only later that I realized my Apple Computer critic was simply looking at the "object world" from a different perspective: to him, what characterizes an object is what it *does*, not what it is. Identification and documentation of attributes come later; the first question is "What does this object have to *do* to exist?"

For example, most of us would immediately accept the notion that a "person" is an object; for some, the essential nature of "person-ness" is the combination of such attributes as height, weight, name, age, and so on. But for others—perhaps those thinking of a "person" object within a corporate environment—the essential nature of "person-ness" is what he or she does. When you're introduced to someone at a cocktail party or social gathering, for example, are you more likely to ask, "Where do you live?" or "What do you do for a living?" Both questions are usually appropriate and socially acceptable, but they reflect two very different perspectives.

Indeed, Apple Computer is not alone in this perspective; many OO enthusiasts use a method of documenting their objects known as "CRC" cards, originally developed by Ward Cunningham of Wyatt Software Services, Inc., in Lake Oswego, OR. "CRC" is an acronym for "class-responsibility-communication," and it addresses three fundamental questions about an object: What class does it belong to? What responsibility does it have? And how does it communicate with other objects?

Identifying the *responsibility* of an object is another way of asking what function(s) it performs; discovering objects by asking about responsibilities thus leads one to focusing on verbs in a problem statement, rather than *nouns*.[16]

What does this have to do with systems analysis and OOA? As mentioned, many systems cry out to be examined from a special perspective; we would be more likely to investigate the elevator system from a functional perspective than the *Small Bytes* system (though, as we will see in Section 9.4, the elevator system is even more amenable to the behavior perspective).

But we also observed in Chapter 8 that the perspective depends a great deal on the mind-set, personality, and orientation of the user: if the user is most comfortable talking about the requirements of his or her system, that may be the most appropriate one to use when discovering objects. *This is particularly common in business reengineering projects, when the user's essential question is: "What business are we really in? What do we really **do** around here?"*

The primary danger of a function-oriented OOA perspective is that it can corrupt the analyst or the user into building a completely functional model of user requirements[17] As a starting point for object discovery, it's fine—but if it leads to a final analysis model that looks like a (HIPO) diagram, or a functional decomposition diagram, or a structure chart, then the OOA process has gone badly awry.

9.4 FINDING OBJECTS: THE BEHAVIORAL PERSPECTIVE

There is one last perspective that can be helpful in discovering objects: *behavior*. Our primary questions here are: How do objects

---

[16]The most eloquent description of the "responsibility-driven" approach to OO analysis and design is provided by Rebecca Wirfs-Brock. See *Designing Object-Oriented Software*, by Wirfs-Brock, Wilkerson, and Wiener.

[17]Don Firesmith points out that a business-oriented "function" can often involve multiple objects.

communicate? With whom? How fast? How do they respond to messages, signals, interrupts, or other forms of communication?

The applicability of this perspective to real-time or distributed systems is obvious. But it can also be helpful if the analyst can entice a group of users to adopt a "role-playing" attitude in acting out the behavior of the overall system. Thus, if the analyst suspects that there is a "customer" class in the system being modeled, he might ask one of the users to pretend that he *is* a customer. It is easy to imagine how questions like, "Who do you interact with?" and "How do you respond when the accounting department sends you an 'overdue invoice' message?" could evoke a healthy analyst-user dialogue to help determine whether "customer" really is an appropriate class for the system.

As we will see in subsequent chapters, a closer examination of the behavior of objects typically introduces one or more additional kinds of diagrams into the OOA process; the most common one is the well-known *state-transition diagram.* In addition, we may find it helpful to draw "object interaction diagrams" or "event communication diagrams" to illustrate the communication between objects. These will be discussed in Chapter 13.

But for the initial task of discovering relevant classes and objects, these diagrams are unnecessary. Instead, we might focus on a simple textual list of the *events* to which the system is required to respond. When interviewing the user in the *Small Bytes* system, for example, the analyst might hear the casual comment, "Well, of course, sometimes we get a request for a sample copy of the magazine; since it's fairly expensive, people want to look at it before they decide to subscribe." The relevant event, then, could be described succinctly as REQUEST-SAMPLE-COPY, and it suggests questions such as: Which object initiates such an event? Which object within the system must respond to that event? Does that "external" event trigger a "chain of events" within the system—and if so, which objects are involved in that chain of events?

Structured analysis veterans may recognize this line of thinking: it is very similar to the "event-partitioning" strategy proposed by McMenamin and Palmer[18] as part of their methodology of "essential systems analysis." Their strategy, which can be used as an alternative means of discovering objects in a system, can be summarized as follows:

---

[18]Stephen McMenamin and John Palmer, *Essential Systems Analysis* (Englewood Cliffs, NJ: Yourdon Press/Prentice Hall, 1984).

1. Develop a list of events or external stimuli to which the system must respond. Cross-check the event list against the top-level context diagram for the system for consistency. Typically, each incoming data flow on the context diagram will correspond to an event on the event list.[19]

2. Draw an initial data flow diagram in which each incoming event is "captured" by a single DFD "bubble." Thus, if there are 100 events for the system, there will initially be 100 discrete bite-size mini-DFDs.

3. Identify the required processing steps for the system to respond to the event in a satisfactory fashion. In some cases, this may involve some immediate computation and an outgoing data flow (back to the external source that created the incoming data flow). In other cases, the appropriate response might involve storing some information in a data store (which will eventually be implemented as a buffer, queue, database, and so on), so that some other (asynchronous) event can use the data for its processing. In some cases, the analyst may wish to identify a "chain" of DFD bubbles that are required to fully process the incoming data flow and respond to the event. At the end of this step for a 100-event system, the analyst will have "fleshed-out" mini-DFDs.

4. Join all the mini-DFDs together. Since the events are presumed to be asynchronous, the "joining," or interface, between the various diagrams consists of the data stores: the various event-processing DFD bubbles will store and retrieve information from common data stores. The result of this step is a *single* DFD; for the 100-event system, the simplest case we could imagine would be a 100-bubble DFD, with data stores that act as buffers between the asynchronous processing taking place in the bubbles.

5. To produce a *leveled* data flow diagram, perhaps partition some of the bubbles downward, in the traditional functional-decomposition fashion. But a more important activity involves "upward" aggregation of clusters of bubbles into

---

[19]There are some exceptions to this simple guideline: some events, for example, may be temporal in nature (i.e., they occur once a day or once every clock-tick) and may not be associated with a data flow. And some data flows may not represent events per se, but may represent necessary data that the system must obtain as part of its processing of an event that was initiated by some other data flow.

"superbubbles" in a higher-level DFD; this process can be repeated until we have reached the level of a single superbubble: the context diagram for the entire system.

The rationale, or strategy, for clustering bubbles together turns out to be object-oriented in nature: look for a group of DFD bubbles clustered around a common data store, and aggregate them upward into a higher-level bubble. From this perspective, the bottom-level DFD bubbles are *functions*, or "methods." The common data store, which the systems analyst would traditionally think of as a relational table, or a flat-file filled with database records, is comparable to the data attributes of object instances in a class. Thus the act of "clustering" is akin to encapsulation: the higher-level bubble that we create is indeed an object.

OO purists are often highly critical of this notion that objects can be discovered by starting with a structured analysis process; the strategy described here (and others like it) is criticized as "objectifying a functional model." Indeed, caution is appropriate: there is no guarantee that objects discovered in this fashion will be "good" objects. There is always the danger that the bubble-oriented structured analysis "mind-set" evident in this event-partitioning approach will dominate through the rest of the modeling process;[20] and there is the practical, managerial question of whether the initial DFDs created with this strategy must be saved as part of the formal project documentation or whether they can be sketched on the back of an envelope and then thrown away when the relevant objects are discovered.

Nevertheless, it *is* important to realize that there is some commonality between the older and newer methodologies; this is a comforting thought for systems analysts who spent their first 10 years practicing structured analysis and who now wonder whether everything they learned is fundamentally incorrect. We will discuss this theme further in Chapter 25.

---

[20]As an example of the potential danger of bubble-oriented thinking, the strategy just described may help the analyst discover objects of encapsulated data and functionality, and it may help identify the communication between objects (represented on a DFD as "data flows" between bubbles). However, the standard DFD has no concept whatsoever of inheritance, and there is a danger that the analyst who views OOA as a kind of "window-dressing" on top of his SA/SD model may completely overlook the concept of class hierarchies discussed in Chapter 10.

9.5 CRITERIA FOR EVALUATING CANDIDATE OBJECTS

Having discovered numerous classes and objects using the various strategies just described, it is important for the systems analyst to pause and subject each "candidate" object to careful scrutiny. As mentioned earlier, there is a tendency for enthusiasm to run rampant: *everything* becomes an object. More dangerously, there is a "macho" attitude that has been observed in far too many DP projects: "my OOA model is better than your model because it has more objects." Indeed, the head of one large Silicon Valley computer company boasted recently in a public forum that his company's latest creation had *ten thousand* classes; while most in his audience gasped with delight, a few grizzled veterans shook their heads in despair. Whether it's bubbles, boxes, objects, or functions that we use as our measure of "atomic" units in a system, smaller is better. Software is hard enough to develop without turning its architecture into a bureaucracy the size of the federal government.

What do we look for when critically reviewing proposed objects in an OOA model? In an earlier book,[21] Pete Coad and I proposed a number of criteria; these will be familiar to many systems analysts who have used data-modeling methodologies based on ERDs:

- *Necessary remembrance.* Make certain that the proposed object has *some* data that it must remember. It's not necessary at this point to identify all the attributes, but it is useful to verify that some do exist.

- *More than one attribute.* If the proposed object consists of only one attribute, then perhaps that's what it is: an attribute in some other object. This is not intended as a "rule," but merely the basis for a "challenge" to the existence of a proposed object. There are indeed legitimate examples of objects containing only one attribute, and there are (especially in real-time and control systems) objects with *no* attributes. But the vast majority of objects will have multiple attributes.

- *Needed functionality.* It should be possible to identify one or more methods, or services, for the proposed objects: the object has to *do* something to justify its existence. As noted, it is possible (though uncommon) for an object to have no attributes,

---

[21]Coad and Yourdon, *Object-Oriented Analysis.*

but it is highly implausible for an object to have no methods or services.[22]

- *Essential functionality.* The functionality, or behavior, that has been identified for the proposed object should be relevant and necessary regardless of the hardware/software technology that will be used to implement the system; otherwise, the proposed object is a *design* object, or *implementation* object, and it should be deferred until a later stage of the project.

- *Common attributes.* All the attributes of the proposed class should apply to each of the instances of the class. If the analyst hears comments from the user such as, "Well, this attribute of PERSON doesn't apply to left-handed people," it's a strong clue that the model should contain a class hierarchy, as described in Chapter 10. In such a case, we probably have one or more subclasses that have been muddled together into a common superclass.

- *Common functionality.* All of the methods, or services, of the proposed class should apply to each of the instances of the class; the argument here is obviously the same as for common attributes.

9.6 GROUPING CLASSES AND OBJECTS INTO "SUBJECTS"

For small systems, the systems analyst may discover only a few dozen classes and objects. As we will see in the next several chapters, these classes may be organized into complex hierarchies and linked together in various intricate ways. But the basic "building blocks" from which the system is composed may be small enough in number that they can be presented to the user in one fell swoop. All the classes and objects could be graphically documented using any of the notational schemes shown in Section 9.1, for example, and presented to the user for review and approval.

But for large, complex systems, this is clearly inappropriate: there may be hundreds, or even thousands, of discrete classes and objects, and it would be overwhelming to have to deal with them all at once. Hence, virtually all OOA methodologies contain a mecha-

---

[22]Consider the dilemma of an object that contains attributes but no services: How can any other object modify or interrogate the value of those attributes? Even more bizarre is the concept of an object that has no attributes *and* no services.

nism for aggregating groups of objects into a higher-level abstraction. In some methodologies, this higher-level unit is called a "subject"; in others, it is called a "package," a "kit," a "cluster," a "subsystem," or a "subassembly." As might be expected, the graphical notation varies, too: some methodologists use an oval, others use a rectangle, and so on.

For consistency, we will use the terminology notation suggested by the Coad-Yourdon methodology: the higher-level abstraction is known as a *subject*, and it is graphically represented with a rectangular box. As Figure 9.8 illustrates, a subject is given an appropriate name, and it may (but does not necessarily) provide a textual listing of the classes and objects it contains.

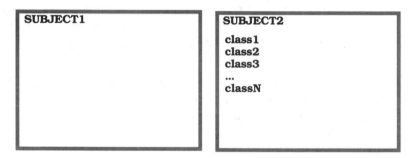

Figure 9.8: Graphical representation of a subject

Note that a hierarchy of classes within subjects is *not* used to represent the familiar superclass-subclass hierarchy that OO methodologies depend on so heavily. Thus we would not expect to see a subject called PERSON, whose component objects are MAN and WOMAN; this would modeled instead using the class hierarchy and inheritance concepts discussed in Chapter 10. Similarly, subjects are not typically used to model "whole-part" hierarchies, which are also discussed in Chapter 10; thus, we would typically *not* create a subject called PERSON and somehow try to show that a person consists one HEAD, two ARMs, one BODY, and two LEGs. Instead, we use the subject concept to combine distinct and discrete, but nevertheless fairly cohesive, classes into a common grouping. Thus, in the *Small Bytes* system, we might decide to create a subject called CUSTOMER, which consists of separate classes for distributors, agents, prospective customers, corporate customers, individual customers, and friends of the publisher who receive complimentary copies of the magazine.

As noted earlier, small systems may not require a "subject layer" for the OOA model; this is a matter of personal preference, and a question of how much detail the user and analyst are willing to deal with. For medium-sized projects, it is quite common to discover the individual classes and objects first and then aggregate upward to create the appropriate subjects. This "bottom-up" approach is quite common for all methodologies; it provides a "top-down" presentation to the user, of the finished model—and it sometimes provides a dangerous illusion that the model was *created* in a top-down fashion.

However, on very large systems, top-down decomposition of subjects into objects may be necessary or desirable for various reasons. The only proviso that must be kept in mind is that the initial decomposition may eventually prove to be faulty; the systems analyst must be prepared, at some later stage in the analysis or implementation of the system, to regroup objects into different subjects to provide a more meaningful picture of the system.

While we have used the term "abstraction" to describe the purpose of a subject, "picture" may be a more meaningful term: *a subject is a way of providing a "view" of some subset of the overall collection of classes and objects.* If one accepts this characterization, accepting too the idea that the subject concept is useful more as a presentation device than a model-creation device, then a related question can be answered quite easily: Are the subjects mutually exclusive, or can a class be represented in more than one subject? If the subject is used as an active part of decomposition and factoring of the system into smaller subsystems (for example, for scheduling, staffing, configuration management, and other administrative purposes), a pure hierarchical factoring would probably be favored. But if it is considered strictly as a "view" of the overall mass of objects and classes, then "overlapping" views should be allowed.

Similarly, what about *levels*, or hierarchies, of subjects? As noted, there is a more fundamental OO-related kind of hierarchy that we will see in Chapter 10; thus, in most cases, a single subject level is sufficient. Indeed, some versions of OOA, such as the one I described in an earlier book with Pete Coad,[23] only allow one subject level; however, most of the popular OOA methodologies in the

---

[23]Coad and Yourdon, *Object-Oriented Analysis.*

field allow, either implicitly or explicitly, as many subject levels as needed by the systems analyst.

Intellectually, of course, the systems analyst is free to do whatever he wants; permission is not required from any of the methodology gurus to decide how many subject levels one will use. On the other hand, most OOA practitioners will eventually use a CASE tool to support their work; thus the presence or absence of multiple subject levels may turn out to be a tangible constraint imposed upon the systems analyst.

9.7 CASE STUDY: THE *SMALL BYTES* SYSTEM

The reader, of course, does not have the benefit of interviewing the end user of the *Small Bytes* system; however, we can imagine the kind of dialogue that might take place between the analyst and user as the analyst reviews the textual description of user requirements presented in Section 8.1.

In the very first sentence, the first noun that catches our attention is "journal." Should we have a class within our model called JOURNAL, or MAGAZINE? We might begin peppering our user with questions: What are some of the data attributes you would use to describe the journal? What do you have to *do* with the journal? and so on. In the course of such a discussion, we might find that what *really* matters to the publisher is the various *issues* of the journal that have been published over the past several years: each issue is distinguishable from all other issues, and there are various pieces of information that we must keep about each issue—how many copies were printed, how many pages it contains, which authors contributed articles to that issue, and so on. It's also easy to imagine some of the things that must be done by, for, or to a journal: subscribers order copies of an individual issue, or enter a one-year subscription that entitles them to a series of issues, and so on. There is little doubt that ISSUE will become a class within our model, but we have not answered the original question of whether JOURNAL is an appropriate class.

Indeed, we may have to postpone our final decision about JOURNAL until sometime later in the project, but for now, we can begin asking some questions. What are some of the relevant data attributes of the journal? It has a name (*Small Bytes*) and a publisher, and a corporate address, and so on. But are these relevant to the system? It would all seem much more relevant if the publisher had several journals, each with its own name, and so on. Similarly, we might ask what functions are associated with the journal as a whole: while verbs like "order" and "subscribe" come to mind immediately, these are associated with one or more issues, not with the journal as a whole. Thus, unless our user has some different insights into the problem, we might conclude that JOURNAL is *not* an appropriate class in our model.

The rest of the first sentence in Section 8.1 contains another important noun: *subscriptions*. Without bothering to identify all the details, it is immediately obvious that SUBSCRIPTION has a number of relevant attributes (when it was placed, to whom it should be sent, etc.) and a number of appropriate functions—one can imagine starting a subscription, canceling a subscription, paying for a subscription, and so on.

Reading on into the second paragraph, we see a reference to "articles" and "authors"; again, it should be relatively easy to convince ourselves that these are appropriate classes. The second paragraph also mentions a nuance that we will discuss in more detail in Chapter 10: some authors already have a subscription at the time they contribute an article to *Small Bytes*. Perhaps this is because they have already contributed an article to a previous issue of the magazine, or perhaps, as the user might point out to us, the author is a "paid" subscriber to the magazine. The noun "subscriber" appears later in the text as well, but our discussions with the user might lead us to include SUBSCRIBER in our model at this point; more importantly however, we need to remember that some people are authors, some are subscribers, and some are both authors *and* subscribers.

Whoops! *People* has just been introduced into the discussion. It seems appropriate to introduce a PERSON into our model. Although we haven't discussed it officially yet, it is obvious already that AUTHOR and SUBSCRIBER are subclasses of PERSON (or "roles" that a PERSON can play), but there may be more subclasses yet to come, as well as some strange combinations we're not yet ready to worry about, for example, What about the larger mass of humanity that consists of persons who are neither subscribers nor authors?

Reading on in the second paragraph, we see a number of other provocative words: "free," "payment," "expiration date," "history," and "year." Most of these seem to be attributes of something else: an expiration date, for example, is clearly an attribute of a subscription.

"Payment" could be a legitimate class within the model, except that the description very clearly states that the publisher does *not* make any payments to authors for their articles. If we anticipated that this policy might change in the future, we might include PAYMENT as an object; otherwise, we would leave it out.

The third paragraph tells us that there is a class called EDITORIAL ADVISOR and hints that we might include a class called TOPIC; it seems that each issue of the magazine contains articles that are all related to a specific topic (or possibly a small group of topics). The third paragraph also tells us that there is more than one kind of article (unsolicited articles) and more than one kind of author (would-be authors). Further discussion with the user might clarify these points: most of the articles are actively "solicited" or "invited" from authors whom the publisher contacts; however, various other authors (many of whom the publisher has never heard of before) may submit unsolicited articles for consideration. Since it is reasonable to assume that these various categories of authors and articles may require different attributes and/or different behavior, we should probably represent them as distinct classes. Similarly, the fourth paragraph tells us that we have different types of subscribers: corporate and individual.

Much of the information in the fourth paragraph is concerned with details of a subscription: price, number of copies, address to which the subscription should be sent, and so on. It also becomes evident that a subscriber may not always be identified by a person's name—but this is a detail that we can probably deal with later.

The fifth paragraph introduces another important noun: *organization*. Apparently, an organization can be a corporation or a government agency, and so on; an organization has an address; and an organization has one or more people associated with it. However, the fifth paragraph also tells us that there are *sites*, which are not the same as organizations: an organization like IBM, for example, has multiple sites, each of which presumably has multiple people.

The next two paragraphs introduce the classes known as *agency* and *distributor*. It's not clear at this point whether the agents and distributors should be considered as subclasses or superclasses or subscriber; however, they are obviously sufficiently different from a "normal" subscriber that they need to be identified explicitly in the model, regardless of the hierarchical class structure we eventually create.

On the other hand, it's not as obvious whether the concept of a "complimentary subscriber" needs to be identified as a distinct class—or whether it can be represented as an ordinary subscriber whose subscription price happens to be zero. Our user might tell us, though, that there are various types of complimentary subscribers: friends, enemies, relatives, gurus, other publishers with whom *Small Bytes* "swaps" subscriptions, and so on. Again, this might be represented with a single attribute—perhaps the same attribute used to distinguish between other categories of paid subscribers. But this is dangerous thinking: the phrase "distinguish between other categories" should be a clue of old-style thinking that depends upon some procedural logic (IF-THEN-ELSE or CASE constructs in a typical third-generation programming language) to carry out the appropriate processing for the different categories. If the categories *are* different—if they exhibit different behavior and have different attributes—then they should be represented by different classes in the OOA model. So we would probably conclude the COMPLIMENTARY SUBSCRIBER is a class in its own right.[24]

Reading on through the description, we see the nouns *renewal* and *payment* and *invoice*. After talking with the user, we might conclude that a RENEWAL is the same as a SUBSCRIPTION; this would be especially tempting to a systems analyst who wants to simplify things. However, the fact that the user does have two different terms suggests that this is a dangerous decision; it is better, at this point, to distinguish between new subscriptions and renewals of subscriptions. If we decide later on that there really is no essential distinction between the two, we can modify the class hierarchy.

Similarly, a *payment* might be considered, at first, as a simple attribute of a subscription. But we are likely to discover, as we get into the details of the analysis, that a payment represents an interaction between a SUBSCRIBER and a SUBSCRIPTION and an INVOICE: among other things, we want to know the date of the payment, which is not an appropriate attribute of SUBSCRIBER *or* SUBSCRIPTION *or* INVOICE; we also note, from the textual description,

---

[24]Some readers will be jumping ahead at this point, and will argue that COMPLIMENTARY SUBSCRIBERS are merely a subset (and thus a sub-class, in OO terms) of SUBSCRIBER. Indeed, this will be the conclusion we reach in Chapter 10, but at this point, we're not trying to build class hierarchies, we're simply trying to identify discrete classes.

that some subscriptions are paid without any invoice ever being sent to the subscriber. Similarly, we will need to record the amount of the payment, but this might not be the same as the subscription amount or the invoice. Finally, we note that a distinction is made between credit card payments and payments by check; for the moment, we will introduce separate classes for each of these.

The user has also told us about single-copy purchases of *Small Bytes*, typically for individual back issues of the magazine. Our instinct, as systems analysts, is probably to treat these as if they were "normal" subscriptions: the subscription period is simply for 1 month, rather than for the normal 12-month period. Still, the fact that the user distinguishes between these single-copy sales and normal subscriptions should leave us feeling a bit nervous; we might be persuaded to include PURCHASE in the OOA model just to keep the user happy. However, we would be even more inclined to do so if the user went on to tell us that some of these purchases involve several *different* back issues of the magazine—for example, the customer orders the January 1989 issue, the March 1990 issue, and the April 1991 issue to fill some gaps in his library collection.

A minor point almost escapes our attention: if the purchase involves multiple copies, a discount is offered. The same is true for normal subscriptions, too, but we glossed over it. Is "discount" an attribute of the SUBSCRIPTION and PURCHASE classes, or is it a class in its own right? The answer would depend on the user: if the user's policy is to determine a discount percentage on an ad hoc basis for each transaction, then we would probably include it as an attribute. If, in responding to this question, our user began describing a "discount schedule" or a "discount table," we would be more inclined to consider it a distinct class. Our user might tell us, further, that the extent of the discount also depends on *which* issue of the magazine is being ordered; some of the older, more precious, issues have a smaller discount.

Finally, we note that some customers place "special orders" for "mini-issues" of *Small Bytes*. This is apparently sufficiently different from a purchase of one or more "off-the-shelf" copies of a standard issue of *Small Bytes* that we should distinguish it as a class of its own.

The final paragraph of the textual description tells us that there are "prospects," which should be identified as a separate class; we will probably identify this later as a subclass of subscriber, though it may eventually stand entirely on its own. Also, the final paragraph refers to a "trial subscription," which is evidently different from a "normal" subscription. This has also been included in the model as a distinct class.

This gives us a total of 25 distinct classes for the *Small Bytes* system, as shown in Table 9.1. It should be emphasized that more classes and objects may be discovered later, and some may disappear.

Table 9.1: Initial classes for the *Small Bytes* system

issue
subscription: new subscription, renewal, trial subscription
article: solicited article versus unsolicited article
author: invited author versus uninvited author
subscriber: corporate, individual, complimentary, and "prospect"
person
editorial advisor
topic
site
organization
agency
distributor
payment: credit card payment versus check payment
invoice
purchase: single copy versus "mini-issue"
discount

9.8 CASE STUDY: THE ELEVATOR SYSTEM

Discovery of objects for the elevator system would proceed in much the same fashion as for the *Small Bytes* system, except that the focus would probably be on the *behavior* of the proposed objects rather than on their data content.

Our initial list of classes and objects, from the textual description in Section 8.2, might look like that in Table 9.2:

Table 9.2: Initial classes for the elevator problem

elevator
elevator-motor
elevator-door
building
floor
summons (or "request")

destination-button (in the elevator)
destination-button-light
arrival-light
summons-button: up versus down
summons-button-light: up versus down
overweight-sensor
floor-sensor
controller(?)

Note that a lengthy parenthetical discussion in the second paragraph of the description tells us that the elevator cannot actually distinguish the presence or absence of individual passengers. For most systems analysts, there is an enormous temptation to include "person" or "passenger" as a class: after all, the whole point of the elevator is to transport people. It is people who push the buttons and cause the elevator to go up or down. But our system is entirely incapable of distinguishing between instances of people; all it cares about is whether an aggregate mass of people (or cats and dogs, for that matter) has caused the elevator to be overloaded, as determined by an "overweight" sensor. So, with reluctance, we have omitted passenger from the model.[25]

Several other nouns are immediately apparent when reading the textual description of the elevator system: "computer," "program," "panel," "circuitry," "interrupt," "input register," and so on. Most of these can be eliminated from the OOA model immediately, for they are obviously concerned with the implementation of the system; if the hardware/software architecture is constrained to behave in the fashion indicated by Section 8.2, then we may need to include appropriate objects in our OOD model, but we prefer to leave them out for now.

---

[25]Some readers will strenuously object to this conclusion. It could be argued that the system can differentiate between instances of the PASSENGER class (e.g., by determining precisely when they get on or off the elevator). It could also be argued that PASSENGERs do have at least one interesting attribute: their weight. And clearly PASSENGERs do have interesting behavior: it is they who push the buttons that cause the elevator to operate. In a "real-world" project, most of us probably would include a PASSENGER object until or unless our users told us that they don't care about passengers. For the purposes of this book, based on the problem description provided in Chapter 8, we have made precisely that interpretation: passengers don't matter.

On the other hand, the noun "controller" is more difficult. While we obviously wish to avoid a specific physical implementation of a controller in our model, it is apparent from the problem that the users are assuming some kind of "intelligence" *separate and distinct from the individual elevators themselves* that determines whether each of the individual elevators should be directed to travel up or down in the building to fulfill a request. However, other implementations of an elevator system could allow each elevator to operate completely independently, for example, when each elevator reaches a floor, it could send a message to the other elevators to determine their direction and position, and decide what to do based on this information. The fact that the user has "specified" the existence of a "controller" to coordinate and synchronize the behavior of the elevators could be interpreted as a requirement, but for the purposes of this book, we will interpret it as a premature commitment to an implementation approach. Thus, while it may reappear in the OOD model, we have decided not to include a CONTROLLER class in the OOA model.

Even more difficult is the discussion of the stop button, red emergency stop switch, and the audible alarm optionally attached to the emergency stop switch. All of us are familiar with such devices, and they clearly have a major impact on the behavior of the elevator. However, the problem description very clearly indicates that these devices are not going to be attached to the computer system we are designing. According to the user's description, the elevator control system does not need to be aware of whether a passenger has pushed the stop button or the emergency stop switch; the system simply uses its door sensors to determine whether the elevator door is open or closed and its floor sensors to determine the elevator's location and direction of travel. The effect of the stop button upon the movement of the elevator door, and the effect of the emergency stop switch on the movement of the elevator between floors, could be seen as an "act of God"; we will not include it in our OOA model.

10

Object Structures and Class Hierarchies

Having identified the basic classes and objects in an OOA model, our next activity is to begin organizing them into hierarchies that will take advantage of the inheritance paradigm of all OO methodologies. In addition, we will look for opportunities to model "whole-part" structures—for example, the phenomenon of a PERSON class composed of ARMs and LEGs, a BODY, and a HEAD.

As we have seen in the case study discussions in Chapter 9, it is impossible to *avoid* thinking about hierarchies during the initial discovery of objects. This point needs to be emphasized: the various activities described in Chapters 9–14 are not intended to be carried out in a sequential, waterfall fashion; inevitably, some of the activities will take place in parallel. However, it is usually easier to begin organizing hierarchies of classes once we have a reasonable (though not necessarily final) idea of what the basic classes are.

After discussing the two common forms of class hierarchy, we will show how they are used on the *Small Bytes* and elevator case study.

10.1 GENERALIZATION-SPECIALIZATION HIERARCHIES

The concept of a superclass and subclass is familiar to almost everyone and has a widespread use far beyond the field of software engineering; indeed, it is precisely *because* of its widespread recognition that it is such a powerful analysis concept, as well as a design and implementation concept in later stages of OO systems development.

Many OOA methodologies use the "superclass-subclass" terminology; others describe the same concept somewhat more obliquely by referring to "the inheritance mechanism." In an earlier book,[1] Pete Coad and I used the terminology of "generalization" and "specialization"; while it may be somewhat less commonly used, it does have the admirable advantage that it can be abbreviated as gen-spec; hence we will continue to use it in this book.

The graphical notation for gen-spec structures varies considerably from one OOA methodology to another. In the Coad-Yourdon version of OOA, for example, the following notation would be used to describe a generalization (superclass) of SUBSCRIBER, and two specializations (subclasses) of PAYING-SUBSCRIBER and COMPLI-MENTARY-SUBSCRIBER (figure 10.1):[2]

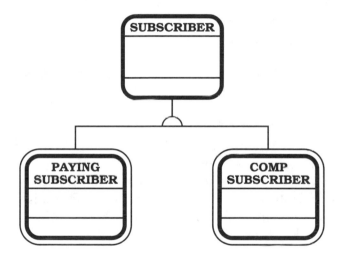

Figure 10.1: A gen-spec hierarchy for subscribers

There is a small subtlety in this example that needs to be pointed out: Figure 10.1 explicitly indicates that there are no instances of SUBSCRIBER per se; the only instances (or objects) occur at the specialization level of paying or complimentary subscribers. This is indicated by the absence of a thin object line on the upper SUB-

[1]Peter Coad and Edward Yourdon, *Object-Oriented Analysis*, 2nd ed. (Englewood Cliffs, NJ: Yourdon Press/Prentice Hall, 1990).

[2]Note that the classes and objects shown in Figures 10.1 through 10.7 do not correspond exactly to the classes and objects for the *Small Bytes* problem in Chapter 9.

SCRIBER icon, and the presence of such thin lines for both of the specializations.

By contrast, the Rumbaugh notation for a gen-spec structure uses a triangular "hat" rather than a semicircle to separate the superclass from the subclass (Figure 10.2):[3]

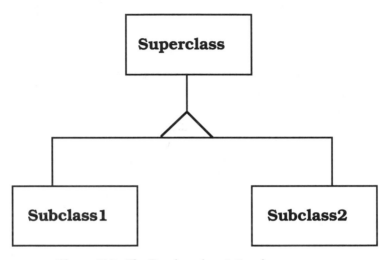

Figure 10.2: The Rumbaugh notation for gen-spec

Booch4 and Firesmith,[5] on the other hand, use a notation in which the superclass is shown topologically at the bottom of the diagram, with directed arrows showing the relationship from generalization to the specialization. A Booch diagram and Firesmith diagram of the subscriber situation shown in Figure 10.1 are presented next, as Figure 10.3 and 10.4, respectively.

[3]James Rumbaugh, Michael Blaha, William Premerlani, Frederick Eddy, and William Lorensen, *Object-Oriented Modeling and Design* (Englewood Cliffs, NJ: Prentice Hall, 1991).

[4]Grady Booch, *Object-Oriented Design with Applications.* (Redwood City, CA: Benjamin/Cummings, 1991).

[5]Donald G. Firesmith, *Object-Oriented Requirements Analysis and Logical Design.* (New York: John Wiley and Sons, 1993), p. 108.

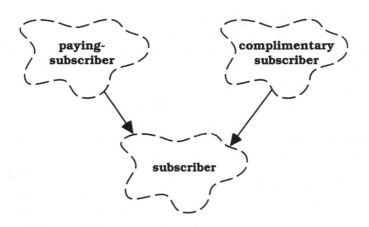

Figure 10.3: Booch notation for subscriber gen-spec hierarchy

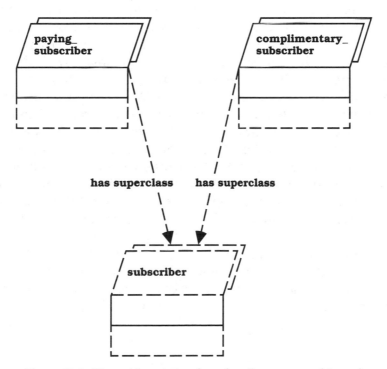

Figure 10.4: Firesmith notation for subscriber gen-spec hierarchy

When viewing the gen-spec structures shown, two questions arise: First, are the specializations mutually exclusive? And, second, does the union of all specializations cover the set described by the generalization? With our subscriber example, the questions are: Can someone be a paying subscriber and a complimentary subscriber at the same time? Are there any subscribers who are neither paying subscribers nor complimentary subscribers?

Some analysts will argue that the answer to these questions should be intuitively obvious for a specific application; others will argue that a typical user is unlikely to care about this level of detail. But it would be convenient to have a graphical notation to answer these questions; sadly, many OOA methodologies—including the Coad-Yourdon methodology whose notation dominates this book!—do not provide it.

The Martin-Odell[6] methodology, on the other hand, provides two different mechanisms for showing gen-spec structures: nested boxes within boxes, and a "triangle arrow" pointing from subclass to superclass. The presence or absence of a bar drawn across the bottom of a box indicates whether or not its enclosed specializations "fully enumerate" all the members of the generalization. With such an approach, we might draw the Martin-Odell diagram for our subscriber situation as shown in Figure 10.5. The diagram indicates that the subclasses of complimentary and paying subscribers are "disjoint"—that is, one can be either a complimentary subscriber or a paying subscriber, but not both. The presence of the horizontal "bar" across the box surrounding individual subscribers indicates that the subclasses contained within the box do *not* "cover" all the instances of the superclass; in other words, *some* of the paying subscribers are individuals, but not all. By contrast, the lack of a horizontal bar across the box surrounding complimentary and paying subscribers indicates that those two subclasses do *cover* all the instances of the superclass above them—*all* instances of a subscriber are described as *either* a complimentary subscriber or a paying subscriber.

[6] James Martin and James J. Odell, *Principles of Object-Oriented Analysis and Design* (Englewood Cliffs, NJ: Prentice Hall, 1992).

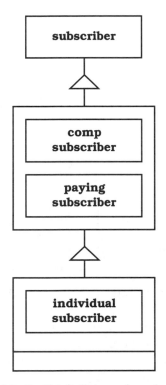

Figure 10.5: A Martin-Odell diagram for subscriber gen-spec

Aside from the overall clumsiness of this notation and the fact that subtyping is being represented in two different graphical forms, the diagram does not provide any obvious visual clues to help answer one of the questions just posed: Are the specializations within a specialization mutually exclusive?[7] Embley, Kurtz, and Woodfield address this with a notation that is reminiscent of Rumbaugh's, but more detailed in its description of the "coverage" of the specializations (see Figure 10.6):

---

[7]In fact, the Martin-Odell methodology explicitly defines the kind of partition illustrated in Figure 10.5 as "a division (or partitioning) of an object type into disjoint subtypes"; in this respect, it is similar to the Coad-Yourdon methodology, which also partitions a class into disjoint subclasses without emphasizing that fact in the graphical notation.

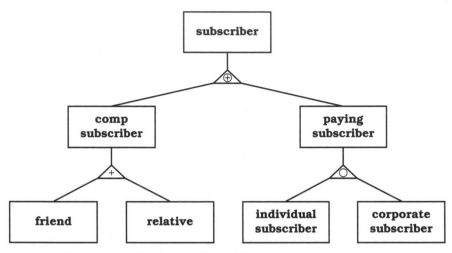

Figure 10.6: The Embley-Kurtz-Woodfield gen-spec notation

This model indicates that paying subscribers and complimentary subscribers are not only mutually exclusive (as indicated by the "+" sign in the triangular "connector" joining subscriber, comp. subscriber, and paying subscriber), but that *all* subscribers are covered by one of these two subclasses (as indicated by the "o" that encloses the "+" sign); more formally, the class of subscribers is *partitioned* into complimentary and paying subscribers. Complimentary subscribers are further specialized, but Figure 10.6 says only that friends and relatives are mutually exclusive; it explicitly indicates that some complimentary subscribers are neither friends nor relatives. Furthermore, Figure 10.6 indicates (by means of the "U" sign in the triangular connector joining paying subscriber, individual and company) that all paying subscribers are either individuals or companies—or *both*.

Whether such an elaborate notation, and such a sophisticated form of generalization-specialization, is needed is something the systems analyst must determine, based on the complexity of the problem he is analyzing, as well as the tolerance of the user for interpreting myriad notational symbols. One problem in this area is that an organization may decide to adopt an OO CASE tool that supports a rich notational scheme, with literally dozens of different boxes, arrows, triangles, bubbles, and so on. While these may be unnecessary for simple applications, it will be difficult for many systems analysts to avoid the temptation of overwhelming the user with excessively detailed diagrams.

Even with the all the details, though, the *concept* of a generalization-specialization hierarchy is quite understandable to the systems analyst, and it is likely to be quite familiar to any software engineer who has used a data modeling methodology in the past. However, the OO perspective on gen-spec hierarchies is quite different from a typical data modeling "subtype-supertype" approach, and it must be emphasized at this point: it is known as *inheritance*. When we show PAYING SUBSCRIBER and COMPLIMENTARY SUBSCRIBER as specializations of SUBSCRIBER, we are explicitly indicating that the two specializations *inherit* all the attributes and methods (or functions) defined for the generalization. While this may have been intended as a programming trick within the early object-oriented programming languages, OOA methodologies explicitly use the inheritance concept as an important modeling tool in user-analyst discussions of the system requirements.

Most of the diagrams don't identify *which* attributes and services are defined for a SUBSCRIBER; all we know is that anything defined for SUBSCRIBER automatically becomes part of the definition of the specializations.[8] But the whole reason for identifying different specializations, obviously, is that they are different! This means that (1) some of the attributes and/or services in the specialization may have a *different* definition from that of the parent from whom they inherit and/or (2) they may contain *additional* attributes and/or services.

This concept of overriding and extending inherited definitions will be discussed in more detail in Chapters 12 and 14. But to illustrate the point, consider the subscription example: one could argue that an obvious attribute of SUBSCRIBER is "address"; we would expect this to be inherited by both complimentary and paying subscribers alike. But we might decide that paying subscribers need to have a "fax-number" attribute, so that the magazine can send information about late-breaking news in the software engineering field, while "fax-number" is judged to be completely inappropriate or irrelevant for complimentary subscribers. In this case, "fax-number" would not exist as part of the definition of the SUBSCRIBER class,

---

[8]Firesmith's detailed classification diagrams *do* provide this level of detail.

but would be included as a distinct, separately defined, attribute for paying subscribers (and all its specializations).

Although the concept of inheritance is common to virtually all OO methodologies, there is one aspect that causes great debate: *multiple inheritance*. All the examples thus far in this chapter involve single inheritance; that is, a specialization inherits its attributes and behavior from a single generalization class. In a large majority of analysis situations, single inheritance is perfectly adequate—and besides, it never occurs to many analysts or users to consider anything else!

However, a simple example of multiple inheritance can easily be illustrated for the *Small Bytes* system; in several of the diagrams shown, we have identified a class known as "individual subscriber." But we also know that the system maintains information about individuals who are *not* subscribers; these were identified as members of the PERSON class in Chapter 9. This could lead us to a multiple inheritance structure such as the one shown in Figure 10.7:

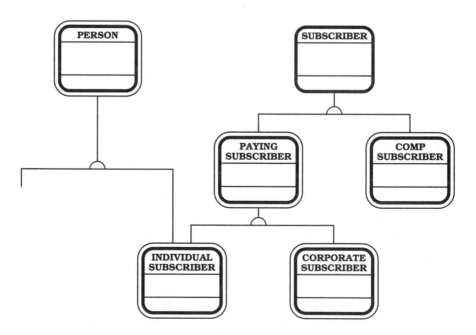

Figure 10.7: Multiple inheritance for the *Small Bytes* system

Thus, the INDIVIDUAL SUBSCRIBER class inherits its attributes and behavior from *both* the PAYING SUBSCRIBER class and the PERSON class. Whether this is the best or most appropriate class hierarchy will be discussed further in Section 10.3; for now, it is sufficient to note simply that it *is* a plausible hierarchy, and that it could be easily explained to a typical user.

On the other hand, multiple inheritance hierarchies can become extremely complicated, though some authors, including Embley and coworkers[9], and Martin and Odell,[10] make no distinction (in terms of complexity or desirability) between single and multiple inheritance; indeed, Shlaer and Mellor don't even mention multiple inheritance in either of their OOA books![11] Don Firesmith, on the other hand, notes the potential danger of *all* forms of inheritance and suggests that it can be even greater for multiple inheritance:

> Understandability can be greatly diminished because all parts of a class are not collected in a single location. If inheritance hierarchies are large, it is often difficult for a software engineer to determine which resources the subclasses are inheriting and from which superclasses they are inheriting those resources. This is especially true of multiple inheritance, in which either the same resource may be inherited through multiple superclasses or incompatible resources may be inherited from different superclasses.[12]

Similarly, Rumbaugh and coworkers make the following observation:

> Multiple inheritance . . . is a more complicated form of generalization than single inheritance, which restricts the class hierarchy to a tree. The advantage of multiple inheritance is greater power in specifying classes and an increased opportunity for reuse. It brings object modeling closer to the way people think. The disadvantage is a loss of conceptual and implementation simplicity. In principle, all kinds of different mixing rules can be defined to resolve conflicts among features defined on different paths.[13]

The issue of "conflicts" is typically the biggest problem with multiple inheritance. To understand the nature of the problem con-

[9]David W. Embley, Barry D. Kurtz, and Scott N. Woodfield, *Object-Oriented Systems Analysis: A Model-Driven Approach* (Englewood Cliffs, NJ: Prentice Hall, 1992).

[10]Martin and Odell, *Principles of Object-Oriented Analysis and Design*.

[11]Sally Shlaer and Stephen J. Mellor, *Object-Oriented Systems Analysis: Modeling the World in Data* (Englewood Cliffs, NJ: Yourdon Press/Prentice Hall, 1988), and Sally Shlaer and Stephen J. Mellor, *Object Lifecycles: Modeling the World in States* (Englewood Cliffs, NJ: Yourdon Press/Prentice Hall, 1992).

[12]Firesmith, *Object-Oriented Requirements Analysis and Logical Design*, p. 88.

[13]Rumbaugh et al., *Object-Oriented Modeling and Design*, p. 65.

sider our subscriber example in Figure 10.7, and assume that both PERSON and PAYING SUBSCRIBER have a separately defined attribute known as *phone-number;* perhaps in the case of a PERSON, the phone number is presumed to be a home, or residential number; for the PAYING SUBSCRIBER, the phone number is presumed to be an office phone number, including a telephone extension. Since INDIVIDUAL SUBSCRIBER inherits all the attributes from both parents, which phone number does it receive?

Of course, if all the classes in Figure 10.7 were being defined at the same time, we could easily eliminate the problem: PERSON should have an attribute called *home-phone-number*, and PAYING SUBSCRIBER should have an attribute called *work-phone-number*. The problem comes from situations where some of the classes were created by different software engineers, perhaps for different projects. As Rumbaugh and coworkers remind us in their comment, OO projects strive for high degrees of reusability, and multiple inheritance amplifies that activity. Thus the project team on the *Small Bytes* system may wish to take advantage of a PERSON class that has already been defined and implemented; there may be dozens of other systems already using it. If it has a *phone-number* attribute, we're stuck with it.

So we may not be able to eliminate the "name conflict" problem in a trivial way. But as Rumbaugh and coworkers note, there are "all kinds of different mixing rules" to resolve the conflicts that would otherwise exist. Meanwhile, although this discussion involves multiple inheritance in the analysis phase of the project, much of the debate occurs during the later stages of design and programming. For example, Jacobson and coworkers note that:

> The main disadvantage with multiple inheritance is that it often reduces understanding of a class hierarchy. The problem arises especially if both ancestors have an operation with the same name, but with different definitions . . . In the majority of programming languages, that support multiple inheritance, the user is forced to redefine the name so that it become unique.[14]

But as Grady Booch observes,

> The need for multiple inheritance in object-oriented programming languages is still a topic of great debate. In our experience, we find

---

[14]Ivar Jacobson, Magnus Christerson, Patrik Jonsson, and Gunnar Övergaard, *Object-Oriented Software Engineering: A Use Case Driven Approach* (Reading, MA: Addison-Wesley, 1992), p. 68.

multiple inheritance to be like a parachute: you don't always need it, but when you do, you're really happy to have it at hand.[15]

We will discuss these, as well implementation problems concerning multiple inheritance, in Chapter 20.

10.2 WHOLE-PART HIERARCHIES

Gen-spec hierarchies are often referred to as *is-a* hierarchies; the hierarchical structure, for example, allows us to say that an INDIVIDUAL SUBSCRIBER *is a* PERSON, and that a CORPORATE SUBSCRIBER *is a* PAYING SUBSCRIBER.

The second major form of OO class "architecture," known as a *whole-part* structure, is often described by the phrase "has-a." It allows us to describe a class in terms of its component parts, or subobjects. Thus a PERSON *has a* BODY, two ARMS, and so on.

The Coad-Yourdon graphical notation for whole-part structures is shown in Figure 10.8:

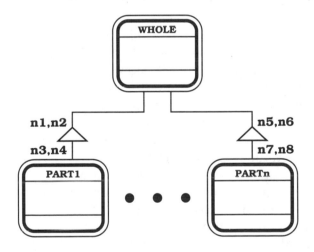

Figure 10.8: Coad-Yourdon whole-part class hierarchy

Thus a "whole" may be composed of many parts, and the analyst can express the cardinality of the relationship between each of the parts and the whole. Note also that the cardinality may be different depending on whether it is being viewed from the perspective of the whole or the part. Thus Figure 10.8 tells us that each instance of the WHOLE class must consist of no fewer than n1 and no more than n2 instances of PART1; conversely, each instance of PART1 may be a part of no fewer than n3 and no more than n4 instances of the WHOLE class. An optional relationship between a whole and a part may be expressed by using a value of zero for one of the lower limits (i.e., n1 and/or n3 in the example). Naturally, Figure 10.8 tells us that the whole-part relationship between WHOLE and PARTn has its own cardinality, which may or may not be the same as the cardinality of the WHOLE-PART1 relationship.

Note that the whole-part structure shown in Figure 10.8 is different from the gen-spec structures of Section 10.1 in one fundamental way: *the parts do* NOT *inherit attributes or behavior from the whole.* Inheritance applies to gen-spec structures, but does not apply to whole-part structures.

When software engineers hear this, their first question is often: "Then what's the use of a whole-part structure? What good is it?" The answer, quite simply, is that it allows the analyst to model (and document) important user policy that cannot be captured with a gen-spec structure. Thus if the user wants to express the policy that a PERSON is a "whole" consisting of exactly *one* head, one torso, zero to two arms, and zero to two legs, a whole-part structure is a convenient mechanism for documenting the policy; it allows us to specify that a headless, four-armed, nine-legged creature is *not* a PERSON.

Software engineers also tend to be curious about the eventual implementation of these structures, even though they are analysis models. Those familiar with object-oriented programming languages like C++ typically have an idea of how the inheritance hierarchies of a gen-spec structure will eventually be implemented; but they are curious about the implementation of whole-part structures. The answer, in most cases, is *pointers*: the "whole" object will have a pointer (or a collection of pointers) to its constituent parts, and the parts will typically have a pointer to the whole to which it belongs.[16]

---

[16]You will soon see that the object relationships discussed in Chapter 11 are also typically implemented with pointers. Indeed, whole-part structures can sometimes be implemented with the mechanisms discussed in Chapter 11; however, since most OOA/OOD methodologies support only *binary object* relationships, it is necessary to have the whole-part structure to support a model that consists of a whole and *many* (i.e., more than one) different parts.

As with the gen-spec structure, each variant of OOA methodology has its own graphical notation for whole-part hierarchies. Rumbaugh and coworkers, for example, use the notation shown in Figure 10.9:

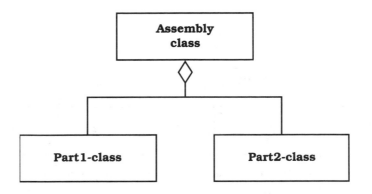

Figure 10.9: The Rumbaugh notation for whole-part hierarchies

Booch's notation, on the other hand, looks like that shown in Figure 10.10:

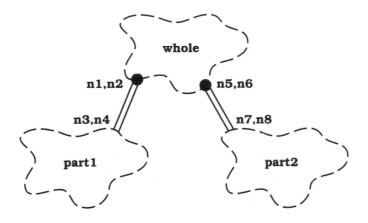

Figure 10.10: The Booch notation for whole-part hierarchies

Firesmith's ADM_3 method provides the following graphical notation for whole-part structures shown in figure 10.11:

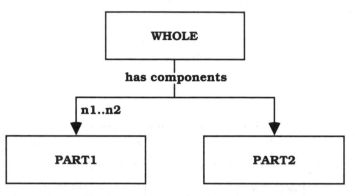

Figure 10.11: The Firesmith notation for whole-part structures

The Martin-Odell notation is exactly the opposite of the Coad-Yourdon notation for gen-spec and whole-part structures: Martin and Odell use triangles to represent gen-spec and semi-circles to represent whole-part hierarchies; the Martin-Odell whole-part notation looks like that in Figure 10.12:

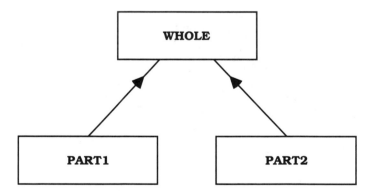

Figure 10.12: The Martin-Odell notation for whole-part structures

Finally, the Embley-Kurtz-Woodfield OOA methodology uses the notation in Figure 10.13 for whole-part hierarchies:

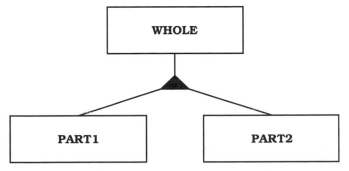

Figure 10.13: The Embley-Kurtz-Woodfield whole-part hierarchy

How do we discover whole-part hierarchies in a systems analysis situation? It usually occurs *after* the discovery of the fundamental classes and objects in the system; our concern is how to connect the classes together into meaningful hierarchies. Most of the time, the whole-part hierarchies will be "intuitively obvious" to the user and/or the systems analyst, but if necessary, each class among the list of fundamental classes can be examined to see if could be regarded as a potential whole—and if so, what parts would it be connected to?

We would expect the parts to have been identified already, as part of the discovery of fundamental classes and objects in the model; however, the search for whole-part hierarchies might help us discover new classes that would otherwise have gone undiscovered. But the systems analyst must beware of going overboard: one can easily invent new classes that have no justification for being in the OOA model.

For example, consider the class PERSON in our *Small Bytes* system. Our fundamental whole-part questions are: "Can we identify parts of a PERSON?" "Can each occurrence of such a part be identified with attributes?" "Do the parts that we propose to add to the model reflect 'real-world' parts?" Naturally, the parts that would come to mind immediately are arms, legs, and so on.—and these parts do satisfy the initial criteria that we have posed. But there are more questions: "Does the system need to keep track of the occurrence of the parts?" "Are the parts within the scope of the system we are modeling?" It's hard to imagine why a magazine subscription system would need to keep track of the arms and legs and bodies of its subscribers. . . .

For completeness, we should consider each class in the model from the opposite perspective—that is, as a potential part. Our basic question is: "What other classes combine with *this* class to form a meaningful whole?" It might occur to us, for example, that a PERSON is part of a SITE and a SITE is part of an ORGANIZATION; these classes already exist in our *Small Bytes* example, but in general, this investigative process might also help us identify hitherto undiscovered classes. Once again, the question of relevancy is crucial: we must ask whether the system we are modeling needs to keep track of the occurrence of the "wholes" that we have proposed.

10.3 CLASS HIERARCHIES FOR THE *SMALL BYTES* CASE STUDY

An important consequence of the creation of class hierarchies in an OOA model is that it forces the analyst (and, by extension, the user) to rethink the work that he has already done. The initial discovery of objects in the *Small Bytes* system, for example, helped reduce an informal rambling of text into an ordered list of objects; but the resulting list was a very high-level abstraction, and as an act of analysis, it was obviously incomplete. More important, it may have been wrong. When we begin focusing on how the various objects may be combined into class hierarchies, we may discover that some objects were poorly named, others did not deserve to exist, and still others had not even been discovered. Even more important, we should realize that our model is still not finished at the end of this stage: the subsequent activities of discovering attributes, relationships, state behavior, and methods (discussed in Chapters 11–14) may require even more changes.

As we noted in Chapter 9, the first step in the OOA process identified some 25 classes. This is certainly not a large number, and we could continue working with the classes in toto as we create genspec and whole-part structures. Most analysts would conduct this next stage of OOA work in a brainstorming fashion, using large sheets of paper, or a blackboard, or Post-it™ notes on a whiteboard, or a CASE tool. In preparing this book, I sketched out the class hierarchies for the *Small Bytes* system on several sheets of normal sized notepaper; the results were then organized into separate *subjects* for presentation within the limited topological space constraints of a textbook.

Thus it was only after finishing the process of creating class hierarchies that the decision was made to group things into four subjects; at this high level of abstraction, we could diagram it as shown in Figure 10.14 below:

Figure 10.14: Subjects for the *Small Bytes* case study

The PUBLICATION subject is relatively simple: we saw, for example, that an ARTICLE published in the magazine is either SOLICITED ARTICLE or an UNSOLICITED ARTICLE; and we saw that one or more ARTICLEs make up an ISSUE of the magazine. This will lead to a relatively simple combination of gen-spec and whole-part hierarchies.

However, there is one nuance that is more difficult to model: our user has told us that each issue of the magazine typically deals with a single TOPIC—for example, the topic of object-oriented methodologies or the topic of GUI CASE tools. Our user also tells us, rather casually, that some topics are perennial favorites—so the topic of OO, for example, might be covered on an annual basis. Thus it might be tempting to model TOPIC and ISSUE as a whole-part relationship: a TOPIC has zero or more component ISSUEs devoted to it.

On the other hand, if pressed, our user might grudgingly admit that sometimes a single issue of the magazine will contain articles on more than one topic. Aha! This means that ISSUE is the whole and TOPIC is the part! What arrangement best represents the world as the user sees it?

After some reflection, we might well decide that a whole-part structure is simply not the appropriate way to model the information we have received from the user: it's hard to make a compelling case for either of the whole-part scenarios proposed here. And this is often the case, when the proposed whole-part structured has only *one* kind of part; there is far less confusion, for example, when we talk about a PERSON whole and its component ARM, LEG, and BODY parts.

Indeed, there *is* a relationship between ISSUE and TOPIC that we want to model; our user tells us, for example, that customers often call to get a list of all the issues of *Small Bytes* that have covered a particular topic. But TOPIC and ISSUE are, in a sense, co-equals; forcing them into an artificial whole-part relationship simply confuses the matter. The important information that we want to represent will come later, in Chapter 11, when we add *relationships* to our OOA model. For now, we model ISSUE as one class hierarchy and TOPIC as a "stand-alone" class, both contained within the PUBLICATION subject; this is illustrated in Figure 10.15:

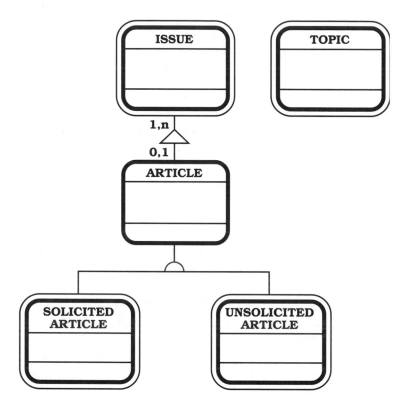

Figure 10.15: The class hierarchy of the PUBLICATION subject

Note the implications of the cardinality of the ISSUE-ARTICLE whole-part relationship. According to our user, an ISSUE consists of between 1 and n ARTICLEs (though this may seem unrealistic, there actually have been issues of *Small Bytes* that consisted of a single, very long article). On the other hand, an ARTICLE is part of 0 or 1 ISSUE. An UNSOLICITED ARTICLE, in particular, is typically *not* associated with any ISSUE when it is first received—and it may never be! On the other hand, the user is adamant that an ARTICLE will never be republished in the magazine, so it can only be part of a single ISSUE.

The FINANCES subject is also quite simple; it contains classes for invoices, payments, discounts, and purchases. The PAYMENT class has a gen-spec structure for credit card payments and payments by check, but in reviewing this, our user suddenly realizes that he forgot to tell us about payments by direct bank deposit; this rarely happens with domestic subscriptions that form the bulk of the magazine's business, but it's quite common for international subscribers to instruct their bank to make their subscription payment directly to *Small Byte's* bank account. Thus our FINANCES subject has the structure shown in Figure 10.16:

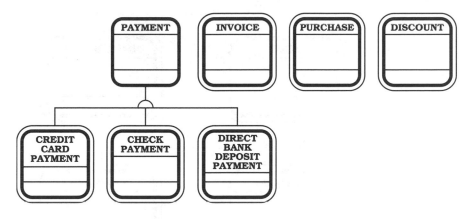

Figure 10.16: The class hierarchy of the FINANCES subject

As might be expected, the most complex parts of the *Small Bytes* OOA model involve subscribers and subscriptions. In our original discovery of classes and objects, we identified various categories of subscribers: corporate subscribers, individual subscribers, complimentary subscribers, and so on. We also distinguished among new subscriptions, trial subscriptions, and renewal subscriptions.

Attempting to put all this into a meaningful hierarchy, it becomes more and more evident that the phrase "corporate subscriber" is describing a relationship between a SUBSCRIPTION and an organization (or possibly a site within an organization); the phrase "individual subscriber" describes a different kind of relationship. Thus it seems appropriate to build one class hierarchy to describe the various creatures that are capable of entering into a subscription and a different hierarchy to describe the various flavors of subscriptions. While doing this, it also becomes evident where to put AUTHOR, EDITORIAL ADVISOR, AGENCY, and DISTRIBUTOR.

Figure 10.17 shows the class hierarchy within the PEOPLE subject.

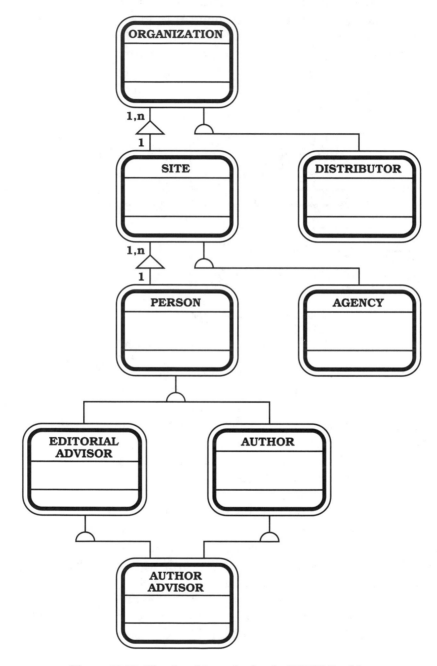

Figure 10.17: The class hierarchy for the PEOPLE subject

Note the various implications of this class hierarchy: a DIS-TRIBUTOR is a specialization, or subclass, of ORGANIZATION; however, an AGENCY is shown as a specialization of SITE, because *Small Bytes* has separate interactions with different branch offices of the same agency organization. Note also that PERSON is shown as a generalization *with instances of its own*; thus our model recognizes the existence of ordinary people, as well as the special subclasses of editorial advisors and authors. Since some editorial advisors are also authors, we have shown a subclass of AUTHOR ADVISOR with multiple inheritance.

Finally, the SUBSCRIPTIONS subject has a class hierarchy of its own. For the time being, we have distinguished between new (first-time) subscriptions and renewals, simply because the user emphasizes the distinction. Later on, when we have a better understanding of the details attributes and behavior of the various classes, it's possible that we could represent the renewal status of a subscription as part of its *state*. But for now, our SUBSCRIPTIONS subject has the structure shown in Figure 10.18:

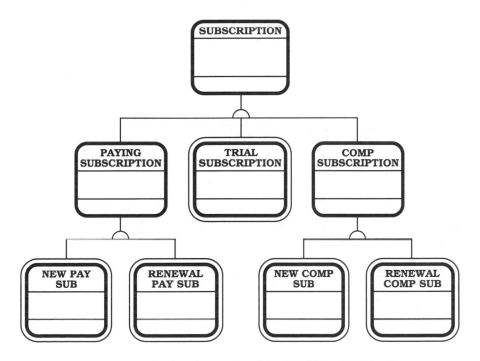

Figure 10.18: The class hierarchy of the SUBSCRIPTIONS subject

10.4 CLASS HIERARCHIES FOR THE ELEVATOR CASE STUDY

From the discussion so far, we should be in a position to quickly and easily identify the class hierarchies for the elevator system. The SUMMONS class, which we identified in Chapter 9, has no specializations or whole-part structures; however, in subsequent chapters, we will document a number of interactions and relationships between the SUMMONS class and the other classes in the model.

The two major class hierarchies involve a FLOOR (which is a part of a BUILDING) and the ELEVATOR (which has a number of component parts). The BUILDING FLOOR whole-part structure is shown in Figure 10.19. Similarly, the whole-part structure for ELEVATOR, and its component parts of MOTOR, DOOR, and so on, are shown in Figure 10.20:

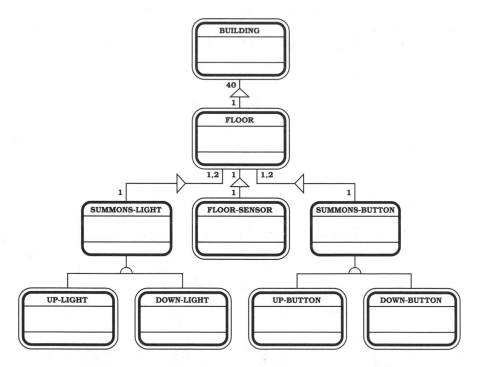

Figure 10.19: The BUILDING-FLOOR whole-part structure

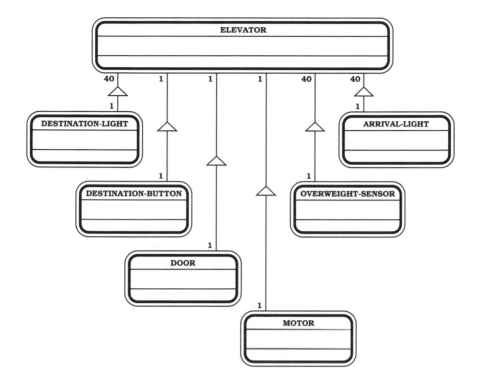

Figure 10.20: The ELEVATOR whole-part structure

11

Object Relationships

In the previous chapter, our OOA model began to take shape with the creation of class hierarchies. In this chapter, we add the next important element: *relationships* between classes and objects. Devotees of data modeling methodologies and entity-relationship diagrams will find this concept familiar; on the other hand, it is interesting that practitioners of OO programming who are now moving up to OOA are frequently unfamiliar with the concept.

Object relationships, as discussed in this chapter, are not the same as the concept of "collaborations" discussed in various OO methodologies. An object relationship is a *static* representation of user policy—for example, a user policy that says, "For every invoice, there must be exactly one customer, and for every customer, there may be zero to many invoices." A "collaboration" between objects, as the term is normally used in OO methodologies, is an *active, dynamic* relationship that typically involves a message being sent from one object to another. As we will see in Chapter 14, the existence of an object relationship almost always implies the existence of a collaboration, but they are nevertheless separate concepts.[1]

We begin with the simplest form of relationship: a binary "instance connection" between two classes. Then we will examine extended forms, and some special cases, of object relationships. Finally, we will illustrate object relationships with the *Small Bytes* and elevator case studies.

---

[1]To put it another way, an object relationship will typically be implemented as a pointer, whereas a message is typically implemented with something more akin to a procedure call.

11.1 BINARY RELATIONSHIPS

Throughout OOA modeling efforts, a crucially important aspect of user policy is described with *relationships* between classes and objects. A SUBSCRIBER in the *Small Bytes* system, for example, is associated with one or more SUBSCRIPTIONs; an ELEVATOR in the elevator case study is associated with exactly one DOOR. It is important for the analyst to discover these relationships, confirm them with the user, and document them in the model.

Such relationships, or "instance connections" as they are called in the Coad-Yourdon versions of OOA, are "static." They do not describe the *behavior* of an object, nor do they describe the *messages* that are used to communicate between objects; these will be discussed in subsequent chapters. Instead, they capture the policy of users when they say, "Every time you have one of *these*, you gotta have one of *those*."

The graphical notation for such relationships is shown in Figure 11.1(a):

Figure 11.1(a): Graphical notation for binary relationships

Notice that the line connecting the two class and object symbols touches the *instance* boundary, not the *class* boundary, of the symbols; it specifically indicates that *some number of instances* of CLASS1 are associated with some number of instances of CLASS2.

The numbers on the diagram describe the cardinality of the relationship, as seen from both sides: thus an instance of CLASS1 is associated with between n1 and n2 instances of CLASS2, and an instance of CLASS2 is associated with between n3 and n4 instances of CLASS1. If a lower-bound integer (that is, n1 or n3) is zero, it denotes an *optional* relationship; otherwise, the relationship is considered *mandatory*. If the upper and lower bounds are the same, the cardinality is expressed with a single integer; a common situation, for example, is the one where each instance of CLASS1 must be associated with one, and only one, instance of CLASS2.

The fact that the cardinality in Figure 11.1(a) is documented from both directions of the relationship emphasizes that the relationship *is* bidirectional; regardless of how we eventually intend to implement this model in a programming language, it is important to document the user's policy regarding relationships between CLASS1 and CLASS2. However, as Rumbaugh and coworkers observe,

> Although associations are modeled as bidirectional they do not have to be implemented in both directions. Associations can easily be implemented as pointers if they are only traversed in a single direction.[2]

A common variation on this notation is the "crow's-feet" symbology shown in Figure 11.1(b):

Figure 11.1(b): Crow's feet notation for binary relationships

Typically, the cardinality notation is read differently on these diagrams than they are on the diagram shown in Figure 11.1(a): the markings closest to a class and object symbol describe the cardinality *as seen by the other class and object*. Thus, we would read Figure 11.1(b) as follows: each instance of CLASS1 is associated with zero to many instances of CLASS2; each instance of CLASS2 is associated with one, and only one, instance of CLASS1.

Of course, there are potentially many other variations on these notational schemes,[3] and the analyst should choose whichever notation works best for his or her situation. Keep in mind, though, that the choice is not only a matter of personal preference, but also a mat-

---

[2]James Rumbaugh, Michael Blaha, William Premerlani, Frederick Eddy, and William Lorensen, *Object-Oriented Modeling and Design* (Englewood Cliffs, NJ: Prentice Hall, 1991), p. 27.

[3]See ibid. for example, for a notation in which the "optional" circle in Figure 11.1(b) is a completely filled, black circle to denote zero or more connecting instances, and an empty, white circle to denote zero or one connecting instance.

ter of whether the organization's CASE tool supports it. And there is an even more important consideration: Does the user understand the notation? For a user weaned on entity-relationship diagrams, Figure 11.1(b) may be preferable. As Martin and Odell point out,

> Entity-relationship diagrams have been used for many years in conventional systems analysis. They show relationships among entity types. . . An object-relationship diagram is essentially the same as an entity-relationship diagram.[4]

Another common variation on the relationship diagrams involves the *naming* of the relationship itself. For example, we could imagine the relationship shown in Figure 11.1(c) in an order-entry system:

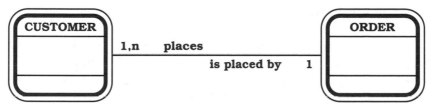

Figure 11.1(c): Another variation in instance connection notation

It is the author's opinion that in the vast majority of cases, this textual description of the relationship is trivial—indeed, so trivial that it insults the reader's (and the user's!) intelligence; furthermore, while the analyst can usually find a (trivial) meaningful term to describe the relationship from one direction, the "inverse" relationship (e. g., "is placed by" in Figure 11.1(c)) is artificial and redundant. However, there are a few times when the textual description can be useful indeed.

Because of this bias, and because of the author's experience trying to explain the "crow's-feet" notation of Figure 11.1(b) to users who had never seen entity-relationship diagrams before, we will use the simplified notation of Figure 11.1(a) for most of the discussion in this chapter. However, the ideal situation would be one where the

---

[4]James Martin and James J. Odell, *Object-Oriented Analysis and Design*, (Englewood Cliffs, NJ: Prentice Hall, 1992), p.83. It is interesting that Martin and Odell illustrate their point with a figure whose caption reads "An entity-relationship diagram on a CASE tool screen. An object-relationship diagram can be represented in the same manner. (Courtesy of Texas Instruments.)" This suggests that the choice of diagramming notation may be heavily influenced by the features of an existing CASE tool, whose vendor is trying to evolve from an older SA/IE methodology into the newer world of OO. This situation is discussed further in Chapters 23 and 24.

CASE tool allows one to switch back and forth between the notation of Figures 11.1(a) and 11.1(b); the difference between Figures 11.1(a) and 11.1(c) could be considered a simple matter of hiding or revealing detailed information—which should be another CASE tool option.

While the cardinality notation of Figure 11.1(a) documents both the "participation" constraints (optional versus mandatory relationships) and the "multiplicity" constraints (e. g., 1:1, 1:N, N:N, etc.), it is usually a good idea to explore these constraints separately with the user. First determine whether *any* relationship exists between a pair of classes; then determine whether that relationship is optional or mandatory, as seen from either side of the relationship; then determine the multiplicity of the relationship.

11.2 EXTENDED RELATIONSHIPS

In the vast majority of cases, the simple binary relationships just described are sufficient to document the user's policy in an OOA model. Indeed, the majority of OOA methodologies do not provide for anything more elaborate than binary relationships.

However, there are a few limited cases where the analyst may feel the need to express relationships involving three, four, or more classes and objects. Such a situation can occur, for example, if the analyst starts with a simple binary relationship and then begins to realize that there is important information that needs to be stored about that relationship.

In a simple order-entry system, for example, the user and analyst might begin by discussing the relationship between a CUSTOMER and a PRODUCT; the relationship might be described as "orders" or "purchases." But it soon becomes evident that we need to keep track of *when* the purchase was made; this is not a proper attribute for either CUSTOMER or PRODUCT, but rather an attribute of the relationship itself. Thus we would be prompted to create a new class and object (assuming that it didn't already exist) called ORDER and document a three-way relationship between CUSTOMER, PRODUCT, and ORDER. Indeed, it might occur to the user that an essential component of a purchase is the SALESPERSON who convinced the CUSTOMER to buy the PRODUCT; thus we might end up with a four-way relationship shown in Figure 11.2:

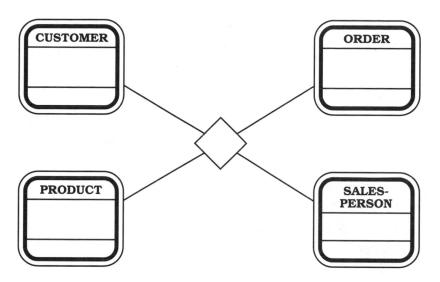

Figure 11.2: A four-way relationship between classes and objects

Note that the relationship (shown by the diamond) is not named and that the diagram does not show the cardinality of the participating members; it is far more difficult to describe, and great care would have to be given to ensure that the notation on the diagram was understandable. Each instance of an ORDER, for example, is probably associated with exactly one CUSTOMER, exactly one SALESPERSON, and one-to-many instances of PRODUCT. But what is each instance of a product related to? How do we describe the relationship from the perspective of a CUSTOMER? As Rumbaugh and coworkers observe,

> Higher order associations are more complicated to draw, implement and think about than binary associations and should be avoided if possible.[5]

Thus we recognize that there are circumstances where n-ary relationships may be useful to accurately model a complex problem; the systems analyst may wish to ensure that his OO CASE tool provides the capability for so doing. But in the overwhelming majority of cases, it will be unnecessary; the situation shown in Figure 11.2,

---

[5]Rumbaugh, et al., *Object-Oriented Modeling and Design*, p. 28.

for example, could be modeled, if necessary, as a combination of six separate binary relationships. The two case studies in this book, for example, will use only binary relationships.

11.3 SPECIAL CASES

N-ary relationships are just one of several special cases of the basic concept introduced in this chapter. For completeness, we discuss several more in this section:

- Many-to-many instance connections
- Recursive instance connections
- Multiple instance connections between classes
- Unary connections between classes
- Consequences of a mandatory connection when adding/deleting instances

11.3.1 Many-to-Many Instance Connections

The basic notation shown in Figure 11.1(a) allows the analyst to describe 1:1 relationships as well as 1:N and N:N relationships. While some analysts (particularly those with a data modeling background) may feel nervous about allowing N:N relationships in an OOA model, they are perfectly legal.

However, it is precisely this kind of situation where the phenomenon discussed in section 11.2—relationships that have attributes of their own—is most likely to occur. Rumbaugh and coworkers suggest that the modeling notation explicitly allow the analyst to describe attributes of the relationship.[6] Thus for the straightforward situation where a CUSTOMER purchases a PRODUCT (ignoring the possibility of a SALESPERSON being involved in the process), we might have begun with a simple N:N relationship as shown in Figure 11.3(a):

Figure 11.3(a): An N:N relationship

---

[6]Ibid., p. 33. Rumbaugh et al. use the term "link attributes" to describe this concept.

As soon as we see the N:N nature of the relationship, we should consider it a clue that an attribute may have been improperly buried within one of the connecting classes.[7] Thus as we have already discussed, it might occur to us that the date and time of the relationship are important; also, the price (amount of money) of the relationship is important to us. Neither of these attributes is legitimately associated with CUSTOMER or PRODUCT. Hence we should consider introducing a new class, PURCHASE, with a new set of relationships as shown in Figure 11.3(b):

Figure 11.3(b): Introducing a new class in an N:N situation

An alternative notation is suggested by Rumbaugh and coworkers, using the concept of "link attributes," as shown in Figure 11.3(c):

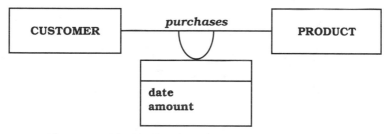

Figure 11.3(c): The Rumbaugh notation for link attributes

On the one hand, this notation may be more descriptive of the actual situation; note that the link attributes are graphically represented as something *different* from a "legitimate" class and object. On the other hand, it introduces two more graphical icons that the user must know how to read and interpret. And it is likely to raise a conceptual question from the user: "If it isn't an object, what the hell *is*

---

[7]We have not yet discussed the attributes associated with a class and object; this is the topic of the next chapter. However, the pedagogical presentation of this material in a typical sequential textbook fashion should not be construed as a necessary sequence of activities in a waterfall project life cycle. In many projects, the user and the analyst may have begun (or possibly even finished) the identification of attributes before or during the identification of object relationships.

it?" In this book, we have attempted to keep the notation as simple as possible and avoid such theological arguments by using the notation of Figure 11.3(b).

Although the model in Figure 11.3(b) is intuitively appealing and almost certainly acceptable to the user, there may be other situations where the analyst or the user strongly argue that it has led to the creation of an undesirable "artificial" object. Thus let's imagine what would have to be done if, for some reason, the user insisted on keeping the basic structure shown in Figure 11.3(a).

The problem, once we consider the situation more closely, is that not all instances of customers have necessarily purchased any products, and not all instances of products have necessarily been purchased by any customers. For the nonpurchasing customers and the unpurchased products, the attributes of "date" and "amount" are utterly meaningless. Hence, if we insisted on attaching those attributes to one of the classes, we would have to create the gen-spec structure shown in Figure 11.4:

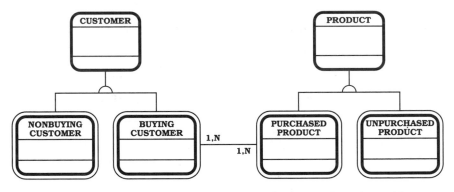

Figure 11.4: Another approach to the CUSTOMER-PRODUCT problem

With this structure, we could consider stuffing the "date" and "amount" attributes into either the BUYING CUSTOMER or PURCHASED PRODUCT class. But the resulting hierarchy is incredibly clumsy, and it is further complicated by the realization that objects will have to change their class during their lifetime, that is, from instances of nonbuying customers to buying customers and from unpurchased products to purchased products. Figure 11.3(b) is by far a simpler alternative.

11.3.2 Recursive Instance Connections

What about relationships between instances of the same class? The situation is often described as a "recursive" relationship; it can be handled by the basic notation of Figure 11.1(a), although additional textual documentation is often useful to avoid confusion.

Consider, for example, a PERSON class for an organization in which we wish to model the fact that some people are managed by others. Figure 11.5 shows a model of this situation; the textual annotation is useful, as can be seen, so that we can distinguish the cardinality of the "managed by" relationship from the "manages" relationship.

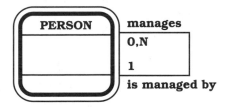

Figure 11.5: A recursive relationship

11.3.3 Multiple Instance Connections Between Classes

All the examples shown thus far in this chapter have involved only one relationship between pairs of classes; indeed, this will be the norm, and a systems analyst could experience dozens of projects without ever feeling the need for anything else. But the methodology and the notation shown in this chapter need not be so restrictive; if the situation calls for it, there can be as many relationships as needed between classes.

For example, let's imagine that we want to keep track of customers who have ordered products, as well as customers who have recommended products to their friends and associates. For the moment, let's assume that we don't need to store any attributes about the ordering and recommendation activities; all we need to know is which customers have recommended which products and which customers have purchased which products. In this case, our model might look like the one shown in Figure 11.6:

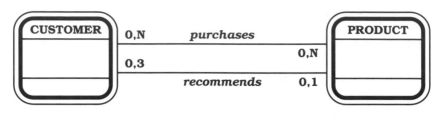

Figure 11.6: Multiple relationships between classes

Note that this is another case where it is convenient to annotate the relationship so that we can tell one from the other. The reason we *must* distinguish one relationship from another, in this example, is that they have different cardinality constraints. Our user has told us that the CUSTOMER-PRODUCT relationship is a straightforward 0:N situation, but the situation with recommendations is somewhat more involved. The user has decided that a customer may not recommend more than three products, and it's possible that he may choose to recommend none; similarly, the user has decreed that a product can be recommended by no more than one customer.

11.3.4 Unary Connections Between Classes

As noted earlier, a relationship between a pair of objects is normally considered bidirectional; although the cardinality constraints may be different from each side of the relationship, it is presumed that the relationship has some "meaning" from each direction.

Jacobson and coworkers observe that this is not always the case:

> As one ObjectOry user, experienced in data modeling, stated: 'If I'm married to my wife, I want my wife to be married to me. So why aren't all relationships bi-directional?' True, but what if you know about the king of Sweden? Does that mean that he knows about you? Normally not. Relations in the real world may be both bi-directional and unidirectional.[8]

If the analyst expects this kind of situation to occur when developing an OOA model with the user, then it should be reflected consistently in the notation. One way to do this would be to include cardinality limits *only* for those directions in which the relationship can be legally interpreted. Thus to describe the relationship between members of royalty and members of the citizen class, we might create a model such as the one shown in Figure 11.7:

[8]Ivar Jacobson, Magnus Christerson, Patrik Jonsson, and Gunnar Övergaard, *Object-Oriented Software Engineering: A Use Case Driven Approach* (Reading, MA: Addison-Wesley, 1992), p. 174 .

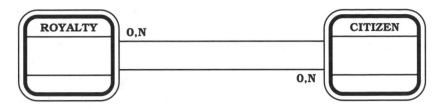

Figure 11.7: Unary relationships between classes

11.3.5 Consequences Of Mandatory Connections When Adding/Deleting Instances

Finally, we note that the presence of a relationship between two classes may imply certain actions when an instance of either class is added or deleted. Suppose that a member of royalty, as modeled in Figure 11.7, dies and his or her instance object is deleted from the class. What happens to the citizens he or she knew? Should they all be executed and deleted? Presumably not. The relationships should be deleted, but the instances of CITIZEN to which they were attached should not (to the great relief of the citizens thus affected).

On the other hand, we might have an OOA model that includes a class called MANUFACTURER and another class called PRODUCT. Assume for the moment that a PRODUCT is manufactured by only one MANUFACTURER, which suddenly goes bankrupt and is deleted from the model. Should the related PRODUCTs also be deleted? What about the case where the PRODUCT is manufactured by multiple MANUFACTURERs, *each* of whom goes bankrupt, one after the other—should the related instances of PRODUCT be deleted when the last MANUFACTURER has disappeared? Depending on the nature of the business, the user's response might well be, "Yes!"

In such a situation, one of the classes could be considered a *controlling* class: if an instance is deleted, then the instances it is connected to via a relationship should also be deleted; the *relationship* itself is known as a *controlling relationship*. This is illustrated in Figure 11.8.

Figure 11.8: Controlling relationships

A similar question arises when a new instance of a class is created, when the OOA model tells us that the class is related to another class. For example, if a new instance of manufacturer is created in Figure 11.8, what can we say about the products it manufactures? If we look closely at the cardinality constraints in Figure 11.8, there is a "chicken and egg" problem: each instance of a manufacturer is required to be associated with at least one product, and each product must be associated with exactly one manufacturer. The obvious interpretation is that an instance of MANUFACTURER and one or more instances of PRODUCT must be created (and linked together) at the same instant.

To some users, this will seem like an irrelevant detail; for others, it will be regarded as a programming question—that is, they might respond to the question just posed by saying, "Do whatever you want when you program it; just make sure it works." But, for some, there may be legal, political, or contractual implications—and they will care deeply about such details. If they care, then we must have a way of representing it in the model.

To pursue the example a little further, let's assume that our user allows us to have PRODUCTs that are not associated with any MANUFACTURER, for example, we will continue to carry an inventory of the PRODUCT even if the MANUFACTURER has gone bankrupt. This means that we will represent the product-to-manufacturer relationship as a 0:1 relationship, and we can delete the "C" notation for the controlling relationship.

Having done this, our model would allow us to *first* add instances of a new PRODUCT without necessarily associating the product with a MANUFACTURER. As a separate step, we could then add instances of MANUFACTURER, and as part of *that* instance creation activity, we could establish the relationship with the appropriate product(s). In this case, the relationship would be called a *dependent relationship* and would be diagrammed as shown in Figure 11.9:

Figure 11.9: A dependent relationship between two classes

From this discussion, it is evident that the details of controlling and dependent relationships involve substantial knowledge about the *state* and *behavior* of classes and objects, which we have not yet discussed. Indeed, many systems analysts prefer to "bury" this detailed information in the diagrams and documents that we will discuss in Chapters 12, 13, and 14 rather than highlight it on the relationships diagrams. But this is a matter of choice; our only advice is that consistency is crucial: if dependent and controlling relationships are documented in the model, they should *all* be modeled on the relationship diagram or in the details of the object's internal behavior and methods. This is likely to be domain-specific knowledge, and it should be documented by the model; otherwise, it may fall through the cracks, and may never be implemented by a programmer who is unfamiliar with the application domain.

11.4 THE *SMALL BYTES* CASE STUDY

In Chapter 9, we saw that there were 25 distinct classes in the *Small Bytes* system; in practice, this means that we should examine some 300 pairwise combinations of classes to see which, if any, relationships exist and should be documented; in general, if there are N classes, there will be N * (N–1)/2 potential relationships.

In practice, a systems analyst is unlikely to exhaustively examine every possible pair; for example, there is usually no need to consider relationships between classes in a whole-part structure or a gen-spec structure. In addition, classes tend to "cluster" in cohesive groups, and the attention of the user and the analyst will naturally be drawn to those clusters. Indeed, as we saw in Chapter 10, some of that clustering has already been accomplished through the mechanism of *subjects*, as shown in Figure 11.10:

Figure 11.10: Subjects for the Small Bytes case study

Thus our first level of examination would consist of looking for relationships between classes within a subject, for example, among the ISSUE, ARTICLE, and TOPIC that constitute the PUBLICATION class. However, there are also some important relationships that cross subject boundaries; for example, without even knowing the details, it is evident that there will be a relationship between some component of the SUBSCRIPTIONS class and some component of the PEOPLE class.

As a common convention, such details are *not* shown at the subject level of abstraction; the analyst might be tempted to add relationship connectors, but the picture would become even more cluttered when we considered adding message connections in Chapter 14. The purpose of the subject-level diagram is to provide a very clean, simple, spare abstraction for the reader—just as we have done with Figure 11.10—and it is best to leave it at that. When we are ready to see the level of detail encompassed by relationship connections, we will need to "drop down" to the level of classes and objects.

For example, let's drop down to the level of the classes and objects within the PUBLICATION subject, which is shown in Figure 11.11.

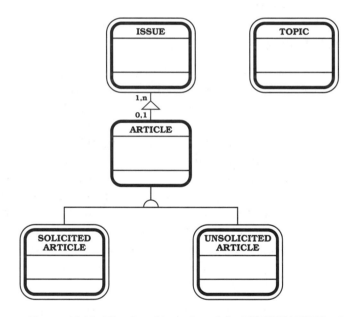

Figure 11.11: The class hierarchy of the PUBLICATION subject

The first relationship we'll consider is the one between ISSUE and TOPIC; our user has told us that every issue of *Small Bytes* is devoted to a single "theme" topic. After some additional discussion, the analyst is convinced that an ISSUE *must* be associated with a TOPIC (there are no "random" issues of the magazine) and that there is never more than one TOPIC, so the cardinality of that part of the relationship is simply "1." From the other direction, we learn from our user that for most of the existing instances of TOPICs at least one ISSUE has been published—and sometimes more than one. But after some discussion, the user admits that the class of TOPICS also includes a "wish list" of "possible" topics for which no specific publication plans have been made; hence the cardinality from TOPIC to ISSUE is 0:N.

What about the relationship between TOPIC and ARTICLE? It stands to reason that any ARTICLE that is associated with an ISSUE, via the whole-part relationship, must also be associated with exactly one TOPIC. But our user notes that some articles are not associated with any issue; this is primarily true for unsolicited articles, but it could also be true for articles that have been invited from famous gurus but that showed up too late to be included in the issue for which they were originally intended. In any case, an article that is not included in an issue is one that has not yet been published; it may or may not be associated with a TOPIC. This is particularly common with unsolicited articles, which appear from unknown parts of the galaxy: if the magazine's editor receives an article entitled, "The Joy of Ada," the first reaction is to assume that it was a deliberate oxymoron and abandon all hope of finding a legitimate topic with which it could be associated.

This leads us to the instance connections shown in Figure 11.12. Note that we have not yet considered the relationships among issues, topics, authors, and subscriptions. Before we tackle those, let's consider the other "intrasubject" relationships in the FINANCES, SUBSCRIPTIONS, and PEOPLE subjects.

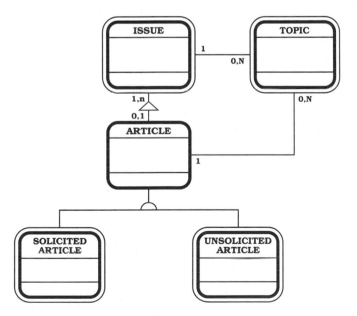

Figure 11.12: Instance connections for PUBLICATIONS subject

Within the FINANCES subject, shown in Figure 11.13, a discussion with the user uncovers a number of interesting facts. An invoice is normally associated with a single payment, but there are rare occasions when an invoice remains unpaid; the unpaid invoice must remain in the system, so that it can be identified, for accounting purposes, as a bad debt. Similarly, there are a few rare cases (especially with international invoices involving shipping charges, or where there is a misunderstanding about the discount to which a customer is entitled) where two or more payments are necessary before the invoice is finally satisfied; however, the user is adamant that there have never been, nor will there ever be, more than three payments for any invoice.

From the opposite end of the PAYMENT-INVOICE relationship, the systems analyst might assume that a payment is made in response to an invoice initiated by *Small Bytes*, but as noted in Chapter 8, many subscriptions arrive with full payment, in which case no invoice needs to be generated. With all this information, we can now document the full PAYMENT-INVOICE relationship.

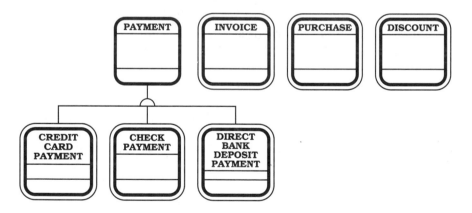

Figure 11.13: The class hierarchy of the FINANCES subject

Similarly, the user tells us that every PURCHASE generates an INVOICE, but from the preceding discussion, we know that not every INVOICE is associated with a PURCHASE (it may be associated with a normal subscription). Similarly, our user reminds us that PURCHASE is an unusual class, which represents a "mini-issue" of *Small Bytes* that has been especially created at the request of a customer who wants several thousand copies. Consequently, the notion of a DISCOUNT does not apply to PURCHASE; there is no relationship between these two classes.

This still leaves the possibility of a relationship among a DISCOUNT, an INVOICE, and a PAYMENT. One could imagine a possible relationship between the three classes if the user offered a discount for fast payment, for example, a 1 percent discount for invoices paid in 10 days or less. However, our user shrugs and says that it's not worth the trouble for the small amounts of money involved; for that matter, the user doesn't bother adding late-payment charges or interest charges for overdue invoices.

So the only possible relationship would be one between DISCOUNT and INVOICE; a discount is offered, as we recall, when a subscriber orders multiple copies. Indeed, this might be a situation in which it would be interesting to consider a four-way relationship involving INVOICE, DISCOUNT, PERSON, and SUBSCRIPTION. However, as noted earlier in this chapter, we have arbitrarily decided to limit ourselves to binary relationships, to keep the methodology and the notation as simple as possible.

Having made that decision, then, the question is: What is DISCOUNT most realistically related to? For that matter, What *is* a DISCOUNT? We have not yet bothered identifying all the attributes of the various classes and objects in our model, but this might be a good time to think a little more carefully—after all, it might be argued that DISCOUNT is simply a parameter, or an attribute, that could be stuffed into some other class.

After some discussion with our user, we learn that a DISCOUNT is not intimately tied to a subscriber—even though it is ultimately the subscriber who enjoys the benefit of the discount. And even though it might be argued that a DISCOUNT is "part" of an invoice (in the sense of a whole-part relationship), it really enjoys a life of its own. And as the user begins to think about it more carefully, he confirms that a DISCOUNT is really "driven" by, or controlled by, a SUBSCRIPTION: the more units of *Small Bytes* that have been ordered as part of a subscription, the larger the discount.

So why not make DISCOUNT an attribute of SUBSCRIPTION? If the discount were decided on a case-by-case basis, on the whim of the person processing the subscription, that might be a reasonable thing to do. To put it more formally, if *knowledge* about how the discount is calculated is *not* within the scope of the system, then it might as well be an attribute. But in fact, this is not the case; our user finally articulates for the analyst what really takes place within the business: there are several instances of discount "policy" (each of which is represented as an object within the DISCOUNT class) that are based not only on the number of units ordered, but also on the time interval during which they are valid. In 1989, for example, *Small Bytes* decided that no discount would apply unless five or more copies of the magazine were ordered as part of a single subscription; in 1990, a new discount policy was established, which offered a lower price if as few as two copies were ordered; and so forth. So DISCOUNT is a "legitimate" class; one of the things its instances know about themselves is when, and if, they are valid.

We could argue that there is a DISCOUNT object associated with every instance of a subscription, even though the discount might be zero in most cases. But our user feels very uncomfortable with this; it does not match his conceptual model of how the business really works. His policy is that a discount can be contemplated only if the "number-of-copies" attribute in SUBSCRIPTION is greater than one.

With all this, we finally end up with Figure 11.14 showing the relationships between the classes of the FINANCES subject. Though we have identified the existence of a relationship between DISCOUNT and SUBSCRIPTION, it has not been shown on this figure.

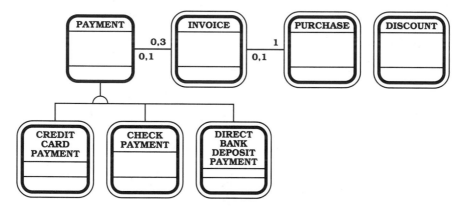

Figure 11.14: Instance connections in the FINANCES subject

The two most complex subjects for the *Small Bytes* system, as we saw in Chapter 10, are the PEOPLE and SUBSCRIPTIONS subjects. But both these involve single class hierarchies, that is, a single class hierarchy of a cluster of whole-part and gen-spec relationships. Assuming that we don't have to model recursive relationships between various instances of PERSON, or various instances of AUTHOR, there should be no other instance connections that need to be documented.

So this leaves us with the relationships *between* subjects, that is, the relationships between a class that has been included in one subject and a class that has been included in another subject. Many of these have already been discussed informally in the preceding discussion, and it is left as an exercise for the reader to complete the model.

The lack of a guided tour through the rest of this section of the *Small Bytes* system is not the result of laziness or exhaustion on the part of the author (Though the author suspects that the reader may be exhausted at this point). The real problem is that the "intersubject" relationships can be shown only by connecting all the class hierarchies together into a single diagram. While the resulting diagram would still be far simpler than most real-world systems (since it still involves only 25 classes), it is too large to fit comfortably within a page of this book. In a real-world project, the systems analyst would probably use a large sheet of paper, or an electronic whiteboard, or some other suitably large drawing space—but the same problem could occur if the model was being developed on a conventional CASE tool whose diagrams are displayed on a typical 14-inch monitor! This is one reason the analyst typically wants great flexibility from the CASE tool, to view only those portions of the overall model that he wants to see at any given time; this is discussed more fully in Chapter 23.

11.5 THE ELEVATOR CASE STUDY

From the discussion of the *Small Bytes* system and a quick review of the elevator model in Chapter 10, it should be apparent that the task of identifying relationships has already been considerably simplified: the model consists primarily of two whole-part structures, BUILDING-FLOOR and ELEVATOR. In addition, we also have a CONTROLLER and a SUMMONS. We don't have to worry about instance relationships between the various components of the two complex hierarchies; all the interesting relationships will occur *across* class hierarchies.

Let's consider these in a pairwise fashion: What are the relationships among, say, BUILDING, ELEVATOR, and CONTROLLER? As we begin considering this, our attention focuses on an interesting aspect of the BUILDING class that we had not considered in Chapter 9 or Chapter 10: there is only one instance of the class. Our user has told us very explicitly that our system will control four elevators in *one* building; while it might be technologically feasible to imagine a "super-system" that controls all of the elevators in a city full of buildings, there is no obvious reason for recommending it. Even if it were technologically possible, it's likely that our user would veto it for reasons of safety, security, and politics—not to mention long-standing tradition.

So there is one instance of BUILDING and four instances of ELEVATOR. Clearly, each instance of an ELEVATOR must be associated with the single instance of BUILDING, and the single instance of BUILDING is associated with all four instances of ELEVATOR. Unlike many other systems, where the relationships could be thought of as "links" that are established and disconnected during the life cycle of the related objects, the BUILDING-ELEVATOR relationships are eternal. For that matter, so are the CONTROLLER-BUILDING and CONTROLLER-ELEVATOR relationships. We could document them in the model for the sake of completeness, but it provides no useful information that was not already well known—we might just as well add some documentation to record the fact that the elevators obey the law of gravity.

So the interesting relationships exist at the lower levels of the class hierarchies, between the components of a FLOOR and the components of an ELEVATOR. To refresh the reader's memory, these are presented again as Figures 11.15 and 11.16:

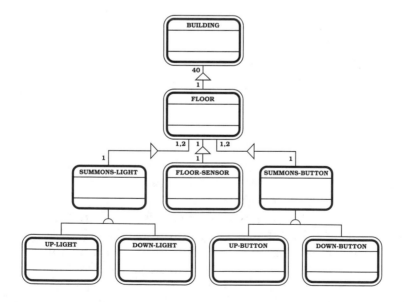

Figure 11.15: The BUILDING-FLOOR whole-part structure

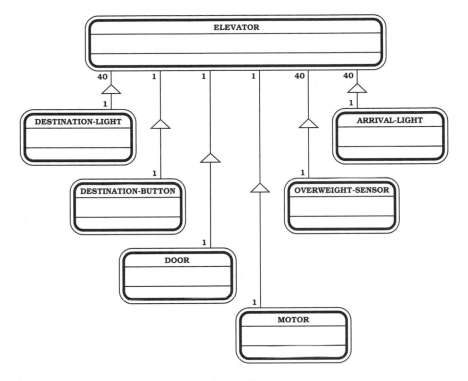

Figure 11.16: The ELEVATOR whole-part structure

From the description of the requirements in Chapter 8, we recall that there is a pair of SUMMONS-BUTTONs on each floor of the building (except for the top floor and bottom floor, which have only one); these allow would-be passengers to request an elevator, and the system is required to turn on an associated SUMMONS-LIGHT to record the fact that the request has been entered. Similarly, we recall that passengers *in* the elevator can push a DESTINATION-BUTTON, for which there is an associated DESTINATION-LIGHT to demonstrate to the passenger that his or her request has been accepted by the system.

So there *is* a relationship between components of the class hierarchies that could be documented, that is, a 1:1 relationship between SUMMONS-BUTTON and SUMMONS-LIGHT and a 1:1 relationship between DESTINATION-BUTTON and DESTINATION-LIGHT. But, again, these are permanent, fixed associations there is no question in anyone's mind as to which instance of DESTINATION-BUTTON is associated with which instance of DESTINATION-LIGHT. For the anal compulsive analyst, it might desirable to document these relationships on our model, but the user and most observers would consider it a nuisance that clutters up the model and obscures the really useful information.[9]

Indeed, there is only one potentially useful relationship that is not already documented in a whole-part structure: the relationship between SUMMONS-BUTTON and DESTINATION-LIGHT. Many of us have ridden elevators in which a would-be passenger's pressing of a SUMMONS-BUTTON not only lights up the associated SUM-MONS-LIGHT, but *also* lights up the appropriate DESTINATION-LIGHT within the elevator cabin; in other elevator systems, the pressing of a SUMMONS-BUTTON may cause ARRIVAL-LIGHTS on the panel above the elevator door to light up. In either case, the intention is to tell the passengers within the elevator not only which floors have been requested by their fellow passengers, but also which floors have been requested by external would-be passengers.

However, a careful reading of the requirements in Chapter 8 tells us that this feature has not been requested by our user; we might diplomatically request that this additional "functionality" be considered, but if the user refuses, we have no choice but to document what has been requested.[10]

So our final conclusion is an interesting one: aside from the "fixed" relationships whose documentation would add nothing useful to the model, there are no other relationships that reflect important user policy. This is actually not so surprising when we think about the nature of the syste all the "action" is in the *communication* between the objects. This will become clear when we discuss object behavior and object methods in Chapters 13 and 14.

---

[9]Some software engineers might argue that this is too harsh a judgment. In the next chapter, we will see that the relationships between objects could be considered part of the *state* of an object, and is thus very much like an attribute; indeed, it will eventually be implemented as a "pointer" in most programming languages. The fact that the relationship between an instance of ELEVATOR and the single instance of BUILDING is fixed, permanent, and "global" does not eliminate the fact that the relationship exists. On the other hand, as may be evident to the reader already, what makes the relationship interesting is not its static existence, but rather its dynamic behavior. In other words, what we *really* care about, in terms of the relationship between ELEVATOR and BUILDING (and most of the other classes in this problem) is the *messages* they send to one another. This will be discussed in Chapters 13 and 14.

[10]Here is an interesting question: What are the consequences if the user changes his mind about this feature after the system has been developed? Aside from adding the instance connections between SUMMONS-BUTTON and DESTINATION-LIGHT, what has to be changed in the code? Although we have not yet discussed object behavior and object methods (the subject of Chapters 13 and 14), the knowledgeable reader can already guess what will have to be done: the SUMMONS-BUTTON object will have to send a "turn yourself on" message to DESTINATION-LIGHT in addition to the "turn yourself on" message that it already sends to SUMMONS-LIGHT. Presumably, no changes would be required to the DESTINA-TION-LIGHT object, since it doesn't care who sends it the message to turn itself on.

12

Object Attributes

It will come as no surprise that an OOA model must include a definition of *attributes* for the classes and objects. The model we have developed in the previous three chapters has grown progressively richer and more complex, but it is the attributes that truly begin to clarify the *meaning* of a class, by adding finer-grained detail about the abstractions wc are modeling.

Attributes describe data-related information that is hidden inside the class and object, invisible to the outside world. As we will see further in Chapter 14, attributes are manipulated by *methods* (or services) in the class and object. Thus attributes and methods are the yin and yang of a class and object: attributes describe the *state* of an object, while methods describe the active *behavior* of the object.[1]

As we saw in Chapter 9, the typical graphical notation for classes and objects usually involves a simple textual listing of the attributes within the object boundary; this is illustrated in Figure 12.1.

Figure 12.1: Showing the attributes in a class and object

[1]Attributes are also used to describe an object with nonstate variables; in addition, attributes are typically used as the means of implementing the object connections described in Chapter 11, in the form of pointers.

In this chapter, we will discuss the strategy for identifying attributes in a class and object; then we will discuss the placement of attributes in a class hierarchy. This inevitably leads to a process of *revision*: we learn so much about the true nature of the classes and objects during the discovery of attributes that class definitions or class hierarchies are modified to better model the true nature of the application. Finally, we will return to our discussion of the *Small Bytes* case study and the elevator case study.

12.1 DISCOVERING ATTRIBUTES

OOA provides no magical technique for discovering the attributes that an object requires to do its job. The task is essentially the same as it would be in any form of systems analysis: the analyst must study the application itself, interview the user, and try to learn as much as possible about the true nature of each class and object in the model.

However, there is one interesting aspect of an OO mind-set: during the search for attributes (and to some extent, in the search for basic objects, too), the analyst investigates each class and object from a "first-person" perspective.[2] That is, the analyst suspends reality for a moment and pretends that he or she *is* the object; this leads to questions such as the following:

- "If I am a subscription object, how am I described, in general?"
- "As an elevator object, how am I described in this problem domain?"
- "As a DESTINATION-BUTTON object, how am I described in the context of this system's responsibilities?"
- "What do I need to *know* to survive as an ISSUE class and object in the *Small Bytes* system?"
- "As an ARRIVAL-LIGHT class and object, what state information do I need to remember over time?"
- "What states can I be in as an ARTICLE class and object in the *Small Bytes* system?"

This perspective is quite different from that seen in other methodologies, where the analyst and user regard functions or enti-

---

[2]Such an approach is also referred to as anthropomorphism and "personification."

ties as inanimate creations, whose definition and behavior is typically described in third-person comments: "What do we have to do to that thing?" or "What are the attributes we assign to an elevator entity?"

Note that some of this information may have been discovered during the initial analysis activities discussed in the previous chapters. The reader may recall that we informally mentioned some of the potential attributes during other aspects of the discussion—for example, our decision about what kind of class hierarchy to create may have been guided by our instinctive knowledge of what attributes would eventually have to be added to the model. In the textbook discussion, we did not add those attributes to the model during the information discussion, but in a real project, they probably would be added. If the information is available, we might as well record it—as long as the process of recording does not distract us from the main work at hand.

Note also that while we are likely to do a reasonably complete job of defining attributes, there is no guarantee that it will be perfect. As we have discussed throughout this book, prototyping is an essential strategy for double-checking our formal analysis work and discovering details that were overlooked during the creation of the OOA model.

12.2 PLACING ATTRIBUTES IN A CLASS HIERARCHY

Attributes are discovered, as we have seen, by mentally climbing inside a class and object, putting on the clothes it wears, and trying to understand what defines it. If we are looking at a "stand-alone" class and object, then its attributes continue to live within its encapsulated walls; once we have defined the attributes, our job is done (until we consider object behavior and object methods in the next two chapters).

But as we saw in Chapter 10, many of the classes in an OOA model participate in a class hierarchy composed of gen-spec structures and whole-part structures. If we were to go through the attribute-discovery process in a strictly top-down fashion, we would simply observe that attributes in the high-level gen-spec structures are automatically "carried down" and inherited by the subclasses below them.

However, there will be many situations where attributes are first discovered in the subclasses. For each such attribute, it is important to stop for a moment and ask: How high *up* in the hierarchy should this attribute be carried? The attributes should usually be placed as high as possible in the hierarchy, so that their definition is carried down to all subclasses below them.

12.3 REVISING THE CLASS HIERARCHY

Inevitably, the detailed process of assigning attributes to classes and objects will lead to a more complete understanding than was possible in the earlier stages discussed in Chapters 9, 10, and 11. So we should expect some revisions of class definitions, and some rearrangements of the class hierarchies to result from this step of the OOA model.

As part of the careful definition of attributes, the analyst should define its legal values; in the case of numeric attributes, for example, this typically involves defining a range, or upper and lower limits, precision, accuracy, units of measure, frequency of update or calculation, and so on. But in the course of confirming this with the user, the analyst may learn that some attributes have a value of "not applicable." This is a clear indication that the class and object we have been investigating is not a simple, stand-alone class, but rather a gen-spec structure in disguise. We might as well recognize this fact and revise the OOA model accordingly.

For example, suppose we had identified the class ARTICLE in the *Small Bytes* case study and were now identifying its attributes. The user might tell us that one of the attributes is the date when the article is due to be received from the author—because the normal course of action is for the magazine's editor to first call the author and invite him or her to write the article; since it is being planned for a specific issue, we need to have a deadline when the article will be received. But, as the user observes, this is not applicable for the case when an article arrives without warning from an author with whom the magazine has had no previous contact. It is this "not applicable" value to the "deadline-date" attribute that might first give us the clue that ARTICLE has, in fact, a gen-spec structure.

Similarly, we might discover at this stage of our analysis that a class and object has only one attribute; while it may have previously seemed plausible as a full-scale legitimate class, we might well decide now that it deserves to be an attribute in some other object. But this must be done carefully; sometimes, for example, a class may have only one attribute, but may have some important behavior encapsulated with that attribute.[3]

Consider, for example, the case of the DOOR class in the elevator problem. Everyone knows that an elevator has a door, it hardly required any thinking or justification to include in the model originally. But when we begin focusing on the attributes of the door, it may occur to us that the *only* relevant attribute is its state: open or closed.[4] Does this mean that "door-state" should be an attribute of elevator? Perhaps this would appeal to the analyst or the user, but it occurs to us as well that a door has behavior: it knows how to open itself and close itself, and can presumably do so if so instructed.

On the other hand, during the analysis of the elevator problem, the discussion of floor sensors and overweight sensors might have led the analyst to propose a class and object called WEIGHT. During the attribute-discovery process, though, it is unlikely that we would be able to think of more than one attribute for WEIGHT; indeed, most of the discussion would probably revolve around the proper units (pounds, kilograms, tons ,etc.) and the legal values (e. g., no more than 2,000 pounds). Indeed, it should have been evident even during the initial object-discovery process discussed in Chapter 9 that WEIGHT does not deserve to exist on its own, but now is our chance to put it wherever it belongs (probably an attribute of ELEVATOR).

Note also that the (binary) relationships between classes and objects are typically implemented as attributes, too; as we noted in Chapter 11, they are part of the *state* of an object. These "relationship-attributes" are typically not included in the list of "normal" attributes that we saw in Figure 12.1; their presence is indicated by the relationship line connecting the class to another class.

However, this is a good time to take another look at the relationships themselves. Our user might point out to us one of the many instances at the other end of the relationship line has a special meaning, for example, it is the newest one, or the oldest one, or the

---

[3] In the extreme case, an object may have *no* attributes. It may have no state memory; it may simply exhibit behavior. For example, a simple elevator button may not have to remember its state, but may simply send an "I've been pressed" message when the user presses the button.

[4] Other attributes, such as the door's height, width, color, weight, and so on are interesting for elevator passengers to observe as they stand facing forward, studiously avoiding the gaze of their fellow passengers—but they are not likely to be relevant to the system we are designing.

highest-priority one. If this is the case, it is usually a strong clue that we need to add an appropriate attribute to the affected class and object.

For example, our *Small Bytes* system has a relationship between AUTHOR and ARTICLE; our user has told us that some authors write more than one article, so it is a 1:N relationship.[5] This is illustrated in Figure 12.2:.

Figure 12.2: The AUTHOR-ARTICLE relationship

In the course of this discussion, the user might casually point out to the analyst that it's very important to be able to distinguish the most recent article that an author has submitted to the magazine. This perspective—namely, distinguishing among the *set* of relationships between two classes—helps us identify an attribute that might not otherwise have been obvious. In this case, it indicates that we need a "date" attribute associated with ARTICLE; chances are, we've already thought of this during our investigation of ARTICLE by itself. But if it was overlooked, we would now be prompted to add it.

12.4 THE *SMALL BYTES* CASE STUDY

Discovery of the attributes in the *Small Bytes* system begins with the class hierarchies and instances connections that were documented in the previous chapters. The attributes for the FINANCES subject are shown in Figure 12.3:[6]

---

[5] If we allow for the possibility that an article can be written by multiple authors, then it is an N:N relationship.

[6] Figure 12.3 was produced by one of the popular object-oriented CASE tools, OOATool™, from Object International, Inc. OOATool allows the user to group a number of classes into an aggregate known as a "subject," and each subject can be assigned a unique number. The subject boundary is shown as a shaded rectangle surrounding all the enclosed classes and objects; the subject-number is shown in the corners of the subject-rectangle.

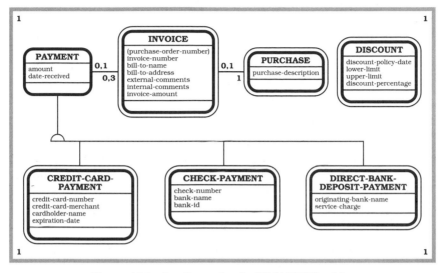

Figure 12.3: Attributes for the FINANCES subject

Most of the attributes are straightforward, and there is little question where they should be placed. However, note that the INVOICE class has an attribute that has been placed in parentheses: a "purchase-order-number" attribute. Our user tells us that most invoices are straightforward and require only the obvious information of invoice-date, invoice-amount, and so on. However, some customers require a purchase order number; any subsequent requests for payments, or any disputes with the customer's accounting department, will inevitably require the purchase order number.

However, since most customers don't need or require such a number, it has been shown as an optional attribute. One could argue that this is a case of the "not applicable" situation described earlier; the analyst might even be tempted to create a gen-spec structure to distinguish between those invoices that have a purchase order number and those that don't.

On the other hand, the presence or absence of the purchase order number is entirely at the discretion of the customer; the *Small Bytes* system doesn't need the information, and doesn't care if it has been supplied. It would be more appropriate to think of the attribute's definition as either "none supplied" or an alphanumeric string.

Note also that the invoice class contains a "bill-to-name" and "bill-to-address," which should cause us some concern. Our user explains that sometimes the invoice is sent to a different person from the subscriber to whom the issues of *SmallBytes* will be sent; however, most of the time, the "bill-to" and "ship-to" information is the same.

The distinction between "bill-to" and "ship-to" isn't the problem here; after all, the "ship-to" information will probably be located in the SUBSCRIPTION class elsewhere in the model. The real problem is that we are burying name and address information in the INVOICE class, when we have a perfectly good class called PERSON to hold that kind of information. Thus it suggests that there should be an additional instance connection in our model, which we didn't recognize in Chapter 10, between INVOICE and PERSON. Thus we should remove the name and address attributes from INVOICE; the instance connection from INVOICE to PERSON will eventually be implemented as a "person-ID" pointer.

The PUBLICATIONS subject is shown in Figure 12.4; its attributes are straightforward and require no additional explanation.[7]

---

[7]Note that we have not explicitly shown a "key" attribute in any of the classes in Figure 12.4. In most OOA methodologies, *every* object is presumed to have a unique, system-generated identifier, which can be used as a "key attribute" to retrieve it. For those who are more comfortable with conventional database methods, it might be convenient to indicate one or more of the user-defined attributes as "key attributes." Thus the key for ISSUE would probably be the concatenation of volume-number and issue-number; the key for ARTICLE would be title, or title concatenated with date-received.

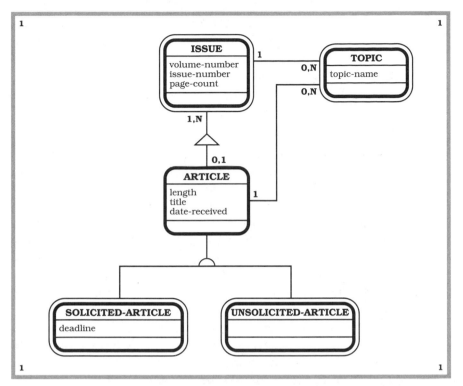

Figure 12.4: Attributes for the PUBLICATIONS subject

The discovery of attributes for the PEOPLE subject is more difficult; our first effort is shown in Figure 12.5. As usual, many of the attributes are obvious and straightforward; however, some questions arise:

- What attributes does an author have? On the surface, it is evident that an author is intrinsically different than an "ordinary" person—but what makes it so? Conceivably, our user might tell us that we need to keep some additional information such as the author's home phone number, which would not be necessary for the superclass. But what *really* distinguishes an AUTHOR from a PERSON is the kind of instance connections it can have (e. g., with ARTICLE) and the special privileges he or she enjoys (e.g., receiving a year's complimentary subscription to the magazine). It's not clear yet how we are going to handle this; let's defer any final decisions until Chapters 13 and 14.

- Similarly, what attributes should AGENCY and DISTRIBU-TOR have? Indeed, what distinguishes an AGENCY from a DISTRIBUTOR? Why do they each have a proposed attribute of "discount-percentage" when we already have a class called DISCOUNT?
- Why has DISTRIBUTOR been made a subclass of ORGANI-ZATION, while AGENCY is a subclass of SITE?

The more we think about these questions, the more we realize how sloppy our original class hierarchy was—and how we must have been guided by our user's informal mental model that was never precisely articulated. So it behooves us to begin asking a number of detailed questions to learn what's really going on.

The first thing that we learn is that the user has mentally distinguished between DISTRIBUTOR and AGENCY because a distributor consists of one site with whom all communication takes place, but an agency consists of a number of distinct sites, each of whom operates independently. Thus the distributor in India consists of (as far as *Small Bytes* is concerned) one office in New Delhi; it may have several people attached to it, but there is only one site. The EBSCO agency, on the other hand, has dozens of offices (sites) across the United States; each one seems to operate in complete ignorance that the others exist, and each has its own independent dealings with *Small Bytes*. The only thing they have in common is the name of their common parent company; hence the user instinctively thought of AGENCY as a subclass of SITE.

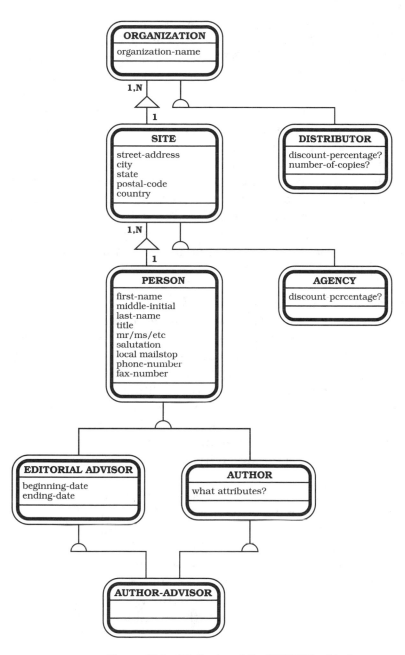

Figure 12.5: Attributes of the PEOPLE subject

But with this additional explanation, it now seems more appropriate to consider *both* DISTRIBUTOR and AGENCY as subclasses, or specializations, of ORGANIZATION. They both have component SITEs; it just happens that (1) the magazine has never taken advantage of the fact that the various agencies have a common parent and (2) distributors have only one site, as a matter of common practice. But this kind of analysis leads to a phenomenon that is common to all systems analysis projects, regardless of whether OO, SA, or any other methodology is practiced: the user recognizes an opportunity to change his policy in the middle of the project. "Maybe we should encourage our international distributors to have multiple sites within their country and offer them an additional discount for more aggressive marketing activities," he muses. "And maybe we should contact the head office of each agency when one of their branch offices sends us a subscription—we could offer them a larger discount for volume deals!"

But this brings up the question of discounts again; why does it exist as an attribute when we already have a DISCOUNT class? Obviously, the reason that agencies and distributors deal with *Small Bytes* in the first place is that the discount is their way of making a profit; this is very different, conceptually, from the discount that an ordinary subscriber enjoys when he buys multiple copies of the magazine. Indeed, agencies receive a discount on *each* subscription they deliver, regardless of whether it is for a single copy or multiple copies. Distributors, on the other hand, are presumed to receive more than one copy (otherwise, why would the magazine bother dealing with them?).

The real problem is that we have assumed, up to this point, that DISCOUNT is associated directly with a SUBSCRIPTION: if you buy two copies of *Small Bytes*, you get a certain discount, regardless of whether you're Santa Claus or Genghis Khan. But an agency's discount is associated directly with the agency itself, which places a subscription on behalf of some other person. Similarly, the distributor's discount is associated directly with the distributor and is applied to whatever number of copies the distributor receives.

12.5 THE ELEVATOR CASE STUDY

Most of the classes and objects in the elevator system have very simple attributes; as we have already seen, what distinguishes this system is its dynamic behavior, rather than its static data characteristics.

Thus we would expect that a relatively brief set of discussions with our user would identify the key attributes of BUILDING, FLOOR, and so on.

Note that in the case of FLOOR, one attribute is crucial: a "floor-number" to distinguish between the instances of the class. By contrast, BUILDING needs no such attribute, as long as we are confident that there is only one instance of BUILDING and that this requirement will never change.

For the SUMMONS-LIGHT class, we can only imagine one obvious attribute: a binary "on/off" attribute indicating the current state of the light. Note that SUMMONS-LIGHT is an abstract class with no instances of its own; the actual instances of summons lights are shown as subclasses. Naturally, the "on/off" attribute is inherited by both UP-LIGHT and DOWN-LIGHT subclasses, but that makes us pause for a moment: What's the difference between the two? Indeed, why should we even bother distinguishing between an UP-LIGHT and a DOWN-LIGHT: Why not collapse them into the superclass and refer to everything simply as a SUMMONS-LIGHT?

This is not the sort of thing the analyst is likely to discuss with the user. The user's reaction to this kind of metaphysical thinking is likely to be, "Up is up, and down is down. You don't have to be a rocket scientist to understand that they're *different*." And he would then point to the physical implementation of lights on a real elevator to emphasize his point.

But it's a real dilemma for the analyst: it's hard to imagine that UP-LIGHTs and DOWN-LIGHTs could have different attributes.[8] And it's hard to imagine that they would have different "methods" (which we'll discuss in Chapter 14 in more detail): the only thing a summons light has to know how to do is turn itself on or off—and one would assume that such a method would operate in the same way regardless of what kind of summons light it was operating upon.

And yet. . . our instinct tells us that the user is right: there *is* a fundamental difference between the up lights and down lights. What could it be? *Aha!* The difference is who they "talk" to: an UP-LIGHT can receive messages from an UP-BUTTON and nothing else; a

---

[8] Some elevator aficionados might point out that it's common for the "up" summons button to be lighted with a red bulb, and the "down" button to be lighted with a white bulb, or vice versa. But this is more a question of physical-mechanical implementation; it's hard to imagine that we would put this kind of detail into an analysis model.

DOWN-LIGHT communicates with a DOWN-BUTTON and nothing else. Imagine the chaos that would ensue if UP-BUTTONs began sending spurious messages to DOWN-LIGHTs! Ironically, our decision in Chapter 12 *not* to model the 1:1 instance connections between SUMMONS-BUTTON and SUMMONS-LIGHT may have made it a little more difficult for us to see why UP-LIGHT and DOWN-LIGHT need to be modeled as distinct subclasses.

Next, we consider FLOOR-SENSOR. At this point, it may be a little difficult to recall what it does; we take another look at the relevant section of the user's textual description of the problem:

> *Floor sensors*: There is a floor sensor switch for each floor for each elevator shaft. When an elevator is within eight inches of a floor, a wheel on the elevator closes the switch for that floor and sends an interrupt to the computer (there is a separate interrupt for the set of switches in each elevator shaft). When the computer receives one of these (vectored) interrupts, its program can read the appropriate memory mapped eight-bit input register (there is one for each interrupt, hence one for each elevator) that contains the floor number corresponding to the floor sensor switch that caused the interrupt.

Good grief! The analyst does his best to skim over all this talk about switches and interrupts and computers and input registers to get to the heart of the matter: What is a floor sensor? After some careful thought, the analyst decides that a floor sensor is an object that is intelligent enough to know that it has been "enabled" (by virtue of an elevator coming within 8 inches of itself) or "disabled" (by virtue of the elevator leaving this 16-inch zone). So we need only a single attribute to represent this in our model.

But this makes us realize something interesting that wasn't apparent when we modeled the instance connections in Chapter 12: there is a relationship between ELEVATOR and FLOOR. We might describe it as an "is-at" relationship: an elevator *is at* floor N. . . or an elevator is at *no* floor, because it's in the "twilight zone" between floors. Thus as mentioned earlier in this chapter, careful consideration of attributes often causes us to revise the "architecture" of the OOA model.

Similar consideration of the remaining classes in the elevator problem indicates that most of them have a single attribute describing a binary state: on/off, enabled/disabled, or (in the case of a DOOR) open/shut. The attributes of the BUILDING class hierarchy resulting from this analysis is shown in Figure 12.6:

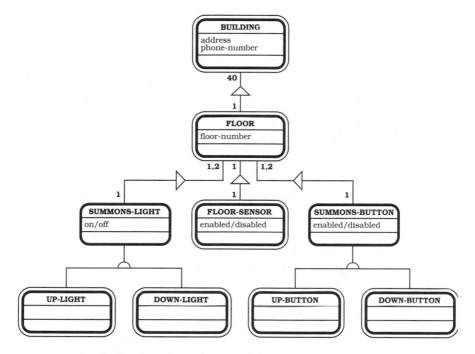

Figure 12.6: The attributes of the BUILDING hierarchy

13

Object Behavior

In previous chapters, we discussed the *static* characteristics of classes and objects: objects have "structure," they have relationships with other objects, and they have attributes that clarify their internal meaning.

But objects are also *dynamic:* they have "behavior." An externally visible manifestation of this behavior is the sending of messages to other objects, which we will discuss in Chapter 14. However, first we need a way of modeling the behavior itself; this will be accomplished in this chapter with an approach virtually identical to the *state-transition* diagram from structured analysis methodologies.

Until recently, models of a system's time-dependent behavior were important only for process control, telephone switching systems, high-speed data acquisition systems, military command and control systems, and other such examples of real-time systems. Some of these systems are passive, in the sense that they do not seek to control the surrounding environment, but merely react to it or capture data about it. Many high-speed data acquisition systems fall into this category (e. g., a system capturing high-speed scientific data from a satellite). Other real-time systems are more active, in the sense that they seek to maintain control over some aspect of the surrounding environment. Process control systems and a variety of embedded systems fall into this category.

Systems of this kind typically deal with high-speed external sources of data, and they must provide responses and output data quickly enough to deal with the external environment. An important part of specifying such systems is the description of what happens *when*.

For business-oriented systems, on the other hand, this issue has traditionally not been so important. Inputs may arrive in the system from many different sources and at relatively high speeds, but the inputs can usually be delayed if the system is busy doing something else. A payroll system, for example, does not have to worry about interrupts and signals from external radar units. Typically, the only timing issues that we see in such systems are specifications of response time.

However, we are beginning to see some large, complex business-oriented systems that *do* have aspects of real-time behavior. If the system is dealing with inputs from thousands of terminals, as well as high-speed inputs from other computer systems or satellite communication facilities, then it may have the same kind of time-dependent issues that a classical real-time system has. Hence, although you may not have to deal with such problems in every system you build, you should be familiar with the modeling tools for time-dependent behavior

We begin by discussing the concept of object states; then we will examine a popular modeling tool used to explore this component of the OOA model—the object life-history (OLH) diagram. Finally, we will return to our familiar case studies to see an illustration of the modeling technique.

13.1 OBJECT LIFE-HISTORY DIAGRAMS

A typical object life-history diagram is shown in Figure 13.1(a). This diagram shows the behavior of a typical telephone answering machine; it would be useful if we wanted to regard the entire answering machine as a single object, *or* if we were modeling the behavior of a "controller" object whose purpose is to coordinate and synchronize the behavior of other objects that control such activities as the rewinding of the message tape, and so on.

The major components of the diagram are *states* and arrows representing *state changes*. There are a variety of alternative notations for such diagrams; one common one is shown in Figure 13.1(b). While it is equivalent in content to Figure 13.1(a), it has the minor disadvantage of looking too much like a data flow diagram. To avoid confusion and to maintain consistency with common notation used by several commercial methodologies, we will use the notation of Figure 13.1(a) throughout this book.

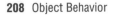

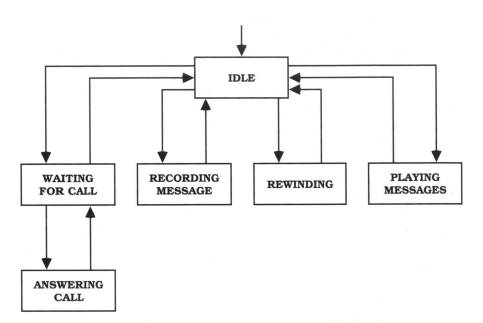

Figure 13.1(a): A typical object life-history diagram

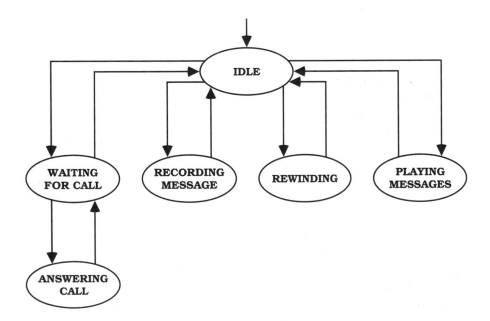

Figure 13.1(b): An alternative object-life history diagram notation

13.1.1 Object States

Each rectangular box represents a *state* that an object can be in. Webster's *New World Dictionary* defines a "state" in the following way:

> A set of circumstances or attributes characterizing a person or thing at a given time; way or form of being; condition.[1]

Thus typical object states might be any of the following:

- Waiting for user to enter password
- "door open" or "door closed" for an elevator door
- "expired" for a Small Bytes subscription object
- "Accelerating" for an engine object
- "moving up" for an elevator object
- "has a subscription" for a Small Bytes person
- "paid" for an invoice

Note that one of these examples involves the object *waiting* for something to occur and is not expressed in terms of the object *doing* something. This is because our object life-history diagram is being used to develop an "essential model" of the system—a model of how the object would behave if we had perfect technology. One aspect of perfect technology is the assumption that our computer operates infinitely quickly, so any processing or computation that the object has to do, or any action that it has to take, will be done in zero time. Thus any observable state that the object is in can only correspond to periods of time when (1) it is waiting for something in the external environment to occur or (2) it is waiting for a current activity in the environment (moving, accelerating, etc.) to change to some other activity.

This does not mean that our objects are incapable of taking action or that we do not intend to show those actions. It's just that actions, which happen instantaneously in our perfect technology model, are not the same as states, which represent observable conditions that the system can be in. Thus a state represents some behavior of the system that is observable and that lasts for some finite period of time.

---

[1] *Webster's New World Dictionary*, Second College Edition (New York: Simon & Schuster, 1980).

Note also that our diagrams show the *internal behavior* of individual classes and objects. Thus each class has its own separate diagram that describes its own internal microcosm. It is also possible to imagine a life-cycle diagram for the entire system, which would represent the aggregate life history of all the objects within the system. However, except in rare cases, such a diagram would be far too complex to work with: there could easily be hundreds, if not thousands, of individual states for the system as a whole.

A more practical compromise would be to create a "life-history" or "state-transition" diagram to describe the behavior of collaborating *groups* of objects. For example, consider a MAN object and a WOMAN object; each has its own internal life-history model, but we may be more interested in the life history of the collaboration between the two—beginning with no association whatsoever and progressing through dating, marriage, and possibly even divorce. In effect, this involves developing a life-history model of the *relationships* between classes and objects; Shlaer and Mellor recommend this approach.[2] However, we can also model the behavior of the connections (or relationships) from the perspective of the individual classes and objects which participate in those relationships; since that is what our users will typically focus on most closely, those are the only life-history diagrams we will discuss in this chapter.

13.1.2 Changes of State

An object that existed in only one state would not be very interesting to study: it would be static, and we would depend instead on the kind of models we discussed in previous chapters. Indeed, the information systems that we typically model may have dozens of different states. But how does an object change from one state to another? If it has orderly rules governing its behavior, then typically only certain kinds of state changes will be meaningful and valid.

We show the valid state changes on our OLH diagram by connecting the relevant pairs of states with an arrow. Thus Figure 13.2 shows the behavior of an object that can change from state 1 to state 2; it also shows that when the object is in state 2, it can change to

---

[2]Sally Shlaer and Stephen J. Mellor, *Object Lifecycles: Modeling the World in States* (Englewood Cliffs, NJ: Yourdon Press/Prentice Hall, 1992).

either state 3 or back to state 1. However, according to this OLH, the object cannot change from state 1 *directly* to state 3. On the other hand, the diagram tells us that the object *can* change directly from state 3 back to state 1. Note that state 2 has two successor states. This is quite common in OLHs; indeed, any one state might lead to an arbitrary number of successor states.

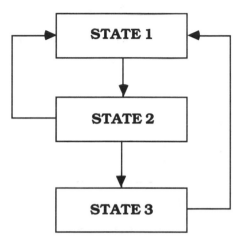

Figure 13.2: Changes of state

While Figure 13.2 gives us some interesting information about the time-dependent behavior of an object, it does not tell us something that may turn out to be very important: what the object's *initial* and *final* states are. Indeed, Figure 13.2 is a steady-state model of an object that has been active forever and will continue to be active forever. Most objects do have a recognizable initial state and a recognizable final state; this is shown in Figure 13.3.

The initial state is typically the one drawn at the top of the diagram, although this is not mandatory; what really identifies state 1 in Figure 13.3 as the initial state is the "naked" arrow that is not connected to any other state. Similarly, the final state is often the one drawn at the bottom of the diagram, but this is not mandatory. What really identifies state 5 as the final state is the absence of an arrow leading out of state 5. In other words, once you get to state 5, you aren't going anywhere!

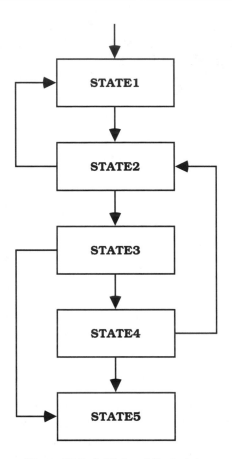

Figure 13.3: Initial and final states

In most systems, an object can have only one initial state; there may be some circumstances where an object has multiple initial states depending on some condition. But while a single initial state is common, it is necessary in most systems to allow an object to have multiple final states; the various final states are mutually exclusive, meaning that only one of them can occur during any one execution of the system in which the object resides. Figure 13.4 shows an example in which the possible final states are states 4 and 6.

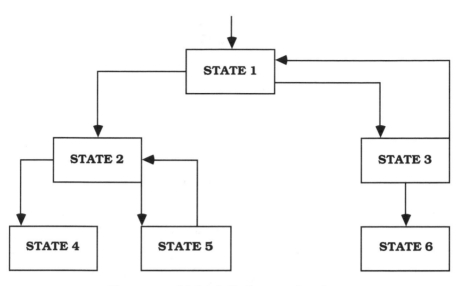

Figure 13.4: Multiple final states of an object

Since we are using OLHs to build an essential model of the system, we also assume that state changes occur instantaneously; that is, it requires no observable time for the object to change from one state into another state. When the designers and programmers begin to build an *implementation model*, this will be a real issue: it typically *does* take a few microseconds for a computer to switch from one processing activity to another, and they must ensure that it happens quickly enough that the environment does not get out of control.

13.1.3 Conditions and Actions

To make our OLH diagram complete, we need to add two more things: the *conditions* that cause a change of state and the *actions* that the object takes when it changes state. As Figure 13.5 illustrates, the conditions and actions are shown next to the arrow connecting two related states.

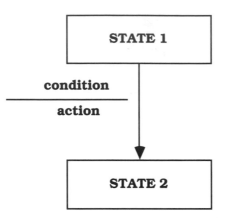

Figure 13.5: Showing conditions and actions

A condition is some event external to the object itself that the object is capable of detecting; it will typically be a message from another object. This will typically cause the object to change from a state of waiting for X to a new state of waiting for Y or carrying out activity X to carrying out activity Y.

But as part of the change of state, the object will typically take one or more actions: it will produce an output, display a message on the user's terminal, carry out a calculation, send one or more messages to other objects, and so on. Thus actions shown on the OLH diagram are either responses sent back to the object that causes the state change via a message connection or calculations whose results are remembered by the object.

13.2 PARTITIONED DIAGRAMS

In a complex system, some objects may have dozens of distinct states; trying to show them all on a single diagram would be difficult, if not impossible. Thus just as we used leveling or partitioning with subjects and their component class hierarchies, we can use partitioning with OLHs. Figure 13.6(a) shows an example of two levels of state-transition diagrams (STDs) for a complex object.

Note that in this case, any individual state of a higher-level diagram can become the *initial* state for a lower-level diagram that further describes that higher-level state, and the final state(s) in a lower-level diagram correspond to the exit conditions in the associated higher-level state. In other cases, the systems analyst may need to show, explicitly, how a low-level OLH diagram exits to an appropriate place in the higher-level diagram.

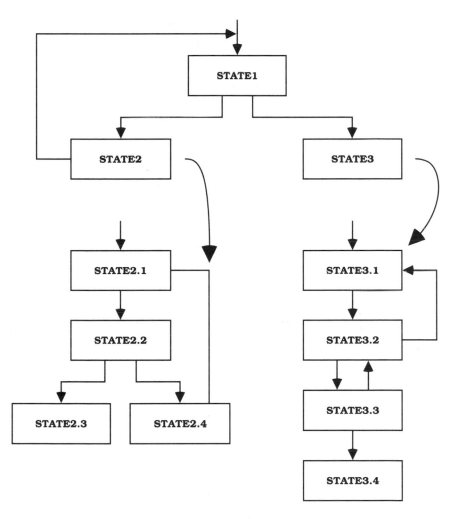

Figure 13.6(a): Two levels of STDs

An example of the need for a partitioned OLH diagram might be the automated teller machine (ATM) found in most banks; an OLH for the ATM object whose job is to synchronize the behavior of the various components of the ATM is shown in Figure 13.6(b).

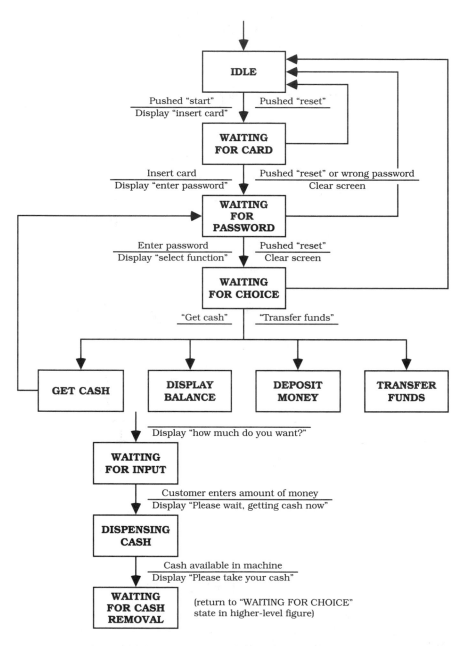

Figure 13.6(b): A partitioned OLH for an ATM machine

13.3 BUILDING THE OBJECT LIFE HISTORY DIAGRAM

Now that we have seen the notation for OLH diagrams, we briefly discuss the steps in building one. You can follow either of two approaches:

1. You can begin by identifying all possible object states, representing each one as a separate box on a sheet of paper (or on your favorite CASE tool). Then you can explore all meaningful connections (i.e, state changes) between the boxes.

2. Alternatively, you can begin with the initial state, and then methodically trace your way to the next state(s), and then from the secondary state(s) to the tertiary state(s), and so on.

Your approach will be dictated, in many cases, by the user with whom you are working, particularly if the user is the only one familiar with the behavior of the object. In any case, when you have finished building the preliminary OLH, you should carry out the following consistency-checking guidelines:

- *Have all states been defined*? Look at the object closely to see if there is any other observable behavior or any other condition that the object could be in besides the ones you have identified.

- *Can you reach all the states*? Have you defined any states that do not have paths leading into them?

- *Can you exit from all the nonfinal states*? As mentioned, the object may have one or more final states with multiple entrances into them, but all other states must have a successor state.

- *In each state, does the object respond properly to all possible conditions*? This is the most common error when building an OLH model: the systems analyst identifies the state changes when normal conditions occur, but fails to specify the behavior of the object for unexpected conditions. Suppose the analyst has modeled the behavior of an object as shown in Figure 13.7; he or she expects that the user will press a function key on his terminal to cause a change from state 1 to state 2 and a *different* function key to change from state 2 to state 3. But what if the user presses the same function key twice in a row? Or some other key? If the object behavior is not specified, there is a good chance that the designers and programmers will not program for it either, and the resulting system will exhibit unpredictable behavior under a variety of circumstances.

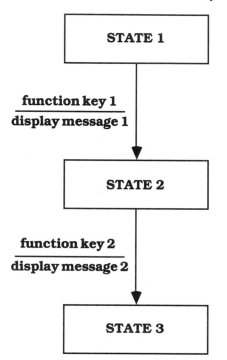

Figure 13.7: An incomplete OLH

13.4 THE RELATIONSHIP TO OTHER MODEL COMPONENTS

The OLH diagram can be used as a modeling tool by itself, as the user and analyst explore the details of each object in the system. However, it can be, and usually should be, used in conjunction with those other tools. This is illustrated in Figure 13.8; note that the *conditions* in the OLH typically correspond to *incoming* messages to class and object 2 in a separate "object communication diagram." Similarly, the *actions* on the OLH correspond to *outgoing* messages on the object communication diagram. This will become particularly apparent when we explore *messages* between objects in Chapter 14.

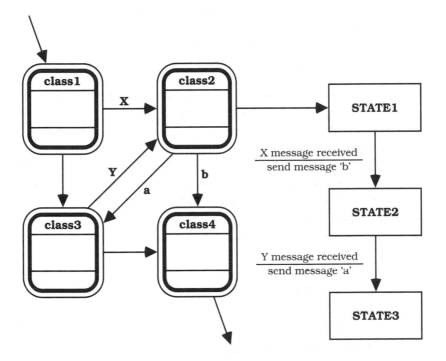

Figure 13.8: Relationship between OLH and object communication diagram

13.5 THE *SMALL BYTES* CASE STUDY

The first thing that occurs to us when we look at the OOA model we have developed thus far for the *Small Bytes* system is, "Wow! Do I really have to create an OLH diagram for every one of these classes and objects?"

This is a matter of some debate among OO methodologists. At one extreme is the camp that says, "Absolutely! You'll be struck down by the great Object-in-the-Sky if you don't develop a formal object life history of every class and object in the system!" At the other extreme is the laissez-faire camp that feels the diagrams shown in this chapter are more work than they're worth, that they are a distraction for the end users, and that the "business policy" that they capture could just as easily be incorporated into the description of *methods*, which we will discuss in the next chapter.

We take a middle ground in this book: OLH diagrams are useful for *all* objects in *some* systems, and typically for *some* objects in *all* systems. As we will see in the next chapter, OLH diagrams are useful as an informal brainstorming tool to help discover the existence of methods that might not otherwise be obvious; for that purpose, they could be casually sketched on the back of an envelope, and then thrown away when no longer needed.

But for the purposes of *this* chapter, the OLH diagrams serve the important purpose of documenting and explaining the complex behavior of classes and objects that would otherwise remain an amorphous mystery. The skeptic might say, "So what? It's great that the OLH helped you understand what the class and object are doing, but why does that mean you have to save it as part of a formal model?"

The most important answer is that the OLH helps verify the correctness and consistency of other parts of the model. It does so by focusing attention on two questions:

- What state does an object have to be in before it is capable of accepting, and responding to, a particular type of message?
- What state does an object have to be in before it can establish an instance connection (or break a connection) with another object?

Of course, in some cases, these questions may be trivial, and may require no deep thought at all. But if the object's behavior is complex, then it will be very important to ensure that it has been studied carefully—in which case, the OLH diagram should become part of the formal model of the system. This, in turn, means that there should be some way of storing it in a CASE environment, cross-checking it against other model components, and so on.

Thus, from a methodological perspective, a reasonable compromise between the two extremist camps described is: make the OLH diagrams an optional component of the model. Develop OLH diagrams only for those classes and objects whose behavior seems intrinsically complex after initial discussions with the user; in any case, don't bother with OLH diagrams of classes and objects that have only one or two states. For especially complex systems, where there are complex interactions between collaborating clusters of objects, consider life-history diagrams for the *relationships* that connect those objects.[3]

With this perspective, we conclude that most of the classes and objects in the *Small Bytes* system are sufficiently simple that they don't require a formal OLH diagram. Within the PUBLICATIONS subject, for example, we have the class hierarchy and object relationships shown in Figure 13.9, as first discovered in Chapter 11:

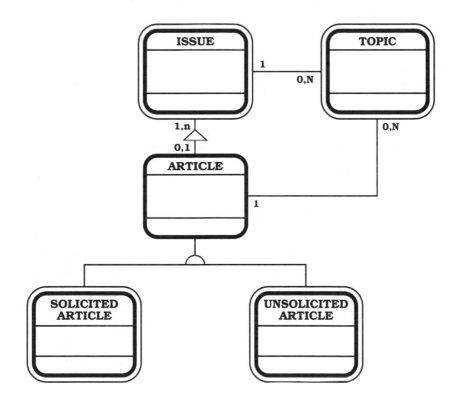

Figure 13.9: Class hierarchy for PUBLICATIONS subject

---

[3]An interesting point: the vast majority of OOA CASE tools don't support the concept of life-history diagrams for relationships (although some accomplish the same thing by allowing the user to create "associative objects").

What states can an ISSUE be in? The user's first response is automatic: "Either it's been published, or it hasn't been published!" The analyst's immediate instinct is to ignore this naive statement: of *course* the issue is either published or not-published: that would be determined by comparing the publication date (comprised of volume number and issue number) with today's date. The analyst's attention is focused instead—just as the reader's is likely to be—on the instance connections between ISSUE, TOPIC, and ARTICLE.

But the user is not so easily dismissed; the distinction between the states of published and not-published is not so trivial.[4] Indeed, says the user, there is a whole *series* of stages, or states, through which an issue of the magazine goes before it can be considered published. It begins as a gleam in the editor's eye; then, once it has been officially "launched," it is associated with a topic. Then comes such activities as this:

- Authors have been contacted, so the editor has some rough idea of the number of articles to expect (assuming a reasonable estimate of "attrition" from authors who fail to deliver). But it's impossible to tell how many pages the issue will consist of, because some authors write very short articles, and others write very long articles.
- Some of the articles have been received from the authors and uploaded into the magazine's desktop publishing system. But since we haven't gotten all the articles, we still don't know how many pages there will be.
- All the articles have been received and/or we have abandoned hope that we will ever get an article from some of the authors. At this point, a relatively final page count can be estimated, which can be used to tell the printer what quantity of paper should be ordered; this occurs several weeks before the final "camera-ready copy" is sent to the printer, but the printer needs that much lead time to deal with his suppliers.
- With the articles in hand, and with a tentative title for each article (which may or may not match what the authors have suggested—most authors propose unbelievably dull titles for their own articles), the graphic artist can be contacted to begin designing a "layout" for the first page of each article;

---

[4]To make matters worse, the user is married to the analyst in the real-world system from which this case study was drawn and has the annoying habit of following the analyst into the bathroom to harass him with problems like this while he is taking a shower.

this consists of a combination of photo-quality clip art and a bunch of fancy fonts for spelling out the author's name and the article's title—all which can be merged into the desktop publishing system in which the "body" of the articles are being edited and formatted.

- All the articles have been edited and formatted, so we now have a much more precise page count for the issue.

- The graphic artist finally comes back to us with his designs for each article. Invariably, he misspells the title and the author's name, but that is only a minor convenience. What the editor really has to watch out for is that the graphic artist sometimes gets carried away and designs a two-page "spread" for the opening of an article. This not only screws up formatting, page breaks and page counts, but it also implicitly presumes that the article can start on an odd-numbered page of the issue. It never occurs to the graphic artist that any of this could be a problem.

- After the editor has recovered from this shock, a final page count can be computed. But since the page count has to be a multiple of four (because the printer prints the magazine on large sheets of paper, which are then folded cleverly into the proper size), the total length of all the articles will then have a major impact on the two remaining components of each issue: the publisher's introduction at the beginning of the issue and the book reviews at the end of the issue. It's normally expected that these items will each be one or two pages, but sometimes the book review disappears entirely because of the page-count constraints; on the other hand, sometimes there are two book reviews so as to fill up the requisite number of pages.

- After the book review and introduction have been supplied and edited, the editor adds the final "boilerplate" material: the cover page, table of contents page, inside back cover (which may be the final page of the last article, or a subscription form, or even blank) and the outside back cover.

- *Then* it goes to the printer and can effectively be considered "published."[5]

---

[5]"Well," says the user, "that's not *really* true. The printer sends back 'blues' that have to be checked to make sure that nothing got dropped when the camera-ready copy got transferred onto film. Then we have to give the printer a final order for the number of copies we want and hope that neither they nor we were too far off on the estimate of how much paper to order. And then. . ." to which the analyst might well say, "*Enough!*"

If you have followed all this, it may have occurred to you about halfway through these nine states that our analyst has completely bungled the job so far. What's this about a printer? Where is that in our model? What's this about a graphic designer and a "design" for each article? Who ever said anything about an "introduction" and a "book review"? Our OOA model is missing a number of critical objects!

The user's response is predictable: "Oh. Well, I guess I forgot to tell you. . . but I assumed it was obvious. . . I mean, if you had *looked* at the magazine, you would have seen it. And besides, what's this got to do with the subscription system, which is what I thought you were working on?"

We leave it to the reader as an exercise to amend the class hierarchy to incorporate all this new information presented by the user. But before you get carried away with dozens of new classes, remember the user's final comment: What do your proposed new classes have to do with the overall *purpose* of the system?

Whatever you decide, it's evident that focusing on the life history of an object can do much more than just fill in some microscopic details; it may help spot major errors and omissions, and it can even lead to a complete reexamination of the problem.

Let's consider one more class from a life-history perspective: SUBSCRIPTIONS. The class hierarchy we developed in Chapter 10 is shown again in Figure 13.10. Having seen what happened when we examined an ISSUE more closely, we should not be surprised if we get a whole new perspective from our user when we ask the obvious question: "What happens to a subscription? What states can it be in?" Here's what our user says:

- "Well, of course, we *begin* by creating a new subscription when someone decides to subscribe. . ."

Aha! thinks the analyst. That means that the first "change-of-state" involves creating a new instance of a SUBSCRIPTION. It's beginning to look like the classical "create-read-update-delete" sequence.

But then the user pauses for a moment, looks off into space, and says, "Well, that's not actually true. . . sometimes it goes like this. . ."

- In some cases, we pick unsuspecting victims to whom we send a "trial" subscription for a few months—to see if they would like to subscribe on a regular, full-time basis.

- In other cases, we may have sent out a large-scale promotional offering a three-month trial subscription. Thus sometimes a person will decide on his own to initiate a trial subscription.
- Naturally, some of these trial subscriptions "convert" over to regular "paying" subscriptions. But some of them don't; they lapse and expire just like any other subscription.

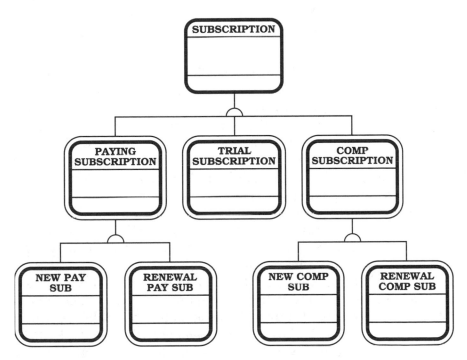

Figure 13.10: The SUBSCRIPTIONS Class Hierarchy

- And then, of course, we get the regular paying subscriptions from lots of people who have not gone through the trial subscription phase.
- In any case, once a "normal" subscription begins, it runs for a certain period of time until it's renewed or it expires. During this time, of course, the customer sometimes changes his address, his name, his company, his phone number, and goodness knows what else.

- Oh, I forgot: we have complimentary subscriptions too. They're basically the same as any other subscription, except (of course) they're free as far as the subscriber is concerned. But there is one difference: we decide whether we're going to renew such subscriptions on a complimentary basis. Normally, this is done on an annual basis, but sometimes it happens during the year—for example, if a comp subscriber moves without bothering to give us his new address, and doesn't notice he's missed a couple of issues, then we conclude that he must not want it badly enough to warrant sending it to him.

What does all this tell the analyst? First, we can breathe a sigh of relief: it doesn't appear that the user has surprised us with some new classes that we didn't know about. But one of the things this stream-of-consciousness description *does* tell us is that *objects can change the class to which they belong.* An instance of a trial subscription becomes an instance of a paying subscription (or it remains ultimately in the state of an "expired" trial subscription). A new paying subscription becomes a renewal paying subscription, and so forth.

You may recall from Chapter 10 that the analyst had some doubts about the class structure shown in Figure 13.10 when he first created it: What's so special about the distinction between "new" and "renewal" paying subscriptions, anyway? Let's defer consideration of that question for a moment, for there is an even more fundamental question: Why is it that our model presumes that *one instance* of a SUBSCRIPTION goes through all these states, possibly including even a change of the class to which it belongs? Why not look at the problem a different way: What if each state change "spawns" a new instance of an object, leaving the original instance intact?

The distinction is significant, as we'll see in a moment. But let's repeat the question: Why did we model it that way in the first place? The answer is devastating: *because that's the way the user is doing it in the current system!* The user currently has, as we recall from Chapter 8, a jury-rigged system consisting of a flat-file database program and a few spreadsheet programs on a Macintosh. It turns out that in that system, there is one physical copy of each subscription record; all the state changes just described are managed through a complex and ill-documented set of "status codes" buried within the record.

And the user is already aware of some of the consequences of that choice; as we mentioned, the distinction is significant. Each of the states in the life of a "-subscription" typically has a beginning date and an ending date, as well as various other attributes such as subscription price. But the current physical system has only one data field in each subscription record for start-date, end-date, subscription-price, and so on. The practical consequence of this approach, then, is that there is no "audit trail" showing the very object life history we are now trying to document.

So the notion of "spawning" new objects is perhaps a very practical approach. In terms of life cycles, we could imagine how the analyst might interpret part of the process described by the user: "When a TRIAL-SUBSCRIPTION object receives a message indicating that its associated SUBSCRIBER wants to convert to a paid subscription, then (1) it changes its state to 'frozen' and (2) it sends a message to the PAYING-SUBSCRIPTION class, asking it to create a new instance of itself with appropriate initial values."

But spawning new instances of an object does not mean that we need to have the elaborate class hierarchy shown in Figure 13.10. We are left with the question we deferred a few moments ago: What's so special about the distinction between "new," "renewal," "trial," and "complimentary" subscriptions?

At first glance, there is a strong temptation to collapse the entire hierarchy into a single class called SUBSCRIPTION. After all, they seem to have the same attributes: starting date, ending date, and so on. Obviously, the subscription price for a trial subscription and complimentary subscription is zero, but aside from that, it's the same attribute used to store a nonzero price for the paying subscribers.

But wait! This is a classic example of a programmer mentality—burying a "status code" by embedding it in a numeric data field. One could legitimately argue that for complimentary subscribers, *there is no "subscription price" field*—it simply isn't a relevant attribute. After all, that's what "complimentary" means: there is *no* price associated with the subscription. This is probably true of trial subscriptions, too, although our user points out that sometimes a promotional campaign will offer a trial subscription at a reduced "nuisance" price of $1.98, to discourage starving graduate students and other riff-raff who will never be able to pay the full price.

Why does any of this matter? Because one can imagine the kind of programming that would result from squashing all these into one SUBSCRIPTION CLASS. In one of the methods, there would be program logic that said, effectively, "IF the subscription price is zero,

THEN assume it's a complimentary subscription and do such-and-such; ELSE if the price is greater than zero but less than 50 percent of the full price, THEN assume it's a trial subscription and do this-and-that; OTHERWISE assume it's a paying subscription, and do the real stuff." As we will discuss in Chapter 21, object-oriented code filled with IF-THEN-ELSE statements is usually a danger sign that the class hierarchy was poorly organized.

In any case, it's in the *methods* that we are likely to see the substantial differences between the various subclasses of SUBSCRIPTION. The renewal policy is different for each; the strategy for soliciting renewals is different for each—different letters, different discounts and special offers, and so on—and it may even differ for first-time renewals as opposed to second-time and third-time renewals.

So what conclusion do we draw from this? First, the object life-history perspective has made us rethink the *Small Bytes* system in much more detail; it's virtually impossible for the systems analyst not to have a deeper understanding of the user's requirements after going through this process. In terms of the ISSUE class hierarchy, we have learned that there may be many more classes than we had originally suspected. In terms of the SUBSCRIPTIONS class hierarchy, we may well have concluded that the basic hierarchy is adequate; however, we might well decide to follow the "spawning" approach described earlier, in which case it would be appropriate to show instance connections between the various subclasses (each instance of a trial subscription is related to zero or one. . . or maybe more than one?. . . instance of a paying subscription, etc.).

13.6 THE ELEVATOR CASE STUDY

An interesting aspect of the elevator system is that while the *system's* behavior is obviously rather complex, the behavior of the various classes is relatively simple; indeed, our discussion of the binary-valued attributes for these classes in Chapter 12 leads us to believe that most of them will all have two states.

Looking at the BUILDING class hierarchy, for example, there is no need to spend any time on the BUILDING class itself. It has only one state, as far as this system is concerned: it exists. We might be tempted to say the same thing about a FLOOR; after all, we don't expect to see a floor dancing around, exhibiting different kinds of behavior.

But recall from Chapter 12 that our examination of required attributes uncovered an instance relationship between FLOOR and ELEVATOR: an elevator is either "at" a floor or is not at a floor. But this is a symmetric relationship: a floor either has an elevator within eight inches of it or it does not. This suggests that a floor oscillates between two states, as illustrated in Figure 13.11:

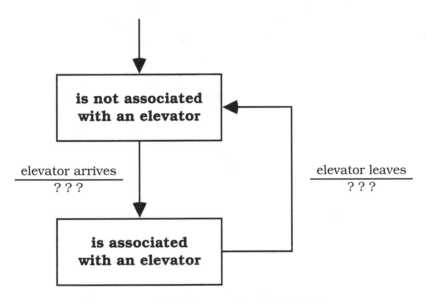

Figure 13.11: OLH diagram for the FLOOR class

This is not very profound, and we might be tempted to avoid inclusion of this OLH diagram in the formal model of the elevator system; as mentioned earlier in this chapter, many software engineers include OLH diagrams only for those classes whose behavior is nontrivial.

But before we throw Figure 13.9 into the wastebasket, let's ask a few questions. First: How do we know that the "arrives" condition and the "leaves" condition has occurred? We recall the answer from Chapter 12: it is the FLOOR-SENSOR that knows that such an event has occurred; although we haven't discussed the details of messages and methods yet (don't peek at Chapter 14 yet!), it is evident that the FLOOR-SENSOR will have to send a message to ELEVATOR or FLOOR, or possibly both.

What should a FLOOR do once it knows that an ELEVATOR has arrived in its vicinity, or departed to another floor? In the vocabulary of OLH diagrams, what *actions* need to be taken when the FLOOR changes state? The immediate thing we notice is that the instance connection between floor and an instance of ELEVATOR should be established or disconnected.

Naturally, our primary attention in such a scenario will be focused on the ELEVATOR: we expect the elevator to open or close its door appropriately. But that is the responsibility of the ELEVATOR; it has nothing to do with FLOOR. On the other hand, a FLOOR knows its component parts; it knows that it is attached to either one or two SUMMONS-LIGHTs and SUMMONS-BUTTONs. So, while the ELEVATOR goes on its merry way, the job of the FLOOR is to send a message to the appropriate SUMMONS-LIGHT to turn itself off (if the elevator has just arrived), and to enable/disable the SUMMONS-BUTTON. This will all be documented, as we will see in Chapter 14, with appropriate message connections.

14

Object Services

Thus far, we have concentrated on the modeling of the class hierarchies, the instance connections between classes and objects, the attributes and internal behavior of the objects. Now we focus on the final component of the OOA analysis model: the *services* and the *messages* between classes and objects.

In an earlier book,[1] Peter Coad and I used the term "service" to describe this component of a class and object, instead of the more commonly used term "method" from object-oriented programming languages. The term "service" was chosen because we thought it would be more meaningful to nontechnical users; others have used the equally attractive term "operation" to describe the same concept. However, it is clear that the OOP and OOD implementation technology has invaded the pure world of systems analysis; most systems analysts I have seen using OOA during the past few years have tended to use the term "method." Indeed, just as innocent users have acquired a veneer of computer literacy by spouting terms like "byte" and "LAN," so it seems that the more erudite of our user community even know what a "method" is. But not all users have been thus tainted, so we'll continue the fight; we'll use the term "service" in this chapter.

A service is the processing carried out by an object when it receives a message specifically directed to it; the presence of the service within the object is shown graphically in Figure 14.1(a). Messages, as we will see later in this chapter, are documented with an arrow from the sending class and object to the receiving class and object.

[1]Peter Coad and Edward Yourdon, *Object-Oriented Analysis*, 2nd ed. (Englewood Cliffs, NJ: Yourdon Press/Prentice Hall, 1990).

Figure 14.1(a): Graphical representation of a service

An alternative notation, favored by Booch and others, empha-sizes the fact that the services serve as the external interface to other classes and objects, as shown in Figure 14.1(b): [2]

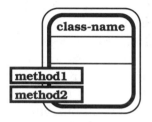

Figure 14.1(b): Alternative notation for a service

Most OOA methodologies assume that the services document-ed with diagrams like Figures 14.1(a) and 14.1(b) are services that are available for, and defined for, each instance in the class. This raises an interesting question: What about the possibility of services that are associated with the class as a whole, but *not* with individual instances? The distinction may be too subtle for the user to care about (which is probably why it is omitted from some OOA method-ologies), but an OO programmer can immediately anticipate why this might be useful: it might be preferable, for example, to allow the class to create new instances of its objects, but not allow instances within the class to spawn additional instances of themselves; or we might want to query the class to determine the number of instances

---

[2]Note that this implies that *all* of the methods are "visible" or "exported." But in most applications, some of the methods will also be "private" or "internal," that is, only accessible to other methods within the same class, or perhaps within the same class hierarchy.

it contains.[3] This is one of several embellishments on the basic idea of services and messages, which we will discuss in more detail shortly.

From a methodological perspective, we must first discover what services are required by each class and object; while this is often straightforward, there are some useful strategies that come in handy for the more obscure cases. Next, we will document the messages used by classes and objects to communicate with each other. And, finally, we must specify the user's detailed business policy for each of the services we have identified. As usual, we will return to the *Small Bytes* and elevator case studies at the end of the chapter, to illustrate some of these issues.

14.1 DISCOVERING REQUIRED SERVICES

How do we determine what services a class and object require to carry out their required behavior? There are five "fundamental" kinds of services that are now described in more detail:

- "implicit" services, such as create, modify, search, and delete
- services associated with message connections
- services associated with instance connections
- services associated with attributes
- services suggested by the object life-history diagrams

14.1.1 Implicit Services

Virtually every class and object in an OOA model will need a set of services to create a new instance of itself, to modify attributes within its instance, to select an instance based on a "key word" identifier, and to delete an instance. These are known in the Coad-Yourdon methodology as "implicit" services and are typically not even shown on the OOA diagrams.[4]

---

[3]This raises a host of related possibilities, then: we might imagine attributes that are associated with the class, but not with its instances; this could be useful for keeping a global variable such as "last account number assigned" in a CUSTOMERs class. We might want to have different notation to show messages sent to class-only methods versus class and object methods, although one could also argue that the sending object should not have to be aware of this distinction. In any case, these nuances have been omitted from the presentation in this book.

[4]Ideally, this would be an option that the analyst could specify when working with his CASE tool. Sometimes the implicit methods are important and need to be seen and discussed. Most of the time, though, they simply clutter up the diagram and need to be hidden. So the question is really one of deciding what gets hidden and what remains visible: this is a CASE issue, not a methodology issue.

As always, the details will vary from project to project, and from system to system. But the details are typically just that: details. We will discuss the specification of a service's detailed processing requirements in Section 14.3. For now, the question is simply: Does the class and object require a service to create, delete, modify, and select its instances? If so, then to the extent that we want to show them at all on our object diagrams, they should be written into the list of services shown in Figure 14.1.

Actually, the issue of "modifying" an object is usually deferred at this point; the only thing we can imagine modifying is the individual attributes within an object, and it's unlikely that we would have a list of services called "modify attribute x," "modify attribute y," and so on. The modification is usually the result of a message connection that has already been identified as part of an application-specific "event" that the user can describe; this is discussed further below.

14.1.2 Services Associated with Message Connections

Services and message connections go hand in hand: the discovery of one typically leads to the discovery of the other, and as a result, both are added to the model in parallel. As we have seen in previous chapters, it often becomes evident during the development of the OOA model that one object will need to "talk" to another object; thus we may have begun sketching in the message connections (using notation that we will describe further in Section 14.2) even before the services have been fully identified.

The strategy is quite simple: if you see that a message is being sent to an object, then that object needs to have one or more services to receive the message and carry out the appropriate processing. For now, all we need to do is give the service a name and include it on our diagram; the details will come later.

14.1.3 Services Associated with Object Relationships

In Chapter 11, we discussed the concept of object relationships, or instance connections, as part of the *static* model of classes and objects. However, there is almost always a "dynamic" component as well: except in rare cases, the *specific* connections between an instance of class A and an instance of class B will be established and broken (or "disconnected") as the objects execute. Hence, we may need appropriate services in one, or possibly both, objects involved in such a relationship.

Again, the details are project specific: sometimes the making and/or breaking of a connection will be the result of processing some other message. In our *Small Bytes* system, for example, we might imagine that an AUTHOR object would send a message to the SUBSCRIPTION class (or perhaps to the COMPLIMENTARY SUB-SCRIPTION subclass) to create a new instance, to provide the author with a year's free subscription. The response from that message would probably include an "object-identifier" of the newly created complimentary subscription; this would allow the AUTHOR object to effectively establish the required relationship.

So in many cases, then, the relationships that we documented on our model in Chapter 11 serve as a cross-check to ensure that we have not left out any required services. For each such relationship on the model, the analyst should ask: "What service allows this relationship to be established? What service causes the relationship to be disconnected?"

14.1.4 Services Associated with Attributes

As noted, various services will be needed to allow external objects to access and modify an object's internal attributes. For the most part, this should evolve in a natural fashion by considering the implicit services, the message connections, and the instance connections.

Hence, the attributes also serve as a checklist: after the analyst is reasonably sure that he has found most of the required services, he should ask the following questions for each attribute: "Does the attribute need to be accessed or modified by anything *outside* the object I am looking at? If so, what service accomplishes this?" Note that, completely aside from the principle of encapsulation and infor-mation hiding, some attributes may be entirely "private" to the object in question: no matter what kind of messages are sent to it, it may refuse to divulge its secrets about certain attributes.

For real-time systems, there is often another perspective: Do any of the attributes need to be "monitored" to determine their cur-rent value on a periodic basis? For both real-time and non-real-time systems, do any of the attributes act as "triggers"—that is, Is the object supposed to do something when their value exceeds some threshold or strays outside some range of values? Whether this is determined internally or externally, it may suggest the need for additional (possibly concurrent) services.[5]

14.1.5 Services Suggested by OLH Diagrams

In Chapter 13, we noted that a careful investigation of the life history of each object can reveal not only the object's detailed behavior, but also some "global" characteristics of the system. One of those global characteristics is the discovery of services that might not have been obvious otherwise.

The basic life history for any object, as suggested in Chapter 13, might begin with a "create-read-update-delete" sequence; these states are already covered by the "implicit" services discussed in Section 14.1.1. But if there are any additional states—as there typically will be in any but the more trivial objects—then they, too, must be handled by appropriate services.

The services are intimately associated with the "conditions" and "actions" of the life-history diagrams. In the straightforward case, as we discussed in Chapter 13, the condition that causes a state change will be an incoming message; and the action that results from the state change will be an outgoing message (typically based on whatever calculations the object has to carry out internally). The incoming message must be received by a service, and that same service is typically involved in creating the outgoing message.

14.2 DOCUMENTING MESSAGE CONNECTIONS

Now that we have discussed the concept of messages, let's look at the graphical notation. A message sent to a specific instance (or to a set of instances) within a class is shown graphically in Figure 14.2(a);

---

[5]But the overall architecture of the system might be quite different, depending on whether the threshold condition is discovered internally or externally. Consider, for example, a PERSON object that has an attribute of "temperature." The "external" scenario involves a DOCTOR object sending a message, periodically, to the PERSON, saying, "Tell me your temperature. Then I'll determine whether you're sick." The "internal" scenario effectively has the PERSON saying to himself, "I know my own temperature. I'll damn well decide for myself whether I'm sick, and if I am, *then* I'll tell the doctor." In either case, the PERSON has to have a method that can determine the current value of temperature, and perhaps update it with the latest thermometer reading.

a message sent to the class itself is shown in Figure 14.2(b).[6] Although the arrow points in only one direction (from the sender to the receiver, obviously), *it implies two-way communication*: that is, the receiver is expected to respond in some appropriate fashion to each message it receives.

Figure 14.2(a): A message sent to an object

Figure 14.2(b): A message sent to the class

Obviously, most systems involve a great deal of communication between the various classes and objects; thus we are likely to see the kind of diagrams shown in the earlier chapters annotated with message connections. If we remove the instance connections and some of the other details, what's left is often called an "object communication diagram."[7]

[6]Note that the graphical distinction between Figures 14. 2(a) and 14.2(b) is quite small: the arrow has simply been extended a few millimeters into the receiving object-symbol, until it touches the interior boundary of the class. This might be easily overlooked by a user or analyst glancing casually at the diagram, and there is a natural temptation to use entirely different forms of arrows. But as we will see, there are many other nuances of message connections—and if we use a different graphical icon for each, there can be a dozen different shades, colors, patterns, and thicknesses of arrows between objects. We have deliberately adopted a minimalist notational convention in this chapter and throughout most of this book

[7]Isn't this the same as a data flow diagram from structured analysis? Well, not quite: the bottom-level DFD involves "bubbles" that communicate via "data flows" to other bubbles. But the bubbles are presumed to be pure function; meanwhile, the standard DFD has another notation to represent the "data store," or a collection of pure data. And the arrows connecting bubbles and data stores are presumed to be unidirectional, without the added assumption of a "response." However, if we aggregate a cluster of such DFD bubbles, together with the data store they operate upon, we can represent it as a single bubble in a higher-level DFD; this is common practice with "leveled" data flow diagrams, regardless of whether the leveling is performed

Note that the arrow connects to an unspecified spot in the middle of the receiving class and object—roughly at the belly-button, rather than the head or the feet. In most OOA methodologies, there is no significance to the topological placement of the arrows; to make the diagram look presentable, it might be convenient to attach the arrow to the top, sides, or bottom of the receiving class and object.

But there is one obvious problem with this: it's not clear which service the message is being sent to. Also, the notation does not indicate what information (or parameters) are being supplied to the receiving object, nor does it indicate what information the receiving object communicates back to the sender. In many cases, this is a level of detail that neither the analyst nor the user wants to see on the diagrams; however, if it turns out to be important, then the notation originally shown in Figure 14.1(b) may turn out to be more convenient. An example, with additional annotations to show message parameters, is shown in Figure 14.3:

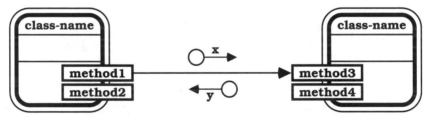

Figure 14.3: A more detailed message connection

Whether this level of detail is more appropriate for analysis or design is a matter of personal choice; some analysts and users would rebel at the detail of Figure 14.3, and others would argue that they can't live without it. As noted earlier, it should be implemented as a flexible option in the CASE tool that supports OOA and OOD.

There are additional details that may or may not require special documentation. As noted earlier, the simple message connection is sent from an instance of one class to an instance of another class; hence the message must indicate *which* instance it is intended for (usually by specifying a unique object identifier or "keyword" attribute). But it's also possible for a message to be sent to multiple

top down or bottom up. Because the bubbles in the intermediate-level DFDs do represent encapsulations of function and data, they could be considered virtually the same as the object communication diagrams shown in Figures 14.2(a) and 14.2(b). However, this does not mean that such high-level DFD bubbles are "good" objects: if the bubble-partitioning rationale is based on functional decomposition, it is quite possible that the functions and data stores encapsulated within the high-level bubble will be an unrelated hodgepodge.

instances (e. g., to all the SUBSCRIPTION instances which are due to expire in the next three months) or to multiple classes within the system. Presumably, those details will become evident when we study the sending service's detailed policy description; we have chosen, somewhat arbitrarily, *not* to show it on the object communication diagrams.

What about a message sent from one service to another service within the same object? We could imagine drawing this in the fashion shown in Figure 14.4; this is a familiar to object-oriented programmers, whose languages allow messages to be sent to "self" or "this."[8]

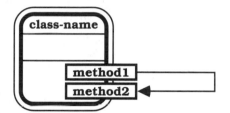

Figure 14.4: An object sending a message to itself

Because most of us have grown up in a "von Neumann" world of single-CPU sequential processing systems, we have another built-in assumption about message connections: we assume that the sending object pauses until it has received a response to its message, and we assume that the receiving object goes back to sleep once it has made its response. In addition, there is an even more subtle assumption that the receiving object will only be responding to one message at a time.

But in a "perfect technology" model, none of these constraints is imposed; if the constraint exists at all, it must be associated with the application itself, as described by the user. Thus we might imagine a scenario where the sending object continues to compute, asynchronously, while the receiving object is doing its job. And we might imagine a scenario where the receiving object responds appropriately to a message and then continues computing. And we might want to distinguish between those objects that can process more than one message (and more than one *type* of message) from those that behave in the more traditional "single-thread" fashion.

---

[8]This requires no change in the notational scheme, but some analysts might reject the concept as being too "purist." "If a method needs to invoke another method in the same class," one analyst retorted to me after looking at Figure 14.4, "it can bloody well make a good old-fashioned subroutine call." I decided not to argue the point.

All these scenarios could be appropriately documented on the object communication diagram—each with its own form of message arrow, as well as additional annotations to describe the behavior of the sending and receiving objects. Indeed, this might be quite valuable for certain types of real-time systems, but for other types of systems, it would lead to such an overwhelming array of graphical symbols that a Ph.D. in computer science would be required to read the diagrams. And, with the exception of some real-time systems, there is an important point to emphasize: most of these "scenarios" involve what the user would regard as "low-level" details. Hence, they should not be visible on the diagrams at all; they should be hidden within the detailed description of the services themselves or in some other supporting textual information within a CASE repository.

14.3 SPECIFYING SERVICES IN DETAIL

Having identified the necessary services for each object, and having documented the message connections between objects, we are left with one final task: describing the detailed behavior of each object. Our advice in this area is simple: continue doing this part of the job the same way you've done in the past.

Each service describes a *function* to be carried out upon receipt of a message. If the objects have been well defined, then each service will be small and highly cohesive; we will discuss this further in Chapter 21. Thus it should be possible to describe the user's business policy for each service compactly in some semi-formal notation or in a paragraph or two of narrative text.

Most organizations already have some standards in this area: some use "structured English," others use action diagrams, flowcharts, Nassi-Shneiderman diagrams, decision tables, or even a high-level language like Ada. If it worked well before, *and* if the objects have been well-designed, then the same approach should continue to work well with OOA.

Of course, some services may turn out to be complex; even though the service can be identified with a simple phrase, perhaps the details of its requirements are extremely elaborate. In this case, the traditional methods of functional decomposition should be used. Thus it may turn out to be useful to document the details of complex services using structure charts, data flow diagrams, or various other notational schemes from structured analysis/design and other conventional methodologies. Aside from the question of methodological purity (i.e., Has OOA been somehow tainted by allowing the use of a structure chart to model low-level details?), there is also the question of CASE support: Does the CASE tool support both object diagrams and structured analysis diagrams? We will discuss this in Chapters 23 and 24.

14.4 THE *SMALL BYTES* CASE STUDY

To document the service layer for the *Small Bytes* case study would fill almost an entire book: each of the 25 classes is likely to have 5 to 10 services, each of which would take a page to describe in detail. Indeed, if this were a real project, many software developers simply wouldn't bother: having reached the level of detail provided by the previous chapters, they would simply begin implementing the system by writing code.

Assuming that the services could be implemented directly in a reasonably powerful 4GL, or a high-level language like Ada or Smalltalk, this might not be such a bad idea. It's highly unlikely that the user would ever read the code to confirm the correctness of the "policy" expressed by the services, but on the other hand, it's also somewhat unlikely that a typical user in a small publishing organization would read 100–200 pages of service descriptions, no matter how they were documented. Since the system is not carrying out life-critical functions (for example, nobody is going to die instantaneously if a subscription is processed incorrectly), the consequences of a misunderstanding of the user requirements are not so dire. And if a service is omitted (because the analyst/implementer didn't think of it, or the user forgot to mention it), a 4GL development environment would probably make it fairly easy to add a new service, even after the service was fully implemented.

This appears to be an argument against the rigor and formality of a full-blown OOA approach. But rigor and formality have to be balanced against the political reality of a situation where the user wants to see something implemented *now*. If it would take an additional month to identify all the services for the *Small Bytes* classes, and to document their requirements—during which time there are no tangible results to demonstrate—then the project runs a non-trivial risk of being canceled by an impatient user. The best of all worlds would be an evolutionary prototype, in which the service specifications were written in a high-level language that could be directly executed.

In any case, we will illustrate some of the issues of the service layer of the *Small Bytes* system by examining the required services for a subscription. We recall from Chapter 10 that the SUBSCRIP-TIONS subject has the class hierarchy shown in Figure 14.5:

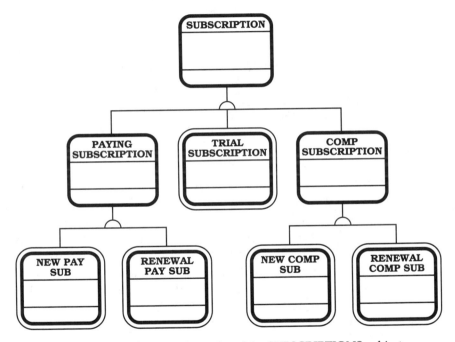

Figure 14.5: The class hierarchy of the SUBSCRIPTIONS subject

Let's start with the abstract superclass at the top of the hierarchy. The basic attributes and services for SUBSCRIPTION might look like the example shown in Figure 14.6:

Figure 14.6: Attributes and services for SUBSCRIPTION class

Note that we have shown attributes of "for-whom" and "invoice" enclosed within square brackets; this is an informal notation to indicate that we expect to see object relationships, or instance connections between SUBSCRIPTION and PERSON, and between SUBSCRIPTION and INVOICE; when we reach the design stage of our OO development project, it is quite likely that these instance connections will be implemented in the form of pointers that will exist within the object alongside the other attributes.

The services shown for SUBSCRIPTION are often known as "CRUD" services (for "create," "read," "update," and "delete"); they are sometimes referred to as "implicit" or "built-in" services, that is, the kind of services that we would expect to see for *every* class.

What kind of user policy would we expect to see for the "create a new subscription" service? One possibility is shown in Figure 14.7:

CREATE SUBSCRIPTION using this-person, start-date, end-date, number-of-copies, subscription-price, amount-paid.
Send message to PERSON: does this-person exist?
    If not, send message to PERSON class to create new instance
Create new instance of SUBSCRIPTION class and initialize with values of this-person, start-date, end-date, number-of-copies, subscription-price.
Is amount-paid equal to subscription-price?
    If not, send message to INVOICE class to create new instance

Figure 14.7: Specification for create new subscription

Because of the inheritance hierarchy, this service will be inherited by all the subclasses of SUBSCRIPTION. Thus we need to ask the user whether the same subscription-creation policy applies to all the subclasses; if not, we need to provide a new service that will override the definition of the superclass service. For example, it's reasonable to assume that PAYING SUBSCRIPTION in Figure 14.5 will inherit *exactly* the specification shown in Figure 14.7; perhaps a TRIAL SUBSCRIPTION should, too, if the user's policy is simply that a trial subscription is granted at a lower price than a "normal" subscription. But a COMPLIMENTARY SUBSCRIPTION definitely needs a new service; by its very definition, there is no money to be paid (which also means that the attributes of subscription-price and amount-paid do not really belong in the SUBSCRIPTION superclass), and there should never be any attempt to "connect" the subscription to an INVOICE.

Even more questions arise when we examine the subclass RENEWAL PAYING SUBSCRIPTION. It might be appropriate to simply inherit the service shown in Figure 14.7, but the name doesn't seem appropriate—what we're doing here is not creating an entirely new subscription, but merely a new instance of a renewal. . . of a subscription that already exists!

It's easy to change the *name* of the service in Figure 14.7 (which we should have done from the very beginning) to more appropriately describe what the service is doing—namely, creating a new instance of the class to which it is attached. But more important is the subtle implication of our user's last comment: a renewal is "linked" to the original subscription (or the previous year's renewal) that spawned it. At the very least, this will highlight an instance connection that we might not have seen before: instances of RENEWAL PAYING SUBSCRIPTION are connected to other such instances, and/or to instances of NEW PAYING SUBSCRIPTION.

When we have finished a similar analysis of the other services, it might become apparent that, in fact, there is no difference between a "new" subscription and a "renewal" subscription except that a "new" subscription has no previous subscriptions to which it should be linked. In this case, we might conclude that our class hierarchy should be simplified, as shown in Figure 14.8:

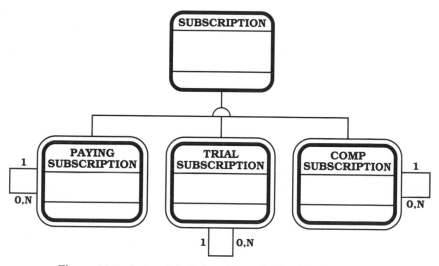

Figure 14.8: A simplified class hierarchy for SUBSCRIPTION

The presence of this new instance connection means that the "create a new instance" service has to be clever enough to figure out *which* previous subscription it should be connected to. Sometimes this is obvious, for the *Small Bytes* subscriber effectively says, "I have a subscription which expires on December 31st; please renew it." But in other cases, especially with some of the subscription agencies that deal with *Small Bytes*, it is far less obvious: the user may innocently believe that he or she is creating a completely new subscription, and we will need to depend on the "create a new instance" service to be clever enough to determine whether there are any other existing instances associated with the same subscriber, for which the expiration date implies that the new transaction is actually a renewal.[9]

---

[9]Sometimes the situation is even more obscure: subscriber A from company X has a subscription that expires on December 31. On December 15, an innocent-looking subscription form appears from a subscription agency indicating that subscriber B, also from company X, wants a subscription beginning January 1, and that subscriber A's subscription should be terminated. It might not be apparent that what's *really* happening here is that subscriber A is leaving the company and has turned over his or her subscription to subscriber B. So what's really happening is a combination of a name change and a renewal.

There is one last *major* service that we have overlooked; it was suggested by the discussion, which talked about a subscription "spawning" a renewal subscription. One of the most important things that a subscription knows about itself is when it expires! And, from an object-oriented perspective, it is the subscription that should be smart enough to do something *before* it has expired, for example, generate a series of renewal letters to the subscriber, beseeching him or her to send in a renewal check.

14.5 THE ELEVATOR CASE STUDY

Rather than examining an individual class and its services, as we did for the *Small Bytes* system, we will take a different approach with the elevator system: let's look at the message communication *between* services. This is, in fact, quite likely what an analyst would do when discussing this system with a "real" user: the classes and their respective services are, for the most part, quite simple. It is the *interaction* between the classes and objects that is interesting.

The model shown in Figure 14.9 assumes that the elevator is "smart" enough to know that it has reached a floor sensor; thus the "thread" of 11 messages is initiated when this event occurs. Naturally, the user might have an entirely different opinion about the requirements of his elevator system; thus this model would simply be the starting point for discussions and negotiations with the user.

The other important thing to note about this model is the presence of a "controller" class. In Chapter 9, we argued that a "controller" is not part of the "essential" requirements for an elevator system, even if the user described it in his narrative description. Indeed, that is still the author's opinion—and the arguments for eliminating the controller become more persuasive when we see the consequences of including it in the model. Note that the vast majority of the messages in Figure 14.9 occur between elevator components and this mysterious (and quite artificial) controller; note also that it is a "singleton" class—that is, there is only one instance of the controller, which hardly makes it an interesting class.

As an exercise, the reader is invited to consider the changes that would be made to Figure 14.9 if the controller were eliminated. In such a scenario, the elevator components would be communicating directly with one another, and the two services presently embedded within the controller class would presumably be moved within the elevator class.

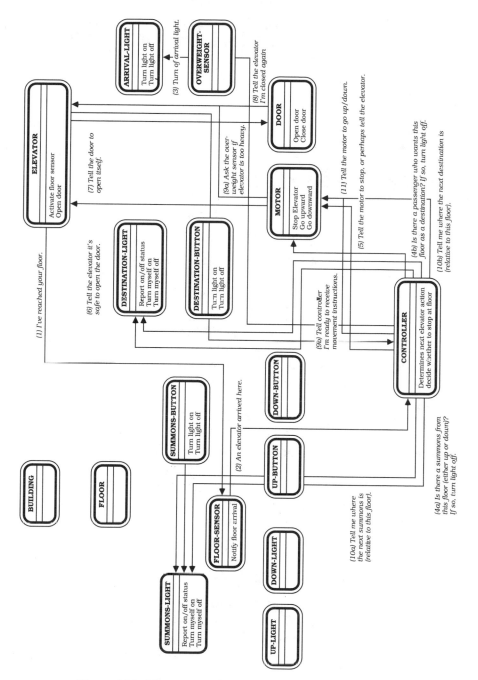

Figure 14.9: Messages and services for the elevator system

247

PART IV
OBJECT-ORIENTED DESIGN

15

Overview Of OOD

After spending the last several chapters discussing issues of systems analysis, we are now ready to move into the world of design. With older methodologies, this was an entirely different world: different notation, different vocabulary, different CASE tools, and so on. With OO methodologies, the boundary between analysis and design is blurred and indistinct; this may have been accidental in the early days of OO, but now it is a conscious and deliberate feature of the methodology. This is particularly true, as we noted in Chapter 3, for prototyping environments, and where the software engineers have a common development environment for *all* their project activities. If one asks the project team whether they are doing analysis, design, or programming at any particular instant in the project, their answer is likely to be "Yes."

In this brief chapter, we provide an overview of the design and construction activities in an OO project. Subsequent chapters then deal with a number of detailed issues involving OOD notation, strategies, goodness criteria, and so on.

15.1 WHAT DOES OOD CONSIST OF?

Ever since the first waterfall methodologies were conceived, software engineers have made a distinction between analysis and design. Analysis is concerned with *what* the system must do; design is concerned with *how* the requirements will be implemented.

Analysis, as we have suggested in the previous several chapters, usually takes place with the assumption that "perfect" technology is available; design usually takes place with the conscious or unconscious assumption that the system will be implemented on hardware platform X, under operating system Y, and with programming language Z.

While this distinction is usually helpful in separating the various issues that the software engineers have to worry about, Shlaer and Mellor make the interesting observation that

> . . . this two-way separation between Problem and Solution, What and How, or Analysis and Design, is overly simplistic. Instead, there are many layers of problem-solution pairs between an application and the computer science abstractions that implement that application. Rather than distinguish between analysis and design by problem/solution, and so on, we should instead distinguish on the basis of subject matter, that is, by *problem domain*.[1]

The situation has become further muddled by the fact that issues that were traditionally considered "pure" design in the 1970s and 1980s have now moved into the area traditionally reserved for analysis. A good example of this is the user-interface component of a system: in olden days, we might show the user a mock-up of report layouts and input screens on a dumb terminal, but it was all pretty simple; the *hard* part was figuring out how to make it work with a telecommunications package like Consumer Information Control System. Now the tables have turned: if one has a GUI-builder package, implementation may be rather straightforward; the hard part is figuring out, with the user, what the windows and graphical icons should look like.

Even with all these problems, though, it remains useful to think of design and analysis as distinct activities. They may be overlapped; indeed, they may be taking place at the same time in a typical project. The detailed "subactivities" may have changed, as has happened with GUIs. But there is still a fundamental distinction between *what* and *how* that most software engineers recognize. Indeed, the danger of *not* recognizing this distinction is that the analyst or (shudder) the user may begin to incorporate far too many assumptions and con-

---

[1]Sally Shlaer and Stephen J. Mellor, "A Deeper Look . . . at the Transition from Analysis to Design," *Journal of Object-Oriented Programming*, January 1993, p. 16.

straints about the implementation technology into the statement of requirements; most readers, for example, would agree that this has been done with the elevator case study discussed in this book.

So what is design—and in particular, what is object-oriented design? Fundamentally, it consists of three things:

- *Notation*—so we can communicate our ideas about the design to other members of the project team, and to interested outsiders
- *Strategies*—so we don't always begin each project as if this is the first time the human race has ever considered tackling a problem of this kind, and so that the designs for common domains of problems will begin to fall into familiar "patterns" of solutions.
- *Goodness criteria*—so we can have an objective way of evaluating a design to see if it should be accepted, rejected, or revised

These are discussed in more detail in the paragraphs that follow.

15.2 OOD NOTATION(S)

Analysis methodologies have been moving toward graphical representations of user requirements for the past decade, but design methodologies have had this characteristic for an even longer period of time. Even before structured design popularized the concept of structure charts in the mid-1970s, software engineers were using HIPO diagrams, flowcharts, and a variety of other diagramming representations. Thus it should not be a surprise that OOD also uses a graphical modeling notation.

The question is: What kind of representation do we need, and how different must it be from the OOA representation we saw in previous chapters? Since design is more concerned with implementation, it should not surprise us to see certain OOD methodologies that have representations for "tasks," "modules," "processors," "queues," and other familiar hardware/software components. Nevertheless, most OOD methodologies make a fundamental assumption: the OOD notation should be as close as possible to the OOA notation.

With this in mind, we will explore some common OOD notations in Chapter 16.

15.3 OOD STRATEGIES

Given a set of requirements, as documented with an OOA model, how does the software engineer go about contriving an OO design? Where does he start? What steps does he take? What kind of "framework," or "architecture," should he expect to end up with?

A highly creative software engineer might answer, "Who cares? Whatever happens . . . will happen. *Que sera, sera*." And many software engineers are rather proud of the fact that their design is intrinsically different from the design that might have been created by another software engineer on the planet. But this is the attitude of the artist, the craftsman who enjoys "hand-crafting" the solution to every problem. One of the objectives of OOD and all other methodologies is to introduce some consistency and predictability into the software development process. We will probably never reach the point where 100 software engineers, given the same set of requirements, will come up with exactly the same design, but it would be nice if their efforts fell into three or four predictable patterns.

In the meantime, we may have a more immediate problem: some software engineers come up with no design. They are stymied, and don't know where to begin. One of the objectives of the design strategies discussed in Chapter 17 is to remedy this form of "writer's block."

15.4 OOD GOODNESS CRITERIA

While some software engineers may find it impossible to derive any design from an OOA set of requirements, the other extreme is worrisome for many managers: if 100 designers propose 100 different designs, how do we know which one is best? Or, if we can't determine "best-ness," how can we avoid those that are worst? On a more practical basis (assuming that most managers don't have the luxury of a 100-person design competition for every project!), how can we evaluate the *one* design proposed by the lone designer on the project? How do we know if it's any good?

In some organizations, this kind of discussion degenerates into emotional arguments about "efficiency," "elegance," "flexibility," and so forth. But most software engineers will agree that there are some well-known practices (or "patterns," to use the term suggested in Section 15.3) that simply don't work: every time a system exhibits those patterns, horrible testing and maintenance problems ensue.

Older methodologies, such as structured design, have a well-established set of design criteria; among these are such well-known concepts as *coupling* and *cohesion*. We will see in Chapter 21 that there are similar guidelines for OOD—and that some of these guidelines are essentially the same as for older methodologies, while some have a distinctly unique OO "flavor."

15.5 OTHER ISSUES

What else does the software engineer have to worry about, once he leaves the warm, fuzzy world of analysis? Obviously, even the design created by an OOD methodology is not the final product of a software project: we must translate the design into some programming language, and then test the resulting code.

This book does not discuss the details of object-oriented programming per se; however, it is important to realize that the programming language can have a significant impact on the design process, as well as the mind-set of the designer. Indeed, even the methodology can be affected: several commercial forms of OOD in the marketplace in the early 1990s are evidently influenced by the methodologist's knowledge of, or preference for, such languages as Ada, Eiffel, C++, Smalltalk, and so on. These language influences will be discussed in Chapter 20.

Testing has not disappeared, either: no matter how elegant the OOA and OOD models, and no matter how powerful the OOP programming language, object-oriented systems still need to be tested. What's different about testing in an OO environment? What testing strategies exist? We will discuss these questions, as well as the relatively limited set of answers to those questions, in Chapter 22.

16

OOD Notation

Before we plunge into the details of OOD strategies and guidelines, we need to discuss notation. How does the designer explain what he is doing? What kind of notational representation does he need to explain what he is doing?

Some may argue that notation is not all that important—that it is the *ideas* that count. But an eminent architect, Christopher Alexander, sums up the importance of notation with the following comment:

> If you can't draw a diagram of it, it isn't a pattern. If you think you have a pattern, you must be able to draw a diagram of it. This is a crude, but vital, rule. A pattern defines a field of spatial relations, and it must therefore always be possible to draw a diagram for every pattern. In the diagram, each part will appear as a labeled or colored zone, and the layout of the parts expresses the relation which the pattern specifies. If you can't draw it, it isn't a pattern.[1]

By now, the reader is probably well aware of the recommendation we will make in this book: *wherever possible, use the same notation for OOA* **and** *OOD.* This will strike some "old-timer" methodology users, for example, those who grew up with structured analysis and structured design, as rather revolutionary, so the chapter begins with an explanation and justification of that recommendation. Next, we investigate the additional things for which the designer might need a graphical representation in OOD; and finally, we examine some examples from the various methodologies of Booch, Rumbaugh, Firesmith, and others.

---

[1]Christopher Alexander, *The Timeless Way of Building* (New York: Oxford University Press, 1979).

16.1 THE ARGUMENT FOR USING THE SAME NOTATION

In an earlier book,[2] Peter Coad and I argued that the *same* notation could be used for OOD as for OOA—that is, the same graphical symbols for classes and objects, gen-spec and whole-part structures, instance connections, methods, and messages.

Why is this a good idea? Simply because people who speak different languages have a difficult time communicating their ideas to one another; it's hard enough when the discussion involves tangible things that one can point to, and even more difficult when the discussion involves abstractions. A graphical diagramming notation is a language, just as various current and former nations and ethnic groups have used hieroglyphics and ideograms to record their thoughts. If analysts and designers each have their own unique language, then the organization must invest in two sets of training courses, manuals, CASE tools, and so on—and it must either invest in "interpreters" to translate between the two groups, or it must invest additional time, effort, and money to make each group bilingual.

This is not simply an issue of philosophy or metaphysics: it has real consequences. One of the reasons the waterfall life cycle has been perpetuated and exacerbated in many organizations is that the activities carried out in each phase use such a different set of words and symbols. Translating the analysis diagrams into design diagrams is a painful chore; going *backward* from design diagrams to analysis diagrams is even more painful. Thus the typical systems development organization has no enthusiasm for a project life cycle that allows for "bouncing back and forth" from analysis to design; there is a sharp demarcation between the two, and much (though not all) of that demarcation is based on the underlying notation. By using the same notation, it becomes technologically feasible to consider an iterative, or "spiral," life cycle in which the project team progresses from analysis to design and coding, and then back to analysis again.[3]

For confirmation of the problems in this area, listen to the project team members in your own organization as they move through

---

[2]Peter Coad and Edward Yourdon, *Object-Oriented Design* (Englewood Cliffs, NJ: Yourdon Press/Prentice Hall, 1991).

[3]Of course, there may be various other reasons why the project has to adopt a more conservative waterfall life cycle—for example, because the software is being developed on a contract basis and the customer demands it. This is particularly common in situations where the customer knows that the analysis effort will be done by one software organization and the design/implementation will be done by a different one.

analysis, and then into design, using an older methodology such as structured analysis and design. While drawing data flow diagrams in the midst of structured analysis, one often hears the analysts say things like, "Next week, we're going to bubble on down to the bottom level." Such a statement evokes little reaction from the team members: after all, it simply means continuing on down to a lower level of detail, *using the same notation.*

But then comes the fateful day when the project leader says, "Now, we're going to start transitioning into design." The fact that "transitioning" has been used to describe an ongoing process rather than an instantaneous state change is interesting; the project team members are likely to complain that, for several weeks (or months), they are in the "twilight zone" *between* analysis and design. They have some bubbles (data flow diagrams) in their analysis model and some boxes (structure charts) in their design model, and it's often difficult to see a correspondence between the two.

16.2 WHAT ELSE DOES THE DESIGNER NEED?

While the argument presented in Section 16.1 sounds good, it's usually not enough to persuade veteran designers. "We're working with implementation-level technology," the designers will say, "and we need to be able to represent a number of technology-related issues in our notation." This implementation perspective typically demands a number of things from the OOD notation:

- *Visibility.* The designer wants to specify the degree to which the attributes and methods of a class and object can be seen in other parts of the system. Typical choices here are

Public	The attribute or method can be accessed and/or modified by any other object in the system. Obviously, it's much more common to make a method public than to make public the attributes within an encapsulated object.
Private	The attribute or method can be accessed only by other methods within the same class and object.
Protected	The attribute or method can be accessed by methods in the same class, or in any subclass below it. This takes advantage of the normal inheritance method associated with OO methodologies.

Friends   The attribute or method can be accessed by a specific list of classes and objects elsewhere in the system.

- *Persistence.* A class and its objects may persist for a period as brief as the receipt and processing of a message, or for the duration of a user's session with the system, or for as long as an eternity. This is typically not an issue for the analyst, whose assumption of "perfect technology" *includes* the assumption that an object will exist forever. For the designer, though, it may be important to indicate what actions are required to make an object persistent, and how such objects will be deleted.

- *Exceptions.* What happens if an object encounters an error situation? In the analyst's perfect technology model, the primary errors that we need to worry about are those caused by the user himself—associated with erroneous data, illegal commands, and so on. But the designer must worry about errors associated with faulty technology (read/write errors, memory faults, power failures, and so on) as well as errors caused by bugs in other objects. At a minimum, every object needs a way to respond to *any* message by effectively saying, "Message not understood" and let the sender decide what to do; similarly, it must have appropriate intelligence to decide what to do if its own messages are not understood by other objects in the system.

- *Containment.* Especially the containment of objects within various physical "packages." Depending on the technology, the designer may have to specify how objects are grouped into physical "records," and he may have to specify how methods are contained within "modules," how executable objects are grouped into "tasks," or "packages," and so on. *Logical* containment (for example, the notion that an organization contains employees) is also important, but has probably been modeled already by the analyst in the form of whole-part structures.

- *Concurrency.* As mentioned in Chapter 14, there are a number of scenarios that we can imagine for the coordination of messages between objects; the designer may find it important to specify these in his OOD model. For example, can an object continue computing after it has sent a message, but before it has received a response? Can an object continue computing after it has responded to a message? Can the sending and receiving object be "active" at the same time? Can an object receive and process more than one message at a time?

- *Collections.* A class, as we first saw in Chapter 1, is a template for objects that have the same attributes and methods. But this is a logical concept; the designer may need to express it in physical terms. Thus it may be important to provide OOD notation to describe lists, bags, sets, and parameterized types such as lists of integers. The designer may wish to take advantage of (and use some standard notation for) standard set operations such as the union of two sets, the concatenation of two sets, the difference (exclusive OR) of two sets, and so forth.

- *Constraints.* In a formal software engineering methodology, the designer may wish to specify various "constraints" that will help ensure the correctness of his system. Thus he may wish to say, "the following conditions must be true before object X receives a message of type 'a', and the following conditions must be true after message 'a' has been processed and a response generated." In most methodologies, these constraints would typically be expressed as preconditions and postconditions; the designer is describing the *state* of the object or of the entire system prior to its receipt of a message, and upon completion of message processing—in terms of the values of attributes, the existence of instance connections, and so on. Such constraints might be described textually, in a form ranging from narrative English to a formal mathematical description, or they might be described graphically using state-transition diagrams, state matrices, and so on. For the overall OOD model, it might be useful to indicate which classes and objects have formal constraints specified, and which do not.

Note that *all* the issues just listed could turn out to be analysis issues—especially in real-time systems. Most commonly, though, they fall into the designer's lap and are resolved during the design phase of the project.

16.3 EXAMPLES OF OOD NOTATIONAL REPRESENTATIONS

It should be no surprise that every one of the commercial OOD methodologies has its own approach to the notational issues described in Sections 16.1 and 16.2. In many cases, these differences reflect the methodologist's assumption about the kind of applications for which they are intended, for example, real-time, embedded control systems, business data processing, and so on. In other cases, they reflect the methodologist's assumption about the programming language that will be used—for example, Ada, C++, or Smalltalk.

While this last point may seem obvious, it has profound implications: some OOD methodologies (and their associated notation) have evolved "from the bottom up," whereas the Coad-Yourdon OOD methodology evolved "from the top down." Thus some methodologists *began* by documenting good principles of object-oriented programming, as practiced in C++, Smalltalk and so on, and *then* they "moved up" to consider the issue of object-oriented design. The Coad-Yourdon methodology, on the other hand, began with notation for OOA, and then asked the simple question: "Do we need anything more to document the design?"

All this may have some practical significance in an organization about to adopt OOA and OOD. An analyst who has familiarized himself with the OOA notation presented earlier in this book will probably be perfectly happy with the suggestion that the same notation can be used for OOD. But a programmer who has spent the last several months coding in C++, and who is now told that he must "get formal" by learning OOD, will have a different reaction: he wants to be assured that every clever programming trick that he has learned in C++ has a corresponding graphical notation in the OOD methodology. Otherwise, he will complain that OOD doesn't work— because it doesn't allow him to "say" the things he knows he will want to express at the code level. Ironically, the same situation existed in the early 1970s, when FORTRAN and COBOL programmers were first being exposed to structured design: if the structure chart notation didn't express everything that could be expressed in code, then it was typically rejected.

So the choice of a specific OOD notation and methodology may be based largely on the culture and mind-set of those who are supposed to use it; indeed, this is probably a larger factor than the question of whether it will be applied to a real-time system or a batch payroll system. With this in mind, we will briefly discuss the notation of several commercial forms of OOD methodology.

16.3.1 Comments on the Coad-Yourdon OOD Notation

The Coad-Yourdon OOD notation, as noted earlier, is exactly the same as the OOA notation. Consequently, there is no support for the various design-level issues summarized in Section 16.2. This has the advantage of not tying the designer to any particular programming language or operating system environment, but it has the obvious disadvantage that it fails to address significant issues as the designer approaches the lower-level implementation details.

16.3.2 Comments on the Rumbaugh and Coworkers OOD Notation

Rumbaugh and coworkers provide some useful advice for the *strategy* and the *process* of design, but propose no additional graphical notation; one is left to assume that the same notation introduced for the analysis part of the methodology will also be used for design. The process of design is described by Rumbaugh as follows:

> During the system design, the overall structure and style are decided. The *system architecture* is the overall organization of the system into components called *subsystems*. The architecture provides the context in which more detailed decisions are made in later design stages. . .
>
> . . . The system designer must make the following decisions:
> - Organize the system into subsystems . . .
> - Identify concurrency inherent in the problem . . .
> - Allocate subsystems to processors and tasks . . .
> - Choose an approach for management of data stores . . .
> - Handle access to global resources . . .
> - Choose the implementation of control in the software . . .
> - Handle boundary conditions . . .
> - Set trade-off priorities . . .

Often the overall architecture of a system can be chosen based on its similarity to previous systems . . . [4]

---

[4]James Rumbaugh, Michael Blaha, William Premerlani, Frederick Eddy, and William Lorensen, *Object-Oriented Modeling and Design* (Englewood Cliffs, NJ: Prentice Hall, 1991), pp.198–199.

It is interesting that the various examples of systems architectures used by Rumbaugh and coworkers in this discussion are illustrated with data flow diagrams.[5] And it is interesting that the discussion of the various design decisions that the systems designer must make involves only one informal, illustrative, diagram. Our conclusion is that the Rumbaugh methodology, like the Coad-Yourdon methodology, uses the same notation for both OOA and OOD.

16.3.3 Comments on the Booch OOD Notation

The Booch OOD methodology includes a rich notation that covers virtually all the issues listed in Section 16.2; indeed, the only criticism that can be offered is that it is so rich that it may be somewhat difficult for the novice OO practitioner to use. However, it should be emphasized that the methodology, and its associated notation, were specifically intended for design, not for analysis. Booch makes the following observation about analysis and design:

> There are many different kinds of analysis methods, some of which are suitable as front ends to object-oriented design . . .
>
> Structured analysis is an attractive front end to object-oriented design primarily because it is well known, many people are trained in its techniques, and many tools support its notation. However, structured analysis is not the optimal front end to object-oriented design . . .
>
> The current trend in analysis methods is toward object-oriented analysis, as typified by the work of Shlaer and Mellor and Coad and Yourdon . . . [6]

Thus given Booch's OOD notation, the software engineer has a question exactly the opposite of the one we just posed: rather than asking what *more* we need to support OOD, the analyst would look at Booch's notation and ask, "What can we do *without* while we are modeling the essential user requirements?" As a practical matter, an organization is unlikely to "drop" a subset of the Booch notation during OOA, and then add it back again during OOD (although a CASE tool might provide this kind of methodological control); hence there may be some danger that analysts using the full-blown Booch nota-

---

[5]However, while this book was being prepared in mid-1993, rumors circulated through the field that data flow diagrams were destined to be removed from future versions of the Rumbaugh methodology.

[6]Grady Booch, *Object-Oriented Design* (Redwood City, CA: Benjamin/Cummings, 1991), p. 201.

tion will indulge in some implementation issues in their discussions with users who are trying to focus only on analysis requirements.

16.3.4 Comments on the Firesmith OOD Notation

In Don Firesmith's ADM_3 methodology, it appears that issues of design and construction of the system are intended to be documented in a design language called OOSDL. As Firesmith describes it;

> The object-oriented specification and design language, OOSDL, was primarily developed to improve the specification, design, and documentation of object-oriented software applications. OOSDL is a strongly typed, quasi-formal, textual, object-oriented specification and design language roughly based on the Ada programming language. . . . Although OOSDL could reasonably be used as an implementation language if production-quality compilers were available, it is intended to be used earlier, during specification and language-independent design. OOSDL specifications and designs are intended to evolve incrementally as analysis and design progresses.[7]

As will be noted in Chapters 18 and 19, Firesmith's methodology provides no explicit guidance for the development of the human interface, for it is assumed that the same approach can be used for the human interface as for the "domain" component of the application. No explicit guidance is given for the design of the database, for ADM_3 assumes that an object database will be used and does not support the use of relational databases. There is no question that OOSDL provides the mechanisms to express everything that the designer would want to express about the implementation of his system; the only question is whether one needs to be able to do so graphically, or whether a textual representation is sufficient.

The irony is that the software engineer is almost overwhelmed by the variety of diagrams that the ADM_3 methodology provides at the analysis level. There are no fewer than 15 different kinds of diagrams and 14 "basic node shapes" (banners, boxes, buildings, circles, clouds, data_stores, diamonds, hexagons, ovals, off_page_connectors, parallelograms, trapezoids, rectangles, and rounded_rectangles). The methodology includes the following five types of diagrams "for system-level requirements analysis and design."[8]

---

[7]Donald G. Firesmith, *Object-Oriented Requirements Analysis and Design: A Software Engineering Approach*, (New York: John Wiley and Sons, 1993), p. 323.

[8]Ibid., p. 494.

- System semantic nets (SSNs)
- System interaction diagrams (SIDs)
- System composition diagrams (SCMDs)
- System state-transition diagrams (SSTDs)
- System event timing diagrams (SETDs)

And there are nine types of diagrams "for software-level require-ments analysis and design":[9]

- Context diagrams (CDs)
- Assembly diagrams (ADs)
- General semantic nets (GSNs)
- Interaction diagrams (IDs)
- Composition diagrams (CMDs)
- Classification diagrams (CLDs)
- State-transition diagrams (STDs)
- Control flow diagrams (CFDs)
- Event timing diagrams (ETDs)
- Module diagrams (MDs)
- Submodule diagrams (SMDs)

One might worry about the practicality of implementing a methodology that requires 15 diagrams in an organization of mere mortals. But it should also be noted that not all the diagrams are used all the time; most developers use only a small subset. Also, it should be noted that many of the diagrams are minor variations of one another—so the OO developer does not really have to memorize 15 totally different kinds of diagrams.

In any case, the main point here is that Firesmith seems to be recommending the same (large) set of diagrams for both analysis and "high-level" design of an entire system and/or the software component of that system. When the designer is prepared to deal with issues that would traditionally be considered "detailed design," the ADM_3 methodology switches over to the text-based OOSDL language.

[9]Ibid., p. 510

16.3.5 Comments on the Embley-Kurtz OOD Notation

Like the Coad-Yourdon methodology, Embley, Kurtz, and Woodfield have concentrated primarily on OO analysis rather than design. This statement is not intended as a criticism of their methodology; after all, their book explicitly describes itself as an *analysis* approach, and does not include the word "design" in the title. In a brief appendix, they make the following comment:

> For design we should fully formalize the information contained in the OSA [Object-oriented Systems Analysis] model targeted for implementation. For each ORM [Object Relationship Model], we should write the general constraints in a formal language. For state nets, we should replace high-level states and transitions with lower and even lower level states and transitions until they become "executable" in our target design domain. . . . By pushing the OSA model down to this "executable" level, a formal model of OSD can be represented using the original modeling constructs of OSA.[10]

As a result, we can obviously conclude that the same diagramming notation is intended to be used for OOA and OOD; however, we must offer the same criticism that is leveled at the Coad-Yourdon OOD methodology: its notation does not cover most of the specific design-level issues described in Section 16.2.

16.3.6 Comments on the Martin-Odell OOD Notation

Unlike the Embley-Kurtz methodology, Martin and Odell describe their approach as an "object-oriented analysis and design" methodology. However, it is the author's impression that the bulk of their approach focuses on the analysis activity; only 3 chapters out of 29 chapters and 5 appendices are specifically concerned with design. At the beginning of the first of these chapters, the authors state:

> The particular approach to object-oriented analysis presented in this book models the way people understand and process reality— through the concepts they acquire. . . in this book, the design scope is restricted to software applications. This chapter applies the knowledge gained from object schemas and maps them into the *structural* aspects of object-oriented programming languages.

[10]David W. Embley, Barry D. Kurtz, and Scott N. Woodfield, *Object-Oriented Systems Analysis: A Model-Driven Approach* (Englewood Cliffs, NJ: Yourdon Press/Prentice Hall, 1992).

The next chapter presents ways of mapping event schemas for designing the *behavioral* aspects of an OOPL.[11]

The notion of mapping components of the analysis model directly onto an OOPL is intriguing and may be even more attractive if one assumes that an automated code generator can accomplish the task mechanically. However, it is not the author's purpose to question the efficacy of the Martin-Odell methodology per se; suffice it to note that it introduces virtually no additional graphical notation for the design phase of the project. Also, as with the Coad-Yourdon and Embley-Kurtz methodologies, it is appropriate to note that the design-level issues listed in Section 16.2 are not covered by the Martin-Odell notation.

16.3.7 Comments on the Shlaer-Mellor OODLE notation

Sally Shlaer and Steve Mellor use a graphical diagramming notation called OODLE (an acronym for *Object-Oriented Design LanguagE*) that involves four kinds of diagrams that are separate and distinct from the various analysis diagrams introduced in their two OOA books. In describing their notation, the authors listed the following objectives:

- The notation must represent the fundamental concepts of OOD (including encapsulation of data, inheritance, and polymorphism) in an intuitive manner.
- Data typing should be strongly emphasized and represented. Experienced designers take careful account of data types, regardless of the level of support for typing in the intended implementation language.
- The design notation should not seek to represent all possible constructs (and combinations of constructs) of a programming language or languages. It should concentrate on fundamental language-independent concepts such as visibility of operations, partitioning of code, invocation and exceptions. At the same time, the notation should be rich enough to support key design decisions that need to be accounted for to render the design into an implementation language.

---

[11]James Martin and James J. Odell, *Object-Oriented Analysis & Design* (Englewood Cliffs, NJ: Prentice Hall, 1992), p. 403.

- The notation should be susceptible to language-specific implementation.[12]

After further discussion of what should and should not be included in an OOD notation, the authors introduce four diagrams:

Class diagram. A class diagram depicts the external view of a single class. This diagram is based on notations of Booch and Buhr, but shows considerably more detail of the external specification.

Class structure chart. The class structure chart is used to show the internal structure of the code of the operations of the class. This chart is based on traditional structure charts, enhanced to show additional concepts pertinent to object-oriented development.

Dependence diagram. The dependence diagram depicts the client-server (invocation) and friend relationships that hold between the classes.

Inheritance diagram. The inheritance diagram shows the inheritance relationships that pertain between the classes. This diagram is derived from the information modeling notation of OOA.[13]

A generic example of the OODLE notation is shown in Figure 16.1:

---

[12]Sally Shlaer and Stephen J. Mellor, Object Lifecycles: *Modeling the World in States* (Englewood Cliffs, NJ: Yourdon Press/Prentice Hall, 1992), pp. 201–202.

[13]Ibid., p. 204.

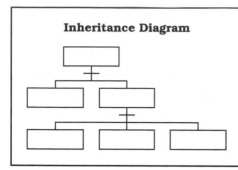

Inheritance Diagram

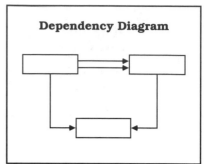

Dependency Diagram

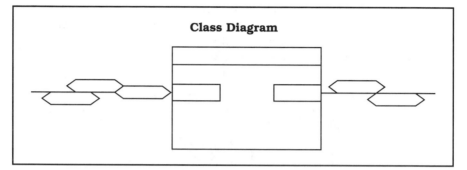

Class Diagram

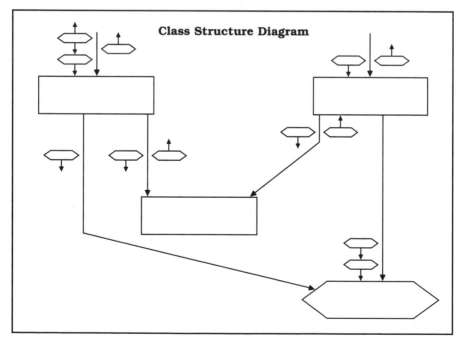

Class Structure Diagram

Figure 16.1: An example of Shlaer-Mellor OODLE notation

17

OO Design Architectures

Alhough we noted in Chapter 16 that there is a wide variety of OOD graphical notations, design is more than drawing pictures. As Grady Booch observes,

> Designing is not the act of drawing a diagram: a diagram simply captures a design. If you follow the work of any engineer—software, civil, mechanical, chemical, architectural, or whatever—you will soon realize that the one and only place that a design is conceived is in the mind of the designer.[1]

But once the design has been conceived and documented with appropriate notation—whether on a scrap of paper, or on an elegant CASE tool—what should it look like? What kind of architectural "shape" should it display: Should it be skinny or fat?

There are two primary reasons for asking this question. First, we have an intuitive sense that the designs for common types of applications should fall into easily recognizable "patterns." As Christopher Alexander observes in *The Timeless Way of Building*,

> If I consider my life honestly, I see that it is governed by a certain very small number of patterns of events which I take part in over and over again.
>
> Being in bed, having a shower, having breakfast in the kitchen, sitting in my study writing, walking in the garden, cooking and eating our common lunch at my office with my friends, going to the movies, taking my family to eat at a restaurant, having a drink at a friend's house, driving on the freeway, going to bed again. There are a few more.
>
> There are surprisingly few of these patterns of events in any one person's way of life, perhaps no more than a dozen. Look at your

[1]Grady Booch, *Object-Oriented Design, with Applications* (Redwood City, CA: Benjamin/Cummings, 1991).

own life and you will find the same. It is shocking at first, to see that there are so few patterns of events open to me. Not that I want more of them. But when I see how very few of them there are, I begin to understand what huge effects these few patterns have on my life, on my capacity to live. If these few patterns are good for me, I can live well. If they are bad for me, I can't.[2]

This doesn't necessarily mean that the design for a common type of application—for example, a payroll system—*must* follow a certain pattern, but it would make life easier for the software manager who would like to minimize the risk that would otherwise be associated with evaluating the quality of a totally new, harebrained design for that application. We will return to this theme in Chapter 21, when we discuss goodness criteria for OO designs. For now, let's just say that it would be nice to have some "standard" architectures so that designers don't have to reinvent the wheel every time they are faced with a new problem.

For some designers, the problem is more severe: they can't reinvent the wheel, for they can't conceptualize *any* design for the problem they have been given. In this sense, the notion of standard architectures is analogous to a cookbook: if you want to bake a chocolate cake, start with these ingredients and follow these steps. A cookbook doesn't guarantee success, for it still relies on the experience, judgment, and common sense of the person following the steps (as is evident with such instructions as "stir until well mixed," "season to taste," and so on), but it's better than flailing around in the kitchen with no idea of what to do.

This situation is more common than one might think: when software engineers first make the transition from a function-based structured design methodology to an object-oriented design approach, they have no familiar landmarks to guide them. As noted elsewhere in this book, the old-style designer is likely to look at an object diagram and ask, "Where's the top?" The designer wants to see the "control" module, so that he can "trace" the architecture by looking for the "afferent" and "efferent" legs of the structure chart, and so on. In the new world of OOD, what should the designer be looking for? What sort of "shape" should he expect to emerge from his design efforts?

[2]Christopher Alexander, *The Timeless Way of Building* (New York: Oxford University Press, 1979).

17.1 AN OOD ARCHITECTURE

Given this need, it is rather surprising that many of the textbooks on OO design pay little attention to this issue of architecture; much of the discussion seems to be focused on issues of packaging objects into modules, and so on. But the Smalltalk community has developed a simple, but elegant, metaphor for such an architecture; it is known as the "Model-View-Controller" architecture, or MVC. Essentially, it suggests that a typical OOD architecture will have three main components: a group of classes and objects that *model* the underlying application itself; a group of classes and objects that provide a human-interface *view* of those model-related classes; and a group of classes and objects that *control*, or synchronize, the behavior of the others.

The Coad-Yourdon OOD methodology uses a very similar concept, with one additional component; it is shown in Figure 17.1.

Human Interaction Component (HIC)	Problem Domain Component (PDC)	Task Management Component (TMC)	Data Management Component (DMC)

Figure 17.1: The Coad-Yourdon OOD architecture

The basic idea of this architecture is simple but crucial: it calls for using the same classes and objects that were documented in the OOA model and then surrounding them with additional classes and objects to handle the implementation-related activities of task management, data management, and human interaction. Unlike classical methodologies, where we basically "throw out" the analysis model and begin afresh with a new design model, this OOD architecture has, as its central theme, *salvaging* the OOA model and using it as the heart of the design model. Obviously, our ability to do this is greatly enhanced if we use the same basic graphical notation for OOA and OOD.

Three of the components in Figure 17.1 are essentially the same as the Smalltalk MVC approach: the human interaction component (HIC), problem domain component (PDC), and task management component (TMC). The fourth component deals an ugly reality that most software engineers must accept: no matter how elegant the architecture of the object-oriented software that runs on the CPU, it must interact with "legacy" data on a database that was designed 5, 10, or even 20 years ago. Some of this data may exist in "flat-file" databases, some may be in a relational form; indeed, there is a tiny possibility that some of it may reside in an object-oriented database management system, but that it is a rare phenomenon as this book is being written in early 1993. Hence we need a separate architectural component—the data management component (DMC)—to transform objects into database records or tables.

With this explanation, the idea of a separate DMC certainly doesn't sound very radical; similarly, having a separate HIC seems reasonable, because the human interface is a separate and distinct (and, these days, enormously important) issue. But there is a crucial consequence of such an approach: it suggests that the central "application-oriented" classes and objects in the PDC should not be aware of the "outside world" and should not have to know how to interact with that world. Without conscious attention to this philosophy, we could end up with an OOD architecture in which each class and object (1) knows how to interact with the end user at his PC or terminal and (2) knows how to read and write its permanent data values to and from a disk file. Such an approach would work, and might run a few microseconds faster than a design built around the architecture of Figure 17.1,[3] but it would be quite vulnerable to changes in the human interface or database, and it would complicate the internal structure of the classes and objects which previously only had to be aware of their essential application-oriented details.

We will examine the HIC in Chapter 18, and the DMC in Chapter 19. While the TMC component may be quite important in certain real-time applications, its job is performed more and more often these days by operating systems and/or run-time environments that handle the details of multitasking, task synchronization,

---

[3]To be honest, we must admit that there will be some situations where the architecture suggested in Figure 17.1 will be *much* less efficient than some other one, for it involves a substantial amount of communication between the PDC class, the HIC classes, and the DMC classes via message connections. In certain real-time situations, this performance penalty may be unacceptable.

and so on; for the overwhelming majority of software engineers today, there is no need for an explicit TMC in the design architecture, and we will not discuss it further in this book.[4]

17.2 CHANGES TO THE PDC

In many cases, the analysis model developed in Part II of this book can be "dropped" into the PDC components of the OOD architecture with no further changes; indeed, this is one of the most elegant features of the OO analysis and design methodology. But there are some circumstances where modifications are appropriate; in an earlier book,[5] Peter Coad and I discussed a number of circumstances, of which the more noteworthy are these:

- *Reusable design/programming classes.* When he examines the class hierarchies of the OOA model that has initially been placed in the PDC component, the designer may see opportunities to take advantage of existing classes and objects in his implementation library. Ideally, this situation would be recognized during the analysis effort; in practice, though, it occurs more frequently during design and implementation. In any case, this would involve changing the PDC to treat appropriate OOA classes as subclasses of the preexisting library classes, and taking full advantage of the ability to inherit preexisting attributes and methods within those library classes.

- *Grouping domain-related classes together, establishing a common protocol.* The designer may wish to gather a number of distinct classes together and treat them as subclasses of a newly created superclass that provides a common "protocol" for communicating with the DMC or with other external system

---

[4]Note, though, that even in the PDC model, there may be classes and objects whose purpose is to coordinate and synchronize the *sequencing* of other objects. But this involves "logical" sequencing, rather than the implementation-oriented *physical* sequencing that the TMC would have to be concerned about. The perfect technology OOA model assumes that each object can carry out its activities in zero time, and that (if appropriate) each object can have its own dedicated CPU, which can communicate with other objects in other CPUs with no overhead. It is only in the design model that we worry about the fact that the entire system may have to run on one CPU and that some objects may have to have a higher priority than others, because their tasks are more urgent.

[5]Peter Coad and Edward Yourdon, *Object-Oriented Design* (Englewood Cliffs, NJ: Yourdon Press/Prentice Hall, 1991).

components. Such a "grouping" approach may also turn out to be useful as a library management mechanism.

- *Accommodate available inheritance.* If the OOA model took advantage of multiple inheritance, and if the designer knows that the system will eventually be implemented in a programming language that supports only single inheritance, it may be necessary to change the class hierarchies within the PDC. Typically, this involves mapping the original multiple-inheritance hierarchy into whole-part structures or separate single-inheritance hierarchies with instance connections between them. In extreme cases, it may involve "flattening" the original hierarchy and suffering redundant duplication of attributes within various classes. However, in most cases, this problem does not occur because (1) the analysts and users often regard multiple inheritance as "too complicated," and simply avoid it and (2) at the very outset of the project, everyone typically knows what kind of programming language is going to be used for implementation, and all the project activities are based on that level of inheritance capability.

- *Modify the design to improve performance.* Performance can be a concern if there is a great deal of message communication between objects, or if the programming language implements inheritance inefficiently, or for various other reasons unique to the OO approach. The designer may respond to such performance problems by "squashing" two classes together (thus permitting intraobject communication rather than interobject communication) or by violating the principle of encapsulation through global data areas, and so on.

Obviously, such modifications should be viewed as a trade-off rather than an excuse for unmitigated hacking; efficient performance of the software is important, for example, but it should be balanced against the desire to minimize maintenance and testing costs by keeping the PDC as close as possible to the original OOA model.

The concern over performance is an interesting example of the "generation gap" between new-breed OO software engineers and grizzled veterans of older methodologies. The younger generation typically has not heard the following "performance sermon" that has been etched on the forehead of the older folks:

- *Don't create a performance crisis if there isn't one.* Often, the efficiency of the software is irrelevant, especially if it is running on a powerful CPU and interacting with a single user. Most of the "clock time" will probably be spent waiting for input from the user.

- *Don't assume that an OOPL like C++ or Smalltalk is necessarily going to be inefficient.* While there may be a few degenerate instances where an OOPL is 10 times less efficient than a tightly coded non-OOPL, in general the performance penalty is likely to be more on the order of 10 percent. In any case, as the older generation has learned by now, programmers get tired; compilers don't.

- *It's easier to make a working system efficient than it is to make an efficient system work.* Your first concern should be to build a clean, simple design that can be implemented and debugged with a minimum of fuss and bother; whatever performance improvements are necessary at that point will usually involve a small amount of work. On the other hand, if you *begin* with the objective of building the fastest, smallest, most efficient system the world has ever seen, chances are that it will be so intricate and convoluted that debugging will be a nightmare. In short, efficiency and performance are so important that you should save them for last.

- *Eighty percent of the overhead in a typical system is concentrated in 20% of the code.* And in some cases, the situation is even more extreme. Rather than destroying an elegant architecture to save overhead *everywhere*, the intelligent thing to do is find out *where* the overhead is concentrated, by using a performance "profiling" package, and then optimize only that portion.

- *Software engineers are notoriously poor at anticipating in advance where the software overhead will be concentrated.* The best way to optimize is to use some kind of performance monitoring tools to observe the system as it runs; the nature and location of the overhead usually turns out to be a surprise, particularly when a high-level language is involved. This is all the more likely when software engineers use an OOPL for the first time, since its treatment of things like inheritance, dynamic binding, message passing, and so on may look deceptively simple, but may generate a great deal of overhead. Unfortunately, software engineers tend to think that if a piece of code *looks* complicated, it will probably be inefficient, but there is no correlation between mental complexity and hardware inefficiency.

- *The greatest performance improvements come from* **smarter** *solutions, not by squeezing out microseconds and bytes of memory.* This observation was true long before OO technology came along, and it remains true in the OO world, too. As Don Firesmith observes, "Microefficiency may destroy macroefficiency."

17.3 THE SMALL BYTES CASE STUDY

From the discussion in this chapter, our first inclination is to begin creating an OOD architecture base on the one in Figure 17.1 for the *Small Bytes* system. There is obviously no real-time "flavor" to the system, so we don't need the TMC; obviously, we do need the HIC and PDC components.

As for the DMC component, our designer would have to get a fundamental policy decision from the user: Can we build an entirely new database for the subscription system? From the original discussion in Chapter 8, we know that the user currently has a subscription system based on a relatively simple flat-file database; the question is whether that database must be maintained or whether it can be replaced with something new.

In a situation like this, the most obvious question is: What other systems or applications use that database? If there are several such legacy applications, and if they cannot be changed, then we are constrained to continue using the existing database—in which case, the DMC component is necessary. If it turns out that the subscription system is the only application, or if there are other project teams busily rewriting the other applications in an object-oriented fashion, then it may be possible to replace the flat-file database with an appropriate OODBMS. In this case, as we will see in Chapter 19, the DMC becomes almost superfluous.

There is another issue one must consider when looking at the database: How difficult or time consuming will it be to convert the existing database into a new OO format, that is, one that directly supports inheritance, as well as encapsulation of data and methods?

For the *Small Bytes* system, it's hard to imagine that this would pose a major problem: assuming that we can write a translation program (or that the OODBMS has a flexible "import" capability), it should not require more than a few hours to convert even several tens of thousands of records. And, of course, the key assumption here is that a small technical journal is unlikely to have an overwhelming volume of data; the situation would be entirely different, for example, if we were building a subscription system for a national consumer magazine like *Time* or *Newsweek or People*.

As for the PDC, it's reasonable to assume that little or nothing will have to be changed. After considering the performance sermon in Section 17.2, it hardly seems appropriate to bastardize the design of the Small Bytes system to save a few microseconds. The OOA model did not rely on multiple inheritance, so we don't have to worry about that kind of change, and since this is apparently the first OO project the organization has built, it's unlikely that we will find any reusable class hierarchies to take advantage of. Thus our conclusion (which we should feel free to amend later on) is that the original OOA model can be dropped, intact, into the PDC component of the design architecture.

17.4 THE ELEVATOR CASE STUDY

The strategy for designing the architecture of the elevator control system basically follows the same line of reasoning as that laid out earlier with the *Small Bytes* system. However, there are a few areas where we might expect to see some differences.

First, the issue of task management needs to be considered; after all, our system has to control the movement of four elevators, the opening and closing of doors, and the operation of several dozen buttons and lights. On the other hand, our user has given us the strong impression in Chapter 8 that the system will be implemented on a reasonably powerful machine, and it's reasonable to assume that the required response time for all this would be measured in milliseconds or seconds, not microseconds. Furthermore, the one critical real-time phenomenon—responding to the emergency button that an elevator passenger can press—is controlled by a separate mechanical system that has nothing to do with our computer software. So it seems reasonable to conclude that our system does not have to worry about priority interrupts and multitasking (despite all the discussion about such hardware features in Chapter 8), and we can forgo the sophistication of a TMC component in our architecture.

The second key issue involves the DMC: What kind of data is it supposed to manage? From our discussion thus far, there seems to be no need for a database, in the conventional sense of the term: all the objects in our OOA model are "persistent" for the duration of the system's operation, which may be 24 hours a day, 7 days a week, until there is a power failure or some human decision to shut the system down. But if the system is shut down and then restarted on a normal, controlled basis, it's hard to imagine why it would have to remember its previous state. Indeed, the only plausible argument for saving all the analysis-based objects onto some form of permanent storage would be the argument of near-instantaneous backup and recovery in the case of unexpected power failures. While this is a real issue to think about, we will assume for the remainder of this book that our user is content with the standard mechanical fail-safe systems that accompany all elevators and does not require us to worry about it in our system.

That leaves the human interface to worry about . . . but from the discussion in Chapter 8, it appears that the human interface consists entirely of the various lights associated with summons buttons and destination buttons. No mention has been made of an "operator's control terminal" that would enable a supervisory person to monitor the behavior of the elevators on a multicolor GUI-based PC in the basement of the building. It would be fun to invent such an interface, but if it wasn't mentioned in the requirements document, it isn't appropriate for the designers to put it in.[6]

Thus our primary concern with the elevator control system will not be at the architectural level—for it appears that only the PDC component of the architecture proposed in Figure 17.1 is relevant. Our concern, instead, will be with the lower-level details of design and implementation. We will discuss this further in Chapter 20.

---

[6]For those who object to this cavalier statement, keep in mind that (1) the analyst might well propose such a feature during the development of the OOA model and (2) the prototyping approach to building such a system might uncover the need for such an interface when the user first sees how the system operates.

18

Designing the Human Interface

As mentioned elsewhere in this book, there is a common tendency to associate OO methodologies with graphical user interfaces: a system built with an OO approach, it seems, is destined to have windows and scroll bars and colorful graphical icons for the users to click with their mouses. And from the discussion in the previous chapter, one might assume that every class and object in the PDC will have a corresponding "shadow object" in the HIC whose job is to display its contents in an appropriate format in a windows-oriented environment.

But there is more to it than that—or in some cases, less. As we saw with the elevator control system, sometimes the physical devices that are controlled by objects in the PDC—such as the elevator summons lights—constitute the entire human interface. And the human interface may also consist of familiar hard-copy printed reports, character-based screens, touch-sensitive devices, and a variety of other mechanisms for interacting with the user. In short, designing the human interface typically requires a great deal of care and attention.

While the popularity of GUIs has emphasized the importance of the human interface in the past few years, it has always been important—and there has been a wealth of good work in the field through much of the history of the software field. Much of the advice for designing good human interfaces for an OO-style system still depends on "classical" advice, from such gurus as Donald Norman[1] and Ben Shneiderman.[2] Recent books, such as the intriguing collection of

---

[1]Donald Norman, *The Design of Everyday Things* (New York: Doubleday, 1988). Previously published as *The Psychology of Everyday Things*.

[2]Ben Shneiderman, *Designing the User Interface*, 2nd ed. (Reading, MA: Addison-Wesley, 1992).

papers edited by Apple Computer's Brenda Laurel,[3] show the pervasive influence of the "Macintosh metaphor" for human interfaces.

By contrast, it is ironic to note that many OOA and OOD textbooks give scant attention to the topic. Neither Martin-Odell,[4] nor Shlaer-Mellor,[5] nor Embley-Kurtz-Woodfield,[6] nor Firesmith[7] mention the design of the human interface at all in their respective books; the topic fails to appear anywhere in the table of contents or index, although all the authors pay appropriate homage to the importance of prototyping. Rumbaugh and coworkers[8] devote a single page to the topic; Booch[9] offers little formal guidance on how to design the proper classes and objects for the human interface, but provides numerous specific case studies, so that the reader can learn by example. By contrast, Jacobson and coworkers[10] base a great deal of their analysis approach on the concept of "use cases" and have a specific graphical notation (as we saw in Chapter 9) for distinguishing between "interface objects" and other categories of objects.

Of course the reader will observe that this book is not a complete treatise on human interface design per se; our primary purpose is to see how the OOD methodology deals with the human interface portion of a software architecture. As we saw in Chapter 17, it does so by adding a separate component called the HIC, whose classes and objects are responsible for interacting with the end user. In this chapter, we explore the contents and organization of those classes and objects, as well as their interactions with the classes in the PDC.

---

[3]Brenda Laurel, ed., *The Art of Human-Computer Interface Design* (Reading, MA: Addison-Wesley, 1990).

[4]James Martin and James J. Odell, *Object-Oriented Analysis & Design* (Englewood Cliffs, NJ: Prentice Hall, 1992).

[5]Sally Shlaer and Stephen J. Mellor, *Object-Oriented Systems Analysis: Modeling the World in Data* (Englewood Cliffs, NJ: Yourdon Press/Prentice Hall, 1988), and *Object Lifecycles: Modeling the World in States* (Englewood Cliffs, NJ: Yourdon Press/Prentice Hall, 1992).

[6]David W. Embley, Barry D. Kurtz, and Scott N. Woodfield, *Object-Oriented Systems Analysis: A Model-Driven Approach* (Englewood Cliffs, NJ: Yourdon Press/Prentice Hall, 1992).

[7]Donald G. Firesmith, *Object-Oriented Requirements Analysis and Design: A Software Engineering Approach* (New York: John Wiley and Sons, 1993), p. 2.

[8]James Rumbaugh, Michael Blaha, William Premerlani, Frederick Eddy, and William Lorensen, *Object-Oriented Modeling and Design* (Englewood Cliffs, NJ: Prentice Hall, 1991).

[9]Grady Booch, *Object-Oriented Design, with Applications* (Redwood City, CA: Benjamin/Cummings, 1991).

[10]Ivar Jacobson, Magnus Christerson, Patrik Jonsson, and Gunnar Övergaard, *Object-Oriented Software Engineering: A Use Case Driven Approach* (Reading, MA: Addison-Wesley, 1992).

18.1 GENERAL ADVICE ON DESIGNING THE HIC

Whether the designer chooses an architecture based on the ideas of Chapter 17, or something entirely different, one principle should be kept in mind: the portion of the system that deals with the human interface must be kept as independent and separate from the rest of the software architecture as possible. The reason for this is evident: aspects of the human interface will probably continue changing throughout the productive life of the system, and those changes should have a minimal impact—ideally, *no* impact—on the application-specific parts of the system.

Indeed, changes in the human interface will take place even more rapidly during the development phase of the project; indeed, this is one of the most common arguments in favor of prototyping. It is not only common, but highly recommended, that the HIC be developed and prototyped during the same period of time that the other model components are being developed. Indeed, there is a good chance that the HIC will be initially prototyped before the OOA analysis model is even complete. During the early prototyping activities, the user will probably request changes that affect both the HIC and the PDC; thus we might expect to hear comments like, "I want to display a piece of data called X, and I'm sorry that I forgot to tell you before that X is an attribute of object Y; and, by the way, I want X to be displayed in purple." Later on, as the analysis model settles down, subsequent prototyping may concentrate more on the "look and feel" of the human interface.

Partly because of the rapid changes caused by iterative prototyping, and partly because of the intricate detail involved in today's GUI interfaces, there is one piece of advice we can offer to designers with great passion: *don't design a custom-tailored HIC that can only be programmed in a low-level language.* In a language like C++ in many of today's popular operating system environments, it can take as much as six pages of code just to open a window for the user; at this point, the software engineer is likely to be so exhausted that he can't remember what he wanted to display in that window![11] Even though we will offer some cautions and warnings about upper-CASE tools for OOA and OOD in Chapters 23 and 24, there is already a strong trend toward lower-CASE tools for building the human interface in a GUI environment.

---

[11]Of course, if those six pages of C++ code have already been written, and are available to the developer in the form of a reusable class library, then this comment can be ignored.

This means that the designer may be provided with a "GUI-builder" that has the intelligence to generate appropriate classes and objects to manipulate windows and the elements within the windows; the software engineer merely has to provide the "hooks" to connect the human interface component to his application-oriented classes. Some of these GUI-builders may be part of a more comprehensive object-oriented application generator, such as MacApp or NeXTstep; others may be solely concerned with the user interface, such as Flashpoint, Easel, and so on.

The result may be that the designer is unaware of the details of the classes and objects generated by the GUI-builder to manipulate windows and icons; in any case, it is fair to say that the design of the HIC component is highly influenced not only by the operating environment in which the system will eventually run (as well as the designer's desire to allow portability across several such environments!), but also the tools that the designer has available to build the HIC component. This makes it somewhat easier to offer specific advice for building the HIC component within, say, the Windows-3 or OS/2 or Motif or Macintosh environment, but somewhat more difficult to offer generic, environment-neutral advice. Perhaps this explains why so many OOA and OOD authors have avoided saying anything specific about the topic.

18.2 THE HIC DESIGN STRATEGY

In an earlier book,[12] Peter Coad and I described such a "generic" strategy for designing the HIC component for a system, on the assumption that the designer did not have a convenient GUI-builder that would handle the details. That strategy can be summarized as follows:

- *Classify the people who use the system*—the designer may be able to take advantage of gen-spec structures in the OOA model that partition a "person" superclass into various subclasses. If appropriate, consider additional subsets of people by skill level, organizational level, membership in different groups, and so on.
- *Describe the task scenarios of the users*—the task scenarios identify events to which users must respond, and the sequence of

---

[12]Peter Coad and Edward Yourdon, *Object-Oriented Design* (Englewood Cliffs, NJ: Yourdon Press/Prentice Hall, 1991).

activities they must carry out. This is where the "use case" of the Jacobson methodology excels; some designers may choose to accomplish this with an event list, state-transition diagrams, or various other approaches.

- *Design the command hierarchy*—the command hierarchy will define a series of menu screens, or a menu bar with pull-down menu choices, or a series of icons that take action when the user "drops" an object on them, and so on; however it is accomplished, the command hierarchy should respect existing conventions and styles with which the user is comfortable and familiar. Note that the command hierarchy is, in effect, a way of presenting to the user the various methods within the classes and objects—or (to look at it another way) the various messages that the user himself can send to the classes and objects within the system. By organizing the command hierarchy into menus and submenus, and so on, the designer seeks to organize a rich, detailed interface using functional-decomposition concepts of "chunking," and breadth versus depth guidelines.

- *Design the detailed interactions between the user and the system*—the detailed interactions may involve mechanisms for allowing the user to input data fields, as well as choosing between options by "clicking" on radio buttons, check boxes, and various other GUI representations; this can be further augmented with sound, color, and all the high-tech gadgets at the designer's disposal. However, the distinction between a good interface and a bad interface, at this detailed level, has little or nothing to do with GUIs and OO technology. Sadly, many OO designers and many GUI enthusiasts have little exposure to or knowledge of the fundamental principles of good interface design espoused by Donald Norman, Ben Shneiderman, and others.

- *Design the HIC classes necessary to manage the interaction*—the basic class hierarchy for the HIC will typically have a "window" superclass, with appropriate subclasses for each of the different categories of windows to be displayed to the user. In addition, the designer will typically construct a whole-part structure to show the relationship between the window (whole) and the component parts of text/numeric fields, graphic elements, and so on. In many cases, the window class will need a "selector" subclass to deal with such issues as recognizing mouse clicks and drags, selecting a block of text in a text field, and so on.

- *Continue prototyping to ensure the HIC is acceptable to the user—* whatever formal design the designer develops must be exercised in a prototyping environment to ensure that it meets the user's needs. At the same time, this ongoing experimentation will almost certainly provide the designer with many opportunities to rearrange the class hierarchies and message connections between the HIC and PDC to improve the overall quality of the design.

18.3 FUTURE TRENDS IN HUMAN INTERFACES

A windows-based GUI-style human interface is widely accepted as the "state of the art" in many organizations today; there is little argument that such interfaces are more pleasant, more intuitive, and easier for most users to learn. Whether or not such interfaces are really cost-effective in all cases, and whether or not an older-style character-based interface might be more appropriate in some circumstances, arguing against GUIs is roughly as popular as arguing against downsizing.

But the designer must be especially careful not to assume that GUIs will be the ideal human interface forever; it could be a disaster if the *entire* software architecture depends heavily on the assumption that the human interface *must* take the form of a GUI. As this book is being written, we are already beginning to witness the beginning of the next wave of human interface: pen-based computing. Already, it has become evident that the human interfaces of pen-based (or pen-centric, or pen-aware, depending on whose marketing lingo one wants to use) applications have important differences with standard GUI interfaces:

- The "cut and paste" metaphor typically disappears, because the interface is based on *direct manipulation* of objects on the display screen—for example, the user touches an object directly with his pen and drags it someplace else on the screen. As a result, the "clipboard" metaphor disappears.
- The human interface includes a number of "gestures," or shorthand notations, made with the pen, to accomplish common tasks. Many pen-based word processors, for example,

use standard proofreader's notations (for example, the "pig-tail," and caret) for deleting and inserting characters.

- There is much more emphasis on variable-sized fonts for the text fields on the screens. This is not unusual in itself, but the font sizes are *dynamically* variable: the field of data currently being manipulated by the user is displayed in a larger font, for example, because the pen-based machine is being used in a poorly lit environment where the user has trouble reading the data; as a result, the fields of data that are not being actively manipulated can be shrunk to a smaller size.

Of course, as soon as pen-based human interfaces become widespread and common, we will be ready to move on to voice recognition . . . and meanwhile, researchers at Xerox PARC are suggesting the possibility of a three-dimensional user interface to replace today's standard two-dimensional interface. While today's interface is based on the metaphor of a "window" and a "desktop," tomorrow's interface may be based on the concept of a "room," with walls, windows, and doorways into other rooms.

Even before such avant-garde interfaces appear on the scene, the designer must be prepared for the following demands from users:

- *Complete customization of the user interface*—including fonts, colors, icons, screen-savers, and so on. For those familiar with the Macintosh environment (and various imitations thereof), this is second nature, but one must remember that many organizations have lived in a world of dumb terminals and character-based interfaces for so many decades that both the users and the software engineers have become brainwashed into believing that God intended humans to read nothing but 10-point Courier type on a green background.
- *Bite-size user interfaces*—so the user only has to see those commands that are relevant for the kind of work he is doing. Some commercial PC-based spreadsheet commands, for example, have over a thousand commands in their user interface, but the average user typically uses only a dozen. Why not let the user customize his user interface so that he only sees the dozen commands that are meaningful to him?
- *Intelligent "agents" that lurk in the background, watching the user's actions and making helpful suggestions*—for example,

noticing that the user has typed the same string of characters several times and offering to make it a macro (without forcing the user to retype the string yet again!) so that it can be invoked with a single keystroke.

- *Intelligent interfaces that anticipate the user's needs by watching for patterns of behavior*—for example, noticing that the user habitually invokes the spreadsheet package at 4:00 every Friday afternoon to update his departmental budget. After seeing the pattern a few times, an intelligent human interface could anticipate the request in advance—like a faithful puppy dog noticing that you have plopped yourself down in the living room chair and assuming that you would appreciate having your shoes fetched for you.

Customization and bite-size user interfaces should be possible now within the OO paradigm that we have discussed. However, the idea of intelligent agents and intelligent interfaces may cause a more significant change, for it assumes that some (if not all) of the objects in the system are "agents" and are *eternally active, looking for something to do.* We noted this possibility in an indirect way in Chapter 14, when we pointed out that an object could respond to a message and then continue computing; however, most software engineers are so thoroughly indoctrinated in the classic von Neumann style of computing that they automatically assume that objects are *passive* and "wake up" only when they receive a message.

All this suggests that GUI interfaces are just the beginning. Bill Curtis, of the Software Engineering Institute, boldly proclaimed in 1991 that the 1990s would be "the decade of the human interface."[13] And though we are a third of a way into the decade as this book is being written, we have a long way to go before we reach the next millennium!

18.4 THE *SMALL BYTES* CASE STUDY

Before we even begin thinking of the human interface for the *Small Bytes* system, let's remember what the user is dealing with now: a collection of spreadsheet, word processing, and database programs on a Macintosh computer. Thus it's reasonable to assume that the user is familiar with windows, icons, a mouse, and all the usual

---

[13]Bill Curtis, "Usability: The Quality Issue of the 1990s," *American Programmer*, February 1991.

manifestations of a GUI interface. It's also reasonable to assume that the user is a hard-code Macintosh bigot, with built-in assumptions that the new system will be just as "Mac-like" as every other program within that environment. Obviously, it will be important for us to maintain the Macintosh "look-and-feel" in our application.

Unfortunately, there is a disadvantage to the computer literacy our user exhibits: most of the real work in the current system is carried out with a simple flat-file database management system, using two files: a "names" file and an "invoices" file. So the user is familiar with the concept of opening a file, locating a record within the file based on arbitrarily complex search criteria, adding new records to the file, and occasionally deleting records from the file. The user is also aware that there is a conceptual "link" between the records in the invoice file and the records in the names file, although it never seems to work properly with the current system: each record in the invoice file is supposed to contain a unique "record-number" of a record in the names file, which is supposed to make the database management system automatically copy the name, address, and phone number fields into appropriate fields of the invoice record.

The first problem is that we don't want our user to think in terms of "files" and "records," but in terms of "classes" and "objects." But this distinction—and the argument about whether it is simply a matter of vocabulary or something deeper—strikes us, at first, as a diversion: what the user is really seeing, even in the current system, is a *view* of certain relevant data; because of the Macintosh environment, the user can open two windows on the screen at the same time and see a view of a subscriber name at the same time another window displays a view of an invoice. So perhaps we could simply tell our user that the new system will provide somewhat different "views" and avoid the confusing discussion of objects and files.

But here's the rub: the view that the user currently sees when displaying a record in the "names" file is a *combination* of information in the ORGANIZATION-SITE-PERSON class hierarchy that we modeled in Figure 10.17, *plus* information in the SUBSCRIPTION class hierarchy of Figure 10.18. And the view that the user currently sees in the "invoice" file is really a combination of information in the INVOICE class and the PAYMENT class hierarchy of Figure 10.16. Assuming that we want to provide approximately the same functionality in our new system, there is one obvious conclusion to draw from this: the information in a typical "window" class of the HIC is likely to contain pieces of information taken from several different classes (or class hierarchies) in the PDC. To model this carefully, then, we will need to document all the instance connections and messages connections between the HIC window classes and the PDC application classes.

But there is a far more important reason for making this observation: the "windows," or "views," that the user sees in the human interface reflect the various "use cases" (to use Ivar Jacobson's terminology) or *events* to which the user must respond. If we did not approach the problem from this perspective, we would be tempted to take a very simple-minded approach to the HIC for the *Small Bytes* system: every class and object in the PDC should have a one-to-one correspondence with a "shadow" class and object in the HIC whose job is to display the PDC contents and accept any modifications requested by the user.

And, indeed, sometimes this is exactly what we want to do in the human interface—if the PDC object is a "stand-alone" object, or *if* it does not have a required instance connection (or whole-part connection) with other classes and objects in the system. Thus when we look at Figure 11.12, where the instance connections for the classes in the PUBLICATION subject have been documented, we see that the user can, if desired, create a new instance of the TOPIC class without necessarily referring to any other class. If all the classes in the *Small Bytes* system were similarly "unattached" to anything else, our user interface would consist of a series of "create-search-update-delete" windows to allow the user to manipulate everything in the PDC.

But, evidently, things are not this simple: according to the whole-part connections and instance connections shown in Figure 11.15, for example, the user cannot add a new instance of ISSUE without describing the instance(s) of ARTICLE and the instance of TOPIC to which it is related. And although we can enter a new ARTICLE into our system without associating it with an ISSUE, our model tells us that we must associate it with exactly one TOPIC. And this leads to the key point: *our user interface must reflect, and match, the connections so specified in the OOA model*. Thus if we provide the user with a "window" to enter or manipulate an ISSUE, it *must* contain some data entry fields to allow the user to specify appropriate instances of TOPIC and ARTICLE.

Exactly how those fields are laid out on the screen is not our primary concern at this point; nor do we particularly care what color, size, or font is used to display that information. What we do need, at this point, is a list of user interface windows and a list of the PDC classes whose contents may have to be displayed within each window. Note, by the way, that in most cases, our window will have to display most (if not all) of the data fields of the "primary" class the user is trying to access; we typically only need to display the key field(s) of the classes to which the primary class is connected. Thus if the user wants a window that allows a new ISSUE to be entered, we probably need to display all the relevant attributes of the ISSUE class; however, we only need to display the "topic-ID" of the TOPIC class and the "article-ID" (or article-title) of the ARTICLE class.

How do we obtain a list of the necessary user interface windows? It should correspond to the "event list," if we developed such a list when modeling object behavior, as discussed in Chapter 13. Alternatively, we may wish to create an HIC window class for *each* PDC class, together with its "associated" classes (those connected via instance connections or whole-part connections). This may seem like overkill, but it will certainly provide an exhaustive list; through intelligent prototyping, we could choose the window classes of most concern to the user and implement them first.

19

Designing the Database

Together with the human interface, the database is typically a key component of concern for the software designer—regardless of which methodology is used to organize the software architecture. Of course, there are some systems—such as the elevator control system discussed throughout this book—where the database is negligible or nonexistent. But the vast majority of interesting application-oriented systems have permanent data that must be recorded on magnetic disk or tape, or some other device.

In an OO environment, the ideal solution to this issue would be to use an object-oriented database management system (OODBMS); in this case, every one of the "persistent" classes and objects in the software architecture would correspond *exactly* to a database object managed by the OODBMS. Indeed, the designer's primary job, in this environment, would be to distinguish between transient and persistent objects; inevitably, though, the designer's thinking about how best to organize the class hierarchy in the PDC and HIC would be influenced by his knowledge of how to optimize the performance of the OODBMS.

But at the time this book is being written, such an issue is irrelevant for more than 95 percent of the application designers around the world: they are not using an OODBMS, and they have no immediate plans to do so. Indeed, even if they wanted to, it would be impossible: their new application, developed with an OO approach, must interface with existing "legacy" data managed by a relational database management system (RDBMS) or flat-file system. So the primary question, for this part of our design architecture, is: How do the classes and objects in the PDC, HIC, and (if appropriate) TMC "talk" to the database? The answer is that all such communication goes through the classes and objects in the data management component (dmc).

An alternative would be to make each class and object, throughout the entire software architecture, responsible for its own reading and writing activities. Obviously, our chief concern with such an approach is that the entire architecture then becomes dependent upon the database technology; if, for example, the organization changes from a flat-file to a relational database—or possibly even from one RDBMS to another, such as a change from DB2 to Oracle—it would impact all the classes and objects throughout the system.

Thus the approach we use in this book is to make only *one* part of our software architecture aware of the idiosyncrasies of the database. This one part, otherwise known as the DMC, serves as an intermediary with the classes and objects in the PDC, HIC, and TMC. Via message connections, it reads and writes data between the database (in whatever form that happens to be organized) and the objects within the system. The penalty we pay for this kind of "information hiding" (that is, hiding information about the nature of the DBMS) is performance: each "logical IO" to read or write an object involves not only the physical read/write commands, but also an exchange of data (via message parameters) between the DMC and the relevant object elsewhere in the system.

It is interesting to note that, despite the wide variation in vocabulary, strategies, and notational schemes, most OOA/OOD methodologies seem to agree with this basic approach (although the methodologies that focus more exclusively on OO *analysis*, such as those of Embley-Kurtz and Shlaer-Mellor, sometimes make no mention of the database problem at all). Peter Coad and I described the approach in an earlier book,[1] and it is considered to be part of the Coad-Yourdon OOD methodology; similar approaches are found in the Jacobson, and Rumbaugh methodologies, among others. On the other hand, some authors, such as Don Firesmith,[2] ignore the issue altogether in their OOA/OOD methodology; others, like Grady Booch,[3] provide no formal guidance in the development of the data-

---

[1]Peter Coad and Edward Yourdon, *Object-Oriented Design* (Englewood Cliffs, NJ: Yourdon Press/Prentice Hall, 1991).

[2]Donald G. Firesmith, *Object-Oriented Requirements Analysis and Design: A Software Engineering Approach* (New York: John Wiley and Sons, 1993), p. 2.

[3]Grady Booch, *Object-Oriented Design, with Applications* (Redwood City, CA: Benjamin/Cummings, 1991).

base component of the architecture, but provide richly detailed case studies so that the reader can learn by example.

It is also interesting that most OOA/OOD authors focus their attention on *relational* databases. When discussing the use of an OO-base application with an RDBMS, for example, Jacobson and coworkers observe that

> When a programming language is connected to a DBMS, a number of problems arise. The first problem is that in our system all information is stored in the objects. We therefore need to transform our object information structured into a table-oriented structure. This problem is sometimes referred to as the **impedance problem**. The problem is often that the program has too rich a set of types, including those created by the user. All these types must be converted to the more primitive types of the RDBMS....
>
> The impedance problem yields yet another problem, it creates a strong coupling between the application and the DBMS. To make the design minimally affected by the DBMS, as few parts of our system as possible should know about the DBMS's interface.[4]

Similarly, Rumbaugh and coworkers introduce their discussion of relational databases with the comment:

> The use of an object-oriented design transcends the choice of database. You can design hierarchical, network, relational, and object-oriented databases....
>
> You design a database by first performing the analysis steps . . . and constructing an object model . . . and consider[ing] implementation issues. How can we map an object model to database structures and tune the result for fast performance?
>
> The coverage of this chapter is biased towards relational DBMS for the following reasons. Relational DBMS are gaining popularity at the expense of hierarchical and network DBMS. Relational DBMS are increasing their advantage in functionality and flexibility and are catching up in performance. Object-oriented DBMS

---

[4]Ivar Jacobson, Magnus Christerson, Patrik Jonsson, and Gunnar Övergaard, *Object-Oriented Software Engineering: A Use Case Driven Approach* (Reading, MA: Addison-Wesley, 1992), p. 271.

look promising but have not yet reached the commercial mainstream. Logic DBMS also seem promising but are even further away from mass market acceptance.[5]

Martin and Odell echo a similar conclusion, although they sound more hopeful about the commercial success of OODBMS products:

> The goal of relational databases, that of making the data independent of the application, will remain important for much data. We will always need to set up databases that can be used in unpredictable ways. In contrast, OODB establishes data that are used *only with defined methods*. RDB and OODB, then, meet different needs—both of which are important.
>
> In the foreseeable future, OO database technology will not replace relational database technology but will coexist with it.[6]

"Coexistence" between relational and object-oriented databases will almost certainly exhibit some "hybrid" characteristics over the next several years: several of the RDBMS vendors have already begun to add object-oriented features to their products. For example, some of the newest RDBMS packages allow the user to define superclasses and subclasses of entities, although they may or may not provide the full form of inheritance discussed in this book; some provide a mechanism for "triggers" and "stored procedures" that can be associated with the entities, although they typically don't provide the full mechanism of "methods" and message connections as described in this book. Eventually, some of these RDBMS packages may evolve into full-fledged OODBMSs; for now, however, the designer must still treat them as if they were RDBMSs, because that's how the data is fundamentally organized.

In general, the strategy for the DMC component of the software architecture consists of two parts: designing the "data layout" of fields, records, rows, and tables, and so on on the database and designing the methods/services that will be used to access that data. We briefly summarize each of these activities in the paragraphs that follow.

---

[5]James Rumbaugh, Michael Blaha, William Premerlani, Frederick Eddy, and William Lorensen, *Object-Oriented Modeling and Design* (Englewood Cliffs, NJ: Prentice Hall, 1991), p. 366.

[6]James Martin and James J. Odell, *Object-Oriented Analysis & Design* (Englewood Cliffs, NJ: Prentice Hall, 1992), p. 314.

19.1 DESIGNING THE DATA LAYOUT

The details of the data layout obviously depend greatly on the file structure of the DBMS. With a flat-file environment, for example, we would normally begin with the assumption that each class and object in our design would correspond to a separate file on the database. Depending on performance and storage requirements, we could then "back off" that initial strategy by collapsing several classes into one file; on the other hand, a careful job in this area first requires that the classes in the PDC and HIC components be expressed in first normal form—so that any repeating groups within our classes would typically be separated out and put in a file of their own.

However, as noted, the majority of nontrivial applications today tend to operate in a relational database environment. In this case, we would usually begin by translating the classes in our object-oriented model into standard third-normal form; we would then define a database table for each of the third-normal-form tables emerging from this "object normalization" process. Jacobson and coworkers summarize the process as follows:

> A class is mapped onto tables in the following manner:
>
> (1) Assign one table for the class.
>
> (2) Each (primitive) attribute will become one column in the table. If the attribute is complex (that is, must be composed of DBMS types) we either add an additional table for the attribute, or split the attribute over several columns in the table of the class.
>
> (3) The primary key column will be the unique instance identifier, namely, the identifier by which the instance is uniquely recognized. The identifier should preferably not be visible to the user, since changes of the keys for administrative reasons should not affect the user; machine generated keys should be used.
>
> (4) Each instance of the class will now be represented by a row in this table.
>
> (5) Each acquaintance association with a cardinality greater than 1 (for example, [0..n]) will become a new table. This new table will connect the tables representing the objects that are to be associated. The primary keys of these tables can be used in this "acquaintance" table. In some cases, however, we may

have the relation represented only as a column (attribute) in the associated object's table.[7]

It's important to emphasize that a database developed in this way must be examined for performance considerations. To "populate" or "re-create" an object from a third-normal-form relational database, it will usually be necessary to perform several "join" operations across tables. If the performance penalty is unacceptable, then it may be necessary to back off to second-normal form or even first-normal form.

19.2 DESIGNING THE DATABASE SERVICES

Once we have decided how the data will be organized on the database, we must provide appropriate *methods* for retrieving and updating that data. Rather than burying these methods in the PDC classes and objects, we will put them into one or more "Object-Saver" classes within the DMC.

The straightforward approach is to provide a "shadow" class in the DMC for *each* persistent class in the PDC, HIC, and TMC components of the architecture. This Object-Saver class needs to know which file(s) to open, how to position the file to the proper position, which rows and columns to access, and how to update the records or tables with new values.

Each of these Object-Saver classes needs to have a number of methods that can be accessed, via messages, from appropriate classes in the other components of the software architecture:

- a method that can create a new instance of a persistent object by creating new records, or row(s) within relational tables, and so on. The attribute values of the newly created object would be initialized and populated with data values supplied in the parameters of the message that invokes this "create" method.

- a method that can read a specified instance of an object, by reading appropriate records and/or relational rows and "composing" or "constructing" the object instance by filling in appropriate data values in the attributes.

[7]Jacobson et al., *Object-Oriented Software Engineering*, pp. 272–273.

- a method whose job is to tell the associated PDC/HIC/TMC class, via a message, to save itself. The response to that message should be the appropriate data values for the instances that need to be saved.

19.3 COMMENTS ON THE *SMALL BYTES* AND ELEVATOR CASE STUDIES

For the *Small Bytes* project, our assumption is that the new system will have to run on the same Macintosh environment as the old system. Hence the designer will either have to choose a relatively simple flat-file database or relational database that can be accessed directly by C++ or Smalltalk on the Macintosh. This rules out the FileMaker database approach that had been used on the old version of the system—not because FileMaker is a flat-file DBMS, but because it is "self-contained," with its own scripting language, and no interfaces to other programming languages.

Thus this is one of the relatively infrequent situations where the development of the new application *requires* changing the database; this would have occurred regardless of whether we chose an object-oriented approach or a more conventional SA/SD or IE approach. There are, of course, a variety of DBMS choices available on the Macintosh, and the choice of the DBMS would determine the details of our DMC component, following the guidelines in this chapter.

For the elevator system, it is reasonable to assume that there won't be an external database, since everything that the system does can be maintained in the computer's RAM memory. This means, then, that none of the classes and objects shown in the previous chapters would be persistent; if the system were turned off and then restarted, all the classes and objects would be restored to an initialized state without any memory of what summons buttons had been pushed when the system was previously operating.

20

OOP and the Impact of Programing Languages

Programming is where the tire meets the road: after all the abstract concepts of analysis and design, we must eventually transform the bubbles and boxes in our diagrams into a real-world programming language. Naturally, if we have invested all this effort in an object-oriented form of analysis and design, it stands to reason that we will use an object-oriented programming language to implement the software.

Of course, this is not absolutely necessary: as we discussed in Chapter 3, it's possible to mix object-oriented and nonobject-oriented "phases" of a traditional systems development life cycle. Most often, one sees a combination of structured analysis or some other non-OO approach to the systems analysis phase, combined with OOD and OOP. However, it is conceivable that one could carry out OOA and OOD and then follow it up with a traditional non-OO programming language.

Why would anyone do this? It's hard to imagine that anyone would *want* to follow such an approach, but there may be any number of ugly real-world problems: lack of a compiler for one's favorite OOPL on the hardware platform that has been mandated for the project, lack of experience with the OOPL on the part of the programming staff, contractual constraints that preclude the use of an OOPL, severe performance constraints that force the programmers to use assembly language, and so on. Naturally, we sympathize with these problems, but for the purposes of this book, we'll ignore them: most projects that have committed themselves to OOA and OOD can be expected to use a "pure" or at least a "quasi" OOPL.

Indeed, for the vast majority of projects underway as this book is being written, there is very little argument about *which* OOPL will be used. For better or worse, the battle over object-oriented programming languages is ended, and a marketplace winner has emerged: C++.

Of course, there are other choices, choices that most OO enthusiasts (the author included) would argue are far superior to C++: Smalltalk, Ada, Eiffel, and the new, emerging, object-oriented version of COBOL. Smalltalk is favored by some, and it has approximately the same position, vis-à-vis programming languages, that the Macintosh had vis-à-vis MS-DOS and the IBM PC in the mid-1980s: a benchmark, a standard of excellence at which to aim. Ada 83, has some, but not all, the language features that one wants in an OOPL; whether or not it ever becomes a full-fledged, bona-fide OOPL, it is highly doubtful that it will ever be a "mainstream" programming language outside the U.S. Defense Department. Similarly, Eiffel is much more "pure" in its object-oriented features than C++, but it also suffers from minor-league status: few programmers have ever heard of the language, let alone used it.

But it is not our purpose here to defend or criticize any specific programming language; as suggested, various nontechnical factors may have more influence on the choice of the programming language than the presence or absence of object-oriented features. And it is the author's strong opinion that the issue of programming languages will gradually become less and less important throughout the rest of the 1990s as our attention shifts more and more toward code-generating CASE tools. Twenty or 30 years ago, the overwhelming majority of programming was done in assembly language; high-order languages like FORTRAN and COBOL were regarded primarily as tools for engineers, scientists, and business analysts who weren't smart enough to write real programs. Compilers generated assembly language output (which then had to be run through an assembler) because "real" programmers weren't sure they trusted the compilers—and besides, any debugging typically required an assembly language debugger. Today, all that seems rather quaint, and it is likely that the arguments over C++, Smalltalk, Ada, and Eiffel will strike the software engineers of the early twenty-first century as quaint, too.[1]

---

[1] It should also be emphasized that many of the better prototyping tools today generate code in object-oriented languages such as C++ and Smalltalk; in addition, they provide excellent debugging and tracing tools at the higher-level abstraction of the visual programming language upon which the tool is based.

20.1 WHAT FEATURES SHOULD AN OOPL HAVE?

As noted, not all software engineers have the luxury of using a "pure" OOPL; indeed, virtually all common programming languages have some limitations and weaknesses. As Wirfs-Brock and coworkers acknowledge:

> The language in which you will implement your design will be flawed. We are confident of this statement because the perfect language in which to program a computer has not yet been invented. Choosing a language is therefore partly a matter of deciding which flaws are likely to be relatively minor, given the specifics of your task, and which ones are likely to cause serious inconvenience.[2]

Our concern in this discussion is fairly narrow: we are not concerned with the full range of the semantics of the language, but only in those features that support the concepts of object orientation. What is it that the programming language needs in order to translate effectively the OOA requirements and OOD design into a program that can be tested and maintained effectively?

We have also ignored the largest technical factor in the choice of a programming language: some languages are intrinsically better suited to certain applications than others. Engineers and scientists are likely to choose FORTRAN over COBOL as the "natural" language for solving their problems, and software engineers who build business data processing applications are likely to choose COBOL over C++ for their work. Thus a large segment of the software development industry is likely to ignore object orientation at the programming level until (1) a new OO language is invented to serve their needs or (2) their favorite "old" language is enhanced to include OO features.

Regarding object-orientation, our primary concerns are these:

- How does the language allow us to create classes and objects?
- How does the language allow us to create gen-spec structures?
- How does the language allow us to create whole-part structures?
- How does the language allow us to describe attributes?
- How does the language allow us to describe methods?

---

[2]Rebecca Wirfs-Brock, Brian Wilkerson, and Lauren Wiener, *Designing Object-Oriented Software* (Englewood Cliffs, NJ: Prentice Hall, 1990), p. 178.

The degree of support for these features sometimes leads to an overall categorization of the language as "object-oriented" or "object-based," and so on. Booch suggests the following criteria:

> . . . a language is considered object-based if it directly supports data abstraction and classes; an object-oriented language is one that is object-based, but provides additional support for inheritance as a means of expressing hierarchies of classes.[3]

Each of these is discussed in more detail in the next section.

20.2 CREATING CLASSES AND OBJECTS

Obviously, the ability to create classes and objects is central to the idea of object-orientation. Legitimate OOPLs will provide the programmer with a "class" or "object" declarative construct; non-OOPLs, such as the traditional third-generation programming languages, leave the programmer no option but to "fake" a class and object by using more conventional mechanisms such as subroutines or procedures.

Of course, most of our attention will focus on such things as inheritance, visibility of attributes within the object, and so on. However, we want to start with the basics: Does the programming language have a natural mechanism for allowing the programmer to create encapsulated "chunks" of data and procedure? A programming language that allows each procedure/subroutine to have its own local variables is a bare minimum; this would include such languages as Pascal, PL/I, C, and so on. Even the languages that allow global access to data areas, such as COBOL's treatment of data in a DATA DIVISION, frequently provide the mechanism of separately compiled "units," or "packages," or "programs." Thus, while Ada does not directly support such key concepts as inheritance, its concept of packages does provide a very formal and elegant form of encapsulation.

Of special interest in an OOPL is the mechanism that the programmer uses to create new objects and delete objects that are no longer needed. As Rumbaugh and coworkers note,

---

[3]Grady Booch, *Object-Oriented Design, with Applications*, p. 474. (Redwood City, CA: Benjamin/Cummings, 1991), See also L. Cardelli and P. Wegner, "On Understanding Types, Data Abstraction, and Polymorphism," *ACM Computing Surveys*, December 1985.

Some languages, such as Smalltalk and DSM, have classes that are full objects in their own right. In these languages, an operation applied to a class object (called a class operation) creates a new object of the class. Other languages, such as C++ and Eiffel, do not have class objects. These languages have special operations that create new objects. . . .

Different languages use one of two styles of destroying objects that are no longer needed. In some languages, objects are destroyed by an explicit operation (such as *destroy*). The programmer must take care that no references to a destroyed object remain, or memory access errors may result. Explicit memory management is error-prone, so some languages, such as Smalltalk, include automatic garbage collectors that destroy objects that are inaccessible, without requiring (or permitting) any explicit deallocation.[4]

20.3 CREATING GEN-SPEC STRUCTURES

Support for gen-spec, or superclass-subclass, structures is crucial in an OOP, for this is where inheritance comes into play. Supporters of languages like Ada will argue that inheritance is not mandatory for OO-programming and that the programmer can live without it.[5] But that's like saying the average American family can live without television; yes, it's possible, but it puts one so far outside the mainstream of society that it's hard to communicate.

Assuming that the language does support inheritance, the immediate question is: What kind of inheritance? Smalltalk, for example, supports single inheritance, while C++ supports multiple inheritance. For languages that support multiple inheritance, our question is: How are "name conflicts" resolved? That is, if an object inherits identically named attributes from two different superclasses, how is the conflict resolved? (In most cases, the language will consider this to be a syntax error, and the programmer will be required to use unique names.)

Martin and Odell offer an interesting observation on the subject of inheritance:

---

[4]James Rumbaugh, Michael Blaha, William Premerlani, Frederick Eddy, and William Lorensen, *Object-Oriented Modeling and Design* (Englewood Cliffs, NJ: Prentice Hall, 1991), p. 301.

[5]But they also point out that Ada 9X, which is expected to be released in 1994 or 1995, *will* have inheritance.

Support for multiple and dynamic classification is essential. Currently, very few commercial OO systems fully support this, yet our experience finds these objects types extremely valuable during analysis.

Even with single, static classification, the concept of class inheritance has many subtleties. The fact that several different forms of inheritance exist indicates evolution is still in progress. Currently, inheritances is a low-level notion that allows varied effects—not all of them desirable. In the future, a higher-level use of inheritance could give it a structure in the same way that structured programming organizes flow of control. Until then, inheritance—particularly multiple inheritance—remains a tool that must be used carefully.[6]

Wirfs-Brock and coworkers offer some useful suggestions for dealing with both multiple and single inheritance:

If you are using a language that supports multiple inheritance, we have some recommendations for the best way to make use of its features.

- Define the structure of your objects as low as possible within the class hierarchy and encapsulate that structure within classes. Sharing structure from more than one superclass can be a complex problem in some languages.
- If a class inherits a message from more than one superclass, override the implementation of both superclasses. Either define the behavior of the class precisely when it receives the message, by implementing a method by that name in the class itself, or use the language defaults if they give the desired behavior.

If you are using a language that restricts you to single inheritance and you feel limited by it, you can overcome this limitation with either of two possible techniques:

- Choose which of the desired superclasses the new class is most like, and define the new class to be its subclass. At the same time, make your new class a composite class whose components are instances of the other classes from which you wanted it to inherit. Design the composite class to respond to the messages it would have inherited from these other classes. It can respond simply by passing these messages on to the

[6]James Martin and James J. Odell, *Object-Oriented Analysis & Design* (Englewood Cliffs, NJ: Prentice Hall, 1992), p. 431.

appropriate component, delegating those responsibilities to its components.

- Another, although less desirable, approach is again to choose which of the desired superclasses the class is most like. Define the new class to be a subclass of that class, and copy the code you wanted to inherit from the other class. We do not recommend this method except as a last resort; clearly, it involves duplication of effort for both testing and maintenance, and creates all kinds of possibilities for confusion.[7]

20.4 CREATING WHOLE-PART STRUCTURES

As we have seen in earlier sections of this book, whole-part structures are quite useful when modeling aspects of the user's requirements, as well as components of the software architecture. When we reach the programming phase of the project, the question is: How does the language support the whole-part concept?

Most OOPLs don't have an explicit construct to identify wholes and parts, but they provide one of two mechanisms that are quite adequate for the task: *containment* of classes inside other classes and *pointers* from one class to another. In some cases, simply placing the text of a "part" class declaration inside the scope of the "whole" class declaration will do the job.

20.5 CREATING ATTRIBUTES

Obviously, all programming languages allow the programmer to create attributes—although they may be called "variables," "data members," and so on. As noted before, our first concern is the ability to *encapsulate* those attributes, together with appropriate methods, inside an object.

Since the primary objective of encapsulation is to "hide" the attributes from other components of the system, our question about the programming language is: What control does it give the programmer over the *visibility* of the attributes? Languages like C++ provide a variety of visibility schemes; languages like Smalltalk allow one to declare "instance variables" (which are hidden inside each object) and "class variables" (which are accessible to the objects

---

[7]Wirfs-Brock et al, *Designing Object-Oriented Software*, pp.180–181

within the class, as well as their subclasses—but not to the other classes and objects in the system).

To allow for a smooth "mapping" from the OOA/OOD model into code, the language should also allow the programmer to describe "constraints" on the attribute—allowable values, upper/lower limits, data types (integer, character), accuracy, precision, units of measure, and so on.

A very important category of "attribute" is the instance connection between one object and another; as noted in Chapter 11, this could be considered part of the "state" of an object. As with whole-part structures, we would expect most programming languages to implement the concept of instance connections with pointers.

20.6 CREATING METHODS

Finally, the language must provide the programmer with a mechanism for creating methods; since this is a form of "function," or "procedure," or "subroutine," we can safely expect that it will be present in any language that claims to be an OOPL. Similarly, the concept of a "message connection" is fundamentally the same as a subroutine call or procedure invocation—so there is little doubt that it will exist in any programming language. However, the form and "flavor" of methods and messages in an OOPL is substantially different than in older-style programming languages; among other things, non-OOPLs typically don't support polymorphism or dynamic binding. Here is the way Jacobson and coworkers describe it:

> Each object has a well-defined **interface** which specifies which stimuli the object can receive, that is, which operations can be performed on the object. Each stimulus received causes an operation to be performed, where the stimulus is interpreted by the receiving object. If one tries to send a stimulus to an object which has no corresponding operation (i.e., the stimulus is not represented in the object's interface), an error occurs. . . .
>
> Each object is able to receive a specified number of stimuli. The object interprets this stimulus and performs an operation or, perhaps, directly accesses a variable.[8]

---

[8]Ivar Jacobson, Magnus Christerson, Patrik Jonsson, and Gunnar Övergaard, *Object-Oriented Software Engineering: A Use Case Driven Approach* (Reading, MA: Addison-Wesley, 1992), pp. 87–88.

There are two issues that need to be examined closely when considering a prospective OOPL: What kind of control does the programmer have over the visibility of the methods? And what support does the language provide for dynamic binding?

The issue of visibility is essentially the same as with attributes: in some cases, we want to declare "private" methods, or "protected" methods that are only visible to members of the class; in other cases, we are willing to make the method "public" and therefore accessible to any other class in the system.

The issue of dynamic binding is particularly important for reuse: we would like the ability to specify, *at run time*, the identity of the class or object to which a method is sending its messages. Many of the older programming languages have static binding, in which the name and identity of the invoked object must be specified at compile time, or at link-edit time. Languages like C++ allow the programmer to specify whether the binding is static or dynamic, and languages like Smalltalk assume that all object-to-object binding is dynamic in nature.

21

OO Goodness Criteria

Throughout this book, our discussion has implied that there will be only *one* model of user requirements and only one OOD software architecture. Indeed, we will end up with only one such model by the time we begin programming, but there are *many* possible models that will correctly implement a set of requirements. Still some models are better than others, so the question is: How do the analyst and the designer know which model is the best one?

To some extent, the answer is based on prototyping. An initial model may be proposed by the software engineer and sketched on paper or CASE workstation using the diagramming conventions in this book, but if an initial prototype proves unacceptable to the user, or unwieldy to the software engineer, it will obviously be changed. Thus many OO systems developers might argue, quite simply, that the best design is the one that works. Period.

But the real measure of goodness may not be apparent for several years after a system has been put into operation. If there is one thing that the older generation of non-OO mainframe structured analysis practitioners has learned, it's that software lasts forever. Many large organizations around the world are now maintaining application systems that are old enough to vote; indeed, some of them are older than the programmers who maintain them! Even in the Nanosecond Nineties, with CPUs being replaced every year or two, we must still concentrate on building software that lasts.

From this perspective, a good design is one that balances a series of trade-offs to minimize the *total cost* of the system over its entire productive life span. Obviously, we want a system that is reasonably efficient, and we want it to be elegant, user-friendly, portable, and so forth. But we also want it to be reasonably easy to test, modify, and maintain. At least half the total cost of the system—

and often as much as 90 percent!—will be incurred *after* the system has been put into operation. It may not be glamorous or politically expedient, but that's where we should be focusing our attention.

So—how do we help the designer achieve an optimal design? One approach would be to rely more heavily on the idea of standard software architectures, which we discussed in Chapter 17. Thus, if an organization eventually discovers (perhaps through trial and error) an ideal software architecture for the kind of systems it builds, it could then announce to its software engineers, "Henceforth, *all* designs must look like this one!"

Of course, this presupposes that the organization only builds one kind of system, for example, it does nothing but build payroll systems or flight control systems. For the organization that builds a wide variety of applications, the hard-nosed "one-size-fits-all" approach obviously won't work; however, a broader version of this idea, based on the concept of "patterns," can be quite useful, as we will see later in this chapter. Indeed, much of the advice passed on from veteran designers to neophytes has to do with bad patterns: "Don't ever do this, because it leads to incredible problems!"

The object-oriented software engineering field is gradually beginning to accumulate a storehouse of knowledge of this kind: guidelines, rules of thumb, warnings, and "magic numbers" that can be used to evaluate the goodness or badness of a proposed design. To be brutally honest, all this has to be categorized as informal "tribal folklore." It's not that OO software engineers are primitive savages, squatting around the campfire and muttering to one another, "Whenever we have more than three parameters in our message connections, the Object Overlord strikes us down with a lightning bolt, and our children suffer the curse of impotence and bad coupling!" But on the other hand, we have no statistical evidence or scientific experiments to confirm the validity of the various goodness criteria that will be discussed in this chapter.

Ironically, the same criticism was valid for structured analysis and design during the 1970s and 1980s; it was only with the publication of David Card's book, *Measuring Design Quality*,[1] some 15 years after the first book was published on structured design, that we saw a the beginning of a serious, detailed, scientific effort to validate such

---

[1]David Card, *Measuring Design Quality* (Englewood Cliffs, NJ: Prentice Hall, 1990).

concepts as coupling, cohesion, span of control, and so on. It is hoped that it won't take another 15 years for researchers to verify and quantify the goodness criteria for OO principles.

In the meantime, tribal folklore is better than nothing at all. The guidelines presented in this chapter may not be accurate in all cases; indeed, a few of them may eventually be proven wrong. But they reflect the real-world experiences of practicing OO analysts, designers, and programmers around the world And, as we will see, many of the OO guidelines are based on common software engineering principles that *have* been validated within the context of other analysis/design methodologies.

In an earlier book,[2] Peter Coad and I discussed a number of OOD guidelines; we begin by summarizing those. We then summarize the design guidelines proposed by Tom Love, and those proposed by Kemerer and Chidamber.

21.1 THE COAD-YOURDON OOD GUIDELINES

The Coad-Yourdon OOD guidelines are based on extensive discussions and interviews in 1989–1990 with software engineers throughout North America, Europe, and Australia. Some can be categorized as "hard" guidelines, with quantitative metrics; others are "soft" guidelines that must be interpreted by the designer on a case-by-case basis.

The guidelines include the following:

- *Coupling guidelines.* Coupling is a term that was popularized in the mid-1970s with various structured design guidelines; it refers to the "strength" of interconnections or interdependencies between discrete components in a system; as such, it is a "bad" thing, something to be minimized whenever possible. For an OO system, we are primarily concerned with the coupling between classes and objects that are not part of a genspec or whole-part hierarchy; that coupling takes the form of message connections. Of course, the very principle of encapsulation is intended to minimize coupling, but we still look for ways to minimize the number of messages between objects, as well as minimizing the complexity and content of

---

[2]Peter Coad and Edward Yourdon, *Object-Oriented Design* (Englewood Cliffs, NJ: Yourdon Press/Prentice Hall, 1991).

the messages themselves. Coupling is also created by inheritance in class hierarchies, but this is usually evaluated in terms of the cohesion guidelines discussed next.

- *Cohesion guidelines.* Cohesion is also a term popularized by structured design; it remains relevant in the new world of OOD. Cohesion is a way of describing the "togetherness," or strength of association of elements *within* a system component; low cohesion is a bad thing, and something to be avoided. In OO designs, we are concerned about cohesion at three levels: (1) the cohesiveness of individual methods, (2) the cohesiveness of the data and methods encapsulated within a class and object, and (3) the cohesiveness of an entire class hierarchy. At the microscopic level, method cohesion can be evaluated just as it is with structured design: a method should carry out one, and only one, function, and it should be possible to describe its purpose accurately with a simple sentence containing a single verb and a single object. At the intermediate level, it can be evaluated using various guidelines discussed shortly, and at the class hierarchy level, it can be evaluated by examining the extent to which subclasses override or delete attributes and methods inherited from their superclasses.

- *Focusing on the clarity of the design.* Although it must be classified as a "soft" guideline, software engineers generally agree that if they can't *understand* someone's OOD design, then they won't reuse it—and if they can't reuse it, it's bad (or, at least, worse than an alternative design that can be reused). Specified advice in this area includes using a consistent vocabulary for naming methods and attributes, avoiding excessive numbers of "message templates," avoiding "fuzzy" class definitions, and adhering to existing protocols or behaviors of classes.

- *Hierarchy and factoring guidelines.* Good designs are neither too "deep" nor too "shallow" in terms of their class hierarchies. A medium-sized system with approximately 100 classes is likely to have class hierarchies with 7 ± 2 levels of gen-spec and whole-part structures. This may be affected by the programming language, by the use of single inheritance versus multiple inheritance, and so on, but it would be unusual (and probably a manifestation of a bad design) to see class hierarchies 20 levels deep, or only 2 levels deep. Excessive levels of subclasses often occur with overly zealous first-time OOD practitioners who "over factor" their design.

- *Keeping classes and objects simple.* A bad design often has an excessive number of attributes in the classes; there should be no more than one or two attributes, on average, for each method, of which two-thirds should be traceable all the way back to the OOA model. A bad design also tends to have an excessive number of methods in each class; one typically finds no more than six or seven public methods per class, in addition to whatever private methods are necessary for internal housekeeping, and so on.[3] And a bad design tends to have excessive "collaboration" (i.e., coupling) between objects. While it's understandable that an object may not be able to respond to an external event by itself, it should not be necessary to interact with more than 7 ± 2 other objects to accomplish something.

- *Keeping message protocols simple.* Complex message protocols, as noted, are a common indication of excessive coupling between classes and objects. If a message requires more than three parameters, it's an indication of a bad design; the typical problem is that the class hierarchy has been poorly factored. Similarly, the existence of computer science "jargon" in the message protocol typically means that the class is doing something other than what is in the problem domain.

- *Keeping methods simple.* With a reasonable high-level language, it should be possible to write the code for each method in less than a page (which may require one or two screens on a workstation display monitor); indeed, with a language like Smalltalk, it is common to see methods of less than 10 lines of code. If the method involves a lot of code, look at it more closely; if it contains IF-THEN-ELSE statements or CASE statements, it's a *strong* indication that the method's class has been poorly factored—that is., procedural

---

[3]Of course, this can vary substantially, depending on the nature of the application.

code is being used to make decisions that should have been made in the inheritance hierarchy.

- *Minimizing the volatility of the design.* A bad design will exhibit considerable volatility all during the development phase of the project, as well as during the ongoing maintenance efforts; a small change in one class, to fix a bug or add a new feature, causes a "ripple effect" throughout many other classes. It may not be clear what the cause of the volatility is (although it is usually the result of the coupling problems described above), but it can nevertheless be used by the project manager as an unbiased assessment of the quality of the design. With a good configuration management system, the manager should be able to track the "impact analysis" associated with a change to an individual class, and it should be possible to detect a trendline of ever increasing stability as the project inches closer to its deadline.

- *Minimizing the overall system size.* Small is beautiful, big is ugly. A medium-sized application should require no more than a few dozen class hierarchies, each of which may involve a dozen subclasses. If each of the individual classes has half a dozen methods, and if each of those methods involves 10-20 lines of code, the aggregate amount of software is pretty substantial. Unfortunately, there seems to be a "macho" attitude among some software engineers that leads them to think that their prowess and competence will be judged by how many classes they have managed to invent in their system.

- *Emphasizing the ability to "evaluate by scenario."* It should be possible to evaluate the goodness of a design with a "role-playing" exercise, in which the reviewers act out the behavior of individual classes and objects. Thus one reviewer might say to another, "Okay, I'm the XYZ object and I'm sending an 'abc' message to you; what are you going to do with it?" If this kind of exercise proves impossible to conduct, it may indicate that the responsibilities of the various classes have not been well described, or well thought out.

21.2 TOM LOVE'S OOD "PATTERNS"

In Chapter 17, we mentioned Christopher Alexander's notion of "patterns" for evaluating the quality of a design. Although Alexander's work was primarily in the field of architecture—evaluating, for example, the patterns that one sees in the design of a building or a town, patterns that form the basis of a "timeless design"— the ideas can be applied to software engineering as well.

In a recent article, consultant Tom Love suggests that the same principles can be applied specifically to object-oriented systems:

> As I read three of Alexander's books, it occurred to me that we have an unusual opportunity in the software industry. As we are making changes in the development process to accommodate objects, we could simultaneously introduce some of the ideas of timeless design. At the very least, we could use this approach to derive some of the patterns of good object-oriented software design within our respective organizations and agree to adhere to them.

Love then proposes the following list of 22 "patterns" of good OO designs:

1. Objects should not access data defined in their superclasses.
2. Classes should be grouped into defined collections of about twenty classes that have restricted visibility from other classes in the system. All methods should not be made available to all users.
3. Classes near the root of an inheritance tree should not depend upon classes further down in the tree.
4. Methods of the same name in different classes should mean the same thing.
5. Methods with different names should mean different things.
6. Methods should do some work, not just pass the buck to another method. Avoid spaghetti code.
7. An inheritance tree should be a generalization-specialization tree with more specialized capabilities near the leaves of the tree.

[4]Tom Love, "Timeless Design of Information Systems," *Object Magazine*, November–December 1991, p. 46.

8. OO code should have a minimum number of branching statements, no more than one branching statement for every five lines of code.

9. Classes should be easy to describe and visualize. It should be possible to draw a picture of each class to convey its purpose or intent.

10. Classes should have minimum coupling with other classes and maximum internal cohesion.

11. A class tester should be written for every class that fully exercises that class and determines if it does what its specification claims.

12. There should be only one set of user interface classes within a single application or system.

13. The ergonomics group or a designated user shall approve all user interfaces including the choice of graphics, font, and color.

14. A focus group of real users should be assembled every four months during any development project. The project manager must explicitly address any usability issues raised in this meeting.

15. The application or system context should be visible to the user at any time. I should know where I am, where I have been, and where I can go.

16. Even large development projects should proceed in a piecemeal or spiral fashion—every six months a major new capability should be provided in the form of a working system. In other words, development should proceed by iterative enhancement with each iteration taking no more than six months.

17. At any given time, there should always be a list of new features and functions, as well as a list of improvements.

18. Methods should set the value of their instance variables by sending a message—to eliminate coupling among inherited classes.

19. Detailed estimates of runtime performance and memory utilizations should be made for each class (or ensemble of classes) at design time and tracked throughout development.

20. Testing of OO systems should strive to remove the most objectionable error first—looked at from the user perspective.

21. A design when "printed" should require no more than 10 percent of the "ink" of the complete system.

22. A design should be machine checkable, executable, and analyzable.

Obviously, some of these "patterns" are not unique for OO projects, and could just as well be used with other methodologies. And others—such as patterns 13, 14, and 16—are not so much concerned with any design methodology as they are with larger issues of project management and system development life cycles. It is also interesting to note that many of the specific design-level suggestions are compatible with the guidelines concerning coupling and cohesion that were discussed in Section 21.1.

21.3 THE KEMERER-CHIDAMBER GUIDELINES

Finally, we mention the guidelines proposed by Chidamber and Kemerer of MIT. It is interesting that the two researchers characterize their guidelines as "metrics":

> This paper presents theoretical work that builds a suite of metrics for object-oriented design (OOD). In particular, these metrics are based upon *measurement theory* and are informed by the insights of experienced object-oriented software developers.[5]

The guidelines, or metrics, fall into six categories, with "viewpoints" expressed by the two researchers:

1. *Weighted methods per class, with a weighting factor based on static complexity of the individual methods.* "Objects with large numbers of methods are likely to be more application-specific, limiting the possibility of reuse."

2. *Depth of inheritance tree.* "The deeper a class is in the hierarchy, the greater the number of methods it is likely to inherit, making it more complex."

3. *Number of children.* "Generally, it is better to have depth than breadth in the class hierarchy, since it promotes reuse of meth-

---

[5]Shyam R. Chidamber and Chris F. Kemerer, "Toward a Metrics Suite for Object Oriented Design," OOPSLA '91 *Conference Proceedings*, pp. 197–211.

ods through inheritance. . . . The number of children gives an idea of the potential influence a class has on the design."

4. *Coupling between objects.* "Excessive coupling between objects outside of the inheritance hierarchy is detrimental to modular design and prevents reuse."

5. *Response for a class.* "If a large number of methods can be invoked in response to a message, the testing and debugging of an object becomes more complicated."

6. *Lack of cohesion in methods.* "Cohesiveness of methods within a class is desirable, since it promotes encapsulation of objects."

Again, it is interesting to note the overlap between these guidelines, the ones proposed by Tom Love, and the Coad-Yourdon guidelines discussed in Section 21.1. Coupling and cohesion, for example, are evidently fundamental concepts that OO software engineers should watch carefully in their designs.

But it must be emphasized again that all of these guidelines are still at the "proposal" stage. Chidamber and Kemerer conclude their list of metrics with the comment:

> . . . this set of six proposed metrics is presented as a first attempt at development of formal metrics for OOD. They are unlikely to be comprehensive, and further work could result in additions, changes and possible deletions from this suite. However, at a minimum, this proposal should lay the groundwork for a formal language with which to describe metrics for OOD. In addition, these metrics may also serve as a generalized solution for other researchers to rely on when seeking to develop specialized metrics for particular purposes or customized environments.[6]

---

[6]Ibid. p. 210.

22

OO Testing

If programming is where the tire meets the road in a software project, then testing is where we see whether the tire flies off the car as the car speeds down the road. After we have carried out a careful OOA analysis, developed an OOD design, and then coded everything in an elegant OOPL like Eiffel or Smalltalk, how do we go about testing the resulting system?

The software engineer who reviews the literature on testing of OO systems is likely to come to the following paradoxical conclusion: either we know nothing about the subject—so there is no ability to say anything about it—or we already know everything there is to know about the subject, so there is no need to say anything about it. And yet this flies in the face of common sense: testing must be important in an OO system, and there must be something different about the way one performs it.

Yet some books—such as the OOA/OOD texts by Martin-Odell,[1] Embley-Kurtz-Woodfield,[2] and (sigh) Coad-Yourdon[3]—fail to mention the topic at all. To be fair, these books are concerned

---

[1]James Martin and James J. Odell, *Object-Oriented Analysis & Design* (Englewood Cliffs, NJ: Prentice Hall, 1992).

[2]David W. Embley, Barry D. Kurtz, and Scott N. Woodfield, *Object-Oriented Systems Analysis: A Model-Driven Approach* (Englewood Cliffs, NJ: Yourdon Press/Prentice Hall, 1992).

[3]Peter Coad and Edward Yourdon, *Object-Oriented Analysis*, 2nd ed. (Englewood Cliffs, NJ: Yourdon Press/Prentice Hall, 1990), and Peter Coad and Edward Yourdon, *Object-Oriented Design* (Englewood Cliffs, NJ: Yourdon Press/Prentice Hall, 1991).

almost exclusively with the analysis and design activities in a project, but by omitting any mention of testing, they can create the subtle impression that there is nothing special that one needs to say. That impression is compounded when one peruses the excellent OO textbooks of Firesmith[4] and Shlaer-Mellor[5]; testing is discussed as part of the systems development life cycle in each of these books, but in an entirely traditional way, with no changes imposed by the OO paradigm.

It's also interesting to note the tacit assumption made by many methodologists that testing will be easier if the earlier stages of analysis, design, and programming have been carried out in an OO fashion; perhaps that's why we don't need to say anything about it! Rumbaugh and coworkers, for example, make the following comment:

> This book does not cover testing and maintenance. Both testing and maintenance are simplified by an object-oriented approach, but the traditional methods used in these phases are not significantly altered. However, an object-oriented approach produces a clear, well-understood design that is easier to test, maintain, and extend than non-object-oriented designs because the object classes provide a natural unit of modularity.[6]

And Booch notes that:

> . . . the use of object-oriented design doesn't change any basic testing practices; what does change is the granularity of the units tested. Unit testing, in which individual classes and modules are tested, is best done by class implementors and application programmers. Since most classes and modules do not stand alone, the developer must usually create a test scaffolding with which to exercise that unit. In practice, we find it best to retain most old tests and test results rather than throw them away, so that as a particular class or module evolves, these tests can be used as

[4]Donald G. Firesmith, *Object-Oriented Requirements Analysis and Design: A Software Engineering Approach* (New York: John Wiley and Sons, 1993), p.2.

[5]Sally Shlaer and Stephen J. Mellor, *Object-Oriented Systems Analysis: Modeling the World in Data* (Englewood Cliffs, NJ: Yourdon Press/Prentice Hall, 1988).

[6]James Rumbaugh, Michael Blaha, William Premerlani, Frederick Eddy, and William Lorensen, *Object-Oriented Modeling and Design* (Englewood Cliffs, NJ: Prentice Hall, 1991), p. 144.

regression tests. In this manner, changes to a class or module can be tested to assure that the new unit at least provides the same behavior as in its previous version.[7]

Indeed, the only two popular OO software engineering books that discuss testing in detail are those of Berard and Jacobson and coworkers, each of which devotes a full chapter to the topic. Both books strike a similar note; Jacobson and coworkers, for example, begins their chapter with the comment that:

> To test a product is relatively independent of the development method used. This chapter describes testing in a manner comparatively independent from the method, but we will nevertheless see that [Object Oriented Software Engineering] provides some new possibilities, but also some new problems.[8]

And Berard notes that:

> When making the transition to a new technology, we should expect that some of what we currently know will still be important and useful. We can also expect that there will be those things which will have little or no relevance, and still others will have to be modified. This is indeed the case when we investigate the testing of object-oriented software.[9]

So if there are some differences, what are they? What should we be looking for when we test object-oriented systems? This chapter summarizes four key issues:

- the testing strategy
- unit testing
- integration testing
- testing tools and environments

22.1 AN OO TESTING STRATEGY

The final stages of development of any large, complex system—whether or not it used OOA, OOD, and OOP—involves many different forms of testing: system testing, acceptance testing, performance

---

[7]Grady Booch, *Object-Oriented Design, with Application* (Redwood City, CA: Benjamin/Cummings, 1991), p.212.

[8]Ivar Jacobson, Magnus Christerson, Patrik Jonsson, and Gunnar Övergaard, *Object-Oriented Software Engineering: A Use Case Driven Approach* (Reading, MA: Addison-Wesley, 1992), p. 307.

[9]Edward V. Berard, Essays on *Object-Oriented Software Engineering*, Volume 1, (Englewood Cliffs, NJ: Prentice Hall, 1993), p.261.

testing, failure/recovery testing, and so on. And those involved in the process may be deeply concerned with such well-known concepts as "black box" testing versus "white box" testing, static versus dynamic testing, and so on.

Assuming that all these concepts are still relevant in an OO world, one of our biggest questions is: What comes first? Is there a particular *sequence* of testing that one must do for OO systems? This question of "strategy" usually involves a series of terms that are even more familiar to software engineers: unit testing, integration testing, and system testing. Or, to use terminology that became popular during the heyday of the structured revolution, Should one perform "bottom-up" testing or "top-down" testing?

The consensus in the OO community is that a classical bottom-up testing strategy is best . . . but with the recognition that it may be different than in a conventional (nonobject-oriented) project. Shlaer and Mellor, for example, offer the following recommendation, with terminology that could be applied just as easily to non-OO systems as to OO-based systems:

> Each module should be coded and tested separately, and then progressively integrated, each module with its callers or subordinates, to produce the program. This step should be interpreted literally to mean that coding is complete only when the program is also tested as a unit.
>
> . . . *Integration* consists of putting the various programs and data together to produce a system. The integration step starts with programs that have been tested, each by itself, and with data that has been verified, as previously discussed. Integration is the step that verifies that these separate units, each as correct as can be mode on its own, will in fact fit together to make the required system. In other words, integration is the test of the *system design.*[10]

This kind of advice implies that testing of an OO system should follow a fairly conservative "bottom-up" approach: first test the individual objects in isolation, then integrate them into groups (or "programs," or "subsystems"), and then combine the groups into an entire system. However, we have been aware of the potential problems with such an approach for decades; several of these were dis-

---

[10]Sally Shlaer and Stephen J. Mellor, *Object-Oriented Systems Analysis*, p. 106.

cussed, for example, in one of the author's earlier books on structured programming and program design in the mid-1970s:[11]

- From the user's perspective, nothing works until it all works; unit testing provides no visible benefit to the user.
- The most difficult bugs are typically discovered at the end of the testing phase of the project, when budget and time constraints typically put the project team under great pressure.
- Requirements for computer testing resources often increase exponentially as the project goes from unit testing to integration testing to system testing.
- Debugging becomes progressively more difficult as the testing phase continues, because of the "combinatorial explosion" problem.

But there is an additional problem with OO-based systems, as noted in the quotation from Grady Booch: *objects rarely stand alone.* Thus while some testing can be done to ensure that an individual class and object does behave as specified, the relatively "flat" structure of an OO software architecture means that almost all of the "interesting" behavior will involve collaborations of several classes and objects.

Also, most object-oriented programs are "message-driven," and most of the messages are initiated by an interaction between the user and the system; thus the sequence of execution (and object interactions) is difficult to predict; the straightforward testing approaches used in batch applications or even conventional on-line applications simply won't work for an OO application.

What does this mean, in terms of an OO testing strategy? Simply that, whether the project manager likes it or not, integration testing will begin much earlier than in a non-OO project. As Jacobson and coworkers observe,

> In traditional development [integration testing] usually involves a lot of work and comes as a "big bang" at the end of development. In [Object Oriented Software Engineering] integration testing comes smoothly and is introduced early in the development.[12]

---

[11]Edward Yourdon, *Techniques of Program Structure and Design* (Englewood Cliffs, NJ: Prentice Hall, 1975).

[12]Jacobson et al., *Object-Oriented Software Engineering*, p. 325.

As the project team develops more and more of the required objects in a relatively complete form, this integration testing involves hooking together "real" objects to exercise various parts of the system. However, in the earlier stages of development, when few such objects are ready for integration, there is often a greater need for "scaffolding" and testing environments, as we will discuss in Section 22.4. Also, note that many OO projects make extensive use of existing classes and objects from a reusable component library; this often provides a natural scaffolding and enables integration testing to begin even earlier.

So the primary thing that a project manager should expect from the testing phase of an OO project is *more* emphasis on integration testing and *earlier* integration testing; it also means that regression testing and configuration management, discussed earlier in this book, are absolutely essential to maintain control of the testing process. As a result, the project manager may see some benefits that were associated with a "top-down," incremental testing approach long before OO technology came along. On the other hand, the project manager should expect to develop an OO testing strategy that has its own unique characteristics; as Berard observes,

> If we are working with a system that "has no top," then it will be difficult to define such things as "top-down integration testing," "bottom-up integration testing," or "sandwich integration testing." All of these testing strategies assume that there must be a definite "top" and a definite "bottom" for the system. This means that new integration testing strategies will have to be developed.[13]

In any case, though, the early-integration approach of OO testing has some important benefits, over and above the elimination of bottom-up testing problems summarized:

- *Deadline problems can often be handled more gracefully.* No matter how wonderful the OO technology may be, the project may still be late—because project schedules are partially (if not entirely) determined by political negotiations. But if the project is not finished when the deadline arrives, it's usually better to have a partially working, *demonstratable* version of the system than a massive collection of system components that have been fully coded and unit tested, but not integrated.

[13]Berard, *Essays on Object-Oriented Software Engineering,* p. 264.

- *Programmer morale is generally improved.* This is because they, like the users, see tangible evidence at a much earlier point that their system is beginning to show signs of life. This is particularly important on projects that last for more than a year or two; the conventional bottom-up approach typically suffers from a midproject "slump," because the excitement from the beginning of the project is gone, and the deadline is still too far away to worry about.

22.2 OO UNIT TESTING

As noted, OO unit testing is complicated by the fact that objects frequently collaborate with other objects in the system. As Jacobson and coworkers observe,

> To do a unit test of object-oriented code is more complex than to test ordinary (procedural) code. This is a result of the object-oriented approach; the program has a flat structure which makes the program flow and the program state distributed. It is difficult for the developer who is dependent on the objects of other designers to test his or her own. This is at the same time a great advantage; the integration test is normally much smoother than for ordinary code.[14]

Even aside from this issue, there is another problem with OO unit testing; as Booch notes in the quotation earlier in this chapter, the "granularity" is different. Berard elaborates on this point:

> . . . we are dealing with larger program units, e.g., a class. Further, the concept of a subprogram is not quite the same as it is in more traditional systems. Specifically, we tend to separate the specification (interface) for the subprogram from its implementation (body). We refer to the specification as a "method interface" (i.e., an advertised capability in the external interface the class presents to the outside world), and to the implementation as a "method" (i.e., the internal (hidden) algorithm by which the operation is carried out). We often further complicate matters by allowing one method interface to be supported by multiple methods.[15]

What does this mean for the project manager? First, it means that unit testing is likely to be more difficult in an OO project than in

---

[14]Jacobson et al, *Object-Oriented Software Engineering*, p. 316.
[15]Berard, *Essays on Object-oriented Software Engineering*, p. 262.

previous projects—*and that it may not be "finished" in the traditional sense, when the programmers tell you they are finished.* Because it is so difficult to thoroughly exercise an object in utter isolation, some of the bugs that you might expect to find in a "unit test" activity will not be found; they'll pop up later, during integration testing.

Second, because an object is "bigger" than a traditional "module" created with a structured design methodology, unit testing may take longer than the manager would otherwise expect. Remember, this is a question of granularity: an object contains a number of data attributes, encapsulated with a number of methods. Each of the methods might have been the subject of a separate unit testing activity in older methodologies.

To draw an analogy between software units and the units of atomic physics, the methods are like electrons surrounding the protons and neutrons; taken together, an atom is approximately the same as an object. A collection of atoms forms a molecule, with tight chemical bonds; this is approximately equivalent to a cluster of collaborating objects. So, whereas the unit testing of conventionally developed systems begins at the electron level, unit testing of object oriented systems typically begins at the atomic level.

22.3 OO INTEGRATION TESTING

Integration testing obviously begins when objects are connected together. But as Jacobson and coworkers observe,

> . . . object-oriented systems are highly integrated and certain objects are dependent on other objects. Therefore it may be necessary to develop object simulators that simulate the behavior of adjacent objects. These supporting objects may be implemented with only operation stubs.[16]

Thus the primary requirement for effective integration testing in an OO environment is a good suite of testing tools, which are likely to be domain-specific; we will discuss this further in Section 22.4.

But there is something else that needs to be said about OO integration testing: the very nature of the OO paradigm tends to make it more difficult. The primary contributor to this difficulty is inheritance, although Jacobson and coworkers also note that polymorphism can introduce its own difficulties:

---

[16]Jacobson et al, *Object-Oriented Software Engineering*, p. 314.

Test coverage based upon [decision-to-decision] paths . . . is thus much harder because of the polymorphism. You do not see in the code which unit is actually invoked, not even in a strongly typed language. It looks like a stimulus is sent to an instance (of a specific type in a strongly typed language), but during execution, an instance of any class (of the descendants in a strongly typed language) can actually receive the stimulus. In traditional language the operation to be invoked is made explicit. Hence every stimulus in OO-code corresponds to a CASE-statement in procedural code.[17]

Why does inheritance create additional difficulties? Because, fundamentally, a method that has been inherited may find that it is operating in a different context than in the superclass where it was first defined. For example, suppose that the subclass (which contains the inherited method) modifies an instance variable (perhaps also inherited) for which the superclass method assumed certain values; as a result, the method behaves differently in the subclass than it did in the superclass. Or the superclass method may invoke other superclass methods which have been inherited differently in the subclasses; this is a particularly common problem in systems where the subclasses *override* the definition of inherited methods and/or attributes from their parents.

Thus the fact that an object, with its component attributes and methods, works properly does *not* necessarily mean that its descendants will operate properly when a class hierarchy is assembled during integration testing. Of course, the project team can establish various OO programming conventions (which could be added to the OOD guidelines discussed in Chapter 21) to minimize these problems, but the fact remains: the behavior of methods will have to be retested in the context of the subclasses that inherit them.

22.4 OO TESTING TOOLS

As noted throughout this chapter, good testing tools and a testing environment are crucial for OO projects. We have already noted the need for a testing environment that includes "object simulators" or a "test harness" that allows the software engineer to test individual objects within a simulated environment.

---

[17]Ibid., p. 320.

In addition to testing whose purpose is to discover the existence of bugs, OO projects also need tools for debugging—to discover the location and nature of a bug, once its existence has been demonstrated. Booch, for example, notes that:

> . . . we have found that nontrivial projects need debuggers that know about class and object semantics. When debugging a program, we often need to examine the instance variables and class variables associated with an object . . . The situation is especially critical for object-oriented programming languages that support multiple threads of control. At any given moment during the execution of such a program, there may be several active processes. These circumstances require a debugger that permits the developer to exert control over all the individual threads of control, usually on an object-by-object basis.[18]

And Jacobson and coworkers echo a similar comment:

> The requirements for debugging tools are also greater for object-oriented systems. Normally the environments contain support to inspect the object structure during execution and other service packages. This is (usually) a standard in environments for Smalltalk, C++, and Eiffel. These tools are invaluable for fault finding.[19]

The earlier discussion of potential problems with inheritance suggests another category of testing tool, which we originally mentioned in Chapter 5: configuration management tools. Whenever a change is made to an object—whether it is during the development phase of the project or during the subsequent operation and maintenance of the system—it is crucial to determine which objects might be affected by that change. As we have already noted, other objects within the class hierarchy, especially the subclasses beneath the one being modified, are the most likely candidates to be examined. But "adjacent" objects, which communicate via messages to the one being modified, also need to be considered. The actual retesting of these affected objects will involve the traditional testing tools, but the configuration management tools are essential for organizing one's attack on the problem.

[18]Grady Booch, *Object-Oriented Designs*, p. 213–214.
[19]Ivar Jacobson et al, *Object-Oriented Software Engineering*, p. 317

22.5 CONCLUSION

As Berard concludes in his discussion of OO testing issues,

> Much of what we know about testing technology does indeed apply to object-oriented systems. However, object-orientation does bring with it, its own specialized set of concerns. Fortunately, there is a significant amount of research being conducted, and there is already an existing experience base.[20]

But while this research is being conducted, there are still many unanswered questions. Does the testing of OO systems take longer than the testing of non-OO systems? Are more test cases required? Should the project manager expect that the testing phase of the project will require approximately the same percentage of project resources and calendar time? Can one reasonably expect that an OO system will be better tested (i.e., contain fewer bugs) than a non-OO system? It is hoped that, as our experience base continues to grow, we will find the answers we seek. But in the meantime, the lack of widespread use of OO technology means that there is a dearth of practical "field" experience concerning such issues as testing.

---

[20]Berard, *Essays on Object-Oriented Software Engineering*, p. 265.

PART V   CASE FOR OO

23

___

OO Case: What's Needed

Throughout this book, we have emphasized the need for CASE tool support to successfully implement object-oriented methodologies. This chapter and the next explore the issue of CASE in more detail.

There is a tendency, of course, to focus one's attention immediately on a specific product or vendor—especially if you have been using the same vendor's products prior to switching to an OO methodology. The situation is complicated by the fact that several of the OO methodology gurus and textbook authors have their own CASE tool companies; in some cases, the decision to use Brand "X" OO methodology is tantamount to choosing the Brand "X" CASE tool from the same vendor that developed the methodology.[1]

This book makes no attempt to endorse or favor any specific tool or vendor; it should also be emphasized that I have no CASE tool of my own, nor do I have any financial interest in any company that provides CASE tools. A number of reputable vendors are mentioned in the next chapters, and their OO CASE tools are listed; all these are worthy of investigation, depending on one's budget and particular needs.

But before discussing specific products, we first need to establish some criteria. Numerous books and articles have been written

___

[1]There is some merit to this approach: one should *first* choose a methodology and then choose a CASE tool that supports that methodology. Of course, it's preferable to have a choice of more than one CASE tool for the chosen methodology!

on the process of selecting CASE tools in general;[2] our purpose in this chapter is to discuss the issues and evaluation criteria that are specific to OO methodologies.

The key issues for OO CASE tools are these:

- Ability to support appropriate diagramming notation for the basic OO concepts of classes, objects, gen-spec structures, whole-part structures, and so on.
- Ability to hide and reveal portions of the model
- Browsing capabilities
- Consistency checks and error-checking capabilities
- Groupware support
- Code generation
- Integration with other tools, repositories, and so on.
- Modest price

Each of these criteria is discussed in more detail in the paragraphs that follow.

23.1 SUPPORT FOR DIAGRAMMING NOTATIONS

In a book like this, it is not surprising that the first item on the OO CASE checklist is graphical support. While one could carry out object-oriented programming with nothing more than a C++ compiler, it's difficult to imagine a serious form of OOA or OOD without a CASE tool that supports the creation of various diagrams that have appeared in earlier chapters. The issue of graphical support is a familiar one to CASE users, and it is discussed in great detail in standard CASE textbooks.

However, there is one interesting aspect of OO methodologies that should be remembered: while the OO CASE tools are just now appearing in the early to mid-1990s, the underlying OO methodologies are still undergoing a significant evolutionary development. By contrast, the original upper-CASE tools appeared in the late 1980s, roughly a decade after the structured and IE methodologies had

---

[2]See, for example, my *Decline and Fall of the American Programmer* (Englewood Cliffs, NJ: Yourdon Press/Prentice Hall, 1992), Chapter 6, or Carma McClure's *CASE Is Software Automation* (Englewood Cliffs, NJ: Prentice Hall, 1988), or Chris Gane's *Computer Aided Software Engineering* (Englewood Cliffs, NJ: Prentice Hall, 1989), or Andrew Topper's article, "Evaluating CASE Tools: Guidelines for Comparison," *American Programmer*, July 1991.

been published. By the time CASE tools came along, for example, there was hardly any debate about what kind of data flow diagrams should be supported—it was either the DeMarco-Yourdon bubbles or the Gane-Sarson bubtangles. We have not yet reached this stage of methodology development in the OO field; however, there are many more "players" than there were in the early days of SA/SD CASE tools, and the field is evolving rapidly.

This suggests several possible strategies for the organization about to choose an OO CASE tool:

- Choose a CASE tool from the vendor that "owns" the OO methodology adopted by the organization—on the assumption that if the vendor changes its methodology, there is a reasonably good chance that it will make a corresponding change in its CASE tool.
- Choose a CASE tool that provides a great deal of flexibility in its graphical notation, so that it can be adjusted to suit the organization's preferences and needs.
- Choose a "meta"-CASE tool that allows the user to *completely* define the notation, icons, semantics, and other details of the methodology. This choice is discussed in more detail in Chapter 24.

23.2 HIDING AND REVEALING PORTIONS OF THE MODEL

As we have seen throughout the book, OO models can become incredibly complex; thus an important feature of an OO CASE tool is its ability to hide or reveal portions of the model, so that the systems analyst and/or user only has to see the relevant portion. Examples of this capability include the following:

- Hiding or revealing the instance connections between classes
- Hiding or revealing the cardinality information on instance connections and/or whole-part connections
- Hiding or revealing the attributes in a class
- Hiding or revealing the methods in a class
- Hiding or revealing messages between classes
- *Selective* hiding of messages, for example, hiding all messages between "implicit" methods in the classes
- Highlighting messages "threads" between a group of classes
- Hiding or revealing the "parameters" associated with a message

23.3 BROWSING CAPABILITIES

Since OO methodologies place such great emphasis on reusability, it is important for the analyst to have powerful tools to help find potentially reusable classes. At a bare minimum, this means that the CASE tool must have an adequate "find" or "search" capability, but it also means that the tool should allow the user to open one or more windows in a GUI environment, so that a search can be conducted in the midst of various other activities.

A great deal of browsing takes place in a manner quite different from the straightforward searching by keyword: the analyst may wish to browse up and down through the levels of a class hierarchy; he may wish to quickly determine all the classes which a given class uses, or is used by; and so on.

23.4 CONSISTENCY CHECKING AND ERROR CHECKING

Error checking of a large, complex systems analysis model has always been one of the major justifications for CASE technology; this issue existed long before OOA and OOD methodologies became popular. Every software engineer and project manager knows that it is more far more cost-effective to detect a systems analysis error *during* the analysis phase rather than letting it remain undetected until the programming, testing, or operational phase of the project.

The details of error checking depend, of course, on the particular OO methodology chosen. For example, in the Coad-Yourdon OOA methodology, the following basic guidelines exist for checking the consistency of classes and gen-spec structures in a model:

> Each Class-&-Object—
> . . . has a name.
> . . . has a unique name (within the model).
> . . . has more than 1 Attribute.
> . . . has 0 or more Instance Connections.
> . . . has 1 or more Message Connections.
> . . . has unique Attribute names (within the symbol).
> . . . has unique Service names (within the symbol).
> . . .
> Each Gen-Spec Structure—
> . . . has more than 1 Attribute or Service per level.
> . . . has 2 to 4 levels (else getting too complex).

. . . has Attribute names which are unique within ancestors and descendants.

. . . has Attribute and Service names which do not appear across an entire specialization level.

. . . has unique Attribute and Service names in generalizations for each portion of a lattice.[3]

While this aspect of CASE technology may seem obvious, the newcomer to OOA/OOD must remember one thing: some CASE vendors have "jury-rigged" the OO methodology support in their CASE tool. "Well, last month we called this diagram an entity-relationship diagram," the marketing representative may tell you, "but this month we're calling it an object diagram. We even changed the shape of the symbols so that it looks a little more like the kind of diagrams your favorite OO guru recommends."

But does the CASE tool support encapsulation, inheritance, message passing and the other characteristic features of OO? Does it really support the *details*, including all the error-checking features, of your favorite OO guru? Amazingly, some CASE vendors are now promoting their tools as "object-oriented" in nature, and yet the user has no way of *seeing* an object on the CASE tool display screen; all he can do is view the data relationships (via ERDs), the object behavior (via state-transition diagrams), and the object communication (via a recently renamed diagram heretofore known as a DFD). With such tools, beware: you may not get any OO-based error-checking capabilities at all!

23.5 GROUPWARE SUPPORT

As mentioned in Chapter 5, OO software development projects tend to be highly interactive: a small group of software engineers works very closely together, with everyone involved in creation and prototyping of classes and objects in a complex hierarchy.

This suggests that the traditional stand-alone CASE tools will be completely inadequate for an OO project. Of course, most CASE tools are beginning to provide various forms of "groupware" support, but the need is even greater for OO projects. Configuration

---

[3]Peter Coad and Edward Yourdon, *Object-Oriented Analysis*, 2nd ed. (Englewood Cliffs, NJ: Yourdon Press/Prentice Hall, 1990), pp. 175–176.

management, which we discussed in Chapter 5, is the first and most obvious component of a proper groupware environment; the traditional CASE concept of a "shared project repository" is taken for granted, since OO project team members *must* work with a common class library.

Aside from that, powerful E-mail facilities, problem-notification facilities, and other related tools are highly desirable. As Softlab's Robert Rockwell has observed, "Software is more like a mortgage than a house"; that is, software projects consist of a series of negotiated, articulated *agreements*, a tiny percentage of which is eventually expected to execute on a computer. If this is true for classical projects, it is doubly true for OO projects.

23.6 CODE GENERATION

Without code-generation capabilities, an OOA/OOD CASE tool becomes little more than an electronic Etch-a-Sketch toy. We learned this lesson with traditional CASE tools by the end of the 1980s; sadly, we seem to be learning it all over again with OO CASE tools. One reason this is a problem is that a substantial number of the early OO CASE tools were developed by small vendors who lacked the resources to provide code-generating capabilities in their product; some of them evolved from earlier tools to support structured analysis and data modeling—and they had no code-generation capabilities for those tools, either.

Fortunately, this situation is beginning to change; as we will see in Chapter 24, there are now a respectable number of OO CASE tools that generate C++, Ada, Smalltalk, or other OOPL code. This is particularly important for the OO field, since many of the current "true believers" of OO methodology are actually OO *programmers*; if someone recommends that they use an upper-CASE tool that does *not* generate code, they are likely to ignore it and return to their hand-coded OOPL world.

Even if the CASE tool does generate code, there is a danger of anarchy and chaos: if the programmer makes his changes to the generated code rather than to the analysis-level or design-level models, then (by definition) the models and the code will begin to drift apart; sooner or later, the CASE-level analysis/design models will be seen as obsolete or irrelevant and will be thrown away.

23.7 INTEGRATION WITH OTHER CASE TOOLS

Even though OO is a brave new world for many software engineers, OO CASE tools will not live entirely in their own world. There are already a number of extremely important and useful CASE tools that should continue to be useful even if the organization changes its software development methodology. These include tools for metrics, software quality assurance, documentation, testing, and so on, as well as the groupware tools mentioned earlier.

OO CASE tools should be constructed to take advantage of these existing capabilities, and should interface smoothly with them wherever possible. Ultimately, this means that the OO CASE tools will have to be aware of the CASE industry standards such as PCTE, SGML, CDIF, and so on.

23.8 MODEST PRICE

If you were just learning to drive, would you buy a Rolls-Royce as your first car, even if you could afford one? Probably not: you would choose something small, simple, and *cheap*. Chances are that the process of learning to drive would also teach you a lot about what you *really* want in a car. So why should you do things differently with a CASE tool?

When we explain this concept to end users, we call it prototyping. It's the same thing for software engineering people who are using a CASE tool for a new methodology: they need the freedom to try a prototype to learn what they really need. This should sound obvious, but it's amazing how many organizations form an "OO CASE committee" (composed of people who have never used OO or CASE before) that then spends two years before deciding to spend $100,000 on the "perfect" tool.

Unless the organization is *very* sophisticated, my recommendation is that it should spend less than $1000 on its first OO CASE tool. If it seems adequate after the first few weeks of experimentation, then half a dozen units of the "cheap" tool should be acquired to support a pilot project team—or the organization should invest in one or two units of a moderately priced ($5000–10,000) tool. *Then*, after the first one or two pilot projects, there may be enough experience to decide on the perfect tool.

An easy way to determine just how sophisticated the organization is to go the Software Engineering Institute's process maturity assessment. An organization at level 3, 4, or 5 may understand enough about its software process to make an intelligent choice of OO CASE tools, but the vast majority of organizations at level 1 or level 2 should stick with the prototyping approach described earlier.

24

OO Case: What's Available

Although computer historians disagree on the precise details, there is broad agreement that the modern CASE industry was born sometime in the mid-1980s, probably circa 1984–85. Although some fledgling CASE tools had appeared a few years earlier, it was not until the mid-1980s that PCs and workstations had evolved to the point where they would support the memory, CPU power, disk storage, and graphics requirements of the upper-CASE tools. Since then, despite some bad press and industry setbacks, CASE has evolved into a billion-dollar industry and is becoming widely accepted as a mandatory tool for software engineers.

But, as mentioned in previous chapters, the first wave of CASE tools, from the mid-1980s through the early 1990s, supported the software development methodologies that were in vogue at the time. Although one can point to an isolated exception here and there, the overwhelming majority of CASE tools and vendors, as of the end of 1992, support structured analysis and design, information engineering, entity-relationship diagrams, and related software engineering approaches. The venture capital community has invested vast sums of money in many of these vendors, and quite a few are publicly traded on Wall Street and other stock markets around the world. Their heritage, culture, and financial fortunes are based on older methodologies: So what are they to do with the arrival of OO-based methodologies?

In this chapter, we will first characterize several broad categories of CASE vendors—not in terms of upper-CASE versus lower-CASE, or whether they favor client-server architectures or mainframes, but instead how they are responding to the OO paradigm.[1] Then we will list a number of CASE vendors whose OO products merit investigation on the part of organizations who are serious about implementing OO methodologies.

24.1 CHARACTERIZING THE VENDORS

Although it may be an oversimplification, it is helpful to organize the industry of some 300 CASE vendors into four groups with regard to OO support:

- the dinosaurs
- the wannabes
- the new kids on the block
- the meta-CASE vendors

Each of these is discussed in more detail in the paragraphs that follow.

24.1.1 THE DINOSAURS

The *dinosaurs*, quite simply, are those CASE vendors who wish OO would simply go away. These are typically the older, larger, more established and conservative CASE vendors, with annual revenues in the $30 million–100 million range. As mentioned, these are the vendors whose entire cultural heritage is based on some earlier software engineering methodology; it is as difficult for them to give up this heritage as it is for IBM to give up mainframes.

Here are some common phrases and comments you'll hear from this category of vendor:

- "Well, object-oriented may be useful as a programming discipline, but it really doesn't have anything to do with analysis and design. So our upper-CASE product really isn't affected at all."
- "OO is a great academic theory, but nobody in the real world is using it. We make tools to solve practical problems in today's cost-conscious, results-oriented world."

---

[1]However, reviewers have noted that I have a subtle bias toward "upper"-CASE whenever I talk about CASE technology in this book. I plead guilty to the charge: given the overall emphasis on analysis/design methods over programming-level issues throughout the book, the bias toward upper-CASE is not surprising.

- "OO is a great academic theory, but its value hasn't been proven. By the way, we also believe that nobody has *proven* conclusively that smoking is bad for your health."
- "OO is interesting, and we've looked at it, but our customers clearly aren't ready for it. We'll take another look in five years, and if our customers want it, we'll certainly consider adding the necessary features to our product."
- "As far as we can tell, you can continue using the diagrams produced by our CASE tool. After all, an entity-relationship diagram is really the same as an object diagram. So if it makes you feel happy, just replace the word entity with object in all our manuals."
- "Object-oriented? What's that?"

A DP organization that is firmly committed to changing over to an OO methodology will presumably find these responses unacceptable. But the vendor responses may echo the same kind of comments being made within the DP organization itself. We will discuss this further in Chapter 25.

24.1.2 The Wannabes

Most CASE vendors have now concluded that OO is here to stay; to attract new customers and avoid losing their market share, they will have to support OO methodologies sooner or later. But, as mentioned, many of them have an enormous investment—in terms of money, software, and culture—in older methodologies. Their problem is that they want to be—or "wannabe," to use the American slang term—object-oriented, but they really aren't. In the best of cases, the wannabes will be legitimate OO CASE vendors in a few years; in the worst of cases, the wannabes will eventually have to admit that their existing tools have to be completely scrapped and rebuilt.

A recent "position statement" from Intersolv illustrates what will, it is hoped, be one of the "best of cases" scenarios:

> Our experience with the use of OO technology has taught us that there are real benefits available. However, we also believe that the uptaking of OO technology will be gradual and that our customers will require support for traditional means of analysis, design, and generation for years to come. Furthermore, they will require these means to be well integrated with the emerging OO

approach, so that OO techniques and notation may be deployed gradually in their organization, when and where it is feasible to do so. Still, we intend to support multiple sets of OO notation, so that each customer may select the rate and approach to OO; some will prefer evolution, others revolution.[2]

Other vendors, such as Texas Instruments, seem to be philosophically committed to supporting OO in the near-term future; TI, for example, is an active member of the Object Management Group's Analysis and Design committee. At the same time, such vendors seem to be spending a lot of effort trying to persuade their customers that, for the moment, they can mimic an OO approach with IE and SA/SD-based tools.

As Intersolv has suggested in its position statement, some DP organizations will prefer evolution, while others follow a revolutionary approach; this is a theme we will discuss in more detail in Chapter 25. The revolutionaries will probably find that the CASE tools from the wannabes fall short of their expectations for the next few years. The evolutionaries, on the other hand, may find that the wannabes are *exactly* what they want—for, as Intersolv has suggested in its position statement, they will be supporting both OO and non-OO methodologies in the same organization for a period of years, as the population of veteran software developers and aging legacy systems slowly changes from a non-OO approach to an OO approach.

24.1.3 The New Kids on the Block

Several of the CASE vendors listed in Section 24.2 are "new kids on the block," that is, CASE vendors who simply didn't exist until a year or two ago.[3] These vendors never supported the older software development methodologies, and they have no intention of doing so in the future. Their sole basis for existence is support of an OO analysis, design, and/or programming methodology. Obviously, these vendors will be of great interest to the revolutionaries; they may be less attractive to the evolutionaries, for the reasons given earlier.

---

[2]Intersolv's Position Statement," *American Programmer*, November 1992, p. 19.

[3]One of the "new kids on the block" that didn't make it into the vendor list in Section 24.2 is HOMSuite™, available from Hatteras Software, Inc. (phone/fax 919-851-0093). It runs on IBM PC machines under Windows and OS/2, supports Wirfs-Brock, Lorenz, and Gibson methods, generates C++ and Smalltalk skeletons, and retails for $495.

There is another concern about the new kids on the block: because they are new, they are typically small. They may be underfinanced; they may not have developed a mature customer support, training, documentation, or maintenance activity. In short, they may not survive. But as we suggested in Chapter 23, most DP organizations should begin their efforts with OO CASE tools on a limited basis anyway; a few copies of an OO CASE tool from a "new kid on the block" vendor will be extremely useful in helping the DP organization discover its true needs. By the time the organization is ready to buy dozens, hundreds, or thousands of units, the vendor will have vanished from the marketplace or will have grown to a larger, more stable organization.[4]

24.1.4 The Meta-CASE vendors

Finally, there is a category of CASE vendor that potentially allows the greatest degree of power and flexibility for DP organizations wanting to automate their OO methodology: the meta-CASE vendors. Fundamentally, these vendors offer a "CASE tool to build CASE tools," much like the compiler-compilers for those who want to create their own programming language.

This kind of ability is particularly attractive to organizations that don't want to commit themselves to a specific "commercial" brand of OO methodology. As we have seen throughout this book, there are a number of interesting variations on notational schemes, rules, semantics, and philosophies of OO analysis and design. So, a DP manager may decide to mix and match the best of several different OO methodologies, as well as inventing some additional notations of his own.

The disadvantage of the meta-CASE approach is that the tools tend to be quite expensive and sophisticated; it is not the best choice for the small organization that knows little about OO. And there is a subtle, long-term problem: the organization may find that it has gotten itself into the "methodology business" by creating, extending, and thus being forced to maintain its own unique dialect of OO analysis and design. While the OO methodology field may be somewhat chaotic now, there is good reason that it will settle down in the

---

[4]Don Firesmith suggests a good rule of thumb for reducing risk in this area: make sure the vendor has survived long enough to release version 2.0 (or later) of his product. Don't bet the company on version 1.0, for it may be filled with bugs—and the company may not survive until the next product release!

next few years. For most DP organizations, it would be preferable to leave the methodology business and the tool business to those vendors who want to make it a full-time business.

24.2 A REPRESENTATIVE LIST OF OO CASE VENDORS

In an excellent survey of the OO CASE industry,[5] circa 1992, Andrew Topper suggests that the OO CASE industry can be categorized as shown in Figure 24.1:

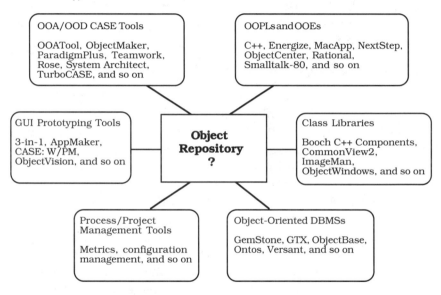

Figure 24.1: Categorizing OO CASE tools

This chapter concentrates on OOA and OOD CASE tools, but a DP organization wishing to make a full-scale investment in OO technology should not ignore the other categories. It is interesting to note that class libraries, OOPLs, and GUI prototyping tools are somewhat more numerous than are OOA/OOD CASE tools and that segment of the tool industry is more mature. On the other hand, the number of OO DBMS vendors is still rather limited, and that aspect of OO technology has been less widely adopted than any of the others.

Topper's survey also includes a list of OO CASE vendors, as shown in Table 24.1.

[5]Andrew Topper, "Building a CASE for Object-Oriented Development," *American Programmer*, October 1992, pp. 36-47.

Platform, Hardware and Software	Vendor Information	Platform; Hardware and Software	Price	Techniques Supported	Generates Code for
MacAnalyst and MacDesigner	Excel Software 515-752-5359 515-752-2435 fax	Macintosh	$1000 to $5000	Booch, Coad-Yourdon, OOMT, and Shlaer-Mellor (OOA)	
ObjectCraft	ObjectCraft 415-621-8306 415-861-5398 fax	IBM PC	$400	ObjectCraft	C++ and Object Pascal
ObjectMaker, CGen, and AdaGen	Mark V Systems 818-995-7671 818-995-4267	IBM PC (Windows), Macintosh, Unix (Sun and HP/Apollo), and VMS	$9000 plus $7850 for C/AdaGen	Booch, Buhr, Bailin, Coad-Yourdon, OOMT, and Colbert	C++, C, and Ada, reverse engineering
ObjectModeler	Chen & Associates 504-928-5765 504-928-9371 fax	IBM PC	$200 to $2000	ERD and class hierarchy diagrams	Skeletal C++
OMTool	General Electric 215-992-6200	Sun SPARC	$2500	OOMT	C++
OOATool	Object International 512-795-0202 512-795-0332 fax	IBM PC, Macintosh, and Unix (Sun)	$2000	Coad-Yourdon	
Palladian design tool	Palladio Software 800-437-0019 414-789-5191 fax	IBM PC (Windows)	$300	Booch '91	
ParadigmPlus	Protosoft 713-480-3233 713-480-6606 fax	IBM PC (Windows), IBM PC (Windows and OS/2), and Unix (Sun, HP/Apollo, and IBM)	$800 $5000 to $25,000	Lekos, Booch, EVB, HOOD, OOAD, and OOMT	C++, Ada, and Object Pascal, reverse engineering
PILOT	Semaphore Tools 508-794-3366 508-794-3427 fax	IBM PC (Windows)	$500		C++
PowerTools	ICONIX Software 310-458-0092 310-396-3454 tax	Macintosh	$1000 to $7500	Booch, Coad-Yourdon, and Shlaer-Mellor (OOA)	Ada and C++
Prograph	TGS Systems 902-455-4446 902-455-2246 fax	Macintosh	$300	Modified DFD	C
Rose	Rational 408-496-3700 408-496-3636 fax	Unix (IBM and Sun)	$4000	Booch	
Software Through Pictures	Interactive Development Environments 800-888-4331 415-543-0145 fax	Unix (Apollo/HP, DEC, Sun, and IBM), and VMS	$5000 to $21,000	Object-oriented structured design (OOSD)	C++, C, and Ada, reverse engineering
System Architect	Popkin Software 212-571-3434 212-571-3436 fax	IBM PC (Windows and OS/2)	$1400	Booch, Coad-Yourdon, and Shlaer-Mellor (OOA)	
Teamwork/OOA, OOD, HOOD, Ada, and C++	Cadre Technologies 401-351-5950 401-351-7380 fax	IBM PC (OS/2), Unix (Apollo/HP, DEC, Sun, and IBM), and VMS	$7500 to $25,000	HOOD and Shlaer-Mellor (OOA and OOD)	C++, C, and Ada, reverse engineering
TurboCASE	StructSoft 206-644-9834 206-644-7714 fax	Macintosh	$1000	Shlaer-Mellor (OOA)	

Table 24.1: Representative OOA/OOD CASE Vendors

It is particularly interesting to see that several of these CASE products are priced under $1000 and that all but two are available for $5000 or less. It is also interesting to note that over 60 percent of the tools have some form of code generation—so the OOA/OOD CASE tool industry has clearly progressed past the point of "bubble-drawing" tools.[6]

On the other hand, conspicuously absent from Topper's list are the "mainstream" CASE vendors such as KnowledgeWare, Andersen Consulting, Intersolv, Bachman, Texas Instruments, and so on. However, several of these vendors have already announced their intention to support OO methodologies over the next few years: Intersolv, for example, is scheduled to release an OO version of their CASE tool at the end of 1993, and TI's OO version of IEF is scheduled for mid-1994.

Author-consultant James Odell has provided an additional list of OO CASE vendors, which includes the vendors shown in Table 24.2. Industry directories, research reports, and trade magazine evaluations will gradually begin including OO CASE tools as the OO methodologies gain prominence and eventual dominance in the field; among the better directories are Applied Computer Research's "Guide to Software Productivity Aids," and *Software* magazine's annual directory of CASE products. In the meantime, it should be reassuring for the project manager and software engineer to learn that there *are* tools and that they are improving every day.

[6]Note also that the industry is in a constant state of flux. For example, between the publication of Topper's article and the preparation of this book, ObjectMaker and ParadigmPlus, shown in Figure 24.1, added support for Firesmith's ADM_3 method; Cadre added support for the Rumbaugh method; Iconix has announced support of Jacobson's ObjectOry method; the Palladian design tool was sold to Rational (where it is now known as ROSE for Windows); and so on.

TOOL	VENDOR	COMMENTS
ObjectOry	Objective Systems SF AB Box 1128, Kista, Sweden S-16422 phone: +46-8-703-4530	Supports Jacobson method runs on IBM PS/2, DECstation, and various UNIX configurations
SES/Objectbench	SES 4301 Westbank Drive, Bldg. A Austin, TX 78746 phone: 512-328-5544	Supports Shlaer-Mellor runs on Mac and UNIX configurations
Objecteering	Softeam One Kendall Square, #2200 Cambridge, MA 02139 phone: 617-621-7091	Supports own "Class Relation" approach runs on Sun, DEC, HP, UNIX configurations
Toolbuilder	IPSYS Software 28 Green Street Newbury, MA 01951 phone: 508-463-0006	Supports many OO methods executable generation of C++, Ada, COBOL runs on Sun, Apollo, HP, DEC configurations
Graphtalk	Rank Xerox AI & CASE Division 7, rue Touzet Gaillard 93586 Saint-Ouen Cedex, FRANCE phone: +33-1-494-85085	Supports IE, NIAM, HOOD, Merise, SADT, etc. configurable meta-CASE tool runs on Sun, DEC, RS6000, UNIX, OS/2 configurations
DEC Design	Digital Equipment Corp. 55 Northeastern Boulevard Nashua, NH 03062	Supports many OOA approaches, including Coad-Yourdon generates fully executable C++
Ptech	Associative Design Technology 200 Friberg Parkway Westborough, MA 01581 phone: 508-366-9166	Supports Martin-Odell method generates C++/Ontos runs on Silicon Graphics, Sun, DECstation, UNIX configurations
ObjecTime	ObjecTime Ltd. 340 March Road, Suite 200 Kanata, Ontario, CANADA K2K 2E4 phone: 613-591-3400	Supports Bell Northern Research real-time, event-driven OO methodology has OO state charts, generates Smalltalk, C, C++ runs on Sun, HP
Stood	Techniques Nouvells d'Informatique Technopole Brest-Iroise ZI du Vernis, Case postale 1 29068 Brest Cedex, FRANCE phone: +33-9-805-2744	Supports HOOD (version 3.1), supports Ada, C, C++ runs on UNIX, RISC, X windows configurations

Table 24.2: James Odell's list of OO CASE vendors

PART VI   HOW TO GET STARTED

25

Revolution Versus Evolution

This final section of the book is concerned with the strategies and tactics for successfully introducing OO into a software development organization. To draw a hardware analogy, changing from an older methodology to OO is not like going from a 386-based PC to a 486-based machine; it is more like going from an MS-DOS system to a Macintosh or from an IBM MVS operating system to the UNIX environment. What we are talking about is more than just change—it is *abrupt* change, a discontinuity from older methods and habits.

We have mentioned throughout this book that the OO paradigm is seen as a revolutionary change by some software engineers and by others as an evolutionary step beyond the older methodologies. In this brief chapter, we will discuss the fundamental strategic choice that an organization must make between revolution and evolution; whatever the personal biases of the software engineer or the software manager, the choice must be made carefully for the OO paradigm to succeed in the organization.

In Chapter 26, we will discuss the political pros and cons of OO methodologies, in an attempt to address the question that we saw in the *Software Development* survey in Chapter 2: Is it time to do OO *now*? For some organizations, the question is not whether OOA is a superior methodology for analysis, but rather whether there are sufficient training and consulting resources available to help the organization use it successfully.

Indeed, *training* is a key factor in making OO work, and it is the subject of Chapter 27. A metaphor will help illustrate the problem: if you already know Spanish, the training required to learn Italian is rather simple and brief. But if you're fluent in Spanish and now want to learn Japanese, it's an entirely different training process.

In Chapter 28, we review an overall organizational "battle plan" for implementing OO; this serves as a conclusion for the entire book.

25.1 THE ARGUMENT FOR REVOLUTION

In some software organizations, OO is regarded as so different from the old way of developing systems that it is hard to describe it as anything other than a revolution. The programming languages are different, the terminology is different, the notation is different, and (most important) the mind-set is different.

To some extent, this is a question of how much variety and flexibility the organization is accustomed to. If the organization is accustomed to working with a dozen different brands of minis and micros, several different operating systems, and several different programming languages—as most organizations are forced to these days—then the introduction of yet another language and development paradigm may not cause much fuss.

On the other hand, a number of the larger business data processing organizations, as well as a significant number of scientific and engineering organizations have been doing things *one* way, with *one* programming language, *one* operating system, *one* brand of hardware, and *one* development methodology for a decade or more. For the business data processing organization, the "one-universe" environment may have included COBOL, IBM mainframes, MVS operating systems, and a structured analysis/information engineering methodology; for an engineering shop, the combination may have been a VAX minicomputer, C and UNIX, and the Hatley-Pirbhai real-time structured analysis methodology. For these folks, and many others like them, the introduction of OO is like putting piranha into the family bathtub.

Sometimes the revolutionary aspect of OO technology is unavoidable, for it comes along with a number of other revolutionary buzzwords: downsizing, client-server technology, cooperative processing, GUIs, and so on. Whether or not OO improves software productivity by an order of magnitude, it has rarely, if ever, been the direct cause of a 10-fold reduction of staff in the software organization. Downsizing, PCs, and client-server technology, on the other hand, *do* tend to have this brutal effect. Since the late 1980s, the computer trade magazines have been filled with stories of million-dollar mainframes being replaced with $10,000 PCs and stories of 100-person DP empires being sacked *en masse* and replaced with 3 PC programmers.

So if someone begins talking about OO as a revolution, it's a good idea to see if they mean OO will be *leading* the revolution or will just be part of a larger revolutionary army. If, indeed, OO is the primary topic of discussion—that is, the primary issue is whether OO analysis/design methodologies should replace SA/SD or IE methodologies—then the question of revolution versus evolution is an interesting one to consider. Even within this narrow domain, revolution may turn out to be necessary—for the same reason it's necessary on the hardware side: a heavily entrenched "culture" that has spent the past 20 years doing things a certain way is not likely to embrace a different approach that may threaten its security and its very jobs. Software development organizations in some companies have become enormous bureaucracies, so involved with their committees and procedures and paperwork that they have forgotten the job they were supposed to be doing. A revolution—whether it's based on OO or something else—may be the only way of shaking the organization up and getting it to make some dramatic changes.

A revolution may also be necessary to avoid letting the OO paradigm become more and more corrupted by the older methodologies. One sees this phenomenon especially often in organizations trying to use old CASE tools to carry out OO analysis and design. "Well," says the analyst, "I know the XYZ tool calls this an entity-relationship diagram, but it's pretty close to an object diagram, so we'll just fake it." On the one hand, this spirit of flexibility is commendable, and every software engineer knows that sometimes he has to do the best he can with the tools available. However, what happens if the analyst discovers that the XYZ tool doesn't support multiple inheritance . . . or *any* inheritance . . . or some way to graphically represent the encapsulation of data and function within an object . . . or messages between objects? At some point, we have to 'fess up and admit it: the OO paradigm has gotten lost in the morass of old methodologies, old tools, and old thinking. Sometimes, it seems, maybe the best thing to do is to burn the old methodology manuals and throw the old CASE tools out the window (or send them to our fiercest competitor).

Aside from the politics involved, the idea of throwing old manuals and tools out the window involves only money; the real problem with the revolutionary approach comes when someone suggests throwing the old *people* out the window, too. There is a common, though unspoken, feeling that "old" software engineers (who may or may not be old in biological years, but who are old in their ways of developing software) are obsolete, and can't be salvaged. Someone who has spent the past 20 years writing COBOL or FORTRAN, using a functional decomposition design methodology, will *never* successfully learn an OO methodology and an OO programming language— or so the argument goes, from the mouths of the revolutionaries.

In many cases, this is clearly a generational argument. These older software engineers are members of the Woodstock generation, and they still remember who Richard Nixon ran against in 1972; like Bill Clinton, their music is stuck somewhere between Fleetwood Mac and Crosby, Stills and Nash. The younger generation entering the software field today is the Nintendo generation; everything about their world, *including their software development methodology*, is different.

But sometimes the argument involves money, power, and various aspects of classical political struggles. The older generation, which may still favor SA/SD, is the generation in power in the typical software organization. These are the folks who may still be defending COBOL and the mainframe; these are the folks who typically earn twice, or three times, as much as the younger generation of hotshot C++ programmers. Is it any wonder there should be a conflict? And is it any wonder that many of the methodological arguments have a hidden agenda, and seem to have no technical basis whatsoever?

25.2 THE ARGUMENT FOR EVOLUTION

What does the older generation have to say for itself? We'll have to skip over the more interesting issues of whose music is better and whether Woodstock really was a cosmic event. What does the older generation have to say about the introduction of OO?

The arguments tend to fall into two categories: (1) there are a lot of old ideas that still have merit, and that can be salvaged in a brave new world of OO, and (2) there is a lot of old "legacy" software and data that *must* be salvaged in the brave new world of OO. This generation is also more likely than the younger revolutionaries to identify a third theme: (3) there are a lot of old software engineers who not only *should* be salvaged for humanitarian reasons and because of the enormous investment the company has made in them, but who *can* be salvaged, for they can eventually be "converted" into OO-people.

The issue of salvaging old methodological ideas into the new OO methodologies is primarily a question of degree and priority—it's not an "either-or," black-and-white world. As we have seen throughout this book, there are a number of fundamental software engineering principles that remain valid in the OO world; however, they might not have the same emphasis or dominant theme. And while *principles* such as striving for a system of highly cohesive, loosely coupled components remains the same, the *strategies* for accomplishing those principles have changed drastically. The older generation recalls that encapsulation was described rather elegantly by David Parnas in the early 1970s as "information hiding," but it will usually admit that the methodologies of the 1970s typically didn't do a very good job of accomplishing information hiding.

As for salvaging the legacy systems, the older generation is likely to argue that that's nonnegotiable: most organizations have tens of millions of lines of old code and disk farms full of DB2-based databases; the thought of all this disappearing is simply inconceivable. Of course, this discussion can get us into the broader technopolitical arguments of downsizing, reengineering, and so on, and depending on the organization, we may find a spectrum of choices, ranging from one extreme of scrapping *all* the old software, to the other extreme of scrapping nothing. Realistically, though, most organizations simply can't afford to throw out a 25-year investment in legacy applications, nor can they scrap their databases overnight.

Whether the OO revolutionaries like it or not, their new OO systems will have to operate in some kind of harmony with legacy software and legacy data built with older methodologies. Indeed, the vast majority of OO methodologies accept this without argument; as we saw in Chapter 19, there are straightforward strategies for interfacing object-oriented software with flat-file and relational-file databases. As for the legacy software itself, it is becoming more and more common to see object-oriented "wrappers" that surround the old code without throwing it away.

What about the third issue—that is, scrapping the older generation of application programmers and systems analysts, weaned on older methodologies? Here again, the older generation will argue that it is not a binary issue. The ability of a large group of software engineers to learn, assimilate, and practice OO technology will probably follow a normal distribution: some will make the transition right away, some will never learn, and the vast majority will muddle along and slowly make the transition over a period of several years. The older generation also notes that OO is not the first new technology to come along—and while it may appear radically new and different from the other software methodologies *du jour*, those commonplace methodologies and technologies were once equally strange and alien. When entity-relationship diagrams and relational database technology was first introduced, it was a *major* culture shock for most organizations, but we gradually assimilated it. Structured design and structured programming were as radical and controversial in the early 1970s as OO is in the early 1990s.[1] Ten years from now, OO will seem commonplace and boring, and we'll all be arguing about some new controversial idea.

25.3 THE LIKELY FUTURE

Smaller software organizations may wish to consider the revolutionary approach. This is a practical approach if there is not much history that needs to be thrown away, for example, very little legacy software, very little accumulated experience of old methodologies and practices. As noted, there is something to be said for making a "clean sweep"; if nothing else, it generates an air of excitement and gets the adrenaline flowing.

---

[1] In 1972, I was stopped at the Montreal airport and asked by a customs official what I was planning to do on my visit to Canada. When I told him I was conducting a seminar on structured programming, he asked in a bored tone of voice what that meant. It was late at night, and my flight had been delayed several hours; I was not in the mood for a pleasant philosophical discussion. So I answered abruptly, "It means programming without GOTO statements." The customs official jerked upright and uttered, with a look of astonishment on his face, "*Mon Dieu!* But that is not possible!" It turned out that he had been taking a FORTRAN course at the local university, to learn a new career. I had shaken his faith in basic principles to the core; it took a long discussion before he was willing to let me into his country with my radical ideas.

For larger DP shops, the issue of OO revolution is likely to be subsumed into the larger revolutionaries issues of the day. If the former director of Systems Development was lukewarm about OO, it's a good bet that the new director—who was also responsible for throwing out the mainframe and introducing the first GUI-based client-server system—will be outspoken in its support.[2] And if the "old guard" manages to retain its hold on power, it may downplay the importance of OO, regardless of its technical merits.

Aside from these larger political issues, it is safe to predict that in most large DP shops, OO will take the evolutionary route—simply because that is the way that almost all technological innovations are introduced into society. True revolutions are few and far between; even those innovations that are announced as revolutions usually have a long evolutionary history.[3] And the history of our own field, as mentioned earlier, has been one of evolution: technologies like structured programming, relational databases, virtual memory, and so on have typically spread slowly through the industry over a period of 14–20 years.

But to be successful, an evolutionary movement into OO has to be planned carefully. The first thing we need to do is see what obstacles and roadblocks might prevent it from succeeding; this is discussed in the next chapter. Then we will discuss the required training of existing software professionals before laying out a full "battle plan" in Chapter 28.

---

[2]Aside from the politics, there is a natural reason for this marriage: as mentioned elsewhere in this book, OO methods are typically a better "metaphor" for modeling a client-server, GUI-based system. So if the organization is prepared to endure the revolution of GUIs and client-server, it should also be prepared to embrace the revolution of objects. Indeed, to do otherwise may doom it to failure.

[3]For an excellent discussion of this point, with examples going back to the steam engine, the cotton gin, and other major innovations of the Industrial Age, see George Basalla's *The Evolution of Technology* (Cambridge: Cambridge University Press, 1990).

26

Is Now the Time for OO?

In some cases, the issue is not so much *if* OO should be adopted, but simply *when*. At one extreme, some of the more outspoken OO advocates argue that it's too late to jump on the bandwagon: if you're not developing your systems from an OO perspective already, they'll tell you, don't bother. Wait for the next revolution to come along. For most organizations, though, the normal assumption is that *now* is the time to get started with OO. The technology is here; the tools are available; the arguments described in Chapter 2 are fairly persuasive. Let's get started!

But is this really the right time for *your* organization to jump on the OO bandwagon? Would it be better to wait for a couple of years? To some extent, the answer to this question depends on the organization's choice of an evolutionary versus revolutionary attitude to OO. But while the term "revolution" usually carries an implication of impatience, this need not be the case: we could calmly and rationally decide that *next year* is the right time for our OO revolution.

Still, why would anyone want to wait? We got a glimpse of some possible answers to this question in Section 2.5 of Chapter 2. In this chapter, we explore a number of "timing" questions for the cautious DP organization to consider. These include:

- Is the OO paradigm sufficiently mature?
- Is a good support infrastructure available?
- Do adequate OO tools exist?
- Is the DP organization sufficiently sophisticated and/or mature to take advantage of OO technologies?
- Are the applications being developed by the organization the kind that will effectively use the OO paradigm?

- Will users understand OO models any better than the SA or IE models they have used before?

- Can the organization's programmers, designers, and systems analysts "unlearn" their old habits and learn new OO techniques?

- Is the competition using OO? There may be a "window of opportunity" to acquire a competitive advantage by embracing an important new technology before the other competitors in your industry.

26.1 IS THE OO PARADIGM SUFFICIENTLY MATURE?

For many DP organizations, OO technology is so new that it's scary; the terminology, concepts, tools, and other aspects of the paradigm are unfamiliar. Worse, there is a concern that it's *so* new that the paradigm has not been sufficiently well described, nor its benefits sufficiently well demonstrated.

On the one hand, this is a rather odd reaction to OO technology, because some of it dates back a decade or more; C++ and Smalltalk, for example, were first introduced in the 1980–81 period and were under development for years before that. Companies like Apple Computer were writing the bulk of their system software in an object-oriented version of Pascal as early as 1982, and OO has been the subject of major computer conferences since as early as 1986.

On the other hand, the methodologies of object-oriented analysis and design do seem relatively new. While many of the leading experts and gurus can legitimately say that they were thinking about OOA/OOD years ago, virtually all the books referenced throughout the discussion in *this* book were published in the 1990–93 period (with the exception of the first of the Shlaer-Mellor books). And, as has been evident in the discussion of Part II and Part III, there is still enormous variation (and some contradictions, as well) between the notation, strategies and semantics of the various OOA/OOD methodologies.

The contrast with the older methodologies is striking: it's as if someone recommended that you learn a new spoken language, and then added casually: "Oh, by the way, there are 12 different dialects of this language—and a compliment in 1 dialect is likely to be a curse in 1 of the other dialects. We don't have a dictionary for this language yet, because we can't get anyone to agree on terms. But don't worry: it's a very important language, and eventually, *everyone* will be speaking it!" Even assuming that you had complete faith in the accuracy of the last sentence of this recommendation, wouldn't you be inclined to wait for a while?

In many ways, the OO "revolution," circa early 1993, is roughly where the structured revolution was in 1979. But there are two differences. First, most of the structured revolutionaries had worked together in the same company at one point, so there was more commonality to their vocabulary, graphic notation, and concepts. And, second, nobody ever put structured techniques on the front cover of *Business Week*. OO methodologies are emerging today from various consultants, methodologists, academicians, tool-builders, and others—many of whom come from utterly different backgrounds, and many of whom have an "ax to grind." And, as we pointed out at the beginning of this book, OO suffers from an enormous amount of over-hype.

A proactive, risk-taking organization may view all this as a benefit: there is an opportunity to seek the kind of synthesis attempted in this book and grab the best from several different methodologies. A more conservative organization may well decide to wait another few years until the marketplace nominates two or three methodology "favorites."

26.2 IS THERE A GOOD SUPPORT INFRASTRUCTURE FOR OO?

There is another consequence of the newness of OO technology: it's hard to find the resources needed to implement it successfully. A large DP organization needs a number of "soft" resources such as textbooks, consultants, training courses, magazines, and conferences—as well as "hard" resources such as CASE tools, compilers, class libraries, and so on.

If your DP organization is located in the heart of Silicon Valley, or any other high-tech "Silicon Gulch," it's reasonable to assume that the support infrastructure that you need is all around you. But what if you're the DP manager of a large bank in Hong Kong? Or the DP manager of a small engineering shop in southeastern North Dakota? Chances are you can find an adequate supply of COBOL programmers, DB2 consultants, MVS textbooks, and even a couple of adult education courses on data flow diagrams at the local community college. But none of this is any help if you're trying to move into OO.

Fortunately, the situation has improved tremendously in the past few years. OO conferences like OOPSLA now have training vendors on the exhibit floor, along with CASE tool suppliers, compiler vendors, and consulting firms. Various special interest magazines and journals carry advertisements for the services of OO consultants and training firms. And as for textbooks, as noted earlier, there has been a virtual explosion of OOA and OOD textbooks since 1990. There aren't as many as one would expect to find for the older methodologies, but they *do* exist.

Nevertheless, infrastructure is critical, and the savvy DP manager will give it serious thought before he commits his organization to the OO revolution.

26.3 DO ADEQUATE OO TOOLS EXIST?

In addition to the soft resources, a commitment to OO requires a good set of "hard" tools. A C++ compiler is just the beginning; as we discussed in Chapters 23 and 24, full-scale CASE tools are essential for success with OOA and OOD.

While Chapter 24 listed nearly a dozen OO CASE tools, it is still a relatively short list—and most of the vendors are relatively small firms, with little or none of the track record of the more established CASE vendors. Indeed, some conservative DP organizations may prefer to wait until their favorite "big" CASE vendor finally offers decent OO support before jumping on the OO bandwagon.

In addition to the basic tool capability, a big issue for long-term success with OO will be the existence of a proper *repository* for storing the models developed with OOA and OOD. It should be an "open" repository, so that the models created by one vendor's tools can be retrieved and manipulated by another vendor's tool for some other part of the software development process. Indeed, it would be ideal if a project team could choose CASE tools from three different vendors—A, B, and C—to carry out one phase of the project like OOA, using a common methodology, such as the Booch or Rumbaugh or Coad-Yourdon method.

But this issue of an open repository is not a new one: various proposals have been introduced over the past several years, including IBM's ambitious AD/Cycle effort. At the time this book was written, all those efforts could accurately be described as limited successes (at best) or utter failures (at worst). While some of these efforts (such as DEC's COHESION environment, HP's Softbench, and the European PCTE environment) may eventually succeed, there is an interesting irony: many of these repository efforts are based on older methodologies. Thus the underlying "metamodel" for the repository is typically based on entity-relationship diagrams *and does not support the fundamental OO concepts of inheritance, encapsulation, and message passing.*

Presumably, all this will improve as time goes on. But for now, the conservative DP manager can count the stand-alone OO CASE tools with code generators on the fingers of two hands. The risk-taking manager may say, "One good tool is all we need," while the conservative risk-avoider may say, "Let's wait for a couple more years until the tool situation improves."

26.4 IS THE DP ORGANIZATION SOPHISTICATED ENOUGH?

As we have seen in this book, OO methodologies involve concepts such as inheritance and encapsulation—which the software engineers in many older-style organizations might find difficult to learn.

But our concern here is not the native intelligence of the software engineers or the speed with which they can learn new technical concepts. Our concern instead is with the overall rigor, formality, consistence, and *maturity* of the overall software development process used by the organization. If the organization thrives on anarchy, and is populated by cowboy programmers, it will *love* OO technology because of the emphasis on prototyping. But it is also likely that OO will be a disaster, because it will introduce one more dimension of instability into the organization.

A number of process maturity models have been proposed over the past few years, including those developed by Howard Rubin, Roger Pressman, Capers Jones, and the Software Engineering Institute. It is not our purpose to defend or compare any of these specific models, but they all have a common theme: at the lowest levels of process maturity, the problems are much more fundamental than choosing a sexy new design methodology. Proper project management, configuration management, estimating, reviews, and software quality assurance procedures are usually much more critical. In short, if the organization is at level one (the "initial" level) on the SEI scale, it probably doesn't need OO as much as it needs some basic skills. The prudent manager can probably get *much* more improvement, in terms of productivity and quality, by investing in the basics.

26.5 DOES OO "FIT" OUR APPLICATIONS?

At this stage in the development of OO technology, there are ample case studies from the entire spectrum of applications: business, scientific, engineering, batch and real-time, big and small. OO is a "generic" approach to developing systems that can be effectively used almost everywhere.

Where does it *not* fit? If your OOA model has only one class and object, and if the methods within that class are so complex that they require half a million lines of code, chances are that the OO approach is not the best one for the problem. Thus a "pure" number-crunching problem that involves little or no data, but *lots* of functionality—or a "pure" database problem that involves complex data relationships but virtually no computation—might be examples of situations where it would be hard to justify an OO approach.

In most DP organizations around the world, there is a fundamental technology shift that fits so comfortably with the OO paradigm that it is hard to avoid it; this shift is variously described as "downsizing," "cooperative processing," "distributed processing," "client-server systems," and "GUI-based systems." The hardware platforms, the operating systems environment, and the user interface virtually forces the software engineer into an object-oriented modeling.

On the other hand, the organization that finds itself still building monolithic batch systems, or mainframe-based on-line systems with dumb terminals, will probably not find the OO approach as useful. And while one sometimes gets the impression from the industry trade journals that mainframes have entirely vanished from the earth, some organizations are still doing very well with them, thank you very much. And while Macintosh bigots (the author included) like to think that computing is impossible without a graphical user interface, there are still millions of on-line applications for which a simple character-based user interface may be the most cost-effective approach. For these organizations, it may be prudent to wait a few years to jump on the OO bandwagon.

26.6 WILL USERS UNDERSTAND OO MODELS?

OO programming and OO design can be carried out without any direct impact on the users during the development phase of a project—aside from the prototyping and GUI aspects of an OO system. But it is OO *analysis* that represents a major change, in terms of modeling user requirements. What if the users don't like the models?

Some users have never seen *any* analysis models before; others have been inundated with data flow diagrams, entity-relationship diagrams, state-transition diagrams, and various other bubbles and boxes over the past decade. Their question is likely to be: "Why should I change?" It may be sufficient to tell them that OO is the latest and greatest thing; it may be sufficient (and even honest!) to tell them that OO is necessary for modeling of the GUI-based, client-server systems they want so badly.

But what if they refuse? Or what if the analysis methodology is mandated by some kind of contractual requirement imposed upon both users and analysts by some external Evil Force (such as a government standards body)? In this case, most DP organizations would still feel content to use OO methods for the design and implementation phases of their project, but this leaves the problem of translating the non-OO analysis model into a proper OO design model. Few, if any, CASE tools support this kind of methodological transformation; chances are that the software engineers will have to do it manually. As mentioned in Chapter 3, the danger is that the software engineers will do it only once, with dubious efforts to verify the one-to-one mapping between the models; during the heat of the prototyping activities, nobody will bother updating both models consistently.

Nevertheless, many DP managers would probably elect to begin "seeding" the organization with the revolutionary fervor of OOD and OOP, with the hope that it would eventually spread "upstream" to the analysis activities at some later point. Indeed, the same thing happened in the 1970s with structured techniques. Even though we will argue in Chapter 27 that the *training* of OO techniques should proceed from the top down, that is, from analysis "down" to programming, the political forces in some organizations force the introduction of new systems methodologies to take place in a bottom-up fashion.

26.7 CAN THE TECHNICIANS CHANGE THEIR WAYS?

As mentioned in Section 26.4, the biggest problem may be with *organizational* maturity, not *individual* maturity, when it comes to introducing OO. Nevertheless, a common concern of some DP managers is that their existing staff may not be smart enough (or may be too "locked in" to their current way of doing things) to be able to assimilate OO techniques successfully.

As mentioned in Chapter 25, the "revolutionary" camp is likely to argue that veteran software engineers have somehow been corrupted by older methodologies—and that they won't be able to learn the new OO way of life. The author sides with the evolutionary camp, which believes that even if some of the veterans find it difficult to change, they will eventually do so; the ease and speed with which this occurs may depend a lot on the kind of training that is provided, which we will discuss in Chapter 27.[1]

Nevertheless, it is certainly true that some DP managers will find themselves in a rather extreme position, for example, with a staff of assembly language programmers who have been maintaining vintage-1972 applications for the past 20 years, and for whom even COBOL would be severe culture shock. Whether or not such technicians are capable of learning OO techniques may not be the primary question: they may simply refuse to do so—or they may take so long to do so that the "window of opportunity" will have been lost.

26.8 SUMMARY

All the scenarios described in this chapter are "real," in the sense that they have occurred in consulting engagements in which the author has been involved. Obviously, the convergence of *several* of these problems may be enough to preclude OO technology for the rest of this decade, but in most cases, the existence of one or two major problems may turn out to be a good argument for postponing the revolution for a year or two (as long as this doesn't turn into an endless series of excuses to postpone OO forever). For software engi-

---

[1]Of course, if management provides no time for training, then it will be almost impossible for today's veterans to learn about OO (or any other new technology). To the extent that today's DP organizations are driven by short-term schedule pressures, any movement into new technologies like OO will be slowed.

neers who have just celebrated their 21st birthday, a year is an eternity; for a DP organization that has been dealing with technology revolutions every year for the past 25 years, a year is just a "blip" on the calendar. And, as we discussed in Chapter 7, OO technology is just one of the "weapons" that the DP organization should be investigating in its efforts to improve productivity and quality. For some organizations, *today* is the time to introduce OO; for others, it might be better to concentrate on, say, peopleware this year and save OO for next year.

27
OO Training

Training and education are important for successful implementation of OO technology—just as they are for any other new technology introduced into a DP organization. Whenever an organization has considered the introduction of CASE, structured methods, relational database technology, client-server systems, or pen-based computing, it has typically acknowledged the need to provide the software engineers and the project managers with appropriate training.

However, the need for education may be greater with OO than with previous methodologies because it requires a substantial shift in the "mind-set" of the software engineer. Structured analysis and design, for example, involves a number of specific terms, graphical notations, and techniques; however, it employs the fundamental principle of top-down functional decomposition, which is likely to already be familiar to most software engineers. The author has been involved in a number of training situations where software engineers look at the diagrams presented in this book, and ask, "Where's the top?" obviously looking for the "control module" or "executive routine" of a hierarchical structure chart.

In this chapter, we explore the type of training and education appropriate for most conventional DP shops embarking upon a new OO methodology. The issues involved here may not be relevant for university students if they are learning OO as their first methodology; on the other hand, since structured design is now being taught at the high school level, and functional decomposition is being introduced in elementary school programming courses, these comments may be relevant for everyone.

27.1 BASIC TRAINING SUGGESTIONS

For most software engineers, a one-day lecture seminar is sufficient to explain the concepts of OOA, and a five-day workshop is sufficient to explain the concepts in detail, discuss them, and practice their application on small classroom exercises. The same is true for OOD and OOP, as well as OO-related project management; thus, the training requirements for a full exposure to OO technology range from a minimum of four days to a maximum of four weeks.

That's enough to get started, with some reasonable chance of applying the technology successfully on a real system. The length of time required to practice the technologies to the point where the software engineer feels comfortable and competent ranges from an absolute minimum of 1 month to a maximum of 3 years. For most veteran software engineers with some prior exposure to programming and older methodologies, this "competence-building" period is likely to be 6–12 months; if it lasts longer than 3 years, it's unlikely that the techniques will ever be mastered. Obviously, these numbers can vary tremendously depending on the software engineer's age, intelligence, motivation, personality, attitude, aptitude, prior experience and habits, and so on, but the organization that expects overnight assimilation of OO technology is in for a rude shock.

Obviously, not everyone in the organization will want or need management-related training; we might assume that the project managers and various levels of supervisory personnel would attend one-day or two-day sessions devoted to OO project management, while the software engineering technicians focus instead on OOA, OOD, and OOP. But this raises an interesting question: What comes first? Ironically, the same question arose 15 years ago, when structured analysis, design, and programming methodologies were first being introduced. The advice today is the same as it was then: begin with analysis, then move down to design and programming, and conclude with testing.

The reasons are the same, too: brilliant programming may end up doing nothing more than helping the project team arrive at a disaster sooner than before. Admittedly, the introduction of prototyping in most OO methodologies makes this argument less persuasive; on the other hand, what many OO developers call prototyping is just hacking. For large, complex projects, it continues to be important to model the requirements properly, and then to model the software architecture properly, and only then to worry about how the code will be written.

The political problems of beginning with OOP and then moving up to OOD and OOA are also the same as they were 15 years ago: there is a danger that the organization might run out of training money before the entire sequence of training courses is finished, and it would be a shame to have done nothing more than introduce a new programming language like Smalltalk without changing the mind-set and the dialogue between the user and the analyst. On the other hand, politics may preclude the introduction of OOA at the outset: the user may simply *refuse* to discuss the requirements of his system from an OO perspective.

27.2 LEVELS OF AWARENESS

The suggestion in Section 27.1 that a one-day lecture or a five-day workshop is "enough" to learn OOA or OOD has a subtle implication: it allows the manager and the software engineer himself to believe that such training is binary in nature: either you know the OO stuff or you don't. As we noted, there is a period of, typically 6–12 months before one really feels competent in the new technology, but the dangerous assumption remains that one can become an "instant expert" in OO by attending a training class or by reading a book like this one.

Until the twentieth century, a number of professions had a concept of apprentice and master; even today, we know that there is a distinction between a "black belt" and a "brown belt" level of proficiency in karate. Why don't we do the same for OO technology, and for all other major technologies that we expect people to use in the software field? Meilir Page-Jones suggests that there are seven levels of expertise in most software engineering technologies:[1]

---

[1]Meilir Page-Jones, "The Seven Stages of Software Engineering," *American Programmer*, July–August, 1990.

1. *Innocent*—has never heard of the technology
2. *Aware*—has read an article about the technology in a trade magazine
3. *Apprentice*—has attended a five-day workshop
4. *Practitioner*—is ready to use the technology on a real project
5. *Journeyman*—uses technology naturally in his work; complains bitterly if it is taken away
6. *Master*—has internalized the details of the technology; knows when he can break the rules
7. *Expert*—writes books, gives lectures on the technology; looks for ways to extend the technology into new areas

Whether there are seven levels, or six, or five, is not the key point here. Indeed, five seems to be a more popular number these days; with all the discussion of the Software Engineering Institute's process maturity model, it should not surprise us to see an adaptation for OO technology. Norm Kerth and Eileen Andreason suggest a five-stage OO process maturity model, as summarized in figure 27.1:[2]

---

[2]Norman Kerth and Eileen Andreason, "Managing the Objects: Management's Role in a Successful Transition to Object Orientation," *American Programmer*, October 1992.

Stages of Transition	Engineering Capabilities	Pitfalls and Mistakes	Software Engineer's Tasks	Manager's Tasks	Impact on Process
Stage 1: Assimilating	Generate interest and enthusiasm.	Rejecting OO thinking without careful analysis; accepting OO thinking organizationwide and mounting a mass transition effort; standardizing on a language or methodology.	Read literature and build paper systems; ask how objects can be applied to the problem domain; develop and discuss a vision of what is possible.	Provide training and access to OO experts; master OO thinking at the big-picture level; create opportunity for engineers to experiment with objects; resist notion to use objects on critical project.	None.
Stage 2: Experimenting	A few people are able to build demonstration systems very rapidly; they are usually human interface intensive.	Standardizing on a language or methodology before experience is acquired; not considering the need for refinement and shipping of demonstration systems.	Master the notions of inheritance and polymorphism; learn to use the language, debugger, and class libraries; develop a habit of solving problems with OO thinking; rethink past problems from OO viewpoint.	Encourage individual exploration and discovery with team discussion; develop a vision of what could be possible; assure that every engineer works through his or her own transition process.	Incrementally growing software seems possible; standard life cycle appears to be obsolete.
Stage 3: Building	Able to see how OO thinking can be used to improve the typical systems the organization builds.	Believing that problem-solving techniques used "in the small" will scale up for use with teams; ignoring quality and professional discipline due to schedule and time pressures.	Select programming tools and languages; experiment with analysis and design methodologies; learn to use OO thinking in a team setting; the practice of incrementally growing software is used as a prototyping tool only.	Learn to manage OO development as a team activity; insist upon quality work and professional practices; use rework and defects as keys for process improvement.	Incrementally growing software is discovered to be not possible in large project and team efforts, so previous standard life cycle is reestablished with some modifications; configuration management and change control need to be revised for objects.
Stage 4: Standardizing	Several projects have been developed using OO technologies; experiences are now part of the culture.	Ignoring the need to develop standards for the use of objects; not recognizing the changes to the software life cycle.	Select a common methodology; participate on standards committees; understand when not to use objects.	Identify meaningful rules-of-thumb metrics and measures; oversee standards refinement effort.	New standards for life-cycle milestones, documentation, and review checklists are developed.
Stage 5: Optimizing	OO development is one of many understood ways to develop software.	Expecting reusable objects will just appear out of engineer's work.	Understand the distinction between building usable objects and product software—each has its own goals, practices, documentation, testing, and measures of success.	Establish a separate function to define, build, deliver, and support software components to be used across the organization.	Reuse of internal and external usable components becomes major part of software design and development.

Figure 27.1: The Kerth-Andreason OO process maturity model

Again, the key issue is not whether there are three levels or five levels in this model; what's important to realize is that people do go through a series of stages as they acquire mastery of a new concept. It's also important to remember that there are plateaus—some people may stay at a particular stage for several months before progressing further upward—and that there can even be "reverse progress" due to disillusionment, lack of management consistency, and so on. Note also that Kerth and Andreason emphasize the pitfalls and key tasks that must be addressed by both technicians and managers at each stage. Achieving mastery at OO is not simply a matter of learning to run faster and faster and faster; it is more akin to crawling, then walking, and then running. At each stage, there are different priorities and perspectives.

It should be noted that the "master" level of proficiency may be represented by members of an in-house training department—that is, the people whose job it is to educate the rest of the staff in OO methods and techniques. Organizations like NASA Ames Research have found that it is quite helpful to use their instructors as in-house consultants to OO pilot projects, making themselves available up to eight hours a week to assist in design workshops, model reviews, walkthroughs, and so on.[3] Indeed, this may evolve into the practice of *mentors*, where those more familiar with the OO technology can act as leaders and guides to shepherd newcomers into the fold.

27.3 MISCELLANEOUS SUGGESTIONS

Most organizations are likely to introduce OO technology the way they have introduced so many new technologies in the past: herd all the software engineers into a training room, subject them to an intense "sheep dip" form of training,[4] and then herd them back to their desks with the instructions that their schedules have been cut in half, because OO has doubled their productivity.[5]

Whether this approach can ever work is debatable; however, it is particularly dangerous with the "evolutionary" approach to OO discussed in Chapter 25. If the training experience basically tells the software engineers that "OO is really like that old stuff, except there are a few new buzzwords you have to learn, and you gotta start programming in C++," and if the CASE tools perpetuate that mental

---

[3]John Connell, private communication, April 1993.

[4]The analogy, suggested originally by Jerry Weinberg, comes from the approach used by farmers to rid their sheep of various infections by dunking them in a bath of disinfectant.

[5]This ignores the all-too-common problem that project managers don't want to release their people for *any* training, because it will interfere with their deadlines. "Just read a couple of magazine articles in your spare time," they might suggest, "and *then* we'll cut your schedule in half, because OO will have doubled your productivity." Here's a simple, but controversial, idea from Tom DeMarco: if you allow your people to accrue vacation days ("you can't take your vacation now, because we're in the middle of a project with a critical deadline"), then you should allow them to accrue training days.

framework, then there is a strong likelihood that the software engineers will continue doing whatever they were doing in the past—with a bit of "window dressing" to convince management that they really are doing up-to-date OO-stuff.

As an alternative, DP organizations should seriously consider a "revolutionary" training approach, *even if they intend to introduce the OO methodology in an evolutionary fashion*. Thus don't teach OO concepts with C++; use Eiffel or Smalltalk instead, because it will *force* software engineers to look at the systems development process from an OO perspective. Don't use traditional CASE tools that have added a few OO bells and whistles; spend the extra money to buy one or two copies of a "pure" OO CASE tools that does *not* support data flow diagrams, entity-relationship diagrams, and all the familiar icons from of methodologies of yore. Such an approach is roughly comparable to a "total immersion" form of learning a new language or an "Outward Bound" experience of putting people into a strange environment where they have few familiar tools and comforts to work with.

Of course, all this will only be relevant for another few years; by then, OO technology will be so pervasive and well understood that it will be taught to kindergarten children as part of their first exposure to computers. Meanwhile, we veteran software engineers, having finally become comfortable with the OO revolution, will suddenly be told that there's a *new* revolution to deal with, and that OO is obsolete. Such is the curse and the blessing of the software field!

28

The OO Battle Plan

After all the theory, and after all the discussion, success with OO requires a commitment, as well as a plan, for action. The software engineering technicians, who are likely to be excited by the new technology, are often ready to make the commitment with no planning at all. And software managers, wary of the siren song of yet another "silver bullet" technology, are sometimes prone to plan forever, without ever making a commitment.

Some of the necessary actions for implementing OO technology have already been discussed in this book: acquiring CASE tools, training the staff, and so on. But there is more: risk management, pilot projects, and a host of other related activities. Introducing OO is like introducing any other major new technology, and it must therefore be planned carefully. And while some technology innovations may have a relatively limited scope—for example, changing the programming language from COBOL to Ada—others can have a ripple effect that extends beyond the ranks of the technicians, into the wider arena of users and managers. A full-scale introduction of OO technology can have as momentous an impact as the introduction of client-server technology.

This final chapter, which summarizes the major management planning activities required for successful implementation of OO, is based on a series of planning steps articulated by Don Firesmith.[1] The activities will be familiar to most managers, and details are available in a variety of other sources. The key concern at this point is simply that we not forget any of them.

---

[1]Donald D. Firesmith, "Take a Flying Leap: The Plunge into OO Technology," *American Programmer*, October 1992.

28.1 OBTAIN INITIAL CONSULTING ADVICE

A small DP organization, with a staff of only a dozen software engineers, might decide to jump on the OO bandwagon with no outside help. After all, there are lots of books (like this one!) and magazines offering information about OO technology, and there are numerous seminars and computer conferences where one can obtain information. "It's no big deal," as one project manager said to the author recently. "We've learned a lot of other new technologies on our own, and I'm sure we can handle this one, too."

Perhaps so. But a large DP organization, with a staff of hundreds or even thousands of people, has a different situation altogether. Because of its size and resources, it has more choices, but for the same reasons, the consequences of a mistake can be far more serious. The consequences of choosing this CASE tool or that one, and this version of OOA methodology or that one, can be far reaching and subtle. Doing this without any previous experience with OO is highly risky; hence, the first step should be to obtain advice and guidance from an experienced, objective outsider.

In many cases, this initial step will include a brief training session to acquaint management and software engineering technicians with the benefits of OO, as well as an overview of the technology itself. But more important is the planning activity that follows: an experienced consultant should have a battle plan similar to the one discussed in this chapter, which will show the key decision makers in the organization what steps are involved, how long it will take, how much it will cost, what benefits are likely to accrue, and what risks must be accepted.

Unfortunately, such advice is sometimes provided by individuals or companies that have a hidden agenda, for example, to sell hundreds of copies of their CASE tool, or to put hundreds of their own consultants on the client site to begin building an application with the latest high-tech OO technology. Ideally, the initial consulting effort should be a "one-shot" engagement, to ensure objectivity, with no commitment of ongoing training, consulting, or software tools from the vendor. Depending on the size of the client organization, the initial engagement should take somewhere between a few days and a few weeks, and the cost should be a negligible percentage of the organization's overall investment in OO technology.

28.2 OBTAIN MANAGEMENT COMMITMENT

Full-scale management commitment to OO technology requires several additional steps, which are discussed in Sections 28.3, 28.4, 28.5, and 28.6. But there is no point beginning these efforts if the organization cannot obtain at least a "gut-level" management commitment that OO is worth considering.

It must be remembered that, for many managers, OO is just another buzzword—like CASE, structured methods, client-server, downsizing, expert systems, reengineering, and a dozen other buzzwords. If it provides quantifiable business benefits, they may be interested; however, even with the prospect of improved productivity and quality, they may perceive political risks that they would prefer to avoid, and they may suffer from the pervasive problem that software people normally associate only with end users: resistance to change. Even if DP management does support OO technology, they may not be *excited* by it; it's just one more decision to make.

This is a crucial issue, and it is often more important for the success of object-orientation in an organization than the technical features of the methodology and CASE tools, or the choice of C++ over Smalltalk. If management is opposed to or blasé about OO technology, then it probably won't work: a grass-roots revolution may lead to some low-level OOPL usage, and a few renegade OO projects, but it will fade away after two or three years, and the organization may return to "business as usual." To make OO really work well, for example, requires a commitment to reusable components, and as we saw in Chapter 6, that requires a rather substantial change in management practices and policies. And on a larger scale, to make OO work requires a commitment of *time*: it will probably be three to five years before the investment pays off.

The willingness to make such a commitment—even though it is a tentative commitment at this early stage—is usually based on a strong feeling by management that things are not going well, or that they *should* be going much better, and, of course, it requires an act of faith that OO technology can be one of the major solutions to the existing problems. In the chaotic world of the 1990s, it's hard to imagine that any DP organization could conclude that it has no problems—but it must be remembered that the perspective of the software engineering technicians is not always the same as that of the managers. Management may have become cynical over the years, and may be resigned to the fact that things will be screwed up no matter what they do; this is sometimes expressed with phrases like, "This is the best of all possible worlds; anything else that we might consider doing would just lead to worse results."

Also, note that management may have decided to invest its time, money, and energy in alternative approaches to improving software productivity and quality. As we saw in Chapter 7, tremendous improvements can be achieved by focusing on peopleware issues, CASE tools, reusability, software metrics, and a variety of technologies that are compatible with OO, but do not *require* OO. And some organizations are so thoroughly involved with downsizing strategies involving client-server systems, networks, distributed databases, and other technologies that they have no time for OO. This can be frustrating for the software engineers in the organization who are passionately committed to OO, but it may make good business sense.

Ultimately, a passionate commitment is crucial for OO to survive the ongoing political crises that the organization face, as well as the more deadly problem of inertia. And while it is unrealistic to assume that *all* the DP management hierarchy will exhibit any degree of passionate excitement toward OO, it is important to find at least one such person. That manager, often dubbed the *champion*, is the one willing to continue popularizing OO in the face of boredom, passive resistance, or outright hostility; in many cases, that manager is willing to risk some of his or her political career by using OO on a pilot project, so that the results can be demonstrated to the rest of the organization.

28.3 CONDUCT PILOT PROJECTS

Like all new technologies, OO needs to be validated and demonstrated to the organization; this is usually done through the mechanism of a pilot project. An organization that has used pilot projects to introduce CASE, or structured methods, or various other new technologies will be familiar with this concept; it has been discussed in various other books[2] and is summarized briefly here.

[2]See, for example, my *Managing the Systems Life Cycle*, 2nd ed. (Englewood Cliffs, NJ: Yourdon Press/Prentice Hall, 1988), or *Managing the Structured Techniques*, 4th ed. (Englewood Cliffs, NJ: Yourdon Press/Prentice Hall, 1989).

A key characteristic of a pilot project is that it should be "medium-sized," within the context of the organization; it should not be too big, and it should not be too small. For most organizations, this typically means a project that will involve half a dozen technical staff members, and one that will last about six months. The danger with a pilot project that is too small is that it won't impress anyone—after all, who needs fancy technology to build a system that your 10-year-old kid could do over the weekend? And the danger of a pilot project that is too big is that (1) it may take years before anyone will see the results and (2) its size and scope may create problems that will be unfairly blamed on OO technology—indeed, OO may turn out to be the straw that breaks the camel's back.

A good pilot project is important and visible, but *not* so critical that its failure will bankrupt the organization; this is another reason for avoiding the overly large pilot project. On the other hand, a pilot project that is buried in the back room of the research labs won't get the attention of the key decision makers in the organization, and a pilot project that is judged to be a frivolous toy won't get the respect of the managers who risk their careers on mission-critical projects.

A good pilot project should be staffed by enthusiastic volunteers who are well trained and well supported by expert consulting assistance. There is no point holding a gun to someone's head and insisting that he or she participate in a pilot project; there will likely be enough problems without worrying about sabotage and sullen resistance. Training of the pilot project team is essential: even if management wants to pinch pennies when it considers the full-scale training plan, it should avoid scrimping on this initial training effort; a full week of training in OOA and OOD is an absolute minimum, and two to three weeks is preferred. Outside consulting is also highly recommended; in this case, it may be wise to ignore the advice in Section 28.1 and choose a consultant associated with the CASE tool used by the project team or a consultant who carried out the initial training for the pilot team staff.

Another important component of a good pilot project is metrics: the team should have additional resources who can devote time to measuring all aspects of the analysis, design, coding, and testing activities. This may turn out to be a part-time job, but it should be carried out by someone who is independent of the technical work itself. At the same time, the schedule should allow for the project team members to record their own observations throughout the project—in the form of logs, diaries, or informal notes. This information can be invaluable for the rest of the organization, if OO is eventually adopted on a full-scale basis.

Obviously, the successes and failures of the pilot project should be publicized. There is a natural political tendency to overemphasize the successes and hide the failures, but this is unfortunate: a great deal can be learned from things that went wrong, and it does not require the fundamental technology used in the pilot project to be thrown out. Indeed, for large organizations, it's a good idea to try two or three pilot projects before a final conclusion is reached about the viability of the proposed new technology.

28.4 DEVELOP A RISK MANAGEMENT PLAN

One of the key benefits of a pilot project is that it provides valuable data for a risk management plan, which should be part of the planning process for implementing any new technology. Risk management is a technology of its own, and is practiced as an offensive weapon by world-class companies, rather than as an act of cover-your-ass, defensive bureaucracy; aggressive companies do not try to eliminate or avoid risk altogether, but focus instead on determining what risks they can afford to take, and how best to manage and control those risks.

It would be foolish, of course, to suggest that OO technology is risk-free. One of the first risk-oriented questions that management will ask is, "What if this stuff doesn't provide the benefits that we keep hearing about?" What if we try this on a large, risky, mission-critical project and it fails? What if it takes longer to implement OO in the organization than originally planned? What if it costs much more than planned? And so forth . . .[3]

In addition to the management-oriented risks, the technicians can usually identify additional risks. What if we can't find decent CASE tools? What if we can't find a compiler for C++ on the machine we use? What if OO leads to performance problems, hampering the run-time efficiency of high-volume on-line systems? What if we choose the wrong OOD methodology, and find three years from now that it's not supported by any of the major CASE vendors? And so forth . . .

---

[3]On the other hand, there are presumably some risks associated with continuing with the current methods, techniques, tools, and technologies. The risks of the "old way" have to be compared with the risks of the "new way."

The passionate defenders of OO technology will be tempted to put their blinders on and ignore many of these risks; they may also become emotionally involved in their defense of OO, making it difficult to carry on an objective evaluation. Conversely, the skeptics and cynics will revel in this activity, for they can conjure up all manner of risks ("What if the sky collapses? What if object-orientation causes cancer?"). Clearly, objectivity and experience are crucial in this area of planning for OO; fortunately, there are now a number of excellent references to help managers assess software risks.[4]

Identifying and quantifying risks are just the beginning; *managing* the risks is an ongoing activity, and it requires a conscious management effort and plan. For the example, the risk associated with OO CASE tools is not one that can be evaluated once and then forgotten; as we saw in Chapter 23 and 24, the "old-guard" CASE vendors are going through an evolutionary process of deciding when and how to introduce OO support in their products; meanwhile, the "young Turks" are introducing brand-new CASE tools, but there is no guarantee that their products (and their very existence) will survive in a highly competitive marketplace. This is especially problematic because neither the CASE vendors, nor the users of CASE tools, can be certain which of the commercial "brands" of OOA/OOD methodology will survive and prosper over the next few years.

Thus a careful OO implementation plan will follow a standard risk management approach of identifying the "top-10" risk items and then tracking them on a regular basis; in monthly status meetings, for example, management should be apprised of the changes in the top-10 list, and should review the plans for mitigating and minimizing those risks.

28.5 DEVELOP A TRAINING PLAN

In Chapter 27, we discussed the importance of training for object orientation. But aside from the philosophical question of whether training is necessary at all, there is the management issue of how to accomplish it. A large DP shop, for example, may have a thousand programmers, designers, systems analysts, and project leaders; the organization probably can't afford to train them all at

---

[4]See, for example, Robert Charette's *Application Strategies for Risk Analysis* (New York: McGraw-Hill, 1990) and *Software Engineering Risk Analysis and Management* (New York: McGraw-Hill, 1989).

once, and it certainly can't afford the disruption of pulling them away from their day-to-day jobs all at once and herding them into a large training facility.

Thus OO training will generally have to be accomplished on a "phased" basis—as it is with any other new technology the organization adopts. The details may be affected by budget considerations, but it is usually influenced even more by the nature of the current work being conducted by the organization. If a project team is already in the middle of a project, for example, it may not make any sense for it to begin any OO training—the team members would have little opportunity to apply the new ideas, and would probably forget most of what they learned by the time they could use the concepts on their next project. The situation is even more extreme in many maintenance situations: What's the point of learning object-oriented analysis if your job involves maintaining a COBOL program written in 1972?

This suggests, then, that training will usually take place on an opportunistic "just-in-time" basis, but that does not mean that the organization should necessarily abdicate all responsibility and allow the training to take place on an ad hoc basis. If OO technology is to be introduced on an entirely voluntary basis (as is typical of organizations characterized by the Software Engineering Institute as level 1 organizations), then the training is probably voluntary as well; as a result, the organization's training department may organize a series of OO seminars, and simply let those project teams and individuals who are interested sign up whenever they have the time. On the other hand, an organization that wants to introduce OO "from the top down," in a carefully controlled fashion, will probably plan the training schedule far in advance.

28.6 DOCUMENT MANAGEMENT EXPECTATIONS

At this point, management should have a lot more information about OO than it did at the beginning of the process—it should have a risk management plan and a training plan, as well as the advice of its consultants and the results from initial pilot projects. At this point, it is important to document management's expectations of the new OO technology, in quantifiable terms, before everyone gets completely carried away with the euphoria of the new technology.

Presumably, one of the expectations of OO technology will be improved productivity. But how much improvement, and over what period of time? Will management be satisfied with a 10 percent improvement, or does "success" ultimately mean a 10-fold quantum leap? Does it have to be accomplished over the next 6 months, or is this part of a 5-year plan?

As we have seen throughout this book, success with OO technology also hinges on some other factors. For example, the productivity improvements from OO may turn out to be highly dependent on reusability. If so, how *much* reusability does management expect? Is this change supposed to happen overnight, or does management expect that it will be accomplished gradually, over a three-year period?

Some of the expectations will involve "soft" factors that may be hard to quantify. For example, OO may be seen as a necessary "enabler" technology to facilitate GUI interfaces for end users—and while everyone is in favor of more user-friendly interfaces, how are we supposed to judge how good a job we've done? Sometimes it means simply that we have to try harder to find a legitimate quantifiable justification; for example, if we can document a reduction in training costs or date-entry errors with the new GUI interfaces, that can be used as part of the justification for OO. And sometimes the process may lead to passing the buck, for example, OO technology may turn out to be *the* necessary enabler for a "soft" benefit like GUI interfaces that the users insist on having, and that they are willing to pay for.

In any case, whatever the expectations are, they should be articulated, quantified, and documented in as much detail as possible. This is important to judge the success of the new technology later on, but it is also important in the early stages to find the "hidden agendas" that some technicians and managers may be holding close to their chest. Technicians, especially, may be clamoring for OO technology simply because it is the latest and most interesting technology around; managers may be clamoring for OO to serve their own political purposes (to discredit a rival manager, etc.).

28.7 DEVELOP AN OO DEVELOPMENT LIFE CYCLE

As noted in Chapter 3, a major part of the OO paradigm involves the concept of prototyping; however, it is possible—if one insists—to use OOA, OOD, and OOP within the most conservative waterfall life cycle imaginable. But since the introduction of OO is likely to challenge or threaten the existing life-cycle "culture" within the organization, it is important that management address the issue carefully as part of the planning process.

Consultants and outside advisors are likely to recommend a prototyping or spiral life-cycle model, perhaps based on Berard's recursive/parallel model or Firesmith's globally recursive model; the younger generation of software engineers, who see OO as part of the "new wave" of computing, are likely to do the same. But if the organization has no previous experience with such life cycles, it may be hard to distinguish between prototyping and unadulterated "hacking." An obvious way to experiment with the concept under reasonably well-controlled conditions is the pilot project approach discussed in Section 28.3.

The change from a waterfall life cycle to a prototyping life cycle is a substantial change in itself, and one could reasonably argue that it should be investigated independently of OO; indeed, there is no reason why one *must* follow an object-oriented approach to use prototyping (although the converse is easier to argue). With good CASE tools and/or a powerful 4GL and "screen painter," it's eminently practical to implement a prototyping life cycle using structured methods or information engineering.

But, as noted earlier, OO and prototyping tend to go hand in hand: if the organization decides to adopt OO, it is usually very hard to resist a prototyping mind-set. Part of this is the result of another "hand-in-hand" phenomenon: OO systems are almost always associated with GUI interfaces, while older methodologies (which followed a waterfall life cycle) were associated with dumb-terminal, character-based interfaces. GUI interfaces demand prototyping; hence OO projects that use GUI interfaces inevitably find themselves operating in this fashion.

28.8 CHOOSE OOA/OOD/OOP/OOT METHODS

Much of this book has concentrated on OOA/OOD methods; a commitment to OO technology requires making some choices in this area. At the time this book was written, there were approximately half a dozen relatively popular (and another dozen or more less publicized, but equally meritorious) OO analysis and design methodologies in use throughout North America and Europe. It is quite possible that some newcomers will join the list over the next few years, and it is also possible that some of those currently in vogue will quietly fade from the scene. But it is likely to be another three to five years before the field narrows to two or three dominant OO methodologies—and by then, an entirely new paradigm may have arrived on the scene!

In the meantime, the typical software organization has two choices: adopt or adapt. The first choice involves choosing one of the commercially available methodologies—for example, the OOA/OOD methodology of Booch, Rumbaugh, Jacobson, Firesmith, Coad-Yourdon, Shlaer-Mellor, Martin-Odell, or Embley-Kurtz-Woodfield—and adopting it, more or less, in its published form. Such a choice must be made not only on the technical merits of the methodology itself, but various other factors such as the availability of CASE tools, training courses, consultants, and so on. And then one must cross one's collective organizational fingers and hope that the methodology prospers in the marketplace, and that one is not stuck with a fate akin to choosing PL/I as a programming language.

The other alternative is essentially the one followed in this book—a conscious act of *synthesis*, taking the best of several different methodologies and merging them together. Despite what one might think of the merits of such an approach, it has traditionally been the common practice of large DP organizations when using older methodologies such as structured analysis and design. It is unlikely that any single commercial methodology will be universally applicable to all sizes, shapes, and types of applications in the full spectrum of DP shops around the world, and even if one could make such a claim, it is unlikely that it would be universally popular. For better or worse, people like to tinker and customize their methodology, just as they like to tinker with the human interface on their GUI-based workstations.

In the past, an organization's decision to "fiddle" with a methodology had little impact on its ability to practice the methodology in a rigorous, consistent fashion, but this has begun to change dramatically with the proliferation of CASE-based methodologies. Of course, most CASE tools allow for a certain amount of customization and flexibility—but only up to a point. Indeed, even relatively cosmetic features such as the shape or color of the icons in the diagrams may be "frozen," with no facility for modification by users of the CASE tool. Thus, if the organization feels strongly that it wants to stray relatively far from the "pure" version of one commercial methodology, *or* if it decides to "mix and match" the features of several different methodologies, it will usually be forced to choose an expensive "meta-CASE" tool that permits a much broader, more powerful form of customization; this was discussed in Chapters 23 and 24.

Of course, if the organization customizes too much, it will end up with an entirely unique methodology of its own; this may have ramifications in terms of training, ability to recruit experienced software engineers, and so on. There is an obvious analogy with spoken languages; in a television-based society like the United States, for example, there is more and more of a tendency for people across the land to speak a neutral, accent-less "television-broadcaster" form of English. But local accents still exist, and they do not prove much of a hindrance to communication: someone from Boston can still communicate with someone from Texas, even though it may require a certain amount of tolerance on both parts. But in other countries, the accents are so different that they become known as "dialects," and the dialects are sometimes so different that they might as well be different languages; the people from one region of China, for example, may be entirely unable to understand the people in another region. This is *not* a situation we want to create with OO methodologies.

28.9 CHOOSE OOP LANGUAGE AND COMPILER

Although the author's bias is very much in the area of analysis and design, it is nevertheless obvious that a commitment to OO technology eventually requires a commitment to a programming language. And although it is conceivable to adopt OOA and OOD within a non-OOPL environment, very few organizations are likely to do so. At the time this book was written, most organizations tended to equate a commitment to OO technology with a commitment to C++. But, of course, there are other choices: Smalltalk, Eiffel, Ada, and (real soon now) object-oriented COBOL.

As with the choice of OOA/OOD methodologies, the choice of a object-oriented programming language is based on many factors—only one of which is the list of technical features for supporting OO concepts. The organization typically must decide, first, whether it wants to make a revolutionary change (e.g., from COBOL to Smalltalk) or an evolutionary change (e.g., from C to C++). It must take into account the availability of trained programmers, ease of training, performance issues, ability to interface with the existing database and telecommunications environment, and so on.

And, of course, it must take into account the availability of compilers for the language. There are numerous compilers for languages like C++ and Ada, and one can be reasonably sure of finding one or two for almost any hardware platform and operating system environment. With Smalltalk, the choice is essentially limited to two vendors: Digitalk and PARCplace Systems.[5] With other languages, the choice may even be limited to a single vendor.

In the next few years, as suggested in Chapter 23, the language issue is likely to become less important—simply because more and more CASE tools will come with robust code-generators. But this may simply shift the emphasis to the CASE tools, as discussed next.

28.10 CHOOSE OO CASE TOOLS AND REPOSITORY

As we discussed in Chapter 23 and 24, a serious investment in OO technology is not recommended unless the organization is willing to acquire adequate tools for its software engineers. This does not mean that every software engineer must have a CASE tool on his or her desk the very instant the organization makes the commitment to OO technology, but CASE tools must definitely be part of the planing process.

Chapter 23 discussed the primary technical issues in selecting CASE tools, and there are numerous "generic" books and technical reports that offer useful pointers for the organization involved in a CASE tool evaluation; Chapter 24 summarized some of the more prominent OO CASE vendors. All this should be taken into account during the planning process, together with one more critical factor: experimentation during the pilot projects. The pilot projects should not only be an opportunity for experimenting with different OOA/OOD methodologies, but also the associated CASE tools.

As noted in Chapter 23, a robust CASE environment depends heavily on a *repository*, and this is doubly important in the OO world because of the emphasis on reusable class libraries. But the organization should be careful not to restrict its attention to reusable *code* libraries; the CASE environment should provide a repository for maintaining analysis and design models, as well as reusable classes and objects in source-code and compiled-binary form.

---

[5]Consultant Adrian Bowles has observed that many people who buy Smalltalk over the next few years will migrate to tools that provide a layer of abstraction above the language; if this is the case, then tool providers like Enfin should be added to the list.

28.11 IDENTIFY OO-BASED METRICS

As noted in Chapter 21, researchers like Chidamber and Kemerer have begun proposing specific software metrics to evaluate the "goodness" of an OO-based design. Similarly, organizations like the International Function Point User's Group (IFPUG) have begun developing an object-oriented version of the "function point" metric, while other researchers like Tom McCabe have begun developing object-oriented extensions of the cyclomatic complexity metric.

In addition to metrics like these, the organization will need to decide what metrics need to be captured to help *manage* the process of OO-based software development. What kind of units of work need to be measured, and what activities of what kind of project personnel need to be measured? If reusability is a major component of the OO paradigm, it is likely, for example, that more attention will be focused on the reusable class library (How many components are in the library? How often are they used? How many people are involved in maintaining and testing the library components?). Similarly, there will be more people involved in user-interface issues, and various other differences in the mix of people and activities during the project.

The pilot projects, once again, should be seen as an opportunity to experiment with metrics. Indeed, the organization is likely to be utterly unaware of *what* metrics it wants to capture until it sees how the pilot projects unfold. And, as is true of any software metrics initiative, *no* metrics should be considered permanent; as the organization evolves, and as it becomes more mature in its use of OO technology, the metrics should change, too.

Software metrics has become a "hot" technology in the past few years; there are several excellent textbooks on the subject, including those of Capers Jones, [6] Larry Putnam,[7] Tom DeMarco,[8] and Bob Grady.[9] Thus far, the standard treatises on software metrics do not

---

[6]Capers Jones, *Applied Software Measurement* (New York: McGraw-Hill, 1991).

[7]Larry Putnam and Ware Myers, *Measures for Excellence: Reliable Software on Time, Within Budget* (Englewood Cliffs, NJ: Yourdon Press/Prentice Hall, 1992).

[8]Tom DeMarco, *Controlling Software Projects* (Englewood Cliffs, NJ: Yourdon Press/Prentice Hall, 1982).

[9]Robert Grady, *Practical Software Metrics for Project Management and Process Improvement* (Englewood Cliffs, NJ: Prentice Hall, 1992). See also Robert Grady and Deborah Caswell's earlier book, *Software Metrics: Implementing a Company-Wide Program* (Englewood Cliffs, NJ: Prentice Hall, 1987).

have an object-oriented perspective, but this is likely to change over the next few years.[10]

28.12 REVISE SOFTWARE DEVELOPMENT PLAN

All the activities discussed are part of an overall software "process" that the organization uses; the new OO practices and procedures should be consolidated into a single reference document.

Note that a complete software development plan will typically include descriptions of *standards* for analysis, design, coding, and other activities in the project; *reviews* of the various work-products produced during the project; and *documentation* of those work-products. All these need to be adapted for the new OO world.

Of course, the organization is unlikely to have enough experience to develop an adequate "process manual" at the beginning of its adventure in OO-land. Based on the experiences of the initial pilot projects, a condensed version of such a document can be drafted, perhaps in as little as 10–20 pages. Even if it ends up being a document as big as this book, it should be done quickly by a small group that recognizes it is involved in a prototyping effort, too; the document they write should not be considered "stone tablets" that cannot ever be changed, but rather a first draft of an evolving set of process standards.

28.13 A FINAL COMMENT

The activities summarized in this chapter appear rather daunting, but this is often the case with major undertakings. It's far better to have a healthy degree of caution when embarking upon a major organizational transition to object-orientation; treating it like a minor variation on an older software engineering paradigm, something that can be assimilated overnight, is far more dangerous.

In Chapter 26, we raised the question of whether it is too soon for some organizations to embrace OO, especially since the methodologies and associated tools are still in such a state of rapid evolution. But the opposite question is just as relevant: Now that OO has been around for a few years, is it too late to jump on the bandwagon? If an organization has not even begun adopting OO technology until 1993, can it ever hope to catch up?

[10]One such book, due to be published in 1994 by Prentice Hall, is *Object-Oriented Software Metrics*, by Mark Lorenz and Jeff Kidd.

Optimists and pessimists are likely to have entirely different answers to such a question; the author casts his vote with the optimists. If you have absorbed and understood everything in this book, you're ready to start. And you might as well start now; delaying the decision by a day will just add one more day to a process that is bound to take several years. If you're worried that you're not the first in your industry (or your state, or your country) to adopt OO, at least take solace in knowing that you're not the last. Perhaps the best advice on adopting new technology in our rapidly changing computer field comes from a Minister of Education in India, as he addressed his colleagues at a conference which was considering the use of computers in schools:

> Our initial backwardness, our late arrival on the scene, and the small investments we made in the past need not remain as our handicaps but can be turned into our most valuable advantages if we make the right decisions now, order judicious investments and march forward with determination.

> Vikram Sarabhai
> *Proceedings of the National Conference*
> *on Computers in Education and Training*
> New Delhi, India

With what you now know about object-oriented technology, you too can make the right decisions, order judicious investments, and march forward with determination. Godspeed on your journey!

Index

B

C